America, Inc.

AMERICA,

INC.

**WHO OWNS AND OPERATES
THE UNITED STATES**

MORTON MINTZ &
JERRY S. COHEN

THE DIAL PRESS   NEW YORK   1971

For our families and parents

ACKNOWLEDGMENTS

We are indebted for help graciously given by more persons than we could possibly name, something like a legion of economists in the government and the universities, lawyers, reporters, and others. Certainly, the pioneering efforts of Dr. John M. Blair, the former chief economist of the Senate Subcommittee on Antitrust and Monopoly contributed greatly to this book. In addition, the kindness shown us by a relative few is so great that we want very much to thank them by name. They include the staff of the Senate Subcommittee on Antitrust and Monopoly and, particularly, Patricia Y. Bario, Jack A. Blum, John J. Flynn, Walter S. Measday for editorial help; Raymond D. Watts, associate counsel of the Senate Select Committee on Small Business; Harrison F. Houghton, formerly assistant to the director of the Bureau of Economics for the Federal Trade Commission; Anne N. Barrett; and the late Edward J. Reilly. Finally, for having shown endless patience and good nature, we wish to thank our wives, Nina M. Cohen and Anita Mintz, and our children, Daniel, Elizabeth, Catherine, and Caroline Cohen and Margaret, Roberta, and Daniel Mintz.

MORTON MINTZ
JERRY S. COHEN

CONTENTS

INTRODUCTION

The management of power in a complex society is built around institutions. In our country, the most enduring, coordinated and generic manager of power is the corporate institution. Controlling great wealth and metabolized by the most fungible of factors—the dollar—the modern corporation possesses a formidable unity of motivation and action with great stamina. Much of what passes as governmental power is derivative of corporate power whose advocacy or sufferance defines much of the direction and deployment of government activity. The federal government is replete with supportive programs—subsidies, research, promotional, contracts, tax privileges, protections from competition—which flow regularly into the corporate mission of profit and sales maximization. So much of government resources is allocated and so much government authority is utilized to transfer public wealth into corporate coffers that Washington can be fairly described as a bustling bazaar of accounts receivable for industry-commerce.

It is important to recognize the multiple approaches to power which characterize the modern corporation, particularly the top two hundred companies that lead the economy. With limited liability for its owners and diffused responsibility of officers and directors, the corporation derives its strength at the outset from what it *gets,* not from what it *receives.* Its inherently acquisitive nature permits easy justification for wide discretion as to when and how to use or not to use the many permutations of its power. Critical impacts on other people and institutions proceed both from the use and non-use of corporate power. How clear have been the consequences, for example, of the historic non-use of insurance industry leverage vis-à-vis the auto industry's hazardous vehicle designs.

The non-use of legitimate power has rarely been popularly evaluated for accountability. So many direct or indirect corporate impacts are of this order. Introducing the internal combustion engine early in the century for mass production in automobiles did not cause much of an air pollution problem. Year after year of rising automotive production with 100 million motor vehicles on the road, the same engine becomes a health menace to Americans. Inaction in 1910 and inaction in 1970 toward the same engine type are completely different displays of corporate behavior. Different magnitudes of hazards to health and property and greatly enhanced industrial capability produce vastly different ethical conclusions. As Alfred North Whitehead wrote: "Duty arises from our potential control over the course of events. Where attainable knowledge could have changed the issue, ignorance has the guilt of vice."

Our legal system has just begun to trundle after the massively tortious impact of willful defaults in preventing known destructions of peoples' rights. For decades, with compliant regularity, the law has permitted so narrow an evaluation of corporate performance—balance-sheet performance—that wide areas of industrial depredations have escaped the law entirely. Historically, many of our country's struggles have been challenges of the corporate power to define the area of its accountability. This was true of the Populist and Progressive movements as well as the challenges of organized labor and the regulatory state of the New Deal. Against these and lesser buffetings, the corporation, with its peerless resiliency of bending now and consolidating later, prevailed only to increase its power.

The corporate institution proved relentless to its adversaries, including the regulatory state, through an impressive variety of stratagems. How else could zoning and urban renewal have become such intimate adjuncts to corporate renewal and enrichment? How else could a progressive income tax become a mechanism of transferring corporate risk and cost through innumerable loopholes to the individual taxpayer or transforming the corporate income tax into a private sales tax? How else to explain the web of procedural obstacles, such as the tyrannical standing requirements that blocked people from access to their own government? How else, indeed, to explain the staggering violence of corporate pollution against innocent people's property and health with virtual impunity? How else can be explained an electoral process putting year after year a greater premium on wealth and corporate indentures?

In no clearer fashion has the corporation held the law at bay than in the latter's paralysis toward the corporate crime wave. Crime statistics almost wholly ignore corporate or business crime; there is no list of the ten most wanted corporations; the law affords no means of regularly collecting data on corporate crime; and much corporate criminal behavior (such as pollution) has not been made a crime because of corporate opposition. For example, willful and knowing violations of auto, tire, radiation, and gas pipeline safety standards are *not* considered crimes under the relevant statutes even if lives are lost as a result. The description of an array of corporate crimes in this forthright book reveals a legal process requiring courage, not routine duty, by officials to enforce the laws against such outrages. The law is much more comfortable sentencing a telephone coin box thief to five years than sentencing a billion-dollar price-fixing executive to six weeks in jail. In one recounting after another, the authors pile up the evidence toward one searing conclusion—that corporate economic, product, and environmental crimes dwarf other crimes in damage to health, safety and property, in confiscation or theft of other peoples' monies, and in control of the agencies which are supposed to stop this crime and fraud. And it all goes on year after year by blue-chip corporate recidivists.

Why? It is easy to answer—"power." But that is the beginning, not the end, of understanding. It is relational power—related to the amount of goods and services and workers employed in a community or about the country. For as long as the corporate mission is production and employment, the law has treated with laxness industrial-commercial damage to consumer-citizens as the "price of progress" or as limited deviations from the norm or as indifference instead of willful in motivation and therefore insignificant. The retention of the slave mentality that the master who does not beat his slave is compassionate can be disastrous in a technological society that can destroy itself domestically by its own inadvertance or knowing indifference. The fact that Chairman James Roche of General Motors does not want his company to have a carcinogenic or genetic effect on the American population has little to do with the enormous damage of GM's plant and vehicle pollution which he and his company are starving of known or knowable remedies. Mr. Roche may privately plead insufficient authority to apply GM's huge resources to its environmental pollution, but he cannot justify his refusal to initiate as a leader. The excuse that there is a diffusion of power in a corporation and no locus of specific responsibility has long been a preconceived strategy of insulating company leaders from having to make such decisions.

Indeed, the entire corporate mechanism is patterned to insulate officials from specific accountability. This pattern is being increasingly refined. Delaware, the nation's corporate Reno for easy chartering of the biggest corporations, now permits corporate officials to be reimbursed by their company even for criminal fines. The federal grand jury hearing evidence of hundreds of knowing violations of U.S. offshore drilling regulations in the Gulf of Mexico was asked this year by federal prosecutors only to indict the company of offense, the Chevron Oil Company, not any of Chevron's executives. Rarely is the law invoked against corporate violence, but when it is, the prosecutional penalty or equitable remedy is applied to the corporate shell and not to those officials who make corporate policy. It is almost axiomatic that irresponsibility toward public interests becomes institutionalized whenever the making of decisions is so estranged from any accountability for their discernible consequences.

Further, the *style* of violence and fraud that flow from corporate activities enhances their perpetuation without countercorrection. Unsafely designed automobiles, pollution, harmful food additives, and other contaminants embody a silent kind of violence with indeterminate, unpredictable incidence per victim. That impact does not provoke immediate sensory response of pain or anguish directed at the source of the harm. Such harm does not depend on its motivation for its impact. And it does not come in the anthropomorphic form that is apparently so necessary to motivate action. Corporate-induced violence illustrates in compelling fashion the biological obsolescence of human beings toward machine, chemical, or other injurious exposures emanating from the technology of corporate groups. Our sensory apparatus, adapted to cruder and older forms of visible hazards, cannot detect carbon monoxide or radiation until it is too late. Soon, this widening gap between the obsolete mechanisms of man's physiology and the multiple, cumulative impacts of his technology may mark the confines of the struggle for planetary survival— even should peace between nations prevail. The mind of man must abstract what is happening more rapidly, for the body of man provides few early alert signals.

Corporate fraud and other economic crimes similarly escape the normative perception that would be applied, for example, to a pickpocket by most people. From educational to media systems, people are not afforded adequate opportunities to learn about and ethically evaluate price-fixing, adulterated citrus juices, hams, and poultry, deliberately fragile bumpers, unperformed but billed-for services, suppression of life-giving innovations, and many other crimes which bilk the consumer, in Senator Philip Hart's estimate, of some $200 billion yearly.

For decades the myth of the market's invisible hand was thought to work adequately to maximize consumer values. During the past generation, a new theory of self-correcting mechanisms—countervailing powers or economic pluralism—gained acceptance. One power bloc, it is said, substantially curbs the excesses of another power bloc, whether they be big sellers, big buyers, big unions, big government, or the collective feedback of ultimate consumers. Both these theories had an intellectual neatness to them that mesmerized many academic analysts into avoiding the arduous task of testing them against empirical reality. This is not to say that both theories have no connection with reality. The question inescapably is how much reality. Both types of political economy, and they do overlap in concept, can be driven toward their limits for justice only by the daily vigilance of advocacy equal to the distorting or suppressive forces.

During the past six years, the realities of the corporate condition have begun to spill into the public domain. Congressional hearings, federal and state investigations, court testimony, investigative reporters, lawyer-activists, and the assertion of the poor's miseries, from migrant workers to slum dwellers, into the nation's consciousness amount to something more than their parts. What can be learned from these materials is what this book is about. The invisible hand has been replaced too often with the mailed fist encased in the corporate purple. The countervailing power turns out to be mostly an accommodating power which transfers the results of corporate abuses from one point on the market or the environmental or governmental continuum until they land on the point of least resistance—the consumer-citizen-taxpayer. A burgeoning technology is giving corporations more power than they choose to exercise responsibly. Witness, for example, the domestic chemical and biological warfare called, too charitably, pollution. Concentration of economic power develops momentums of abuse in political, social, educational, and union areas. Laws and antitrust and regulatory frameworks have been symbols rather than arms of democratic governing, while the corporate regulatees control the public regulators.

What of it? Morton Mintz and Jerry Cohen face the question directly by detailing the harm actually done to citizens' health, safety, incomes, and freedom. Their examples are not merely illustrative; they are representative of epidemic, not episodic, conditions. They call for an end to official secrecy surrounding corporate crimes and incompetence that weights the taxpayer with corporate socialism. The authors' documentation points to the need for systematic government assembling of data on corporate behavior so that long-enacted laws can be enforced and new policies forged. Reading business periodicals and relying on *Fortune*'s 500 information provide entirely too casual a data base for antitrust policy planning and enforcement. A thorough data base would put an end to the restrictive association of "crime" to street crime while extending doctrinaire permissiveness and anarchy to corporate crimes of the rich.

This book pleads for a recognition that preventable business depredations cannot be excused by acknowledged corporate benefits. These depredations are part of a raging corporate radicalism which generates technological violence, undermines the integrity of government, breaks laws, blocks needed reforms, and repudiates a quality-competitive system with substantial consumer sovereignty. If radicalism is defined as a force against basic value systems of a society, then the corporate state is the chief protagonist. In this context, however, the book's title, *America, Inc.,* while reflective of the corporation's dominance, may obscure the continuing stamina of the ideals of the society which run contrary to the behavior of the present political economy. Many Americans, if apprised of how Union Carbide operates here and abroad in producing pollution and job hazards, would disagree strenuously with that company's recent advertisement arrogantly boasting: "When they look at us, they see a little of you. . . . And it's all quite simple, Overseas, we're you."

All this is not to declare that the noncorporate society is innocent. But a society's compassion tends to rot from the top down, and the exemplary power of the propertied institutions in either direction cannot be overemphasized in either the moral or depraved tone set for other groups and individuals. It was of lesser consequence, perhaps, when corporations adhered to narrower lasts. Now, however, corporate involvement pervades every interstice of our society. Companies are deep in the dossier-credit, city-building, drug, medical, computer intelligence, military, and educational industries. The most intimate functions of government, including education, health, and military theater contracting, are engaging companies and with these engagements come the parochial value system and insulation of the corporate structure. These are not temporary involvements but permanent presences. They point to the old Roman adage—"Whatever touches us all should be decided by all."

The central question, then, is what changes are necessary to direct corporate resources toward respecting the values and pleas that are beyond the balance sheet's morality? And what are the instruments to achieve these changes? Authors Mintz and Cohen urge a deconcentration of corporate power in two principal ways—thorough antitrust action and the federal chartering of corporations to rewrite the compact between the corporation and its creator—the state—which has been virtually unchanged for a century. In point of fact, the charter can make the grant of corporate status conditional on a responsiveness to well-defined public interests and a social accounting of corporate performance. The charter can establish structural receptiveness to official accountability, detailed disclosure, and rights of access by the various constituencies including victims. The authors propose other democratizing forces—the use of routine government procurement in stimulating innovation such as less polluting vehicles, consumer class actions, campaign financing reform, surcharging polluters, disclosure of more product and service information to consumers, and other basic changes to attenuate irresponsible uses of power. They also point to new technologies which permit smaller plant size without sacrificing efficiencies, thereby seriously questioning the conventional wisdom that efficiency requires giant corporations.

But even solid structural changes have a way of concentrating old power in new forms sooner or later unless there is a continual assertion and defense of individual rights and responsibilities within the corporate institution itself. Like the medieval peasants who never knew they were serfs, scientists, engineers, accountants, lawyers, physicians, and other corporate-employed professionals rarely realize the extent of their disenfranchisement inside their company government because their roles are defined so narrowly for them. These professionals are usually the first to know the consequences of corporate policies, but they do not have the protected rights vis-à-vis management to exert their professional missions. (Actually, the blue-collar unionized laborer has far more contracted rights with management.) They cannot muster the strength to blow the whistle when their company acts in ways clearly injurious to the public's wellbeing. So millions of defective cars roll off the production line, drugs are huckstered and food additives sold without adequate testing, tenants' and sharecroppers' rights are overridden by absentee management, miners have their health depleted by companies which receive tax depletion allowances, the land, air, and water are filled with carbon monoxide, mercury, lead, cadmium, and untold numbers of other contaminants, and those inside the companies stay silent or actively promote and defend such acts or defaults. The professional employees who would speak out anticipate the consequences and do nothing. As long as the internal authority of the corporation remains unchallenged, any external pressures will have minimal and temporary impact. It is just this absence of internal rights that partly explains the successful resistance of the corporation to external disciplinary attempts. The other insulating factor is the absence of legal responsibility on the part of officers and management officials for corporate impacts. Even in the most personally oriented legal sanctions for investor protection administered by the Securities and Exchange Commission, only a handful of stock exchange and brokerage house officials—all relatively low-level—felt the arm of the law in the midst of recent manipulation, illegalities, and self-dealing which for dollar sums made the debacle of the Twenties small by comparison.

Thus, against the growing sensitivity about corporate predations, willful or negligent, there is more than routine attention to be attached to the proposed, but later rejected, code revisions affecting corporate officials by the National Commission on Reform of Federal Criminal Laws. These proposals would permit imposition of accountability for corporate conduct and law compliance on the individuals responsible for such company decisions. The entire range of legal sanctions against both the corporate structure and its officials has to be reconsidered, as the commission has begun to do, beyond just simple civil-criminal fines toward a more flexible array of civil-criminal sanctions tailored to maximum deterrence. Suspension of corporate managers and board members, temporary bans on corporate advertising because of deceptive practices, required publication of violations to inform consumers who have been harmed or deceived by culpable conduct, and imposition of environmental bankruptcy for a company continually contaminating its neighbors' environment are some suggestions that may effectively deter illegal behavior.

Together with such internal changes, the emergence of full-time, independent corporate monitors, staffed by lawyers and other skilled professionals in Washington and state capitals, would have lasting effect. Such citizens' firms would simply invoke powerful strategies of citizenship against industrial and commercial abuses and advocate in forums of decision-making programs for necessary change.

The modern corporation is the engine of the world's largest production machine. If it is to be more than a mindless, parochial juggernaut, the hands of diverse human values and trusteeships for future generations must be exerted on the steering wheel. There should no longer be victims without representation. In any *just* legal system a victim would have the right to decide with others the behavior of the perpetrator and his recompense. The corporate framework cannot be wished away or simply placed in a different crucible—such as government—and result in an equitable deployment of its resources and creativity. If it did not exist, the corporate entity would have to be invented in some form to collect capital, retain labor and generate the outputs. As the consequences of corporate neglect mount more visibly, the popularization of the corporate condition through initiatory democratic rights, coupled with remedies and representation both on and within the corporation, are sure to become pivotal public issues in the coming decade. What the authors of this relentless book are saying to Americans is what Americans ought to be saying to themselves.

RALPH NADER

Washington, D.C.
December 1970

America, Inc.

The law locks up both man and woman
Who steals the goose from off the common,
But lets the greater felon loose
Who steals the common from the goose.

—Anonymous

PROLOGUE

Calvin Coolidge once told us that "the business of America is business."[1] The fashion has been to judge this notion quaint. But the late President is owed something better than condescension. He should be thanked for laying down an Orwellian stepping-stone to a perception of our true condition: Big Business *is* government.

To govern, the *Oxford Universal Dictionary* says, is "to rule with authority . . . to direct and control the action and affairs of (a people, etc.) . . . to hold sway, prevail . . . manage, order . . ." The constitutional government (a summary phrase intended to embrace the national and state and local governments) rules, directs, controls, sways, prevails, manages, orders. So does the giant corporation. This is an entity utterly unlike the ordinary business.

The constitutional government levies taxes. So, under a different name, does the giant corporation. "Men in America were so conditioned that they felt differently about taxes and about prices," the late Thurman W. Arnold said in *The Folklore of Capitalism*. "The former was an involuntary taking; the latter a voluntary giving. . . . No one observed the obvious fact that in terms of total income of an individual it made no difference whether his money went for prices or taxes."[2]

In the period 1960–1966 consumer prices increased 14.1 per cent. This elicited protests. But the protests were directed largely at obtaining relief from the burden of taxes. Few perceived a relevant connection with inflated corporate profits which, after taxes, had increased 88 per cent, or six times as much as prices. What was little grasped, to put it another way, was that the price increases were substantially attributable to a *profit* inflation. Unit labor costs in manufacturing could not be blamed. These had gone up only 2.1 per cent.

President Nixon, at his first press conference on January 27, 1969,

1

rejected "the suggestion that inflation can be effectively controlled by exhorting labor and management and industry to follow certain guidelines." Rather than intervene in price and wage decisions he would, he said, fight inflation with fiscal and monetary policy. The response of giant corporations to the Nixon signal illuminated the gap between them and ordinary businesses. In the President's remarks they divined a change in the rules of the game. No longer would they face, as they had in the Johnson Administration, the prospect of being summoned to the White House to be exhorted and pressured to restrain price increases. Promptly several giant corporations effected a series of price increases. The result was that eight months later copper, for example, was up 24 per cent. Zinc was up 11 per cent. Steel mill products, on the Wholesale Price Index, climbed 4.5 points.[3] Little had changed in the three decades since Thurman Arnold wrote *The Folklore of Capitalism*. Public frustration did not take the form of demands for action to lower synthetically inflated prices, because these were perceived as "voluntary giving" rather than private taxes. Instead, public pressure welled up against public taxes, these being "involuntary taking."

In 1967 the nation's bill for repairing automobiles was running at an annual rate of between $5 billion and $6 billion. Edward Daniels, a specialist in auto insurance claims, estimated that $1 billion of the total was accounted for by the abandonment of bumpers that were functional for bumpers that were ornamental.[4] These, General Motors acknowledged, met its standards if they protected surrounding sheet metal from the impact of a collision at a speed, if it can be called that, of 2.8 miles per hour.[5] The $1 billion should be seen essentially as a tax levied in the form of elevated insurance rates. With hardly anyone noticing, the industry took another billion dollars in 1968 when it raised prices for "captive" parts—those obtainable only from the maker of the car—and other replacement parts.[6]

When it sends men to war or to a penal death chamber the constitutional government takes life. The giant corporation also takes life. This is as dimly perceived as the similarity between a tax and an artificially high price. Because of this the corporation escapes blame and even criticism. Thought is given instead to the mysterious ways in which God moves His wonders to perform. The auto industry—meaning mainly

General Motors—has provided memorable examples. Consider energy-absorbing steering assemblies. These prevent crushing of the driver in event of accident. Advanced designs were patented in the 1920s. Yet a curious apathy persisted until recent years, although a very large price in blood was being paid.

Finally the industry was embarrassed and prodded by hearings held in July 1965 by Senator Abraham A. Ribicoff (D–Conn.); by the publication, a few months later, of Ralph Nader's *Unsafe at Any Speed*;[7] by the unexpected disclosure of the harassment of Nader by private detectives retained by GM, and by the awkward publicity that attended these matters. Stirred at last, the industry decided it could offer the energy-absorbing assemblies, first on certain 1967 models and then on all new cars manufactured after December 31, 1967. The National Highway Safety Bureau made a preliminary calculation of what this promised. If all rather than a negligible proportion of the motor vehicles in use were equipped at that moment with the safety devices, Deputy Director Robert Brenner said, "instead of 53,000 annual traffic deaths, there could be less than 40,000, a saving of 13,000 lives a year."[8] The prevention of injury would be on a vastly greater scale, the steering assembly accounting for more than 40 per cent of all injuries to drivers. Lowell K. Bridwell, while Federal Highway Administrator, said that over past decades "hundreds of thousands" of drivers had been killed by unyielding steering assemblies. "Most of these deaths need not have occurred," he told the Senate Commerce Committee.[9] His indictment has not been seriously challenged.

Nader said it would be "insulting" to auto industry engineers to suggest that they could not have perfected the steering device for mass produced automobiles over a decade ago.[10] What he called the "suppressed creativity" of industry engineers had found other outlets. On the road are many millions of cars with cleverly designed hood ornaments, phallic bumper guards and other pieces of protuberant metal. While director of the National Highway Safety Bureau, Dr. William Haddon provided manufacturers with evidence, including color photographs, of needlessly grave and hideous wounds.[11] Yet vast numbers of Pontiacs, to take an obvious example, continued to be armed with protruding center grilles shaped like meat cleavers. Seeing such a car, a pedestrian should be advised to be extra nimble in getting off the road, or the warpath. While doing so he might contemplate whether his fate was in the hands of the mighty rather than the Almighty.

Turn to an item as humdrum as windshield wipers. Naked they had always come. No one was offended. Especially in the era of the miniskirt there were more erotic distractions. However, General Motors decided that sales of its more ostentatious cars would be helped by concealing the wipers. In part, GM accomplished this by putting an upward curve in the rear of the hood and the adjoining fender corners. Unfortunately, this means that a front-end accident thrusts one or more of these pieces toward glass rather than steel. The result is that with a moderate impact the windshield breaks, adding $100 to the cost of repair. Inexorably, the cost of insurance rises, even for owners of cars with naked wipers. Thus GM has exercised a private power to tax. Suppose the accident is severe. The hood or fender then is rammed through the windshield into the passenger compartment.[12] GM may also have exercised a private power to imperil life.

Other industries also merit attention. Let us turn first to the pharmaceutical industry. During the 1950s epidemics of serious and fatal staphylococcus infections were widespread. The most prominent cause was an exuberant overprescribing of antimicrobial agents, the sulfonamides and the early penicillins, that allowed proliferation of strains of bacteria resistant to treatment. Although the epidemics subsided with development of a new class of penicillins, the semisynthetics, a threat of new proliferations of resistant strains became apparent in the late 1960s. Dr. Calvin M. Kunin, a specialist in the treatment of infectious diseases and chairman of a National Academy of Sciences–National Research Council review panel on fixed combinations of antibiotics, has warned of possible peril to "all society."[13]

The pharmaceutical industry was mainly responsible for creating the danger and, for fifteen years, perpetuating and expanding it. (To be sure, the Food and Drug Administration, which in 1970 finally secured a withdrawal of such irrational mixtures from the market, had disgraced itself by ever allowing the products to go on sale. This was an act so tainted that a federal grand jury undertook an investigation of the official involved. But the corrupting force was the industry; and the fount of the bitter-end resistance to withdrawal again was the industry.)

One of the therapeutically irrational but lushly profitable mixtures combined, in fixed ratios, two antibiotics, penicillin and streptomycin. The "widespread" and "indiscriminate" use of such products, which was a direct result of industry promotion, "almost led to disaster," Dr. Kunin

4

said. But not until June 1970, when further resistance would have been futile or counterproductive, was an administrative and court battle abandoned by Wyeth Laboratories, one of two prescription-drug divisions of American Home Products, which in the preceding year was the nation's ninety-fourth largest industrial corporation. Similarly, the Bristol-Myers Company—until the FDA, in a rare act of courage, faced it down—used a massive promotional campaign to encourage physicians to switch their loyalties from other effective agents to Dynapen, a semisynthetic penicillin, even though overuse of such an admittedly excellent medicine needlessly increased the risk of staph epidemics.[14] The Upjohn Company enlarged the peril with Panalba, yet another therapeutically irrational but exceedingly profitable mixture of antibiotics (tetracycline and novobiocin). As if this was not enough, the commissioner of the FDA testified that Panalba annually caused hundreds of thousands of needless injuries, a few of them lethal.[15] Similarly, the needless use of streptomycin, usually in combination with penicillin or with a sulfonamide, creates a needless risk of irreversible deafness in some patients, particularly children. In passing, it may be noted that this entire situation probably could not have developed had not the pharmaceutical industry been able to govern a significant element of the medical profession. Such control was achieved, and is maintained, through devices that create dependency and stifle criticism, including gifts to medical schools and the placement of vast quantities of lucrative advertising in the *Journal* of the American Medical Association and other medical publications.[16]

A giant corporation can affect the quality of life and the environment just as surely and profoundly as an elected government. In 1964 in Los Angeles County 3.5 million motor vehicles were daily burning more than 7 million gallons of gasoline and depositing about 800,000 pounds of contaminants into the atmosphere. Even before this, physicians, in a single year, had advised ten thousand persons in vulnerable health to move away. In June 1964 S. Smith Griswold, the county's air pollution control officer, put major blame on the auto industry. "Everything that the industry is able to do today to control auto exhaust was possible technically ten years ago," he told a meeting of the Air Pollution Control Association in Houston. "No new principles had to be developed; no technological advance was needed; no scientific breakthrough was required."

The speech set off an intricate series of events beginning with a visit by Ralph Nader to the Justice Department. He argued persuasively that, though it may have been done inadvertently, Griswold, an engineer, had provided the groundwork for a case of product-fixing as clearly in violation of the antitrust laws as price-fixing. In January 1965 the Department served the industry with initial demands for records. Samuel Flatow, an Antitrust Division lawyer who since has died, was assigned to lead an investigation. His findings were so serious that a grand jury was convened in Los Angeles. The grand jury heard evidence from July 1966 to December 1967. Finally Flatow requested permission to ask the grand jury to return an indictment. Washington refused the request. But on January 10, 1969—in the late twilight of the Johnson Administration—the Department filed a civil complaint charging the four leading manufacturers and the Automobile Manufacturers Association with having conspired to impede development and installation of anti-pollution devices and technology. The enormity of the charge should require no elaboration. It speaks, unspeakably, for itself. The suit never was tested in an open trial. It was settled in the fall of 1969 with a consent decree. As is customary with this remarkable legal invention, the defendants were enabled to avoid saying whether they had committed the offenses charged by the government while promising not to commit the same offenses thereafter.

It is natural that the power to tax, take life, and drastically affect the environment should be present in a giant corporation. It is natural, that is, in an entity with the proportions of a sovereign state. General Motors is the world's largest industrial corporation. Its annual revenue is greater than that of any foreign government except the United Kingdom and the Union of Soviet Socialist Republics, and greater, as well, than the gross national product of Brazil or Sweden. In 1965 GM's sales of $20.7 billion "exceeded the *combined* general revenues of the state and local governments of New York, New Jersey, Pennsylvania, Ohio, Delaware, and the six New England states."[17] This figures out to $2.3 million per hour, 24 hours a day, 365 days a year (by 1969 it was 2.8 million). On the same hourly basis, its profit after taxes was $242,649.[18]

Thurman Arnold, who in the New Deal was Assistant Attorney General in charge of the Antitrust Division of the Department of Justice, once characterized the Ford Motor Company and Chrysler Corporation as "satellites of General Motors. General Motors will let them live as long as they do not grow too much at its expense."[19]

Major international implications flow predictably from corporations that are big enough to be fairly compared with nations. Here is a ten-billion-dollar example. In the late 1950s the demand for steel declined. By 1958, a recession year, mills in the United States were operating at less than 50 per cent of capacity. Yet in August of that year the industry *raised* the price by $4.50 a ton. Only a concentrated industry (or a monopoly) could do that. In the six member countries of the European Coal and Steel Community, steel producers behaved quite differently. They also had experienced a decline in demand. But they reacted with *lower* prices. So it came about that the United States, which had been exporting more steel than it was importing, reversed its role and entered the 1960s as a net importer. For many years American mills operated at less than two-thirds of capacity. Yet prices remained rigid or were slightly increased. In Europe, where prices fluctuated with demand, steelmakers operated continuously at or near capacity. To be specific: In the years 1960–1963 the export price of American steel was held at $126 to $127 a ton. In the same years in Europe the export price fell from $147 in 1960 to $93 in 1963. Claims of higher costs in the United States do not stand up. For one thing, coking coal was substantially cheaper in this country and iron ore was no more expensive. The foregoing is a summary of the background that Professor Egon Sohmen gave the Senate Subcommittee on Antitrust and Monopoly for this astonishing finding:

> Had the [American] industry worked at capacity during the early sixties, and had it exported the additional steel at world market prices, the additional export revenue (taking into account the fact that steel prices on the world market would have been somewhat lower as a consequence) *would have eliminated the U.S. balance-of-payments deficits during these years.* One need hardly go into the details of what the United States would have been spared in this event.[20] [Emphasis supplied.]

A few of the details should be given. In the years 1960–1963 the aggregate deficit in the balance of payments was $10.6 billion. There would have been no deficit at all had the steel industry, in each of the four years, sold an additional 30 million tons of steel at world market prices of at least $90 per ton. Indeed, a $200 million surplus would have

7

accrued. Professor Sohmen testified that the industry could have succeeded in this competition "without difficulty." Even the $10.6 billion understated the stakes. Sohmen explained why:

> If steel prices in the United States had uniformly been at the lower world market levels, many important American industries using steel (the automobile or the machinery industries, to name a few), could have reduced their prices. This would have entailed a rise in exports of those industries and a fall of competing imports, further improving the U.S. trade balance.

To function effectively and reliably as private governments, giant corporations must govern constitutional governments. During the era of the Progressive movement, which rose in the 1890s and peaked in 1912, "the Republican party of Wisconsin was neither more nor less than a railroad machine," Grant McConnell has written. "In California railroad domination was even more complete. The Southern Pacific virtually owned both parties."[21] Today matters often are handled with more discretion. Aspirations are more modest. Rather than ownership, a potential for control is deemed sufficient. It is, for example, extravagant to want to control every member of a congressional committee on every issue; it is enough to be able to control a crucial vote on important issues. A campaign contribution, offered in an hour of need, can become one of the shrewdest of investments. A timely decision to locate an industrial plant in a particular state or congressional district can earn undying, and tangible, gratitude. No one has dealt with these matters more bluntly than Woodrow Wilson. "The masters of the government of the United States are the combined capitalists and manufacturers of the United States," he said during his first campaign for the Presidency. "It is written over every intimate page of the record of Congress, it is written all through the history of conferences at the White House, that the suggestions of economic policy have come from one source, not from many sources. . . . The government of the United States at present is a foster child of the special interests."[22]

A similar complaint would have point today. In 1968 the Poor People's Campaign came to Washington. The reception was cold. Members of Congress accused leaders of the campaign of wanting handouts or other forms of special treatment. Senator Philip A. Hart (D–Mich.), chairman of the Senate Subcommittee on Antitrust and Monopoly, was struck by the contrast with the reception accorded a segment of industry that, say, has lost an antitrust case in the courts: "There is no hesitancy to ask antitrust amendments to take care of its special problems," he said. "Its arguments win general acceptance. It does not have the bad flavor of the poor, non-corporate petitioners."[23]

In 1969, in the Supreme Court, a segment of the newspaper industry lost just such a case. Profit-pooling and price-fixing under a joint operating agreement by separately owned newspapers in Tucson, Arizona, were declared illegal. Similar agreements in twenty-one other cities thus were threatened. A bill to overturn the ruling was introduced in Congress, and wide congressional support was attracted. Liberals found it just as difficult as conservatives to antagonize such supplicants as the Hearst and Newhouse and Scripps-Howard chains. But the Department of Justice was opposed to the bill. Its testimony on Capitol Hill—cleared by the Budget Bureau, meaning the White House—was forceful. The bill would entrench "absolute monopoly," "flout the basic principles of the free enterprise system" and impair the vital newspaper function of "acting as a watchdog on government," the Justice Department said.[24] One day in the autumn of 1969, Richard Berlin, president of the Hearst Corporation, visited President Nixon at the White House. A few days later the Department of Commerce, out of the blue, endorsed the bill, the Newspaper Preservation Act. Although no one could recall a precedent for the Commerce Department's speaking for the White House on an antitrust matter, it did emphatically speak for Mr. Nixon on this occasion.

Although there is some awareness that the oil and gas industries govern through the executive branch and the Congress, the awakening is a relatively recent development. The principal precipitating cause was the great fuss in 1968 and 1969 about the oil depletion allowance and such extraordinary arrangements as those that allowed Atlantic Richfield to earn a total of $797 million in net income in the years 1962 through 1968, pay no federal tax whatever in the first of those six years, and pay at the rate of 1.2 per cent in the seventh year. The following cases will fill out the literature on government by oil and gas.

The upkeep of President Eisenhower's farm at Gettysburg was paid for by three oilmen—the late Alton W. Jones, chairman of the executive committee of Cities Service; B. B. (Billy) Byars of Tyler, Texas, and George E. Allen, a heavy investor in oil. This has been documented by the late Drew Pearson and Jack Anderson. "They signed a strictly private lease agreement, under which they were supposed to pay the farm costs and collect the profits," the newsmen said in *The Case Against Congress.* They continued:

> Internal Revenue, after checking into the deal, could find no evidence that the oilmen had attempted to operate the farm as a profitable venture. Internal Revenue concluded that the money the oilmen poured into the farm could not be deducted as a business expense but had to be reported as an outright gift. Thus, by official ruling of the Internal Revenue Service, three oilmen gave Ike more than $500,000 at the same time he was making decisions favorable to the oil industry.[25]

One must be exceedingly reluctant to impute a trace of impure motive to the late President. Oilmen were his friends. But one must credit the accuracy of Pearson and Anderson in saying that during his years in the White House, "Dwight Eisenhower did more for the nation's private oil and gas interests than any other President." In 1959, by executive order, Mr. Eisenhower imposed a system of oil import quotas. Reasons of national defense were cited. These proved to be insubstantial at best and preposterous at worst. The quotas severely restricted imports of foreign oil. The principal beneficiaries were the major oil companies. Over the years they managed to defuse every effort to overturn the system. They had what Senator John O. Pastore (D–R.I.) called "raw political power."[26] By 1969 the quotas were costing the public $7.2 billion a year. This estimate, made by Dr. John M. Blair, then chief economist of the Senate Subcommittee on Antitrust and Monopoly, was carefully constructed from data on the comparative prices of American and Middle Eastern crude, laid down on the East Coast of the United States. Before almost deserted press tables at a subcommittee hearing, he showed that the quotas added about five cents to the price of each gallon of gasoline ($35 a year for the average motorist), and almost four cents per gallon to the price of fuel oil ($58.50 a year for an average homeowner with oil heat). These homely statistics drew trivial attention in major news media, which simultaneously were devoting massive attention, day after day, to the surtax. Thurman Arnold would have appreciated the irony. The inflated gas and oil prices were a "voluntary giving." The surtax (which, relatively, involved not very much more—about $9 billion) was an "involuntary taking."

On March 4, 1965, a pipeline carrying natural gas under high pressure exploded near Natchitoches, Louisiana. Seventeen persons were killed. Thirteen acres were devastated. Senator Warren G. Magnuson (D–Wash.), chairman of the Senate Commerce Committee, responded by proposing the first legislation to set federal safety standards for gas pipelines. In 1967, by a vote of 78 to 0, the Senate passed the bill. The unanimity of the vote by no means indicated that the bill was acceptable to the industry. To the contrary, the industry was highly displeased. But it chose to fight in the House. There its strategy was vindicated when the desired evisceration was accomplished in the Committee on Interstate and Foreign Commerce. Members of the defeated minority of the committee took the unusual step of writing a letter to the *New York Times* which was published on May 3, 1968. "In our opinion the bill was essentially gutted at the behest of the gas pipeline lobbies most of whose proposals were adopted verbatim," the congressmen said. They made efforts to strengthen the bill on the House floor but failed. The industry was openly pleased. "Certainly it isn't altogether what we'd like if we'd sat down and written the bill ourselves," a spokesman told *Congressional Quarterly*.[27] Fortunately, the Senate succeeded in significantly strengthening the bill before it became law. Yet the industry still may be reasonably pleased, because Congress has not provided adequate funds for enforcement.

John W. Gardner, the former Secretary of Health, Education, and Welfare, has urged that "each government agency honestly appraise the extent to which it has built an empire rather than served the public. And let it ask how much risk it has taken in fighting for good causes." His tone was not optimistic. "The natural state of the bureaucracy is to be unbloody but bowed," he said. "It would look better with some honorable scars."[28] Gardner should be heeded. The importance of regulatory agencies, and of regulatory operations within the Executive, is too often downgraded or forgotten. They deal with the quality and purity of the air, water, food, and drugs; with the safety of aircraft, trains, buses, cars, trucks, tires, pipelines, chemical warfare agents, atomic energy facilities, medicines, pesticides, and food additives; with radiation from color television sets, microwave ovens, and X-ray machines; with the uses of the public's airwaves, with deceit in the marketplace, with the injection of water into hams, with the potential for power blackouts, and with the prices of power and natural gas.

It should be remembered that unlike the Supreme Court, which publishes majority and minority opinions for all to see, regulatory agencies and Executive regulatory operations sometimes operate in secrecy. A discreet phone call between an official and a corporation can, in an operation such as the Food and Drug Administration, abort a necessary regulatory action. As it is, the subject matter can be so arcane as to defy comprehension by laymen. If the lax procedures standard in the FDA during the reign of the late Commissioner George P. Larrick had prevailed, Dr. Frances O. Kelsey would have yielded to the pressures exerted by Richardson-Merrell, Inc., and let thalidomide go on sale. By the time the capacity of the sedative to deform had been recognized, an estimated ten thousand limbless babies would already have been born to parents living in the United States. "Government itself develops vested interests which become more concerned with self-perpetuation than with social values," Senator Edmund S. Muskie (D–Me.) has observed. "Sometimes economic interests and government agency interests become so intertwined that the public cannot distinguish between the two."[29] Three cases of intertwining:

Since 1938 a manufacturer wishing to market a medicine has been required first to demonstrate to the satisfaction of the government that the product is safe for its intended uses. For almost a quarter-century thereafter, however, there was no requirement of a demonstration of efficacy—meaning substantial evidence that a drug would live up to the claims allowed in the labeling. Predictably, many thousands of ineffective preparations went on sale. "There is no way of measuring the needless suffering, the money innocently squandered, and the protraction of illnesses resulting from the use of such ineffective drugs," President John F. Kennedy said.[30]

In 1962, reacting to the thalidomide warning, Congress enacted the Kefauver-Harris Amendments. Among other reforms, the need for which was developed in two and a half years of hearings by the late Senator Estes Kefauver, these required manufacturers, after a two-year grace period, to submit substantial evidence for the claims of efficacy made for drug products marketed in the 1938–1962 period. These products account for more than 80 per cent of the preparations dispensed today by prescription and over the counter. A crucial role would be played by the director of the FDA's Bureau of Medicine. Yet the post had been vacant since August 1962, eleven months after notice of resignation had been served by the last physician to fill it. Primary responsibility for filling the vacancy rested on Boisfeuillet Jones, then special assistant for medical affairs in the Department of Health, Education, and Welfare. The Commissioner of the FDA at the time, George Larrick, had nominated Dr. Charles D. May, a distinguished pediatrician. However, the doctor had offended the pharmaceutical industry with critical testimony before Senator Kefauver and with an article pointing out that promotion of prescription drugs, including activities indistinguishable from payola, was costing three and a half times as much as all of the educational programs in medical schools. Jones "won the confidence of the pharmaceutical industry by blocking the appointment of Dr. Charles May," *Drug Research Reports* said in June 1964. Even before this, Jones had acknowledged to a reporter what his priorities were. He was looking, he said, for a director of the Bureau who would be "acceptable to the industry, the consumers and the academic world, but [HEW was] not trying to satisfy the industry *per se.*"[31]

Jones's patience was rewarded and his priorities met when, in April 1964, he chose Dr. Joseph F. Sadusk, Jr. Once in office as the FDA's top physician, Dr. Sadusk did everything within his power to frustrate the intent of the efficacy legislation.[32] His services were properly esteemed by his constituency and, after leaving the agency, he became vice president of the pharmaceutical firm of Parke, Davis & Company. At the FDA he had made an almost immeasurable contribution to the unconscionable delay in taking nostrums off the market. Of almost four thousand preparations evaluated for efficacy by the National Academy of Sciences–National Research Council at the FDA's request in the years from 1938 through 1962, a "considerable number" failed to meet one or more—or even all—of the therapeutic claims made for them.[33] As of early 1970 virtually all commercially significant medicines in this group were still on sale, and as of early 1971 most were.

Over a period of three decades producers of hot dogs and bologna increased the average fat content from 18.6 per cent to 32.2 per cent. This gave reason for concern. Large numbers of people consume these foods in vast quantities. They are mainstays for, among others, the poor and school lunch programs and institutions. A decline in nutritional value consequently was a threat to health. In addition, medical authorities warned that a greater intake of animal fats would enhance the bodily environment for heart disease. In December 1968 the Department of Agriculture proposed to limit the fat content of frankfurters and bologna to 30 percent. The meat industry lobbied against the proposal. The Department backed down and proposed a 33 per cent limit, which was what the industry wanted.[34] Only extraordinary counter-pressure— from publicity and consumer forces—led the Department to revert to 30 per cent.

President Nixon was on the side of the public in the hot dog episode. But in key broadcasting issues he has been on the side of the fat and fatuous. Late in 1969 he made two appointments to the Federal Communications Commission. His choice for chairman was Dean Burch, a former aide to Barry Goldwater and chairman of the Republican National Committee during the senator's pursuit of the Presidency in 1964. Mr. Nixon's choice for commissioner was Robert Wells, a broadcasting executive. In making these appointments Mr. Nixon ignored the National Citizens Committee for Broadcasting and other public interest forces—but cleared Burch and Wells with the broadcasting industry.[35] He was by no means the first President to have taken such a precaution with one or another true constituency, but this time the consequences promised to be particularly dispiriting. "Of all those Americans who are trying to get more out of life than they have put into it and who are laying waste their country in the attempt, none has appeared more successful as a group than the broadcasters," the jurors for the *Survey of Broadcast Journalism 1968–1969* said. "In what other business can a moderately astute operator hope to realize 100 per cent a year on tangible assets, or lay out $150 for a franchise that in a few years' time he can peddle for $50 million—should he be so foolish as to want to sell? The most fantastic rewards associated with broadcasting in many instances grow from enterprises that do as little for their fellow countrymen as they legally can."[36]

The television industry has been providing more hours of "education" to an average child before he enters kindergarten than he will spend in college classrooms earning a bachelor's degree.[37] In a single week of evening programs television may continue to offer, as it did by count of the staff of the *Christian Science Monitor* in October 1968, "254 incidents of violence, including threats, and 71 murders, killings and suicides."[38] Assuredly the unrelenting exposure to violence will go on begetting violence, just as exposure to television advertising will go on begetting demands by children on their parents for advertised products. Children will go on being taught, as Commissioner Nicholas Johnson of the FCC put it, "that the single measure of happiness and personal satisfaction is consumption," that "success" derives from the purchase of a mouthwash or deodorant, and all the rest. "What are these network executives doing?" he asked in a statement to the National Commission on the Causes and Prevention of Violence. "What right have they to tear down every night what the American people are spending $52 billion a year to build up every day through their school system . . .?"[39] The "right" is much the same as the "right" of other industry executives to govern.

A few giant corporations dominate most basic industries, which, as a result, are called concentrated industries. At the same time, a relative handful of the same corporations dominate most of mining and manufacturing. This is called overall concentration. The near omnipresence of concentration may be obvious to a casual observer of the economy. But that presence requires emphasis and even reemphasis because of the frequent pretense of influential and sophisticated observers that it isn't there. It is a pretense that inhibits understanding. "Instead of reckoning with large and concrete corporations, economists and government officials prefer to shape policy around large and impersonal abstractions," Bernard D. Nossiter says in *The Mythmakers*.[40] "They think in terms of total demand, total employment; they manipulate broad-gauged tools like taxes, spending and the supply of money and credit." But why has the crucial fact of concentration been snubbed? "This is, after all, a sensitive subject because it involves power," Nossiter says. "For a policy maker to cope with concentration can mean conflict with the strongest institutions in America."[41]

To concentrate economic power in *either* private or public hands is to concentrate political power in the same hands. Concentrated political power, no matter in whose hands, weakens and may destroy democratic institutions. Claims of originality would be unbecoming. The Founding Fathers were fully aware of the dangers of concentrated power in their day—roughly a century before the United States became

15

an industrial nation—and took admirable precautions against it. "The accumulation of all powers, legislative, executive, and judiciary, in the same hands, may justly be pronounced the very definition of tyranny," James Madison said.[42] An accumulation of economic power so great that it becomes political power likewise can be tyranny. We have been adequately warned about the state that functions as a super-corporation. We have been inadequately warned about the super-corporation that functions as a state. In setting antitrust policy, Congress long has recognized "that concentration of industrial power may lead to the police state," William H. Orrick, Jr., said while head of the Antitrust Division of the Justice Department. "Can anyone doubt that the prewar experience of Germany, Japan, and Italy have proven the wisdom of the nation's concern over concentration of economic power?"[43]

But concentration grows. One of those who have expressed concern is Attorney General John N. Mitchell. In a speech on June 6, 1969, he reviewed the record: In the previous two years the number of corporate mergers "more than doubled" and, more importantly, "involved an increasing number of large firms"; the assets of acquired firms increased from $4 billion in 1966 to more than $12 billion in 1968; among firms with assets exceeding $250 million, only five were acquired from 1948 to 1966—compared with six in 1967 and twelve in 1968; increasingly, the largest firms were playing a prominent role in acquisitions, as shown by the statistics for 1968. In that year companies among the two hundred largest made 74 of the total of 192 acquisitions of enterprises with assets of at least $10 million. Mitchell went on to say:

> In 1948, the nation's 200 largest industrial corporations controlled 48 percent of the manufacturing assets. Today, these firms control 58 percent, while the top 500 firms control 75 percent of these assets.
> *The danger that this super-concentration poses to our economic, political and social structure cannot be over-estimated.* Concentration of this magnitude is likely to eliminate existing and future competition. It increases the possibility for reciprocity and other forms of unfair buyer-seller leverage. It creates nation-wide marketing, managerial and financing structures whose enormous physical and psychological resources pose substantial barriers to smaller firms wishing to participate in a competitive market.
> And, finally, super-concentration creates a "community of interest"

which discourages competition among large firms and establishes a tone in the marketplace for more and more mergers.

This leaves us with the unacceptable probability that the nation's manufacturing and financial assets will continue to be concentrated in the hands of fewer and fewer people—the very evil that the Sherman Act, the Clayton Act, the Robinson-Patman Act, and the Celler-Kefauver Amendment were designed to combat.[44] [Emphasis supplied.]

The fear of concentration expressed by the Republican Attorney General differs in no significant respect from the fear expressed by men whom, on other issues, he would not count among his admirers. President Franklin D. Roosevelt said, "I am against private socialism of concentrated economic power as thoroughly as I am against government socialism. The one is equally as dangerous as the other; and destruction of private socialism is utterly essential to avoid governmental socialism."[45] But how distant was this from President Herbert Hoover: "Likewise the basic foundations of autocracy, whether it be class government or capitalism in the sense that few men through unrestrained control of property determine the welfare of great numbers, is [sic] as far apart from the rightful expression of American individualism as the two poles."[46]

President Johnson's Cabinet Committee on Price Stability: "Further merger-achieved centralization of economic power and decision-making may seriously impair the proper functioning of our competitive, free enterprise economy, as well as threaten the social and political values associated with a decentralized economic system."[47] Manuel F. Cohen, while chairman of the Securities and Exchange Commission: "A decision to hold back vital goods and services or to set prices at exorbitant levels then becomes not a simple business decision, but an irresponsible abuse of political power."[48]

The late Senator Estes Kefauver: "Through monopolistic mergers the people are losing power to direct their own economic welfare. When they lose the power to direct their economic welfare they also lose the means to direct their political future."[49] Senator Philip A. Hart, who in 1963 succeeded Kefauver as chairman of the Senate Subcommittee on Antitrust and Monopoly: "In this society of ours, we depend on diffusion of power as the best means of achieving political democracy. . . . If we fail the danger is clear to anyone who has studied history—particularly that of the Axis powers prior to World War II."[50] Senator Gaylord Nelson (D–Wis.), head of a Senate small business subcommittee: "Americans, ever suspicious of concentrated political power, have permitted concentrations of economic power to develop, substantially unchallenged, that would make a Roman emperor gasp."[51]

The late T. K. Quinn, who was a vice president of General Electric: "Big business breeds bureaucracy and bureaucrats exactly as big government does."[52] C. S. Lewis: "The greatest evil is not now done in those sordid 'dens of crime' that Dickens loved to paint. It is not done even in concentration camps and labour camps. In those we see its final result. But it is conceived and ordered (moved, seconded, carried and minuted) in clean, carpeted, warmed and well-lighted offices, by quiet men with white collars and cut fingernails and smooth-shaven cheeks who do not need to raise their voices. Hence, naturally enough, my symbol for Hell is something like the bureaucracy of a police state or the offices of a thoroughly nasty business concern."[53]

The bond between men as diverse as those quoted in these pages is of course a common concern about power which is neither checked nor balanced. We are but pawns of such power. The rulers of the great corporations do not have to stand for election. The individual stockholders, the men and women popularized in institutional advertising, do not have control. "In General Electric the election of directors was only formalized at stockholders' meetings," T. K. Quinn said. "The directors were in every case selected by the officers. We had then, in effect, a huge economic state governed by nonelected, self-perpetuating officers and directors—the direct opposite of the democratic method."[54]

In major respects little seemed to have changed by May 22, 1970, when General Motors held its annual meeting of shareholders in Detroit. But spokesmen for the "Campaign to Make General Motors Responsible" were determined to press GM chairman James M. Roche about how the corporation selected directors. Barbara J. Williams, a black law student, demanded to know why no black person ever had been named to the board.

"No black has been nominated and no black has been elected," Roche said. "Our directors are elected by our stockholders."

Miss Williams asked, "How are they nominated?"

"They are nominated at the annual shareholders meeting just as they were today" (in January 1971 GM did elect a black director, the Rev. Dr. Leon M. Sullivan of Philadelphia).

Miss Williams, who was, of course, trying to bring out how closely held the whole process is, then inquired, "Why are there no women on your Board of Directors?"

Roche replied, again vaguely and circuitously, "Our directors are selected on the basis of their ability to make a contribution to the success of General Motors."

Later, Harry Huge, a Washington lawyer, cut through Roche's semantic maze. "Mr. Roche," he said, "*you* nominate the Board of Directors, because eleven [of twenty-four] members of the Board are your officers and former officers of the Board of General Motors." When Roche demurred, saying he merely "can make my recommendations," Huge challenged him to show that "you don't get your way." He asked, "Have you ever had a recommendation that wasn't acted upon favorably?" Roche said he had—but did not assert that the Board ever had rejected a recommendation of his for the Board.

Geoffrey Cowan, a "Campaign GM" coordinator, elicited an amplification. "Different members of the Board," Roche said, "get together and agree on the proposed candidates submitted to the entire Board for their approval." In politics such a practice commonly is derided as "cronyism."

Yet, even though the GM meeting of 1970 supports Quinn's diagnosis of 1953, that diagnosis must be sharply qualified. In many giant enterprises stockholders have acquired control, or a potential for control. Such stockholders, however, are the great institutional investors, principally banks, insurance companies, mutual funds and pension funds, not individuals. Such stockholders have caused power to pass from a few hands into fewer hands. The situation was illustrated in a staff report for the Subcommittee on Domestic Finance of the House Committee on Banking and Currency.[55] The staff found that in 1967 institutional investors held $1 trillion in assets. Of this sum $607 billion, or 60 per cent, was held by the trust departments of the forty-nine commercial banks which the staff surveyed. Six banks in New York City alone held $64.4 billion. One of these banks, the Morgan Guaranty Trust Company, by itself accounted for $16.8 billion. Each of the six New York banks held stock in the others. And each of the six banks, along with major banks in other principal cities, held stock in and shared directors with companies selling competing products or services. Together, the Subcommittee staff found, the forty-nine banks in the survey held at least

5 per cent of the common stock of each of 147 of the 500 largest industrial corporations. The same banks had a total of 768 interlocking directorships with 286 of the 500 largest corporations, or "an average of almost three directors for each corporation board on which bank director representation is found." Thus concentration has tended to evolve into super-concentration.

Such professed conservatives as Governor Ronald Reagan have faith in the benign nature of business. His adviser on consumer affairs in Sacramento, Mrs. Kay Valory, counsels the disgruntled to seek solace in pamphlets prepared by the National Association of Manufacturers.[56] Not that such faith is unique to the Reaganesque portion of the political spectrum. Such putative liberals as Adolf A. Berle, Jr., also put faith in the benign nature of giant corporations.[57] The expression of such reverence may have taken its finest form in a book which, despite the title, is not always to be found in the libraries of theological seminaries. The book is *United States Steel: A Corporation with a Soul.*[58] The author, Arundel Cotter, official biographer of United States Steel, wrote the book a half-century ago. At the time men in the mills worked a twelve-hour shift six days a week and an unbelievable twenty-four-hour shift every second week. Cotter says that the attitude of Elbert H. Gary, chairman and chief executive officer, toward labor "was well known. He believed in 'leaning over backward' in the matter of giving justice to the worker."[59] More, the corporation "was, in a modified sense, an experiment in popular ownership, the ownership of industry by the worker."[60] Admittedly, firmness on occasion had to be shown: "While the colored man often makes a satisfactory worker if properly 'bossed,' he is unreliable and too often has as his motto, 'never do to-day what you can put off until to-morrow.' "[61] Yet, because his "sense of justice" was "the supreme passion of his life," Gary "treats everyone 'white.' "[62] That being so, "the Steel Corporation is a true democracy."[63] In 1906, when the corporation incorporated the town (later city) of Gary, it brought more than democracy to Indiana. It "made Gary at least an attractive, if not a beautiful, residential town," one which a visitor "is never allowed to leave . . . without seeing the Y.M.C.A."[64] A visitor might also see the "patch," a small section in the heart of Gary "full of saloons and dives." This was oppressive to the corporation. It had not acquired the site "because of some question as to the validity of title" and consequently "has no power of restriction over its development. Gary men have long hoped that some means of cleaning up the section would be found. Prohibition seems to be doing it."[65] In World War I the average wage at United States Steel increased from $905.36 in 1914 to $1,684.58 in 1918.[66] Net income increased from $71,663,615 in 1914 to $199,350,680 in 1918.[67] "Of course, United States Steel made large profits out of the war. . . . But always its officials put patriotism before profits."[68]

Unlike Governor Reagan and Adolf A. Berle, Adam Smith two centuries earlier was an agnostic about the goodness of business. Indeed, Smith wrote of "the mean rapacity, the monopolizing spirit of merchants and manufacturers, who neither are nor ought to be the rulers of mankind."[69] He put his trust in classic competition. This would make the spirit of merchants and manufacturers, rapacious or not, beside the point, because competition would prevent them from becoming rulers. Classic competition is easily described. Here is the model in a lucid definition by John Kenneth Galbraith: ". . . the market where sellers are numerous, capital requirements are modest, technology generally available, entry in consequence not difficult, the products of different sellers largely substitutable and where in further consequence no seller has the power to influence appreciably the price at which he sells. That is to say he has no market power. All sell at an externally and impersonally determined price."[70] This precludes concentration of economic power and therefore of political power in business and industry.

Because General Motors claims to fit the competitive model it is time to refresh one's perspective about GM. This can be done without redundancy. It sells more than half of the automobiles sold in the United States. In 1965 its 735,000 employees, at work in the United States and twenty-three foreign realms, earned $5,448,343,000, or more than double the personal income of all of the citizens of Ireland.[71]

The occasion for GM making the claim that it fits the classic competitive model arose in 1968 when two subcommittees of the Senate Select Committee on Small Business began hearings on "The Question: Are Planning and Regulation Replacing Competition in the American Economy? (The Automobile Industry as a Case Study)." GM's answer was a ninety-eight-page statement, formidably entitled: "The Automobile Industry: A Case Study of Competition." This document was intended to show that "competitive rivalry in the industry, far from being replaced

21

by planning and regulation, has intensified." The statement also undertook to show "the error in any claim that General Motors has market control."

The statement ignored the category of oligopoly, which economists have recognized for thirty-five years. Again, Galbraith's definition: "A small number of firms have the market rivalries semantically associated with competition. But the firms are interdependent in their pricing—the price set by one affects the prices that can be charged by all. And recognizing this interdependence, each firm thinks, inevitably, in terms both of its own good and that of the industry. It avoids setting prices that are mutually destructive; it aims for prices that maximize its returns and by the same token those of others. Since such calculation is imperfect and overt communication illegal, the resulting price may differ from the monopoly price. But it approximates it in some fashion. And . . . rivalry continues in advertising, product improvement, gadgetry and the like where it is not destructive."[72]

The subcommittees submitted the GM statement to some eminent economists, including Galbraith. His comments were acerbic. "The automobile industry with three large and strong firms and one weaker one is cited more often than any other as the classical manifestation of oligopoly," he said. GM should not attempt "to be identified in competitive structure with the apple grower or peanut vendor." That such a statement "could come from a wills and deeds lawyer in the most remote boondock would be surprising," he said. "I confess to total puzzlement as to how this could happen."[73]

Professor Galbraith's total puzzlement may have to do with a dreamy notion he expressed in *The New Industrial State*.[74] There he had astutely recognized that *something* has to protect the country against arbitrary corporate government or, to put it another way, private government without the consent of the governed. But his nomination was the intellectual in politics, the "educational and scientific estate, with its allies in the larger intellectual community."[75] The mocking phrase of Professor Walter Adams of Michigan State University was "platonic philosopher-kings."[76]

But there may have been no need for puzzlement about why General Motors claimed to fit the model of classic competition. To start with, it would have been reasonable to assume that for GM, as for any

22

giant corporation, "competition" is the only figleaf around. GM was being pressed by the chairmen of the subcommittees at the time, Wayne Morse of Oregon and Gaylord Nelson of Wisconsin, both intelligent and tough-minded men. It would be too painful to admit the naked truth, which, as stated by Carl Kaysen, a former colleague of Galbraith's at Harvard, is that "the power of corporate management is, in the political sense, irresponsible power, answerable ultimately only to itself."[77] GM sensibly would avoid the silly claim that it is a democracy run by its 1.3 million stockholders. Could GM lightly concede that it is, in the phrase of Professor Adams, "a self-serving, self-justifying, and self-perpetuating industrial oligarchy"—or *any* kind of oligarchy—but that the educational and scientific estate protects the country? No. In an imperfect world even GM on occasion must settle for the least of evils. Better to say it competes, even if that means being classified with the apple grower and the peanut vendor. Better to wear a fig leaf called "competition," even if it is transparent.

The First Amendment protects what the philosopher Hannah Arendt called "the sense by which we take our bearings in the real world." Survival, she said, requires "men willing to do what Herodotus was the first to undertake consciously, namely, *legein ta eonta,* to say what is."[78] Not even total immersion in the prose of Arundel Cotter, which deserves a prominent place in the treacly annals of corporate religiosity, can detract from the towering importance of the guarantee of a free press. John Kenneth Galbraith said of the American government that it "works far better—perhaps it only works—when the Federal Executive and influential business and the respectable press are in some degree at odds. Only then can we be sure that abuse or neglect, either public or private, will be given the notoriety that is needed. In the time of Coolidge and Hoover, the Federal Executive, business, and the press were united. These are times in our democracy when all looks peaceful and much goes wrong."[79] And so we must look into how the First Amendment is used to check corporate power.

During the 1968 presidential campaign, newsmen questioned Richard Nixon, Hubert Humphrey and George Wallace on *Face the Nation* and *Meet the Press.* It is anything but routinely possible for the public to see newsmen confront those who exercise substantial private power. "The individuals who hold the reins of power in any enterprise cannot trust themselves to be adequately self-critical," John W. Gardner has said.[80] It would be instructive to see, on television, critical questioning of the president of General Motors about the long gestation of the impact-absorbing steering assembly. The president of United States Steel might be asked about the contribution of his industry to the balance-of-payments crisis. The presidents of the Upjohn Company and American Home Products might want to try to persuade us that it was necessary to go to court to prevent interruption of the marketing of antibiotic combinations that expose large numbers of persons to needless injury and even death.

For that matter, leaders of the news media, in an open society, might agree that it would be only fair for them to be publicly questioned about their performance. The outlook for such evenhanded checks on private power is never particularly luminous, but a balanced judgment must be that it is generally and reliably enhanced neither by concentrated ownership of news media, whether on a local, state or national basis, nor by enlarging opportunities for corporations with non-media involvements to control news media. The agencies of mass communication, the Commission on Freedom of the Press suggested two decades ago, "can facilitate thought and discussion. They can stifle it. They can advance the progress of civilization or they can thwart it. They can debase and vulgarize mankind. They can endanger the peace of the world; they can do so accidentally, in a fit of absence of mind."[81] All of which is an elaboration on the recognition that the selection of what to report and what not to report, of what to emphasize and what not to emphasize, of the point in time at which significant disclosures will be made—all such decisions are an exercise of the power *legein ta eonta,* to say what is.

Clearly this is a very special and most important kind of power. In 1968 and 1969 the National Commission on Product Safety held a series of hearings on needlessly hazardous products used in and around the household. One of these hearings concerned unsafe glass doors. These alone were estimated to injure children, sometimes fatally, at a rate of 100,000 per year. The remedy for new construction was simple: the Federal Housing Administration, under its rule-making power for guaranteeing mortgages, had but to require, at an extra cost of a few dollars, the use of extra-strength glass which, if it breaks at all, crumbles into pebbles, rather than splitting into shards. As a practical matter, this would control the practice throughout the home-building industry. Parents of victims came forward to testify, hoping thereby to spare other children. A

Georgia couple told how their daughter, playing at a neighbor's house, had crashed through a sliding door of cheap glass. Her wounds were so severe that she very quickly bled to death. A Capitol Hill policeman told of terrible injury done to his little boy when, in an unfamiliar new apartment, he too went through such a door. It happened that a newspaper story on the hearing was seen by Representative Benjamin S. Rosenthal (D–N.Y.).[82] He was struck by, among other things, testimony showing that the National Association of Home Builders, like the FHA, was not supporting safety glazing, and by evidence that on leaving the government some FHA officials have found a snug harbor in the NAHB. Rosenthal summoned the FHA officials involved to a meeting. This, along with the hearing and the news story, helped to overcome, rather swiftly, their reluctance to act.

It must be noted that many major news media did not cover the hearing although, having been held in the New Senate Office Building, it was not inaccessible. Noncoverage of such important matters is commonplace. News resources—reporters, space and time to accommodate their product—are highly limited. News opportunities are not. The point remains, however, that to be able "to say what is" is to exercise formidable power.

It is right to abhor control by the state of "the power to say what is." It is also necessary to recognize the significant potentials for abuse that lie in private control of the same power. One such potential exists in advertising. Although this is too well known to require elaboration here, an example will not overburden the point. The advertising message that Ultra-Brite "gives your mouth sex appeal" helped to win that "whitener" toothpaste nearly 10 per cent of a $350 million market. The disinterested message of the Council on Dental Therapeutics of the American Dental Association was treated as if it had bad breath. That message was that "whitener" toothpastes may be too abrasive and may increase susceptibility to decay in the one adult in four over thirty-five whose gums tend to recede and expose the vulnerable cementum.[83]

Our principal concern is with ownership of news media by large corporations with conglomerate interests. The problem may be made clear at once with a couple of chilling statistics. Each year occupational accidents kill 14,000 persons and disable—for as long as a lifetime— 2.2 million others. These figures are almost universally acknowledged to be conservative; furthermore, they exclude casualties from occupational disease, such as coal miner's "black lung."[84] Other things being equal, is the prospect for thorough reporting of this situation likely to be as great by a news medium with corporate ties to manufacturing or mining as by a news medium without such ties? We need not deal only in hypotheticals. The case was powerfully laid out on the public record a few years ago when the International Telephone and Telegraph Corporation made (but ultimately abandoned) an effort to acquire the American Broadcasting Companies. Here is a concise contemporaneous description of the two corporations:

> ITT is a sprawling international conglomerate of 433 separate boards of directors that derives about 60 percent of its income from its significant holdings in at least forty foreign countries. It is the ninth largest industrial corporation in the world in size of work force. In addition to its sale of electronic equipment to foreign governments, and operation of foreign countries' telephone systems, roughly half of its domestic income comes from U.S. Government defense and space contracts. But it is also in the business of consumer finance, life insurance, investment funds, small loan companies, car rentals (ITT Avis, Inc.), and book publishing. . . .
>
> ABC was born in 1941. . . . Today ABC owns 399 theaters in 34 states, five VHF stations, six AM and six FM stations (all in the top ten broadcasting markets), and, of course, one of the three major television networks and one of the four major radio networks in the world. Its 137 primary television network affiliates can reach 93 percent of the 50,000,000 television homes in the United States (more in prime-time evenings through secondary affiliates), and its radio network affiliates can reach 97 percent of the 55,000,000 homes with radio receivers. ABC has interests in, and affiliations with, stations in 25 other nations, known as the "Worldvision Group." ABC Films distributes filmed shows throughout this country and abroad. It is heavily involved in the record business, and subsidiaries publish three farm papers.[85]

In proceedings before the Federal Communications Commission, ITT and ABC argued that the network would be granted an autonomous status to assure that ABC news and public affairs would be uninfluenced by other ITT business interests. The minority of three commissioners who fought the proposed merger were highly skeptical, especially because of a "subtle, almost unconscious process":

> ABC newsmen and their supervisors will know that ITT is the boss, and that ITT has sensitive business relations in various foreign countries

and at the highest levels of our government, and that reporting on any number of industries and economic developments will touch the interests of ITT. The mere awareness of these interests will make it impossible for those news officials, no matter how conscientious, to report news and develop documentaries objectively, in the way that they would do if ABC remained unaffiliated with ITT. Some of the newsmen will advance within the news organization, or be fired, or become officers of ABC—perhaps even of ITT—or not, and no newsman will be able to erase from his mind that his chances of doing so may be affected by his treatment of issues on which ITT is sensitive.

Thus, the threat is not so much that documentaries or news stories adversely affecting the interests of ITT will be filmed and then killed, or slanted—although that is also a problem. It is that the questionable story idea, or news coverage, will never even be proposed—whether for reasons of fear, insecurity, cynicism, realism, or unconscious avoidance.[86]

It should be borne in mind that the minority commissioners—Nicholas Johnson, Kenneth A. Cox, and Robert T. Bartley—were emphasizing a *potential* for abuse. Almost every day, men and women of courage and integrity do make their mark on news media owned by large organizations as well as small ones. The Westinghouse Broadcasting Company is part of the conglomerate Westinghouse manufacturing organization, has observed high standards, and has a commendable record of dealing with sensitive issues including consumer matters. On the very morning these words were written the *Washington Post* published a column in which Nicholas von Hoffman sharply criticized WTOP, which is owned by the Washington Post Company, for refusing to sell time for a brief message by the Business Executives Move for Vietnam Peace.[87] In addition, the *Post* has published numerous editorial-page pieces critical of its own performance. But, again, it is the *potential* that is of foremost concern. The environment always to be sought is one which assures that ordinary men, not merely heroes, will reliably do what is necessary. The broadcast media did not do what was necessary in terms of news coverage of developments, many of them dramatic, about the largest prospective merger in the history of broadcasting. They treated the news negligibly when they treated it at all. ABC News "often sounded as if its stories about the mergers [*sic*] were dictated by management," the *Columbia Journalism Review* said. "Journalists can be relieved that two such managements did not get together."[88] Thus the broadcast media lent substance to the concerns of the three commissioners, as well as to the Justice Department, which intervened against the merger. ITT's business operations, the Department said, "are bound to generate enormous pressure to intervene in areas of news coverage which threaten fundamental economic interests of the company."[89]

But if doubt remained about a possible threat to the integrity of news at ABC it was removed by ITT itself when, in an incredible display of potential for abuse, it made brazen efforts to intimidate reporters who were beyond its internal system of reward and punishment. After the *Wall Street Journal's* Fred L. Zimmerman broke the story, the Justice Department's antitrust lawyers, brilliantly led by Lionel Kestenbaum, subpoenaed three reporters—Eileen Shanahan of the *New York Times,* Stephen M. Aug, then of the Associated Press, and Jed Stout, then of United Press International—to testify at a hearing which the Commission had reluctantly convened.

In the aggregate the most serious incidents involved Miss Shanahan. On one occasion, she said under oath, an ITT official relayed a company comment on a development and said "something to the effect, 'I expect to see that in the paper, high up in your story.' " At her office in Washington, Edward J. Gerrity, ITT's senior vice president for public relations, asked Miss Shanahan if he could look at a story she was writing, a request which as a reporter she of course considered "improper." In a tone she described as "accusatory and nasty" he "badgered me" to try to get the *Times* to use the text of a certain FCC order. Gerrity inquired whether Miss Shanahan had been following the prices of ITT and ABC stock. Did she not feel a "responsibility to the shareholders who might lose money as a result" of her stories? Her response was, "My responsibility was to find out the truth and print it." Was she aware that Commissioner Johnson and Senator Gaylord Nelson were working "on legislation that would forbid any newspaper from owning any broadcast property"? (Johnson and Nelson each said that they had never met and had collaborated on nothing.) Gerrity told Miss Shanahan that she ought to pass the (false) information along to her publisher, the implication being that the *Times,* as an owner of radio stations, would see a threat to its own economic interests. There were other incidents of nastiness and misrepresentation, some of them involving John V. (Jack) Horner, ITT's public relations chief in Washington.

ITT offered no rebuttal to the sworn testimony of Miss Shanahan, who, needless to say, is a highly respected reporter. Neither did ITT

concede that it had engaged in improper conduct.[90] Miss Shanahan testified on April 20, 1967. Eight weeks *afterward* Horner was questioning
friends and former employers of Miss Shanahan about her personal and
professional life.[91] Subsequently the FCC affirmed its earlier approval of
the acquisition, again by a vote of 4 to 3. The Justice Department then
filed a lawsuit to block it. On January 1, 1968, while the case was pending, ITT abruptly backed out of the proposed merger to move on to less
troublesome acquisitions. The lawsuit had been appropriately entitled
United States of America v. *Federal Communications Commission.*

Deservedly, there would be a poor market for a book on the theme
that death is an outrage and should be abolished. And if great centralization of economic power is, in a modern technological society, inevitable,
possibly our effort would not have much point. The fundamental question—one which should concern conservatives and liberals alike—is
whether economic concentration is truly necessary. If we must have it,
the outlook for the individual is bleak. He will not have a significant
opportunity to shape the intricate corporate and governmental organizations which control his destiny. The democratic institutions which were
carefully designed to allow him fulfillment increasingly will be seen as
the hollow farce that the New Left asserts them to be.

Not just the New Left. During the 1968 presidential campaign
Richard Nixon, describing complaints of "the alienated," found "a common thread." Although he was of course running it through the eye of a
needle pointed at Democrats in Washington, his rhetoric was more en-
compassing, even if inadvertently. "The power to control decisions
immediately affecting one's life is vanishing. . . . That unique, precious,
indescribable thing—the *individual* human mind, heart and spirit—
is being injured, or neglected, or slighted. . . . What we need is not one
leader, but many leaders; not one center of power, but many centers of
power."[92] Compare this with Jeremy Larner, who was a speechwriter for
Senator Eugene J. McCarthy in his campaign for the Democratic presidential nomination: "The idea is to break power down to small units,
so that people can create more satisfying ways of living. That is why the
cliché of 'control over the decisions which affect our lives' reaches people,
whether it is spoken by Mr. Nixon, Mr. [Richard N.] Goodwin, or Mr.
[Tom] Hayden. But the new class [which is "searching for politics which
can change the quality of life"] is going to find that meaningful participa-

tion is impossible without a radical democratizing of our decision-making institutions. *For the ethic of corporate power is blatantly incompatible with the distribution of power among equal citizens.*"[93] [Emphasis supplied.]

John Kenneth Galbraith contends that concentration of economic power must be accepted; modern technology makes it inevitable. Galbraith argued his case in *The New Industrial State*. It was published, with deserved acclaim for its perception, style and wit, in 1967. This date must be accorded some attention. "I had nearly finished a preliminary draft of this book when President Kennedy asked me to go to India in 1961," he said. "With some misgiving I put the manuscript away in the vault of the bank."[94] He returned to Harvard in 1963. A year later, Senator Hart, the Michigan Democrat who heads the Senate Subcommittee on Antitrust and Monopoly, opened hearings on economic concentration. *The New Industrial State* cites the hearings at a couple of points but, we believe, takes them insufficiently into account. In addition, Senator Hart productively continued the hearings in 1967, the year in which the Galbraith book was published, and each year thereafter, including 1970. The news media generally accorded them slight attention; not unexpectedly, public awareness of them is limited. Yet the Hart hearings provide an abundance of empiric evidence to refute Galbraith's thesis. The facts argue that the new technologies should be leading us not toward more concentration, and to preservation of existing concentration, but to deconcentration. That is their natural thrust.

> Actually, big businesses are generally no more and no less efficient than medium-sized businesses even when the gains wrung by monopoly power are included in efficiency. This is the one general finding in comparative cost studies and comparative profitability studies. . . .
> When we recall that most big businesses have numerous complete plants at various points throughout the country, this finding is not surprising. Why should United States Steel be more efficient than Inland Steel, when United States Steel is simply a dozen or more Inland Steels strewn about the country? Why should GM be appreciably more efficient than say a once again independent Buick Motors?

The foregoing excerpt appeared in an article entitled "The Case Against Big Business."[95] The author was George J. Stigler, of the University of Chicago Law School, who headed the Task Force on Productivity and Competition appointed by Richard Nixon while he was President-elect. Exactly the same point was made—an identical phrase was even used inadvertently—by Professor Walter Adams:

> The unit of technological efficiency is the plant, not the firm. This means that there are undisputed advantages to large-scale integrated operations at a single steel plant, for example, but there is little technological justification for combining these functionally separate plants into a single administrative unit. United States Steel is nothing more than several Inland Steels strewn about the country, and no one has yet suggested that Inland is not big enough to be efficient. A firm producing such divergent lines as rubber boots, chain saws, motorboats, and chicken feed may be seeking conglomerate size and power; it is certainly not responding to technological necessity. In short, one can favor technological bigness and oppose administrative bigness without inconsistency.[96]

If technological efficiency collapses as a justification for concentration, then what justifications remain? "The size of General Motors is in the service not of monopoly or the economies of scale, but of planning," Professor Galbraith says. "And for this planning . . . there is no clear upper limit to the desirable size. It could be that the bigger the better."[97] It will suffice—but only for the moment—to ask, we hope not unkindly, whether those concerned, for example, with planning the preservation of the environment care to entrust that delicate mission to the company which, through its vehicles and plants, produces 35 per cent of the country's total tonnage of air pollution.[98] Or, for that matter, to General Dynamics, General Electric, General Foods or General Anything.

The last remaining major justification for "Brobdingnagian size," as Professor Adams has called it, is that it provides the necessary environment for invention, innovation and technological progress. The empiric evidence simply does not bear this out. An extraordinary proportion of the important, radical developments have come from loners, men who worked outside large organizations or without their support. "The disk memory unit, the heart of today's random access computer, is not the logical outcome of a decision made by IBM management," Arthur K. Watson, formerly of IBM and now ambassador to France, has candidly acknowledged. "It was developed in one of our laboratories as a bootleg project—over the stern warning from management that the project had

31

to be dropped because of budget difficulties. A handful of men ignored the warning. They broke the rules. They risked their jobs to work on a project they believed in."[99] The late Milton Lehman, biographer of Robert H. Goddard, said that this "sickly, frail, unrecognized" inventor had accomplished more than any other in this century and "more than any man, opened the door to the age of space." Testifying before the Senate Antitrust Subcommittee, Lehman said that "the organization" of course frustrated Goddard. Yet, he made his rocket inventions with a total of $250,000 for "the salary of his crew, the cost of his 'hardware,' the fees for his patents, and the maintenance of his household—for more than 40 years. (And if you divide $250,000 by 40, it doesn't leave very much a year for inventing the modern space age.)"[100] Walter Adams and Joel B. Dirlam did an analysis of the steel industry, which is one of the most concentrated in the United States.[101] The findings were dramatic. Professor Adams later gave this summary:

> It spends only 0.7 percent of its revenues on research and, in technological progressiveness, the giants which dominate this industry lag behind their smaller domestic rivals as well as their smaller foreign competitors. Thus, the basic oxygen furnace—considered the "only major breakthrough at the ingot level since before the turn of the century"—was invented in 1950 by a minuscule Austrian *firm* which was less than one-third the size of a single plant of the United States Steel Corp. The innovation was introduced in the United States in 1954 by McLouth Steel [of Detroit] which at the time had about 1 percent of domestic steel capacity—to be followed some 10 years later by the steel giants: United States Steel in December 1963, Bethlehem in 1964, and Republic in 1965. Despite the fact that this revolutionary invention involved an average operating cost saving of $5 per ton and an investment cost saving of $20 per ton of installed capacity, the steel giants during the 1950's, according to *Business Week*, "bought 40 million tons of the wrong capacity—the open-hearth furnace" which was obsolete almost the moment it was put in place.[102]

The natural thrust of the new technologies toward deconcentration, toward smaller units, toward a socioeconomic environment compatible, to repeat Jeremy Larner, "with the distribution of power among equal citizens"—this natural thrust has been frustrated. Instead the unnatural has been occurring, most prominently in the 1960s in the conglomerate merger movement. More than anything else this is a testament to the efficacy of synthetic stimuli. In the government sector these have included tax advantages and a long-standing failure to enforce the antitrust laws with the vigor encouraged by the Supreme Court. In the private sector the synthetic stimuli toward concentration have included such power plays as that after World War II when steel was in short supply. General Electric and General Motors could get steel for appliances. Small and medium-sized producers could not, and in significant numbers they died.[103]

The concentration of economic power is well advanced. There is still time—probably not much—to halt the process and maybe even reverse it. If we fail to act swiftly, those who hold concentrated economic power will bring it increasingly to bear on our democratic institutions. They may come to dominate them. Such a manifestation of self-protection and aggression is their natural thrust. We may learn the hard way, and too late, that a free society and massive concentration of economic power cannot for long coexist. This power can be diffused. Its growth can be stunted. These are feasible goals. We will make suggestions looking toward their achievement. If these suggestions should strike the reader as less than ideal we can only offer him the consolation of Alexander Hamilton. "I never expect to see a perfect work from imperfect man," he said.[104]

1 A TOUR THROUGH A STATE OF CONCENTRATION

Art Buchwald, in one of his most penetrating social commentaries, once looked ahead to the year 1978. By then every company west of the Mississippi River had been merged into a single corporation, Samson Securities. Every company east of the Mississippi had been merged into another corporation, the Delilah Company. To simplify things still more, the heads of Samson and Delilah decided to merge, so that there would be only one corporation in the entire United States. However, a clearance to join Samson and Delilah was needed from the Antitrust Division of the Department of Justice. Here is Buchwald's scenario:

> At first the head of the Antitrust Division indicated that he might have reservations about allowing the only two companies left in the United States to merge.
>
> "Our department," he said, "will take a close look at this proposed merger. It is our job to further competition in private business and industry, and if we allow Samson and Delilah to merge we may be doing the consumer a disservice."
>
> The chairman of Samson protested vigorously that merging with Delilah would not stifle competition, but would help it. "The public will be the true beneficiary of this merger," he said. "The larger we are, the more services we can perform, and the lower prices we can charge."
>
> The president of Delilah backed him up. "In the Communist system the people don't have a choice. They must buy from the state. In our capitalistic society the people can buy from either the Samson Company or the Delilah Company."
>
> "But if you merge," someone pointed out, "there will be only *one* company left in the United States."
>
> "Exactly," said the president of Delilah. "Thank God for the free enterprise system."
>
> The Antitrust Division of the Justice Department studied the merger for months. Finally the Attorney General made this ruling. "While we find

drawbacks to only one company being left in the United States, we feel the advantages to the public far outweigh the disadvantages.

"Therefore, we're making an exception in this case and allowing Samson and Delilah to merge.

"I would like to announce that the Samson and Delilah Company is now negotiating at the White House with the President to buy the United States. The Justice Department will naturally study this merger to see if it violates any of our strong antitrust laws."[1]

Everyone agrees, of course, that if only one corporation controlled the assets needed to manufacture all of our products our economic and political system could be described neither as "democratic" nor "free enterprise." "Corporate dictatorship" would be more accurate. Almost everyone would think it intolerable if only fifty corporations controlled the means to produce all of our products, and most would agree that one hundred would be alarmingly few.

But what about two hundred? Today, two hundred corporations *do* stand astride the economy. And the story of who really runs the United States begins with them, and with the interrelationships of this industrial structure to dominant financial and political forces.

Dr. Willard F. Mueller, former chief economist of the Federal Trade Commission, assessed the importance of the two hundred corporations in November 1969 in testimony before the Senate Subcommittee on Antitrust and Monopoly:

> You may recall that I testified before this committee in 1965 that, should post-war trends in aggregate concentration continue, by 1975 the 200 largest manufacturing corporations would control $2/3$ of all manufacturing assets. Unhappily, we have reached this level ahead of schedule. Today the top 200 manufacturing corporations already control about $2/3$ of all assets held by corporations engaged primarily in manufacturing.[2]

They have reached this pinnacle primarily through mergers—buying their way to the top.

The sheer magnitude of the merger movement makes it difficult to grasp. In 1968 the one hundred largest corporations had a greater share of manufacturing assets than the two hundred largest had in 1950, and the two hundred largest in 1968 controlled a share equal to that held by the thousand largest in 1941.[3]

Through mergers many of the top two hundred corporations have secured strong footholds in the entire spectrum of American industry. Starting in 1964, Senator Philip A. Hart, as chairman of the Senate Antitrust and Monopoly Subcommittee, held six years of hearings on economic concentration that insightfully examined this; and a study by John Blair, former chief economist of that subcommittee, demonstrated that in 1958 the two hundred largest corporations had one-quarter of their employment in industry groups other than their primary one, and 20 per cent of their employment in thirty-five different major industry groups.[4] From 1948 to 1968 these two hundred corporations made over 60 per cent of all large acquisitions in manufacturing and mining, buying up more than 3,900 companies with combined assets in excess of $50 billion.[5]

The impression sometimes given about the merger movement of the past two decades is that it generally involved upstart corporations which challenged slumbering old-line firms. With some exceptions, this simply has not been true. Older corporations, too, have played an active role in the merger game.[6]

Many major industries have long been, and remain, highly concentrated—that is, four firms or fewer produce more than 50 per cent of the goods turned out by that industry. Pick an industry—automobiles, say, or breakfast cereals, aluminum or lightbulbs, tires or containers— and you'll find that four firms or fewer dominate the entire industry.

The significance of the merger movement is that instead of a few firms dominating a single industry, as with the trusts of the old days, we are moving to an economy where the same firms dominate *several* industries. The conglomerate, a convenient way of describing a firm active in several industries or markets, has become like the octopus, with tentacles reaching into a broad range of manufacturing. In 1969, the Blair study was reinforced by the Federal Trade Commission's *Economic Report on Corporate Mergers,* prepared under the direction of Dr. Mueller. It conclusively demonstrated that the one hundred largest manufacturers have come to hold leading industry positions in a score of concentrated industries. They have become dominant—primarily through mergers—in most of the major industry groups in the country, and in most cases they operate in many industry groups.[7]

Dr. Blair has described how the trend toward concentration through merger has caused the disappearance of numerous medium-sized manufacturers that had a single or narrow line of products. At a hearing of the subcommittee he testified (with the numbers in parentheses denoting the rank of corporations among the top two hundred):

> Many independent manufacturers in the electrical machinery group with well-known trade names also have disappeared through acquisition. . . . To cite but a few examples, Bendix, the pioneer in home washing machines, was sold to Avco, in turn to Philco, which in turn was acquired by Ford (No. 87). Speed Queen, with a well-established line of washers, dryers, and ironers, was absorbed by McGraw-Edison (No. 80). . . . Indeed, acquisitions by the 100 as well as other diversified firms have literally decimated the ranks of single-line appliance firms in the last decade. Involved in the acquisitions have been such well-known trade names—which have either disappeared entirely or are used for prestige and goodwill purposes—as "Deepfreeze," "Bendix," "York," "Welbilt," "Gibson," "Speed Queen" "Easy," "Eureka," "Jordan," "Dormeyer," "Servel," "Silex," "Universal,"

Dr. Blair concluded:

"Ever Bright" and "Philco."

> In addition to creating multi-industry conglomerates virtually out of whole cloth, the acquisitions . . . substantially enlarged the size and economic power of many other of our largest corporations. In the process they have also resulted in the disappearance, as independent enterprises, of numerous sizable firms whose names have become landmarks in American industry. Among the acquired companies are many which have made noteworthy contributions to economic progress—as competitors, as efficient enterprises and as innovators. A matter of some concern should be whether the resources they represent will continue to make such contributions now that they have lost their status as independent enterprises and are now only divisions —or less—of what have in effect become giant holding companies.[8]

Around the turn of the century, the trusts became dominant by buying up or taking control of all the companies in one industry. We had steel trusts, oil trusts, meat trusts, sugar trusts. But they were pikers compared to the trusts of today, the conglomerates. Most modern corporations fall into this category. A conglomerate may cut across a few industries—or hundreds of product lines.

Harrison F. Houghton, then assistant to the director of the Bureau of Economics for the Federal Trade Commission, who prepared the chart reproduced on pp. 38–39,[9] told the Senate Subcommittee on Antitrust and Monopoly in 1964:

> In all, Textron has acquired nearly 70 different companies outside the textile industry. As a matter of fact, there are so many different industries

Horizontal and Vertical

TEXTILES
(All resold by 1964)

SUNCOOK MILLS, Suncook, N. H., 1943
Cotton, rayon and other synthetic griege goods, cotton fabrics

LONSDALE CO., Providence, R. I., 1945
Cotton fabric, chambrays, lawns and broadcloth, shirtings, bleaching

MANVILLE JENCKES CORP., Woonsocket, R. I., 1945
Cotton and rayon fabric, taffeta, drapery fabrics, rayon

GOSSETT MILLS, 1946
Cotton and rayon fabric, cotton broadwoven fabric

NASHUA MANUFACTURING CO., Nashua, N. Y. 1946
Cotton and rayon fabric, blankets, pajamas, sheets, pillow cases, bedspreads

THE ESMOND MILLS, INC., Esmond, R. I. 1948
Subs: Clarence Whitman & Sons, Inc.
The Esmond Mills, Limited
Esmond Mills, Ontario, Limited
Esmond Virginia, Inc.
The Wilkes-Barre Mfg. Co.
Infant blankets

R. W. BATES PIECE DYE WORKS, INC. Groversville, N. Y., 1951
Cotton broad woven fabrics

VASS COTTON MILL CO., Vass, N. C. 1951
Cotton Fabrics

AMERICAN WOOLEN CO. New York, N. Y. 1955
Woolen and worsted fabrics, blankets and upholstery fabrics, industrial brushes, wool yarn

ROBBINS MILLS, INC., New York, N. Y. (Incorporated New Jersey) 1955
Rayon and acetate fabrics, gray goods, nylon

INDUSTRIAL BATTING

F. BURKHART MANUFACTURING CO. St. Louis, Mo., 1953
Industrial batting

CAROLINA BAGGING CO. Henderson, N. C. 1956
Industrial batting, padding, upholstery filling, polyurethane foam

Oakland Plant of
NATIONAL AUTOMOTIVE FIBRES, INC. Oakland, Calif., 1959
Cotton pad and batts for automobile seating

AIRCRAFT AND PARTS

M. B. MANUFACTURING CO. New Haven, Conn., 1954
Engine mounts and vibration elimination equipment

ACCESSORY PRODUCTS CORP. Whittier, Calif., 1957
Servo actuators, flight control systems, inertial guidance and navigation equipment

BELL AIRCRAFT CORP. Wheatfield, N.Y. 1960
Defense business, including Bell Aerospace Corp. and 3 divisions. Helicopters, rocket engines, research and development on propulsion systems, space vehicle equipment, etc.

ELECTRONIC EQUIPMENT

DALMO VICTOR CO. San Carlos, Calif., 1954
Airborne radar antennas and related equipment

RYAN INDUSTRIES, INC. Detroit, Mich., 1955
Electromechanical products, photographic equipment, jigs, dies, and fixtures

CALIFORNIA TECHNICAL INDUSTRIES Belmont, Calif., 1957
Electronics

GLOBE ELECTRONICS Council Bluffs, Iowa, 1959
Radio equipment

SCHAFER CUSTOM ENGINEERING Burbank, Calif., 1959
Automation equipment for radio and TV broadcast equipment

ALLEGHANY INSTRUMENTS CO., INC. Cumberland, Md., 1960
Gas regulators, thrust and pressure measuring devices, electronic and electromechanical vibration systems

ELECTRONIC RESEARCH CO. Kansas City, Mo., 1960
Electronic components, radio frequency crystals, related power supplies, airborne radar antennas

Nuclear energy operations of
ALCO PRODUCTS New York, N.Y. 1962

COLLEGE HILL INDUSTRIES Warwick, R. I., 1964
Inertia compensated tape recorders for space vehicles, specialized pressure and inertia switches and pressure-sensing capsules; research in other commercial and defense electronic products

ELECTROCRAFT, INC. Chicago, Ill., 1959
Plugs and jacks

ROBOTOMICS ENTERPRISES, INC. Phoenix, Arizona, 1963
Decades and displays for electronic counters

OPTICAL INSTRUMENTS

SHURON OPTICAL CO. Geneva, N.Y., 1958
Optical lab equipment, including interference filters, spectacle frames, cases and lenses

SPECTROLAB, INC. Hollywood, Calif., 1960
Optical lab equipment including interference filters

MODERN OPTICS, INC. Houston, Tex., 1961
Lenses, optical

CONTINENTAL OPTICAL CO. Indianapolis, Ind., 1963
Spectacle frames, cases and lenses

INDUSTRIAL FASTENERS

CAMCAR SCREW & MANUFACTURING CORP., Rockford, Ill., 1955
Industrial fasteners, rivets, bolts

TOWNSEND CO., New Brighton, Pa., 1959
Industrial fasteners, rivets, bolts, cold-heading machinery, wire-drawing equipment, rivet setting machines and electrical contacts

BOOTS AIRCRAFT NUT CORP. Norfolk, Conn., 1960
Lock nuts, engine nuts

AMERICAN SCREW CO. Willimantic, Conn., 1962
Industrial fasteners: rivets, bolts

TUBULAR RIVET & STUD CO. Wollaston, Mass., 1961
Rivets

FABRICATED PRODUCTS CO. West Newton, Pa., 1960
Specialty building seals, washers, closures and fasteners

BOSTITCH, INC. East Greenwich, R. I., 1966
Industrial staplers and stitchers

HARMIL MANUFACTURING, INC. Downey, Calif., 1966
Sealing washers

IRON AND STEEL CASTINGS

CAMPBELL WYANT & CANNON FOUNDRY CO., Muskegon, Mich., 1956
Gray iron and steel castings for automotive, railroad, agricultural, implement refrigeration, marine and other industries

PITTSBURGH STEEL FOUNDRY CORP. Glassport, Pa., 1959
Steel and alloy castings

CHAIN SAWS

HOMELITE CORP., Port Chester, N.Y. 1955
Chain saws and pumps, electric power plants, centrifugal pumps, gas engines

MEASURING INSTRUMENTS

SPRAGUE METER CO., INC. Bridgeport, Conn., 1961
Gas meters, gas regulators, thrust and pressure measuring devices; electronic and electromechanical vibration systems

RESEARCH

NUCLEAR METALS, INC. Cambridge, Mass., 1959
Nuclear and metallurgical research

FITTINGS AND PRESSURE VALVES

M. B. SKINNER CO., South Bend, Ind., 1961
Service fittings for utilities, pressure valves

LEDEEN, INC. Los Angeles, Calif., 1964
Hydraulic and pneumatic control equipment.

38

EXTRON, INC. 1943-1968 [9]

CONGLOMERATE

DIE CASTINGS

PEAT MANUFACTURING CORP.
Norfolk, Calif., 1956
ferrous die castings

ETAL STAMPINGS

RANDALL CO., Cincinnati, Ohio, 1959
agner Mfg. Co., Sydney, Ohio, 1959
(Subsidiary)
iance stampings and aluminum kit-
utensils

ZENITE METALS CORP.
Blytheville, Ark., 1963
for auto and appliance industry

METAL PIPE AND TUBING

CROWELL TUBE CO., INC.
Lexington, Mass., 1960
-diameter metal tubing

IE TOOLWORKS AND LAKEVIEW
FORGE CO., Erie, Pa., 1965
wrenches, vices and bomb lugs

BATHROOM FIXTURES

-MACK CO., Los Angeles, Calif. 1956
oom fixtures and accessories

METAL WORKING MACHINERY

CISION METHODS AND MACHINES
Waterbury, Conn., 1958
g mill machinery and equipment

BRIDGEPORT MACHINES, INC.
Bridgeport, Conn., 1968
l milling machines

MACHINE TOOLS

TERBURY FARREL FOUNDRY &
HINE CO., Waterbury, Conn., 1958
heading machinery; wire-drawing
ment; rivet setting machines

NES & LAMSON MACHINE CO.
Springfield, Vt., 1963
e tools

THOMPSON GRINDER CO.
Springfield, Ohio, 1967
on grinders

UNDRY SUPPLIES

ANNER MANUFACTURING CO.
Cleveland, Ohio, 1958
ry supplies, industrial hardware for
nd steel foundries, machine tools

AMSLER MORTON CORP.
Pittsburgh, Pa., 1959
rial hardware for iron and steel
ies; metal processing, industrial
es

TOR VEHICLE PARTS AND ACCESSORIES

VAN NORMAN INDUSTRIES
Springfield, Mass., 1958
motive replacement antennae

MILFORD MACHINE CO.
Leesburg, Ind., 1960
shafts and connecting rods

ELECTRICAL TRANSMISSION EQUIPMENT

Underfloor division of
WALKER BROTHERS, 1964
Underfloor line for electrical distribution
system

AMERICAN CROSSARM & CONDUIT CO.
Niles, Ill., 1967
Crossarms, braces, insulator pins

BROADCASTING EQUIPMENT

American Microphone Division of
ELGIN NATIONAL WATCH CO.
Elgin, Ill., 1958
Broadcasting equipment

PAINTS

VITA VAR CORP., Newark, N.J., 1962
Industrial paints and protective coatings

FLOOD AND CONKLIN MANUFACTURING
CO., Newark, N.J., 1964
Paints and industrial coatings

Patterson-Sargent and Allied Divisions of
H. K. PORTER CO., No. Brunswick, N.J.
1965
Paints

BEARINGS

FAFNIR BEARING CO.
New Britain, Conn., 1968
Precision ball and roller bearings

PARKERSBURG-AETNA CORP.
Parkersburg, W. Va., 1963
Ball and roller bearings, oil field production equipment, pre-engineered metal
buildings

PLYWOOD

COQUILLE PLYWOOD CO.
Coquille, Ore., 1955
Plywood

MYRTLE POINT VENEER CO.
Norway, Ore., 1956
Plywood

BANDON VENEER & PLYWOOD
ASSOCIATION, Bandon, Ore., 1956
Plywood

PLASTIC PRODUCTS

KORDITE CORP., Macedon, N.Y., 1955
Plastic products, specialty food and industrial bags

FEDERAL LEATHER COMPANIES
Belleville, N.J., 1956
Proxylin-coated fabric and vinyl coated
fabric

OLD KING COLE, INC.
Louisville, Ohio, 1965
Vacuum and rotary forming of plastic

ABRASIVE PRODUCTS

CLEVELAND METAL ABRASIVE CO.
Cleveland, Ohio, 1965
Iron and steel shot and grit

A. P. De SANNO & SON, INC.
Phoenixville, Pa., 1967
Grinding wheels and abrasive products

BOAT BUILDING AND MARINE HARDWARE

FAEGEOL MARINE ENGINE CO.
San Diego, Calif., 1958
Rights to manufacture marine engines and
turbines

DORSETT PLASTIC CORP.
(Dorset Marine), Santa Clara, Calif., 1960
Inboard and outboard runabout cruisers

SOUTH COAST MARINE CO.
Newport Beach, Calif., 1965
Marine hardware

PASSENGER LINER

S. S. La GUARDIA renamed
S. S. LEILANI, 1956
Tourist passenger line

FURNITURE

Ames Maid Division of
O. AMES CO., Parkersburg, W. Va., 1963
Kitchen and juvenile furniture

Pennant division of
NOVO INDUSTRIAL CORP.
New York, N.Y. 1964
Kitchen and bar stools, juvenile furniture

DURHAM MANUFACTURING CO.
Muncie, Ind., 1964
Folding metal furniture

UNDERWATER EXPLORATION

GERALDINES, LTD., Annapolis, Md., 1962
Products and services for commercial and
underwater exploration

AGROCHEMICALS

SPENCER KELLOG & SONS, INC.
Buffalo, N.Y., 1961
Soybean oil, soybean oil meal, lechitin,
linseed oil, castor oil, linseed oil meal,
livestock feed

S. R. MILLS FEED CO.
Freehold, N.J., 1965
Poultry and livestock feeds

POULTRY FARMING

BYARD V. CARMEAN, INC.
Laurel, Del., 1963
Poultry farm

CAROLINE POULTRY FARMS, INC.
Federalsburg, Md., 1963
Grower and processor of poultry

PHARMACEUTICALS

ZOTOX PHARMACAL CO.
Stanford, Conn., 1961
Pharmaceutical preparations

TILDEN CO., New Lebanon, N.Y., 1961
Pharmaceutical preparations

SHOES

ALBERT H. WEINBRENNER CO.
Milwaukee, Wis., 1960
Men's, boys' and children's shoes

STORM DOORS

BENANDA ALUMINUM PRODUCTS CO.
Girard, Ohio, 1956
Storm doors and windows, awnings, siding
material for building

GOLF CARTS

E-Z-GO CAR CORP., Augusta, Ga., 1960
Electric golf carts

WATCH BRACELETS

SPEIDEL CORP., Providence, R. I., 1964
Watch bracelets, chains, identification
bracelets

WRITING INSTRUMENTS

W. A. SHEAFFER PEN CO.
Ft. Madison, Iowa, 1965
Writing instruments, electronic hearing
aids

ZIPPERS

TALON, INC., Meadville, Pa., 1968
Slide fasteners (zippers)

SILVERWARE

GORHAM CORP., Providence, R. I., 1967
Fine silverware, school supplies and
stationery

DISTRIBUTORS

HENRY W. SAARI, INC.
Seattle, Wash., 1967
Distributor, Bostitch products

EDWARD SICKLES & CO.
Philadephia, Pa., 1967
Distributor, Speidel products

OTHER

NEWMARKET MANUFACTURING CO.
Lowell, Mass., 1954

Walsco-Schott division of
TELAUTOGRAPH CORP.
Los Angeles, Calif., 1956

COMPONENT PARTS CO.
Whittier, Calif., 1959

FUEL ENGINEERING CORP.
Torrance, Calif., 1962

represented by these acquisitions that . . . it was necessary to separate out some 37 different industrial categories, ranging all the way from aircraft and parts . . . to watch bracelets. The most prominent acquisitions were made in aircraft and parts and electronic equipment, acquisitions which gave Textron its present position in the aerospace industry. Textron acquired four aircraft and aircraft parts companies, topped by Bell Aircraft's defense business, including helicopters, one of Textron's most important products. The electronic acquisitions started with Dalmo Victor and numbered 10 in all. . . . Textron also produced four optical companies, including lens makers and frame producers.

Only an ad seriatim listing can carry us through the rest of the multitude of companies Textron acquired: industrial fasteners, castings, measuring instruments, research, valves, diecastings, metal stampings, metal tubings, foundry supplies, bathroom fixtures, paper machinery, metalworking machinery, machine tools (topped by the well known Jones & Lamson Machine Co. of Springfield, Vt.), marine engines, electrical transmission equipment, broadcasting equipment, glue, paint, chain saws, boats, plastics, plywood, juvenile furniture and folding metal furniture, ball bearings, a passenger liner—the SS *La Guardia* (renamed SS *Leilani*), which Royal Little bought purely for an investment, but ended up trying to run on the route from the United States to Hawaii, with no success, so that the Federal Government repossessed the ship—agrochemicals and poultry farms (two of them)— Textron's feed is used to produce Textron's own chickens and eggs— pharmaceutical houses, shoes, storm doors, golf carts, and to cap the climax, one of Textron's most recent takeovers, the Speidel watch bracelet company.[10]

Petroleum companies were at the forefront of the merger movement in the 1960s. Subsidized by special tax advantages they receive from their petroleum operations, such as foreign tax credits and depletion allowances, they have almost entirely taken over the fertilizer industry. Further, they are heavily engaged in coal and nuclear power, chemicals and plastics and many other industries. These "other industries" have been described as follows:

. . . truck manufacturing, auto parts, farm machinery, shipbuilding, paperboard containers, aircraft engines, defense items, highway and road construction, aggregates for concrete manufacturing and road building, heating and air conditioning equipment, paper-plastic cups, plywood, brushes, and real estate. Over $2 billion of assets were involved in such "pure" conglomerate acquisitions, over one-fourth of the total assets acquired during the period [1961–1968].[11]

A TOUR THROUGH A STATE OF CONCENTRATION

A common reaction is "So what?" Isn't it a question of the large, efficient company swallowing up the smaller, less efficient company? Isn't the country better served by these large, efficient enterprises?

A charitable and understated reply is "Nonsense."

Some 4,550 firms disappeared through merger in 1969 alone. Many of them were both efficient and well managed. The high prices they brought reflected this. The buyers were not shopping for dogs, but for diamonds. Caspar W. Weinberger, then chairman of the Federal Trade Commission, summed it up when he told the Senate Subcommittee on Antitrust and Monopoly:

> In addition to the magnitude of the merger activity, a significant trend has developed in the quality of firms which are being acquired: the substantial proportion of the middle range of corporations are disappearing. Between 1948 and 1968 a total of over 1,200 manufacturing companies with assets of 10 million dollars or more were acquired. Overwhelmingly these acquired companies have been well established, healthy firms making good profits. These are precisely the kinds of companies—the viable middle tier—which we would expect to grow in the normal way and thereafter present a real competitive challenge to the top corporation. The disappearance of healthy, medium, middle-size firms is a matter of concern not only for competition but for social and political institutions.[12]

Now, strong but smaller competitors that once kept the biggest companies competitive by nibbling at their toes have joined the family.

Are the giant corporations as efficient as the middle-sized companies they swallow? The executives of the giant outfits would have you believe so, partly because they labor to make themselves believe so. They offer two rationales. One is that bigness is synonymous with business efficiency. The other is that to be fully and properly exploited, modern technology requires giant corporations.

It is somewhat ironic that those who complain most about the inefficiency of bureaucracy in big government feel at home with bureaucracy in big business. Yet bloated size is the common basis for inefficiency in both. As government and corporations grow larger and larger, each becomes more difficult to manage. The top simply is too far removed from the middle and bottom tiers to permit effective use of personnel, equipment, and planning processes. A conglomerate management with responsibility for hundreds of different product lines has an impossible task. Robert Townsend, former chairman of the board of Avis and author of the bestseller *Up the Organization: How to Stop the Corporation from Stifling People and Strangling Profits,* has neatly summed up the situation. "Excellence and bigness are incompatible," he said.[13]

The merging process itself can cause great turmoil in the acquired as well as the acquiring company. A. E. Albright, executive vice president of Stauffer Chemical Company, pointed up the problems:

> There also is probably no acquisition that is ever completely painless from the "people" standpoint. Integrating a group of acquired people, whose ways of doing things are totally different from those of the parent company—their ability to communicate with a larger and more remote headquarters office, their necessary integration into existing labor contracts and fringe benefit programs, and so on—presents problems of great magnitude. . . .
>
> In most mergers, there is duplication of both administrative services and research facilities. Normally, these are eventually integrated with the acquiring company's staff services and facilities; but this, I can assure you, costs a great deal of time, effort, and money.[14]

It is true that an economic argument can be made for operational efficiencies in horizontal mergers—those in which the same products are involved. Such mergers sometimes involve the same distribution system, the same equipment and the same kinds of problems. An argument, although less persuasive, also can be made for efficiency in vertical mergers. Here, different steps in the production of a final product are involved. This is the case, for example, when a copper producer buys a fabricator of copper wires. In such a case, it can be argued that a total manufacturing process is being integrated.

But, as we have seen, most of the mergers over the past two decades have been "conglomerate"—a term that, for want of a better definition, describes a merger that, for practical purposes, is neither horizontal nor vertical. The only argument to be made for such mergers by the newer conglomerate oligarchs is somewhat subjective. They immodestly, if heatedly, claim to be more efficient managers than those of other companies. They also rely on the concept of "synergism." Translated, this means that the whole is greater than the sum of its parts—that two plus two equals five.

An unsophisticated observer may well be skeptical of the claim that a manager of a conglomerate such as Ling-Temco-Vought could run its acquired steel firm, Jones & Laughlin, better than its former manager. Indeed, financial reports indicated it was being run right into the ground when in mid-1970, James J. Ling, the conglomerate's moving force and president, was removed gently from power by his bankers. One need not be a mathematics professor to question whether two plus two equals five. "Show me" would be a polite response and a reasonable one.

The mystique of synergism and the notion of superior management by conglomerates began to fade late in 1968 when the big institutional investors paused to take a second look at the monsters they helped to create. In this period, conglomerate earnings began to decline. Disenchantment set in. And synergism as an excuse for giantism may have died forever in the spring of 1970, when the big conglomerates led the blue chips in the biggest market decline since 1963.

The Federal Trade Commission's *Economic Report on Corporate Mergers,* after closely analyzing individual conglomerates, clearly if indirectly foresaw the 1970 slide: "The recent and past experience of large, rapidly merging firms appears to warrant genuine skepticism as to the potential for management to capably operate large, far-flung diversified enterprises.[15]

The air of superiorty so assiduously developed by the new conglomerates was further discredited in a detailed study of Ling-Temco-Vought, Litton Industries, Gulf & Western Industries, National General Corporation, Leasco Data Processing Corporation, and International Telephone and Telegraph Corporation. Conducted by Representative Emanuel Celler as chairman of the House Antitrust Subcommittee, with the help of Kenneth R. Harkins, its able counsel, the study fills seven volumes of hearings and on a case-by-case basis explores the real reasons for acquisitions. Generally, the reasons were financial and bore no relationship to either efficiencies or new technologies. Certainly, superior management capabilities were not evident.[16]

These hearings encompassed mainly the newer conglomerates. But the claimed rationale of efficiency used by the mature conglomerates to justify merger activity is fully as fraudulent as the "superior management" claims of the newer giants, as we will discover.

John Kenneth Galbraith, in *The New Industrial State,* fostered the cult of giantism. Doubtless this comforts numerous executives of

43

giant corporations. It need not please anyone else. Galbraith built a lyric case on the hypothetical example of a pop-up toaster:

> The central characteristics of modern industry are illustrated by this culturally exciting invention. It would require a large organization, embracing many specialists, to get this product to consumers. Considerable capital would be required. While it is conceivably open to an individual entrepreneur such as myself to have an inspiration, no one would expect a one-man firm to produce such a product. It could be done only by a big firm. All decisions on the toaster—those involving initiation, development, and ultimate acceptance or rejection—are the work of teams of specialists and are exercised deep down in the company.[17]

Professor Galbraith may have been unaware that his hypothetical example had been tested in the real world even before he wrote his book, and had flunked. The test was disclosed by the late T. K. Quinn, a former executive of General Electric. He recalled that a relatively small firm, the McGraw Company, had developed the electric toaster and brought it into the market. He said:

> For many years none of the giant companies were able to come near to matching McGraw's toaster. The result was that in order to break into the market successfully General Electric used its economic power to buy up the McGraw Company so it too could have the advantage of technology developed by a relatively small company.[18]

Nor is this an exception. Quinn credited small companies with discovery and initial production of electric ranges, electric refrigerators, electric dryers, electric dishwashers, the hermetically sealed compressor used in refrigerators and air conditioners, vacuum cleaners, clothes washing machines, deep freezers, and electric irons, including the steam variety. "I know of no original product invention, not even electric shavers or hearing aids, made by any of the giant laboratories or corporations with the possible exception of the household garbage grinder, developed not by the research laboratory but by the engineering department of General Electric," Quinn said. "But the basic idea of this machine came from a smaller firm producing commercial grinders."

Quinn also said, "The record of the giants is one of moving in, buying out and absorbing the smaller concern."[19]

The extensive hearings held by Senator Hart also explored the relationship between size and efficiency.

A TOUR THROUGH A STATE OF CONCENTRATION

A study by Dr. Johan Bjorksten, an economic consultant, indicated that one of every six mergers involving manufacturing firms has failed in that the acquired company generally went out of business.[20] The disappearance of a viable firm from the marketplace after each unsuccessful merger is an ultimate in inefficiency.

But what of the other five mergers? Inasmuch as a key measure of efficiency is profitability, the subcommittee tried to discover if a relationship existed between size and profitability. The conclusion of its chief economist was:

> In short, in only slightly less than a quarter of the thirty industries [studied] increasing size was generally accompanied by rising profit rates. In the other three-quarters the tendency was either in the opposite direction or there appeared to be no relationship whatever. Since a higher rate could be the result of either superior efficiency or greater monopoly power, the failure of the companies with presumably the greatest monopoly power to earn the highest rates suggests the possibility that they may be even less efficient than their smaller rivals.[21]

Several important studies relating profitability to merger rates have come up with the same conclusions: companies relying primarily on internal growth for expansion generally are more profitable than those growing through merger. Indeed, the basic study found that profits tended to fall as the number of acquisitions increased.[22]

Evidence has continued to pile up showing there is little relationship between size and efficiency. A study by the staff of the Cabinet Committee on Price Stability concluded: "This [merger] movement appears to be propelled by special financial and speculative consideration rather than by the pursuit of efficiency through large-scale business organizations."[23]

The *Economic Report on Conglomerate Mergers* of the Federal Trade Commission concluded that the frenzied rate of merger activity "cannot be explained in terms of a quest for efficiency, particularly when large firms merge with one another."[24]

Dr. Walter Adams, an economist with outstanding credentials in the field, has testified:

> Unlike horizontal or vertical bigness which under some circumstances may be conducive to efficiency and technological progressiveness, conglomerate bigness almost never possesses these characteristics. Since by its very nature,

the conglomerate firm is composed of functionally unrelated enterprises, it loses the advantages of specialization and the economies of scale pertaining thereto. It also sacrifices the specialized skills and know-how which in other giant firms may be conducive to research achievements and innovation. In other words a conglomerate firm cannot claim to be society's benefactor through greater efficiency or increased progressiveness. Nor, incidentally, can the conglomerate firm claim spectacular achievements on behalf of its stockholders.[25]

A study presented to the subcommittee by Samuel Richardson Reid, author of the book *Mergers, Managers and the Economy,* concluded that owners of stock in companies that had "natural" internal growth fared much better than stockholders in firms that had grown through conglomerate mergers.[26]

Another expert, Dr. Leon Garoian, Professor of Agricultural Economics, Oregon State University, said after a two-day seminar by merger experts:

> In summary, consensus of the papers prepared for the seminar on conglomerate growth suggests that the efficiency motives for conglomeration are not substantial. . . . Therefore other factors prevail as motives for conglomerate development. Not the least of these are financial motives in efforts to achieve economic power in contrast to market power.[27]

The traditional rationale for bigness centered on what was called "economies of scale." Roughly translated, this means the bigger the plant, the less expensive it is to make a product. But it is now clear from the studies of Professor Joe S. Bain and others that this is not true. Beyond a certain plant size, no further economies set in.[28] Moreover, in most concentrated industries, the divergence between plant size and company size is large.[29] In other words, a giant company achieves efficiency in production not by building a single huge plant, but by operating a group of plants each of which may be small relative to the market. This means that a large number of companies could be broken up without in any way reducing efficiency at the plant level.

The evidence is now overwhelming that giant corporations cannot legitimately claim efficiency by reason of bigness, no matter how efficiency is measured.

The second rationale for giantism, closely related to the argument that bigness equals efficiency, is that bigness is needed to develop and market modern technology. This claim has been so compelling that it has disarmed many political liberals and corporate oligarchs alike. In the words of John Kenneth Galbraith, "a benign providence . . . has made the modern industry of a few large firms an excellent instrument for inducing technical change."[30]

The facts are preponderantly against the claim. Modern technology not only does not require giantism, but actually can be thwarted by it. In a classic work, *Sources of Invention,* John Jewkes and Richard Stillerman studied sixty of the most important inventions of the twentieth century. In 1965, Stillerman, testified at the Senate Subcommittee on Antitrust and Monopoly hearings:

> Our study indicates that modern inventions arise from a wide spectrum of sources. More often than not they originate with inventors who have a persistence amounting almost to an obsession. . . .
>
> According to the modern view of invention, today's individual inventor is ill-equipped to contribute anything worthwhile because he cannot cope with the complexity of modern technology, the ballooning cost of experimentation, and the need for team work by specialists. However, in about one-half of our cases, individual inventors were responsible for the major inventions.

He pointed out that xerography, the revolutionary dry-copying process, came from a patent attorney, Chester Carlson, who struggled through years of frustation before a nonprofit research organization, Battelle Memorial Institute, saw promise in the idea and commenced development. He recalled that the jet engine originated—independently in England and Germany—in the minds of individual inventors who at first could interest neither the aircraft engine firms nor their respective governments in their work.

Stillerman told the subcommittee:

> Though science established the ground work for radio, most of the important inventions, among them Lee DeForest's vacuum tube, Reginald Fessenden's heterodyne, and Edwin Armstrong's system of frequency modulation, emerged from a band of enterprising individual inventors who worked either outside the established firms or organized new firms to exploit their ideas. . . . An English watchmaker, John Harwood, conceived the modern self-winding watch, an idea rejected by the Swiss watch companies when first offered to them. Air conditioning is the offspring of individual inventors, principally Willis Carrier who was employed by a small firm

as an engineer. His employer refused to support his notions for air conditioning, so he formed his own firm to exploit the inventions. Kodachrome arose from the experiments of two musicians, sometimes working in their kitchen sinks between concerts.

What of the trend toward institutionalization of research? Although individual inventors who in earlier days might have remained independent are being absorbed into industrial laboratories, Stillerman observed that we do not know whether this organization of research activity, ostensibly designed to increase the flow of invention, actually does so.

> One cannot overlook the limitations to the conduct of research within an industrial laboratory. Making profits is the primary goal of every firm. Few, if any, firms would support the kind of speculative research in manned flight undertaken by the Wright brothers at the turn of the century after experts proclaimed that powered flight was impossible. Or the risky experiments on helicopters which a horde of optimistic individual inventors carried forward over several decades. Or the early rocket research pursued by individuals with limited financial backing.

His testimony was replete with examples of new inventions and developments that large firms rejected, which is not to say that large firms have not engaged in, and sometimes succeeded in, making and developing new inventions. Stillerman concluded his testimony with these words:

> There is much to be said for the virtues of numbers and varieties of attack in development as well as invention. The more schemes for development, the more firms of all sizes prepared to risk capital on development both simple and complex, the less chance the valuable ideas will lay fallow. Large firms are necessary for projects of great magnitude which a small firm could not afford. But clearly our economy would suffer if all industries were reduced to a few large firms. For missing would be those small firms pursuing developments which a large firm might consider trivial, such as a paperclip and a safety razor; those smaller firms willing to gamble on innovations such as xerography, magnetic recording and the helicopter which large firms in the past chose to ignore; in those smaller firms with an eye on rapid growth whose ingenuity and flexibility equipped them to break into new fields such as transistor technology and insecticides. There will be less tendency for firms to rest on their laurels if the way remains open for aggressive small firms to innovate. The value of competition in stimulating innovation should not be underestimated.[31]

A TOUR THROUGH A STATE OF CONCENTRATION

The Antitrust Subcommittee's exploration of the sources of invention and innovation, filling 800 printed pages, includes a review by Dr. Blair of the extensive data on four particular industries:

> In none of the three important new technologies in steel—oxygen conversion, continuous casting or the planetary mill—did any of the largest producers make any significant contribution in research or development, innovation or invention. The same is true of the continuous process in bread-making. It was also true for the many innovations conceived and introduced into their models by the smaller automobile manufacturers in the days when they were still extant. Such important classes of drugs as the corticosteroids, tranquilizers and antibiotics stemmed from discoveries and ideas of independent scientists, some of whom were fortunate in receiving from the drug companies financial support.[32]

Clearly, bigness is not a necessary prerequisite to invention and innovation. To the contrary, it may well be that highly concentrated industries resist technology and invention unless competition forces them to move ahead. The reasons are not hard to discern. With millions of dollars invested in open-hearth furnaces, the steel industry understandably, even if misguidedly, might resist a change over to the oxygen converter. An auto industry with millions of dollars invested in great stamping plants for steel bodies has limited incentive to embrace the new technologies of plastics, except on a limited basis. Nor is there a mystery about the auto industry's reluctance to abandon millions of dollars invested in facilities for the piston engine in order to produce a more efficient power plant. If the industry eventually adopts new engine technology, and it may, it will do so not with a glad embrace, but with a reluctant yielding to congressional and other pressures that will have become unbearable.

Chrysler's failure to market a gas turbine engine, despite its great promise, helps to explain this premise. As early as 1954, its engineers had licked the tough technical problems. *Automotive News* said in an article dated March 29, 1954, under the headline "Chrysler Solves 2 Big Barriers To Gas Turbine":

> Chrysler Corporation's new gas turbine engine, though not yet ready for general use, removes some of the barriers that have challenged engineers for decades. Chrysler said last week that its turbine engine boasts fuel economy equal to that of conventional engines and that the new unit's

exhaust is cooler than that discharged by the average car. . . . George A. Huebner, Jr., Executive Engineer in charge of research, directed the development designed in laboratory test work on the Chrysler gas turbine. Huebner disclosed that test runs of the turbine powered Plymouth at the company's engineering proving grounds near Chelsea, Michigan, was the latest stage in more than nine years of work on gas turbines by Chrysler Corporation engineers. . . . A Chrysler gas turbine is almost two hundred pounds lighter and has less than one-fifth as many major moving parts as a piston engine of a similar power. . . . The turbine's power is inherently vibration free because combustion is continuous and because its few moving parts rotate smoothly on ball or roller bearings.

If the article had appeared fifteen years later, it would not have failed to note that the gas turbine engine is almost pollution-free.

In 1967, Huebner, then director of the research-product planning and development staff of Chrysler Corporation, appeared before the Senate Subcommittee on Antitrust and Monopoly. He testified that in 1962 Chrysler had decided that sufficient technical progress had been achieved in safety, control and reliability to subject turbine-powered passenger cars to public approval and use in a market evaluation test.

The public trial and the 203 users were enthusiastic, Huebner testified. The reasons he gave for not marketing the engine at that time seem thin in the light of most drivers' experience with the engines in their own cars. He said that with the turbine, slow-speed fuel consumption was not quite good enough; noise, while acceptable to most of the drivers, needed further reduction; greater engine braking was desirable; and a slight lag in acceleration from a standing start had to be eliminated.

This should be contrasted with his answer to a question from Senator Hiram L. Fong, a member of the Subcommittee:

> We demonstrated that we had a power plant which could operate in competition with the piston engine. It could produce approximately the same fuel mileage, the same performance as the piston engine, same control. . . . And in addition it demonstrated that this other characteristic which we had felt were possible in the turbine, the long life, the freedom from oil changes, the freedom from antifreeze replacement, the instant heat, the rest of the things which I mentioned, and above all the clean exhaust . . . that they were there and that they were meaningful and further that we satisfied ourselves that we were not dreaming a hopeless dream, but that what we had produced people liked.

Huebner continued at another point: "Our recommended fuels were kerosene, diesel #1, diesel #2, and gasoline in that order. We asked the users not to use *ordinary leaded fuel*. . . . [Emphasis supplied.]" We have italicized the words "ordinary leaded fuel" in order to call brief attention to another exercise by the auto makers of the equivalent of governmental power. In making decisions about the turbine engine, Chrysler, even if inadvertently, was determining for all of us whether the levels of lead in the air we breathe would rise or fall. Similarly, when General Motors, Ford, and Chrysler decided to improve engine performance with drastic increases in compression ratios, they forced greatly expanded use of gasoline with octane ratings increased by the addition of more lead. And so by the late 1960s motor vehicles were blowing about two pounds of lead *per capita* into the atmosphere, thanks to private government. In the 1970s lead is being taken out of gasoline, thanks to public government.

Just as the turbine engine would have spared us from some of that lead, so would it have spared us from another deadly poison. The turbine, Huebner said, is "relatively freer of carbon monoxide in the atmosphere than human beings' breath."

One might fairly ask why, in 1971, Detroit still does not produce turbine-powered autos. Part of the answer, surely, is the inertia that large investments in obsolete equipment generate in large corporations. This phenomenon, to which we alluded earlier, troubled Senator Hart, as shown in this colloquy which he initiated with Huebner:

> We had testimony last week from persons experienced in the use of chemicals as a source of automobile bodies and I remember raising with them basic hard economic problems that any break-through like this presents a manufacturer, whether it is automobiles or anything else. You have got "x" dollars in plant space appropriate really only for automobile body production. You've got awfully big dies and so although the plastic is appealing, look at all this money we have got tied up. We cannot do it. There has to be the economic justification to throw away the dies and is not this really the problem also with turbine engines? The performance may be pretty close to acceptable, but as you put it, "we have recognized from the beginning that a power plant as new as the gas turbine would be required to fit itself into the existing industry and its capital structure."

Huebner replied:

It is part of the problem but I do not believe that it is going to overwhelm anyone. It is a difficult problem, it is true, and in this field perhaps as much innovation and invention, that is, in the financial field, as much innovation and invention will be required as has been applied to the turbine itself. But tools do wear out and since they were not all brought at one time they are always wearing out and always being replaced. It is a question of facing up, of course, to the fact that it has to be done at one time, but this again is a relative condition.[33]

Do the economics of giant corporations, then, act to stifle marketing of technological breakthroughs?

The Chrysler turbine engine story suggests that the answer is yes. The "technological imperative" rationalization for giantism thus may be merely a mask concealing the true state of affairs. It is bad enough to be prepared to sell our economic and possibly our political freedom for the coin of technology. How ironic if the coin is counterfeit!

More evidence that the new technologies should be leading us to a more deconcentrated society involves computers. Using shared time and other devices, the smallest corporation has access to the miracles of computers. A host of functions—market research, inventory control, payroll processing, information storing—once required thousands of employees. Now computers are available to perform these functions for the smallest producer on terms similar to those of the giant conglomerate. The brains of computers, in fact, have become the servants of all producers. They have made available the work-hours of thousands of employees which the smaller manufacturer in the past could not afford. The computer should be the great equalizer, rather than a force toward greater concentration. This message came through clearly in the testimony of industry spokesmen, including witnesses of computer firms such as IBM and Honeywell, Incorporated, before the Senate Subcommittee on Antitrust and Monopoly.[34]

The same hearings made it clear that the computer was but one of the new technologies that were opening the door to opportunities for small firms. A host of industry witnesses—managers, applied scientists and investment bankers—testified that new technological developments are making it possible to enter rapidly growing industries with even modest capital. For example, in the plastics industry, a process called thermoforming produces a wide range of large and strong structures; yet capital entry requirements and operating costs are low. Small firms use thermoforming to produce camper bodies, boats and refrigerators —and with a degree of efficiency difficult for larger corporations to match.

The hearings led the *Washington Post,* on October 12, 1967, to remark editorially on the economic "myth" that one of the reasons why giant firms have become dominant

> is a unique ability to exploit new developments in technology. Much of John Kenneth Galbraith's book on *The New Industrial State* rests upon those preconceptions. But the facts adduced in the recent hearings of Sen. Philip A. Hart's Antitrust and Monopoly Subcommittee tell a very different story. . . .
>
> Alfred Marshall, the great Victorian economist, used to draw an analogy between competition and the ecology of forests. Business firms, like trees, experience life cycles of rapid growth, retardation, stagnation and eventual decline. Technological change serves as a catalytic element in propelling those cycles, and it is a force for greater competition and deconcentration rather than a lever by which monopolists extend their dominance.

In the steel industry, for example, new technology, such as the electric furnace, can make it profitable for small companies to compete in some areas with the giants. On October 26, 1970, the Wall Street Journal, under the revealing headline "More Steel Users Cut Costs by Purchasing from Tiny New Mills," said:

> Technology is making the minimill increasingly economic. There have long been small steel mills, but they concentrated mainly on high-priced specialty steels. The growth of neighborhood mills, which mostly produce low-priced ordinary carbon steel, began in the last decade as electric furnaces and other newly developed equipment improved.
>
> New developments may help further. An increasingly used chemical process called "direct reduction" reduces iron ore to iron-rich pellets that can be fed directly into electric furnaces without the use of expensive blast furnaces. This frees the small mill from relying on scrap metal when its price is high. . . .
>
> An installation producing two million tons of steel a year with a blast furnace and other necessary equipment might cost $200 million. . . . Using direct reduction, "the same tonnage from a series of electric furnaces would require an investment of only $70 million.". . .
>
> Nuclear Corp. of America, which built the mill here in Darlington [South Carolina], says it can produce steel at $15 to $20 a ton less than the prices that foreign producers and big domestic mills demand.

A classic study prepared by Dr. Blair for the Subcommittee should further lock the door on those who believe giantism and modern technology need go hand in hand. Examining concentration on an industry-wide basis, he found that it generally was declining in industries that sell to industrial buyers (chemicals, fabricated metal products and machinery). In consumer goods industries, it was increasing greatly.[35] Generally, in industries where true technological advances have occurred, the trend has been toward more competition and less concentration. The impact of the new technologies has been resulting in new entry—that is, in smaller firms becoming able to challenge leading firms. Such a result hardly would be consistent with the thesis that new technologies require giant companies.

Concentration, the Blair study also showed, was increasing particularly in "food and kindred products." This was significant because these are consumer goods industries where new technology in any significant amount is absent. Similarly, concentration has risen rapidly in brewing. This is an industry in which dominant companies make the proud claim that they use today the same brewing methods that they used a century ago.

Giant firms in consumer industries are not more efficient or more technologically advanced than many smaller firms, but they do mount expensive advertising campaigns. This—not better products at lower prices—significantly explains their success. Major broadcast networks, magazines, and newspapers have given the giants substantial discounts. This has facilitated the process by which smaller competitors have been extinguished. Two volumes of testimony before the Hart Subcommittee detail the process.[36] Indeed, the Supreme Court has overturned a major merger partly because advertising discounts available to a giant corporation were unavailable to its smaller rivals.[37]

In the advertising game, victory goes not to the swiftest but to the richest. Once again, the giant corporation is shown to be buying, not working, its way to the top. Its success results not from any "technological imperative," but from discriminatory ad rates and a fat bankroll.

One last matter indirectly related to both efficiency and technology requires mention at this point.

Professor Galbraith and others have suggested that only the giant corporations can effectively distribute products on a large scale. Aside from the fact that there is little, if any, documentation for this assumption, there are effective methods of distribution equally available to both the small and the giant corporation. A good example is franchising.

For years, the automobile and petroleum industries have been among those to use this system of distribution. They do this because franchising is a cheap, practical, and efficient method of getting a product to the consumer. Its particular advantage is that the corporation uses the capital of its own distributor. This makes franchising especially attractive to smaller companies, which are able to set up an effective and far-flung marketing system using relatively little of their own capital. Its growth since 1965 has been phenomenal. In 1970, approximately 670,000 franchises were doing approximately $100 billion worth of business.

Unfortunately, the promise of franchising has been abused. A case in point is the manufacturer that takes over outlets once it can afford to do so.

Further, franchising has proved so successful that many conglomerates are following the lead of General Electric when it couldn't effectively compete with McGraw's Toastmaster. They are buying out the successful franchisers. For instance, Chicken Delight now is owned by Consolidated Foods Corporation; Burger King by Pillsbury Company; Burger Chef by General Foods. Even Minnie Pearl must pay homage to her successful suitor, National General Corporation.

Nevertheless, franchising is still available to the smaller corporation as an effective means of getting products into the hands of consumers without a great outlay of capital.

There are, of course, reasons why mergers continue to be effected, even though so many in the past have been profitable neither for the merging companies nor their stockholders, have contributed negatively, if at all, to efficiency, and have retarded rather than advanced technology.

Under the economic rationale of our free enterprise system, the primary motivation of a corporation should be to earn as much money as possible. But corporations are not always motivated by economic laws alone.

Some executives, for example, crave the power that comes from running a large rather than a small corporation. Growth for growth's sake, prestige, revenge—an entire catalogue of human motivations must be superimposed on the economic ones. Sometimes, it may be pure greed.

In a discussion of how Xerox was able to take over C.I.T. Financial Corporation, a *Forbes* magazine article pointed out, almost as an aside, the following:

> Among the biggest gainers will be C.I.T.'s top management. At latest count as of January 1, C.I.T.'s executives held options for 343,000 shares at prices ranging between 28.53 and 43.75. If the merger goes through, they could end up with a combined stock market gain of approximately $10 million, a gain which C.I.T. on its own probably couldn't have achieved for many many years.[38]

Such considerations aside, corporate oligarchs have discovered a new dimension in profit-making. Profits need not be earned only from the products manufactured; they can be earned from the process of merging itself. Involved here are financial manipulations as well as Wall Street psychology. A little background may be helpful.

The secret of the growth of the conglomerate movement centers on "earnings." A company which keeps increasing its earnings, particularly through growth by merger, has been endowed by Wall Street with a high price-earnings ratio. That means simply the relation between the price of a company's stock and its earnings. For example, if a company with annual earnings of $1.00 per share is selling for $50 a share, it has a price-earnings ratio of 50 to 1. If another company's stock with the same earnings is selling for $10 per share, it has a price-earnings ratio of 10 to 1. The trick is to hypnotize the big investors on the stock market into giving one's stock a high earnings ratio. The company with the highly valued stock, then, has the ability to buy up companies with the low-valued stock regardless of their comparative assets. Its strength comes not from its internal structure, but how it is rated by big investors.

There are several basic ways to increase earnings—greater efficiency, acquisitions, and appropriate accounting techniques. If our contention is correct—that conglomerates are not necessarily geared to efficiency—then it becomes clear why many of them must keep gobbling up efficient, high-cash-flow companies. They need their acquisitions' earnings. They also are able to utilize accounting options to inflate these earnings. *Forbes* quoted the head of a leading Wall Street investment firm as saying: "You don't have to be in our end of the securities business very long before you realize that what companies call their earnings can be almost anything they want them to be." The same article related: "A partner of one of the Big Eight firms says frankly: 'Give me the books of almost any company and within a year's time I can double the earnings.' "[39]

Abraham J. Briloff, an accountant, told the Senate Subcommittee on Antitrust and Monopoly how this can be done:

> So it is that when it was the managerial objective to reduce income to an irreducible minimum (consistent with what was then deemed to be the "normal growth curve") we were able to accommodate their "Twiggy-Figure" objectives by giving them LIFO (Last In, First Out) inventories, accelerated depreciation, fast R & D and intangible write-offs of oil company development costs, and the like. . . .

He explained that it was this pattern of value suppression which gave rise to the observation that a balance sheet is like a bikini bathing suit—what it reveals is interesting; what it conceals is vital. He continued:

> It might be fairly asserted that it was this very traditional commitment to "a conservative balance sheet," low-earnings reporting, and high liquidity with low debt, which made life so simple for the flamboyant conglomerators, for the performance oriented new breed of management determined to show flair, synergism, flash, and charisma . . .
>
> You see, when the new breed of managers moved into the flesh-pot of assets nurtured by the traditional management, they were capable of disposing of them at ·huge profits when compared with the vestigial written-down book values—producing still greater earnings exposures by the new management and then when the new management relaxed the old "Twiggy-accounting" constraints, the reported earnings zoomed still more and the high priests of Wall Street were unqualifiedly certain that they had oracular powers approaching the divine. And this could, theoretically, have permitted the chain reaction to continue until all of our economic resources would have been brought within the ambit of the entity capable of being blessed with the highest P/E [price-earnings] ratio.[40]

The *Wall Street Journal,* in a story entitled "Conglomerate Earnings: Credibility Gap," gave an example:

> Merger specialists say that conglomerates "have pointed the way" by acquiring companies with disparate operations and then manipulating accounting rules to their advantage. AMK Corp., a diversified conglomerate, was able to boost its fiscal 1969 profit 74 cents a share over the previous year, for example, simply by three accounting switches. Without these, its profit would have declined by 25 cents a share. Two of these changes were pos-

sible because AMK had just acquired a new subsidiary, John Morrell & Co., a meat packer. AMK shifted Morrell from more conservative to more liberal methods of depreciation and valuing inventory and thereby lowered Morrell's cost and thereby raised total corporate profits . . .[41]

Barron's, a conservative business journal, in an article entitled, "Day of Reckoning? Conglomerates Can't Keep Making Two and Two Equal Five Forever," illustrated how accounting alternatives can make a company look better than it really is:

> Two of the basic principles of accounting are uniformity and consistency, yet Teledyne, Kidde and most of the other conglomerates blithely have used "pooling of interests" for acquisitions effected above book, and "purchase of assets" for companies bought below book. In fact, Gulf & Western somehow managed to use both methods in booking the acquisition of New Jersey Zinc. The accounting technique used is the one that best served their interest in maximizing reported earnings.[42]

The Securities and Exchange Commission announced in 1969 that it may require a change in these "pooling of interest" rules. The result: near-panic by some of the acquisition-minded firms.

The *Barron's* article also described the use of yet one more takeover device:

> Another serious problem for investors arises from the massive use by conglomerates of convertible securities. As Mr. [Meshulam] Riklis so eloquently explained at a recent seminar on how to effect acquisitions, the theory is "that by the time the debentures (Russian rubles) or warrants (Castro pesos) become due, the company you acquired can generate more cash than they are worth."[43]

The Federal Trade Commission's *Economic Report on Corporate Mergers* aptly summed up accounting techniques used to obscure operating results, hide profit declines, and overstate growth in earnings under the heading: "Accounting Principles as Tool of Deception." The report pointed up the basic problem:

> Clearly, no good economic purpose is served by accounting for acquisitions in a way that gives the acquirer the power to control reported earnings regardless of current operating experience. Current merger accounting provides a hothouse environment for acquirers. Even if mergers do not turn out well from an operating standpoint, acquiring firms can often show

higher profits through accounting manipulations. It is ironic that internal growth through new investment may be, purely for accounting reasons, subjected to a more stringent test than growth through merger. As a result, firms investing in new capacity to serve producer and consumer needs may be less favored by the stock market than merger-active firms which do not contribute as much to the real growth of the economy.[44]

The report's summary is instructive:

> It is clear that present requirements for corporate reporting are unsatisfactory and are in need of immediate revision. Various members of the business community are exploiting a range of reporting alternatives that tends to mislead the investing public; this also provides the means for promoting a restructuring of industrial organization in such a manner that the requirements of efficient resource allocation will lack a solid foundation. To view the current merger movement as a single manifestation of entrepreneurial effort to restructure the economy in order to meet the requirements of organizational efficiency is nonsense.[45]

Conglomerate earnings frequently have been attributable to such financial and accounting sleight of hand. Companies have grown because they could make one dollar in earnings look like ten.

Fifty years from now, economic historians looking back at this period of concentration through conglomerate merger may well dub it the "Age of Irony"—an age when inefficient companies ate up more efficient ones, when the American public thus was forced to pay more and more for less and less, all in the name of efficiency and technology. It will be difficult for the historians to understand how industry giants could have deluded themselves into believing that merging two large, inefficient companies would achieve something better than a twice-as-inefficient company.

A prime example is the merger of the New York Central and the Pennsylvania Railroads. The Justice Department opposed it. However, the companies were able to persuade their regulator, the Interstate Commerce Commission, and the courts that the merger should be allowed. Both companies had severe financial troubles. By combining, they argued, efficiencies would become possible and could make the operation profitable.

In June 1970 the roof fell in on those who argued "the bigger the better." The Penn Central Railroad was forced into bankruptcy. Yet just two years earlier, the merger had been hailed as the only way to provide better service for the consumer and financial strength for the two ailing giants.

Apparently, it never occurred to the ICC to determine how big is too big. W. Graham Clayton, Jr., president of a profitable railroad—the Southern—just a few days before the bankruptcy proceeding had warned that there may be a disadvantage in being too big.[46]

Eight years earlier, the late Senator Estes Kefauver had warned, after extensive hearings on his bill proposing a moratorium on railroad mergers, of the dangers inherent in allowing mergers between giant railroads.

He may have had in mind the testimony of John R. Meyer, professor of transportation at Harvard, who accurately predicted: "Indeed, it is difficult to see how any cost economies will be achieved if present unwieldy and large enterprises are merged into even larger and more unwieldy enterprises."[47]

It will be years before the multibillion-dollar tangle of Penn Central is sorted out. But, as Senator Hart remarked after the failure: "While many are fond of the cliché, 'Bigness is not necessarily bad,' it is important to understand that the converse is equally true that 'bigness is not necessarily good.' "

A railroad is, of course, a different animal from a manufacturing concern (although through a holding company Penn Central was in hundreds of other businesses besides railroading). Railroads are referred to as natural monopolies, which suggests that bigness is essential for efficiency. But even under these circumstances, two plus two equals four, not five. The lesson is clear: Inefficiency can't be cured through merger.

Another force behind the merger boom is the merger brokers. They profit from putting mergers together, regardless of the value to the merging firm.

A full-page ad in the *Wall Street Journal* said only: "Barron & Co., Inc. . . . when you want to merge your company—discreetly 215 PE5–9634 Philadelphia."[48]

Barron & Co., Inc. is not alone. *Forbes* magazine, in an article entitled "Diversification's Marriage Brokers," found this situation:

> A few week ago a *Forbes* reporter was talking to a prospective seller
> of the kind of small company that is a real plum in today's booming merger

market. He is the chief executive and owner of a profitable, cash-heavy, family-controlled manufacturing firm with sales in the $20-million to $50-million category, a firm that is the dominant factor in its industry.

The man was irate. "I get a phone call at least once a week from some guy who wants to know if we're up for sale, or if we're interested in buying —and hundreds of finders' letters," he said. "Well, if you ask me, these third parties—I don't care whether they're investment bankers, commercial bankers, management consultants, finders, or what they are—are just so many vultures wheeling around a carcass! . . ."

While the businessman in question is not yet certain that he wants to sell, there are over-riding considerations that eventually will make it all but obligatory for him to do so: estate taxes, management succession and the like. And so, while he hesitates, torn by doubts and rationalizations spawned by a lifetime devoted to the company, dozens of eager merger intermediaries know what he does not yet admit: that it is only a question of time before his little jewel of a company will be offered up to an eager merger market.

The same *Forbes* article helped to explain how profits have stimulated the growth of merger-brokering:

Buying firms are more likely to seek outside advice when they are unable to proceed on the basis of their own experience. They are also likely to benefit more from the third party's sales pitch.

They are willing to pay well for such services. For example, American Home Products recently paid investment banker Lehman Bros. a fee of $916,000 for services during the five years of study and negotiations that led to its merger with Ekco Products Co.

With all this potentially lucrative demand for advice and assistance, accounting firms, management consultants, commercial banks and brokerage houses are all looking for pieces of the action.[49]

Two cases from Senate Antitrust and Monopoly hearings illustrate further why the merger movement will be difficult to halt.[50]

The former Wall Street investment firm of Cogan, Berlind, Weill and Levitt decided insurance companies were ripe for takeovers because all those beautiful surpluses from insurance premiums were, as the firm saw it, just going to waste. So it did a survey of insurance companies which prepared it to try to interest clients in taking them over. First, it "found" Reliance Insurance Company for Leasco Data Processing Corporation. For this it received a $750,000 finder's fee. Then Cogan *et al.* advised its clients, primarily mutual funds, to buy Reliance stock.

This was good advice, because when word of the prospective takeover got out, the stock, surely not by mere chance, tripled within six months in 1968, increasing from 30 in April to 99⅞ in October. The investment firm then retrieved the stock from its clients and made it available to Leasco to assist in the takeover. For this Leasco paid a $46,925 commission. How much the investment firm received from its own clients was undisclosed.

The subcommittee counsel, summing up in an exchange with the president of Reliance, said:

> So on one hand they are finding you, and, having "found" you, they are telling their own clients "here is a good buy" which of course it was, because after they "found" you, your stock went up from around $30 to about $90. . . . And then they can take the stock from their own clients and give it back to Leasco to help with the takeover and make a profit on that.[51]

The president of Reliance agreed this was correct.

In another case, the same Wall Street firm "found" Great American Insurance Company for National General Corporation. For this Cogan *et al.* received a $250,000 consultant fee. It received another $157,000 in brokerage from mutual fund clients which, on its advice, had bought Great American stock.

After effecting the takeover, National General declared a $171 million dividend from Great American stock, 93 per cent of which it then owned. This amounted to $55 per share—22 times the $2.50 dividend of previous years. It was also about three times the amount National General had paid for the insurance company in the first place.

Subcommittee counsel asked the counsel of National General: "Does not this give an awful lot of investment brokers a real interest in keeping the merger movement going, not from any question of efficiency, but just from the point of view of their own profitability?"

He replied that the figures "would certainly indicate that."[52]

Some commentators, including Donald F. Turner of Harvard Law School, the lawyer-economist who once headed the Justice Department's Antitrust Division, have suggested that the merger movement may have the virtue of shaking up stodgy management. However, quite the opposite also may be true. Management may spend so much time and effort fighting off takeovers that the business of running the company suffers. Sometimes beleaguered managements even enter into "defensive" mergers. The process reminds one of the dog chasing its own tail. It may start running, but hardly in a productive manner.

The Signal Companies of Los Angeles, for example, have been called a conglomerate that "just happened." Garrett Corporation had asked Signal to buy it in order to fend off a takeover by Curtis-Wright. Meanwhile, Mack Truck also ran into the arms of Signal to keep from being taken over by unacceptable suitors. As explained by Mack's chief executive officer in 1967: "Mack and Garrett wanted to get married to avoid being raped."[53] Management—good or bad—was not at issue. The merger took place to avoid a takeover battle. Possibly, the following description explains why many companies desire to avoid such battles:

> "The takeover fight," says one investment banker often hired to quarterback acquisitions, "is the one activity down here where there is a clear winner and loser. I always prefer a fight to a smooth deal—after it's over anyway." Standing in his plush lower Manhattan office, with the New York harbor spread out behind him, he flails his arms and his eyes dance as he talks of tactics to frighten opposing bankers, pry information out of proxy solicitors and make allies of the arbitrageurs [an elite corps of tape traders who profit from proposed mergers by playing the difference between the market price of an acquisition candidate's stock and the price per share that the acquiring company is willing to pay for it]. "I suppose you could call some of this dirty," he concedes, "but it is so much fun. How can anything that much fun be dirty?"[54]

We shall leave the question unanswered. But if as much time and effort—whether dirty or clean—were spent on company affairs as on merger affairs, it is a fair assumption that even stodgy management could do a better job.

To defend the merger movement on the ground that it may stir up management is like suggesting that the way to renovate an old house is to drop a stick of dynamite down the chimney.

Certainly, the thought of two hundred supercorporations standing astride the economy is a troubling one. But another serious question needs answering. Who influences the two hundred corporations? To answer this question requires an excursion into the world of banking and, to a lesser degree, other areas of the investment community.

It has been accepted by most observers—and quite properly—that small stockholders do not control corporations.[55] But institutional stockholders *do* influence corporations. *Newsweek* reported in the spring of 1970:

> The institutional investor keeps looming larger. In New York last week, the Big Board released a study showing exactly how much weight institutions swing in the market place.
>
> In its fifteenth transaction study, the New York Stock Exchange supplied specific figures to support the general statement that institutions now account for more than half of all the public trading on its floor. During the first six months of 1969, institutions were responsible for 54.4 percent of the shares traded while individuals for the first time fell below the midpoint with 45.6 percent. In dollar volume, the difference is greater yet. Institutions generated 60.3 percent of the total, individuals 39.7 percent. . . .
>
> A breakdown of the institutional totals shows how much more important mutual funds have become in the past decade. Their share of institutional activity increased sharply—from 17.5 percent of the total in 1960 to 26.6 percent in 1969. The funds thus closed the gap separating them from the biggest institutional investors of all—banks and trust companies, whose share fell from 40.6 percent to 36.4 percent during the decade.[56]

Indeed, the conglomerate hysteria has been partially fueled by the need of the mutual funds to move large blocks of stock quickly in the quest for fast profits. Because of the great blocks of stock the mutual funds control, they have a great influence on the nature and form of mergers. But the mutual funds and most institutional investors are primarily interested in their own profitability, not in control.

J. A. Livingston, syndicated financial columnist of the *Philadelphia Bulletin,* told the Subcommittee on Antitrust and Monopoly:

> Institutional investors—insurance companies, mutual funds, trust companies —rarely act as true owners. If anything goes wrong with a company, the institutional investor wants out. He hesitates to take sides in a proxy fight. He will not exercise his voting or moral power during a takeover. He does not want to get involved. He takes his profit and goes on to something else. It is a love 'em and leave 'em philosophy. And this makes takeovers possible.[57]

The large banks are the biggest of the institutional investors. However, unlike mutual funds and the rest, they *are* interested in obtaining a pervasive control of corporations. Thus, the banks are an integral part of the story of who governs America.

Commercial banks are the major source of corporate capital. Indeed, they have, to a great extent, financed the merger movement. At times when money was tight, they financed corporate takeovers instead of, say, making loans to the building industry. It is not unfair to suggest that in making such choices they furthered goals which were nonproductive instead of socially useful.

Large corporations have first crack at bank loans at the expense of smaller borrowers. During the height of the tight money crisis in 1966, for example, both Westinghouse and International Telephone and Telegraph arranged for substantial long-term loans from traditional lending institutions. It was no secret in 1970 that many commercial banks would lend money only if they received equity positions in the borrowing companies. In any case, money was available to their biggest corporate clients when none was available to smaller companies.

However, a truer measure of the banks' influence on the economy comes from their administration of trust funds. In most cases, these portfolios consist of stock which the bank is free to vote. The Subcommittee on Domestic Finance of the House Committee on Banking and Currency described the situation in a monumental staff study on commercial banks and their trust activities:

> The total impact of commercial bank investment on the American economy is tremendous. It is by far the single most important element among all institutional investors. . . . A total of $607 billion, or just under 60 per cent, of the $1 trillion of institutional investment in the American economy, is held by commercial banks. Bank trust assets alone account for 24 per cent of the total. This $607 billion is nearly four times as large as the next largest category, the life insurance companies, with $162 billion, or 15.6 per cent of the total.[58]

The study pointed out that even these figures understate bank influence because of the close relationship between banks and other institutional investors such as insurance companies, giving the banks an undetermined additional influence over institutional investments other than their own.

The report then elaborated on the leverage banks have on many giant corporations:

Bank-managed investment services are of several types including private trusts, various kinds of employee benefit funds and plans, common trust funds and agency accounts.

These arrangements have enabled many major banking institutions to become by far the largest single holder and voter of stock in some of the largest industrial and commercial corporations in the United States. This situation has led in many cases to both direct and indirect representation on the boards of these corporations by banks. As pointed out above, companies which have previously been characterized as "management controlled," are probably controlled either by banks or by a combination of minority control through bank trust department stockholdings and management control.

Although detailed data are not available in most cases, there is evidence that other factors used along with investment which increase the ability of commercial banks to gain influence and control over other corporations are found in the dealings between major corporations and commercial banks outside trust department operations. This would include the borrowing of large sums of money from the same commercial banks that also control large blocks of the corporation's stock and hold directorships, as well as the use of deposit, stock registration and transfer facilities, and other services of these same banks.[59]

Bank power will continue to grow. The same report pointed out that in 1955 the portfolios of private noninsured pension funds, almost all of which are managed by banks, contained investments in common and preferred stocks of approximately 25 per cent. By 1965, this had increased to more than 41 per cent by book value, and to almost 55 per cent on the basis of market value. During this same period, the total value of pension funds grew from $27.4 billion to $85.4 billion.

It was projected that by 1980, pension fund assets will grow from the 1967 level of roughly $100 billion to $285 billion, with approximately 55 per cent invested in common stocks.[60]

In addition, the subcommittee staff report contains substantial data on the interlocks of commercial banks among themselves and with the largest U.S. industrial, merchandising, and transporation corporations; insurance companies; and communications media. Such interlocks exist to a remarkable degree.

Adding to the problem has been the growth of one-bank holding companies. In order to get around the laws which seek to limit commercial banks primarily to the business of banking, the banks have formed holding companies. In this way a bank controls satellite companies in unrelated lines of business which, in effect, have their own captive bank. Put another way, a number of industrial and service corporations are the captives of a single bank.

Those concerned with issues of law and order may care to reflect on the holding company. Using this wondrous device, the banks easily leap over the barriers erected by federal lawmakers against their entry into prohibited fields of enterprise, the insurance companies escape state regulation of activities that otherwise would be regulated, and the railroads elude the flabby clutches of the Interstate Commerce Commission.

The House Banking Committee has reported that in the fourteen years 1955 through 1968 the number of known but unregistered bank holding companies, both existing and proposed, grew almost sevenfold, from 117 to 783. Bank deposits controlled by these companies increased from $11.6 billion to $108.2 billion, or more than 800 per cent. Between 1965 and 1968 alone, the number of unregistered bank holding companies increased by more than two hundred, while their bank deposits increased more than 600 per cent, from $15.1 billion in 1965 to $108.2 billion at the end of 1968.

The report, released in 1969, said: "Within the last 12 to 18 months, 34 of the 100 largest commercial banks in the United States with deposits of over $100 billion, have formed or announced plans to form bank holding companies. This includes 9 of the 12 largest commercial banks in the United States."[61]

In December 1970, Congress enacted a law to check the growth of bank holding companies. While the law may slow the trend toward more such companies, it offers little hope for undoing what has been done. Indeed, the law promptly began to show signs of being an instrument with which one-bank holding companies may expand their operations into "related businesses."

The banks themselves continue to grow larger through mergers. From 1950 to 1965 there were approximately 2,200 bank mergers in the United States, contributing substantially to an increase in bank concentration. By 1965 a mere one hundred of the more than fourteen thousand commercial banks controlled 50 per cent of all deposits, and fourteen of the one hundred controlled 25 per cent. On a regional or city basis the degree of concentration was even greater. For example, in each of twenty-three states five banks controlled at least half of the deposits. In one state, California, the largest bank controlled nearly 40 per cent of all deposits. In 1960 the four largest banks in the sixteen most important financial centers controlled 60 per cent of all bank assets in those centers.

In April 1970 the Justice Department, recognizing the dangers in single banks that hold substantial stock in different corporations in competition with each other, brought its first lawsuit delineating the anti-competitive potentials in such situations.

The suit named the Cleveland Trust Company, the sixteenth largest bank in the United States in terms of total assets. The Department charged that it held and voted the stock of four major tool manufacturers —11 per cent of Warner & Swasey, 27 per cent of Acme-Cleveland, 14 per cent of Pneumo-Dynamics, and 5 per cent of White Consolidated. All four manufacture automatic screw machines. The Department also alleged that Cleveland Trust held the stock not solely for investment purposes, but also to elect directors and influence management policy decisions. Further, two of the bank's senior officers sit on the boards of the same companies, the suit said.[62]

The ramifications are vast. If the pattern exists elsewhere, the influence of banks would extend from particular companies to entire industries. Pricing and other decisions for principal companies in an industry may be directed not in the individual boardrooms of competing corporations, but from the single boardroom of one bank. And, indeed, there is ample evidence in the staff report of the Subcommittee on Domestic Finance of the House Committee on Banking and Currency about the clustering of competitors around a single bank. Thus, a highly disturbing new question arises about the realities of competition and free enterprise.

We have seen how two hundred corporations control most of the economy and how, in turn, they are influenced by commercial banks and institutional investors. We have seen how the two hundred, usually through mergers, have become giant conglomerates. We have learned that their size generally cannot be justified either by "technological imperatives" or by any form of efficiency.

A TOUR THROUGH A STATE OF CONCENTRATION

The tie-ins of this new establishment with universities and foundations and the military have been treated extensively by other sources,
although a brief comment on the so-called military-industrial complex
may be in order. A handful of companies dominate each of the main
categories of military procurement. Indeed, the degree of concentration
is higher than in non-military industrial categories in the country as a
whole. In no fewer than twenty-two out of twenty-seven military purchasing categories, high seller concentration exists, Murray L. Weidenbaum,
an economist who later was appointed an Assistant Secretary of the Treasury, told the Senate Subcommittee on Antitrust and Monopoly in 1968.
Even this tends to understate the case, because the nature of defense
procurement procedures encourages concentration through the frequent
absence, distortion or enfeeblement of competitive bidding.

The community of interest that develops from a market with a single
buyer, the Department of Defense, and but a few suppliers has been
widely recognized. What has been rarely understood is Dr. Weidenbaum's
point, made to the Subcommittee, that the "defense business has become
quietly, without our really realizing it, one of the regulated industries
of the American economy." He termed "just staggering" the "array of
government review, influence and direction of what in every other branch
of the economy is the prerogative of management."[63] In viewing the
military-industrial complex, consequently, one must take into account
the presence of "clientism," the word used to describe the protective
approach taken by regulatory agencies toward industries within their
purview. At the same time, there is a distinction to be drawn, and it is
not a reassuring one: The Department of Defense being exempt from the
provisions for hearings and the other safeguards which the Administrative
Procedures Act provides for the proceedings of avowed regulatory agencies, it enjoys an unmatched secrecy and freedom from inhibition in its
operations.

For our purposes, to talk of a military-industrial, educational-indus-
trial or labor-industrial complex is to obscure the fundamental question:
who governs the country, including all these aspects of the economy?

The answer is "America, Inc."—a gigantic industrial and financial
complex functioning much like a sovereign government.

America, Inc.'s relation to the elected government is the subject of
the final leg of this tour. It is a pleasant myth that the federal government

acts as a countervailing force to private corporate power. Instead, the opposite commonly is true: government power reinforces private power.

In 1955, in *Monopoly in America: The Government as Promoter,* Walter Adams and Horace M. Gray said that monopoly

> is often the outgrowth of unwise, discriminatory, privilege-creating govern-
> mental measures which throttle competition and restrict opportunity. It is
> the concomitant of unimaginative, shortsighted or corrupt exercise of gov-
> ernmental power. Government today is in many instances a promoter of
> monopoly. It frequently puts together the very power concentrates which
> the antitrust authorities are later called upon to break asunder. In short,
> government often supports, rather than countervails, the forces making
> for concentration and monopoly.[64]

In 1970, the situation was worse than it was fifteen years earlier, when Adams and Gray found sufficient documentation of their thesis to fill 180 pages. The regulated industries—transportation, communication, power, natural resources, and financial—now account for about 15 per cent of the nation's income. Yet the regulatory agencies have become the natural allies of the industries they are supposed to regulate. They conceive their primary task to be to protect insiders from new competition—in many cases, from any competition.

The Civil Aeronautics Board prevents qualified airlines from entering markets they desire to serve. The Interstate Commerce Commission keeps new motor carriers from competing with existing carriers. The Comptroller of the Currency and the Federal Reserve Board prohibit new banks from opening. In none of these fields is there any natural barrier to entry. There may be neither technical nor valid economic reasons for such decisions. Instead, the primary purpose often seems to be nothing more nor less than the protection of the "ins" from new competition by the "outs."

Yet regulators not only curtail competition where it need not be curtailed, but rubber-stamp the rate increases which, with the blessing of law, the railroads and truckers set in open collusion through rate-making cartels.

Subsidies are another government aid to big business.[65] The maritime industry gets subsidies for everything from the building of its ships to the wages paid the crews. In 1970, for example, the very Congress that failed to provide a food-stamp program to feed hungry children voted

$199.5 million in subsidies to shipbuilders, most of which are owned by conglomerates. This was an increase of $81 million over the previous subsidy. Congress also voted $193 million in increased subsidies for ship operations, mostly to help pay the salaries of crews. The big defense contractors get the rights to patents they developed with government funds. As early as 1956, former Attorney General Herbert Brownell, Jr., warned that the use of government research expenditures may not run counter to the industrial trend toward concentration, but in some degree may actually reinforce it. He said, "The disproportionate share of industrial research and development in the largest firms may foreshadow a greater concentration of economic power in the United States."[66]

In the decade and a half since Brownell expressed his concern government spending for research and development has increased approximately 330 per cent—from about $3.5 billion in 1956 to about $15 billion in 1970.

The Internal Revenue Service, too, had its love affair with giant business.

In the early 1960s, General Electric, Westinghouse and twenty-seven other manufacturers of heavy electrical equipment were indicted by a federal grand jury for hard-core price-fixing. Subsequently they pleaded either guilty or no contest. Then under provisions of the antitrust laws, private and public utilities brought thousands of suits for treble damages. Ultimately these cases were settled for almost $500 million.

In anticipation of this, several large electrical companies held meetings with the director and other high officials of the Internal Revenue Service. Out of the meetings came a ruling as outrageous as any that ever has come down from an agency whose rulings often outrage individual taxpayers. The companies were allowed to write off the settlements as "ordinary and necessary" business expenses. As stated by Senator Hart at hearings he held in 1966, "With an existing corporate tax rate of about 50 per cent, the effect of the IRS ruling is to cut in half the actual cost of a settlement or treble damage payment. Thus it lightens substantially the impact on antitrust violators."[67]

The ruling had been made in the face of staff memorandums which urged that no "ordinary and necessary" deduction be allowed. The irony is that if the decision had been otherwise, the matter could have been decided in the courts, where the companies certainly had the resources to go. But once the IRS ruling had been made by Commissioner Mortimer M. Caplin, no one remained who had legal standing to challenge it.

Senator Hart questioned what the Commissioner's attitude would have been had an individual taxpayer decided to deduct a fine for a speeding ticket as an "ordinary and necessary" business expense.

Congress adopted a belated, partial reform in 1969 when, as part of the Tax Reform Act, it disallowed deduction of two-thirds of treble damages, but only in a private suit based on a prior criminal action.

The Food and Drug Administration has done what it can to protect the giant drug companies from smaller competitors. For a number of years the smaller drug manufacturers complained that the FDA compelled them to conduct redundant clinical studies to establish the safety and efficacy of their versions of drugs already on the market. It was claimed that such studies are expensive (often costing more than $100,000) and unnecessary, the safety and efficacy of the drug already having been established to the FDA's own satisfaction by the first applicant for marketing clearance.

By such erroneous and duplicative requirements, the FDA did effectively suppress competition with well-established firms in the drug industry.

The Defense Department, too, did its thing for the big drug firms. It prevented small suppliers from bidding on government procurement of certain drugs for which a "sole source" designation has been established by Defense, the largest single buyer of drugs in the world. Often the designation was for expensive trade-name drugs of major companies—including many medicines which the National Research Council later determined to be inefficacious—rather than for lower-priced generic drugs manufactured by smaller companies.

Following an inquiry by the Senate Subcommittee on Antitrust and Monopoly, nearly one-third of the designated drugs were removed from the sole-source category.

The government also assists giant corporations in keeping their profits high by curtailing foreign competition—even though there is nothing in the law that allows it. Not surprisingly, those who make the loudest speeches against "Big Brother" when poverty programs are expanded or Medicaid is suggested, are the first to run to the same "Big Brother" when their profits are threatened. The following story from the *Wall Street Journal* of January 21, 1970, illustrates the situation:

Nixon Administration officials are considering permitting increased steel imports to help squelch the surge of domestic price boosts.

Coming under critical question, insiders say, is an accord negotiated late in the Johnson Administration, under which steelmakers in Japan and the six European Common Market countries "voluntarily" agreed to limit their sales to the U.S. Members of the Common Market are West Germany, France, Italy, Belgium, Luxembourg and the Netherlands.

"Our steel companies are apparently making use of the agreement to raise prices," one Nixon aide complains, adding that the present Administration so far hasn't made any commitment to the early 1969 pact.

The review of price and import developments is in a very early stage, officials say, adding that they're well aware that pressure from the U.S. mills could kill off any Nixon Administration effort to undo the agreement.

However, in fairness to the short-lived expressed concern of the Administration, it should be pointed out that the Department of Commerce, the eager advocate of giant business, was quick to react. The *Wall Street Journal* reported three days later:

Consideration within the Nixon Administration of letting in more imported goods to hold down domestic price increases represents "fuzzy thinking," a Commerce Department official charged. . . .

Accusing "some of our international economists" of "a dangerous kind of complacency," Mr. Davis [Kenneth N. Davis, Assistant Secretary for Domestic and International Business] said: "All at once, massive imports of any commodity, be it textiles, oil, automobiles, steel, shoes, electronics, and on and on are of no great national concern to these people, just so long as lower consumer prices result.

The government's response to pressure from the steel industry forced foreign companies to curtail export sales to the American market. The effect was to reconstitute a steel cartel under government auspices. Had the steel companies done this on their own, they would have been guilty of a criminal violation of the Sherman Act. The government, through its actions, had now become a coconspirator. However, as yet no injured consumer has brought a lawsuit naming the government as a defendant.

Secretary of Commerce Maurice H. Stans followed a similar course in early 1970, trying to persuade the Japanese to curtail textile sales to the United States. In the meantime, the price of wearing apparel continued to rise.

The major oil companies have been shielded from competition by a series of government actions to protect their price structure. Four volumes of hearings by the Senate Antitrust and Monopoly Subcommittee document the story.[68] For immediate purposes, it is sufficient to acknowledge that, in the name of national security and conservation, the federal government and the states have joined together to limit the amount of oil which can be either produced in this country or imported. This props up the price at unnatural levels. Further, probably illegally, the government has even restricted the amount of oil which can be brought in from Canada—again on the basis of national security. Senator Russell B. Long (D–La.) actually defended this action on the ground that we may be in a war with Canada some day and, therefore, we must not become overly dependent on Canadian oil. What Long didn't say was that too much Canadian oil might drive down the price, hurting his petroleum constituency.

The government helped IBM to become number one in its field in the late 1950s and early 1960s through the device of tailoring government specifications for computer equipment to IBM products. On occasion, IBM employees assisted federal procurement personnel in the actual drafting of specifications. The inevitable result was that, in many cases, IBM just happened to have the only equipment which could meet the specifications.

Government stockpiles also have been used as a device to entrench the interests of giant corporations. During a copper shortage beginning in 1965, stockpiled supplies were ordered sold in three batches in 1965 and 1966, ostensibly so that independent fabricators would get the raw materials they needed to stay in business. Yet when the sales were done, it was the big three copper companies—Anaconda, Kennecott, and Phelps-Dodge—and companies they controlled that ended up with 70 per cent of the stockpile.

The Bureau of the Budget administers the Federal Reports Act, a 1942 law designed to decrease unnecessary paperwork and questionnaires, especially those affecting small business, and to maximize the usefulness to all federal agencies (and the public) of the data that any one agency collects. The Bureau, to facilitate administration of the law, has said that it seeks "the benefit of advice by interested parties outside the Government—those interested either as consumers of data or as respondents to the inquiry." Yet, Senator Lee Metcalf (D–Wyo.) has pointed out that there are neither small businessmen nor consumer representatives on the committees which advise the Budget Bureau. Instead, for example, Charles A. Agemian, an executive of the Chase Manhattan Bank, heads the Committee on Banking. N. R. Wenrich of Merck & Company heads the Committee on Chemicals. Robert H. Stewart of Gulf Oil is chairman of the Committee on Petroleum and Natural Gas.

The examples are almost endless of how public government gives favored treatment to giant business. Public government and private government have joined together in tight embrace. This is the "establishment."

The concept of countervailing power is but another mirage. Power does not countervail. It attracts. Among the powerful, mutual assistance pacts are less painful than prolonged strife.

Faced with such strength the individual citizen should be excused if he feels himself overwhelmed by forces which, like X-rays, he knows exist but cannot discern.

2 HEAR NO EVIL, SEE NO EVIL, SPEAK NO EVIL

Just the same, it is time to remember that the first thing we belong to is humanity. And humanity is separated from the animal world by thought and speech and they should naturally be free. If they are fettered, we go back to being animals.

Publicity and openness, honest and complete—that is the prime condition for the health of every society, and ours, too. The man who does not want them in our country is indifferent to his fatherland and thinks only about his own gain. The man who does not want publicity and openness for his fatherland does not want to cleanse it of its diseases, but to drive them inside, so they may rot there.

—ALEKSANDR I. SOLZHENITSYN, winner of the Nobel Prize for literature, in a letter to the writers' union of the Russian Republic; printed by the *New York Times* on November 15, 1969.

Just as the great novelist wants publicity and openness for the Soviet Union, so did the Founding Fathers want it for the United States. They presupposed, as Judge Learned Hand put it, "that right conclusions are more likely to be gathered out of a multitude of tongues than through any kind of authoritative selection. To many this is, and always will be folly; but we have staked upon it our all."[1] The phrasing of the First Amendment ("Congress shall make no law . . . abridging the freedom . . . of the press . . .") focuses on the obvious threat latent in government. But there was no intention to let others do what government could not do. "Freedom of the press from governmental interference under the First Amendment does not sanction suppression of that freedom by private interests," the Supreme Court said in 1945.[2] Reinforcing this view a quarter-century later, the Court said, "It is the purpose of the First Amendment to preserve an uninhibited marketplace of ideas in

76

which the truth will ultimately prevail, rather than to countenance monopolization of that market, whether it be by the Government itself or a private licensee."[3]

Before discussing the strong trend toward concentration of ownership of communications media, let us look at the evidence of danger to the marketplace of ideas. Ben H. Bagdikian, long a student and critic of the press, reminds us that "one of the greatest exposés of all time was the *New York Times*'s destruction of Boss Tweed's gang, accomplished after the publisher, George Jones, in 1871, turned down an offer of $5,000,000 to suppress the stories. This was pretty crude. Today a syndicate of lawyers and brokers could use the money to get control of a corporation to buy an offending news medium, not just knock out one series of articles."[4] This suggests the peril. A democratic society must have a free exchange of ideas, dissent, diversity. It may survive a concentration of manufacturing assets in a few conglomerate corporations, but it cannot withstand a similar concentration of communications media. The two are sometimes related: the one can beget the other. All the more reason, then, to say with Senator Philip A. Hart, who as chairman of the Senate Subcommittee on Antitrust and Monopoly held extensive hearings on the newspaper industry, that what is involved in media concentration is "power—political and economic." We of course will deal with the views of the Vice President, Spiro T. Agnew.

No less than the performance of other human institutions, the performance of news media benefits from fair-minded observation and analysis. Mechanisms for providing these things are few and inadequate. Rarely do newspaper managements even try, for example, to establish a systematic dialogue with members of their own staffs to assess periodically their shared mission and their performance. Yet so long as some modicum of independence remains among news media there will be some auditing of each other. This is very much in the public interest. "Hardly a working journalist," the *Wall Street Journal* said in 1967 in an article on newspapers, "would deny that one of the greatest weaknesses in coverage exhibited by the American press is its coverage of itself." For our purposes the operative word is "itself." The more diffuse and enlarged the ownership of news media, the greater the potential for inhibitions on straightforward coverage of "itself" by "itself." A CBS that owns the New York

Yankees is not the same "itself" as the CBS that did not own the Yankees. The admirable *Columbia Journalism Review* made the point in its Summer 1968 issue, when it criticized an unidentified executive of WCBS radio in New York "for chastising the news staff for tardy reporting of Yankee baseball scores in a memorandum that said: 'If I have to spell it out for you I will: CBS *owns* the New York Yankees.' "

Before he became a Justice of the Supreme Court, Charles Evans Hughes said that the Constitution is what the Court says it is. So is news what news media say it is. One might say that news, like beauty, is in the eye of the beholder. These thoughts should not be reduced to absurdities. Hughes did not mean that the Constitution could be stretched to give his native state of New York three senators and each of the other states only two. Nor do we suggest that the assassination of a President, say, could be deemed un-newsworthy. But, within extreme boundaries, news is what media say it is. This is said without the slightest taint of cynicism. To the contrary, it is not only an inescapable fact of life that news is what media say it is, but an indispensable precondition for the best performance of newsmen of courage, integrity and intelligence. They must never be bound by imposed rigid formulae or definitions of news. As does the Supreme Court, the media have a charter which allows them to adjust and grow to meet changing needs and changing times. Of course this freedom can be a cloak for cowardice, venality and stupidity. But it keeps open the marketplace of ideas. That makes it infinitely precious.

At the very outset of this book, we said that big business *is* government. There are corollaries to this. One is that there is danger in intrusions into news media by private government as well as public government. Another is that there is an archaic inadequacy in news concepts which center on public government to the near exclusion of coverage of private government. But the impact of news media is so great that they, too, must be considered government. They should be reported, as any government should be reported. Their actions and non-actions can have the greatest consequences. If their judgments are made in fear, are inhibited, or are self-serving, what the Republic receives as news is of a different order than if the judgments are made by men who are free of such restraints—whether the origin is in public government or private government.

The news columns always can be filled. There is no shortage of pap, and routine, safe, and even interesting and useful reading matter. The television tube need never be blank. The networks have an inexhaustible supply of what Commissioner Nicholas Johnson, an appointee of President Lyndon B. Johnson to the Federal Communications Commission, once called "cotton candy" for the mind. Improbable as it may seem today, it was not until after the assassination of President Kennedy in November 1963 that the networks recognized that their nightly national television news shows were important enough to be expanded from fifteen minutes—*fifteen minutes*—to a half-hour. In sum, it is of profound importance—of more importance than many actions of public governments to which the media devote resources, and about which we get exercised—who decides what news is, and under what influences.

"The stifling weight of censorship is to be found, not in the hearing rooms of the Federal Communications Commission, but in the conference rooms of this nation's television networks," Nicholas Johnson has said.[5] He was not suggesting (nor do we) that the networks along with much of the broadcasting industry do not do many brave and good things in the public interest. They do. But the immediate question is whether Johnson documents his charge of censorship, despite the offset of the brave and good things. We believe that he does, with substantial evidence in a proliferation of statements—in Commission cases, testimony, articles, personal appearances and his book, *How to Talk Back to Your Television Set*.[6]

Since one of our fundamental concerns is with concentrated power, we turn first to a point that is troubling mainly because of its *potential* for censorship of a most serious kind. The Radio Corporation of America owns the National Broadcasting Company. It is also a major defense contractor, and as such, is a leading beneficiary of the commitment to, among other items, an anti-ballistic missile system. Johnson, in testimony on Capitol Hill, said,

Many Americans will know what they know about the ABM because they learned it from NBC. And the decision in this country on this issue, as on most issues, will be determined by the mass media and what information they decide to put out to the American people. Once again, I am not charging that there has been any deliberate suppression of information or misrepresentation of views by NBC in the service of the broader corporate interests of RCA. All I am saying is that this potential conflict exists; the power exists if they wish to exercise it.[7]

In an opinion in a Commission case, Johnson pointed out that "Bob Hope's commentary about the Vietnam war seems fully acceptable to the networks. And so do other entertainers' critical observations about protesting college students or gun control legislation. Yet, on the reported ground that "an entertainment program is not a proper forum for social comment," CBS dropped the iconoclastic "The Smothers Brothers Comedy Hour." Is it not the correct conclusion, he asked, "that the only kind of 'social comment' that is unfit for television is that which involves, in Mason Williams' phrase, 'The unpopular opinion/Or anything with teeth'?" Surely not—not *any* unpopular opinion, and not *anything* with teeth. Surely also, however, such a conclusion has some warrant. "The ideas and life-styles endorsed and purveyed by American television are truly 'popular' only with those Americans fortunate enough to be native-born-white-Anglo-Saxon-Protestant-suburban-dwelling-middle-class-and-over-thirty," Johnson said. "Of course this is censorship pure and simple."

In the same opinion, Johnson recalled a proposal made in 1964 by E. William Henry, then chairman of the FCC. Henry wanted to limit TV commercials to the number per hour approved by the industry itself, in the Code of Good Practice of the National Association of Broadcasters. But, as on other occasions when raising the banner of "free speech" fails to "coincide with the industry's monetary self-interests," the NAB would have none of it, Johnson said. Instead, it

> galvanized itself into instant action and after intensive lobbying efforts obtained from the House of Representatives a resolution prohibiting the FCC from enacting the industry's own standards into Commission policy. At the same time, as Chairman Henry pointed out, the licenses of WBAI and the other Pacifica stations [which are noncommercial and listener-supported] had been deferred for three years pending FCC investigation of "programming" complaints sent to the Commission. Although the case was well known throughout the industry, and a real danger existed that a broadcaster would lose its license because of the political, economic, or ideological *content* of its programs, not one commercial broadcaster came to Pacifica's defense.[8]

After the 1968 Democratic National Convention, the problem of news staging drew a good deal of attention, but mainly in print media and at the FCC. On television, Johnson once told a citizens' committee, it eluded serious discussion. And he wondered why the networks don't get some critics on the tube to talk—as they do on the BBC in Britain—"about the quality of the new fall programs." And why, he asked, aren't there programs "about the impact of television on children? The impact of television violence on society? . . . on the quality of advertising . . . the license challenges around the country? . . . Or how about a show on the radiation hazards from television sets, (laughter) or fire hazards?"[9]

In a magazine article, Johnson indicted broadcasters for having ignored, or having been extremely slow and limited in reporting, the role of automobile design in highway deaths and injuries, and other vital consumer matters. "Television," he said, "certainly didn't take the lead in telling us about unfit meat, fish and poultry. (Chet Huntley was found to have been editorializing *against* the Wholesome Meat Act at a time when he and his business partners were heavy investors in the cattle and meat business!)" Johnson continued:

> Did you ever find out from television . . . that a *single* recent price-fixing case involved a "robbery" from the American people of more money that was taken in *all* the country's robberies, burglaries and larcenies during the years of that criminal price-fixing? The crime commission [the Presidential Commission on Law Enforcement] declared that "it is essential that the public becomes aware of the seriousness of business crime." Why is it the news media do not tell you about *these* threats to "law and order"?[10]

Johnson's question about non-reporting of business crime—"crime in the suites," in the incisive phrase of Ralph Nader—is astute. "Public shame is an important aspect of all penalties," Edwin H. Sutherland said in *White Collar Crime*. "This was illustrated in extreme form in the colonial penalty of sewing the letter 'T' on the clothing of a thief. In England the Bread Act of 1836 and the Adulteration of Seeds Act of 1869 provided as a penalty the *publication in the newspaper* of the details regarding the crimes of adulteration of these products; the Public Health Act of 1891 authorized the court to order a person twice convicted of selling meat unfit for human consumption to fix a sign on his place of business of a size to be specified by the court, stating that he had been convicted twice of violating this law."[11] [Emphasis supplied.] In recent years, one of the authors has written for the *Washington Post* a large number of stories involving business crimes. Often these crimes have been most serious. One group has involved false and misleading advertising of prescription drugs, which while deceiving the physician can exploit, injure, and even kill the helpless patient.

Even where prosecutions have resulted in conviction, most news media—including *Time* and *Newsweek,* the networks, and the *New York Times*—have failed repeatedly to recognize the importance of adequate reporting and have ignored the cases or treated them trivially. Unlike a human being, a corporation, which at law is also a "person," cannot be jailed. It has no soul which may face Divine Justice in the hereafter. It must be dealt with in the here and now or not at all. Yet the same news media that meticulously record the misdeeds of human wretches, commonly bringing obloquy to their children, go on and on letting giant corporations elude the therapeutic benefits of public shame that fair reporting might bring. The situation is disgraceful. What holds a greater potential to make it worse than to allow control of news media by these same corporations? "Publicity and openness, honest and complete—that is the prime condition for the health of every society," Aleksandr Solzhenitsyn said. Will concentration give us that?

Julian Goodman, president of NBC, has said that television "is now under threat of restriction and control." Similarly, Elmer Lower, president of ABC News, has warned that electronic media may "face the prospect of some form of censorship." But in protecting the First Amendment in broadcasting, no network executive has been more active, vocally, than Frank Stanton, president of CBS. In November 1968 he went to Atlanta to give the keynote address at the convention of Sigma Delta Chi, the national professional journalism society. He found freedom of the press to be in grave danger. He detected "warning signs . . . all around us." This is bad for the journalist, his mission being to tell the whole story— "all of it, the good and the bad, the beautiful and the ugly, the noble and the ignoble." Yet, "increasingly, attempts are being made to block us in that job." Who was making the attempts? Government. Bureaucrats. Agencies.

With justice Stanton does not go unrecognized as a statesman of the broadcasting industry. In December 1969 he accepted an award for public service from the Advertising Council. Even then, at the Waldorf-Astoria, he renewed the battle. Broadcasting, he said, should be given greater access to the proceedings of Congress. "The only way we can keep the right to know alive," he explained, "is by expanding it, making sure that our citizens know more about government and its actions, not less." One should not lightly dismiss this. One could even be impressed.

The trouble was, Stanton provided an immediate reason not to be impressed by his Waldorf rhetoric. On December 1, 1969, he traveled to Washington to testify in favor of S. 2004, a bill sponsored by Senator John O. Pastore (D–R.I.), chairman of the Subcommittee on Communications of the Senate Committee on Commerce. The bill dealt with the triennial renewal of television and radio station licenses. The Communications Act of 1934 puts a burden on the applicant for a renewal—or for an original license grant or a transfer—to show that approval would serve the "public interest, convenience, and necessity." The requirement had fallen into disuse. Renewals were granted automatically. Lately, however, there had been signs of restlessness at the FCC. It had taken the requirement seriously in cases in San Francisco and Minneapolis–St. Paul which we will discuss later in this chapter. Nothing was more certain to produce hostility in the broadcasting industry and, therefore, in Pastore. And so, with the full support of that constituency, he introduced S. 2004. Without actually saying so, the bill would have assured (it has, fortunately, been consigned to limbo) automatic renewal of existing licenses every three years in perpetuity. There were three days of hearings. Stanton appeared at the first. Television camera crews were on hand to record "the good and the bad, the beautiful and the ugly, the noble and the ignoble." But, Marvin Kitman noticed, CBS "ignored the hearings in their entirety."[12]

One must retain perspective. Corporate censorship in all its forms, including self-censorship by newsmen, also exists in newspapers, magazines, and book publishers. If one is to fault Frank Stanton and CBS for non-coverage of the hearings on the Pastore bill one must also take note of the abundant non-coverage in 1967, 1968, and 1969 of the hearings on the Failing Newspaper (later, Newspaper Preservation) Act held by the Senate Subcommittee on Antitrust and Monopoly (and, in 1969, by the House Antitrust Subcommittee). The purpose of the bill was to exempt from the antitrust laws the *per se* violations of profit-pooling and price fixing for the benefit of separate newspaper ownerships in joint operating agreements. Previous judgments by the courts for violations of the antitrust laws would be retroactively set aside. The immediate beneficiaries would be the two parties to joint operating agreements already existing in each of twenty-two cities. This is fortunate for the publishers. Some of them would have difficulty passing a means test today. Consider St. Louis. The joint operators there are the Newhouse chain, which in 1967 paid a record $51.4 million for the *Cleveland Plain Dealer,* and the Pulitzer Publishing Company, which in 1968 dug up $18 million to buy KVOA–TV in Tucson and KOAT–TV in Albuquerque. In Madison, Wisconsin, the joint operators, incorporated as Madison Newspapers, are Lee Enterprises, Inc., owner of the *Wisconsin State Journal,* and the *Capital Times.* In 1968 the rate of return on equity for the owners of Madison Newspapers was a lush 22 per cent. In Columbus, Ohio, the joint operators are Scripps-Howard and the Wolfe family, which Philip Hart, the subcommittee chairman, told the Senate when the bill was before it, is the largest landholder in the state of Ohio. He was only just when he called the bill a "poverty program for the rich." Among the publishers who came to Washington, their gold alms cups unsheepishly extended, were many who had shown little editorial sympathy for poverty programs for the poor. They were the Bleat Generation.

This was not all, or the worst. The bill tends to subvert the First Amendment by making it legal for established publishers to engage in monopolistic practices against which weekly newspapers and other potential rivals cannot compete. The measure "is most probably not a newspaper-preservation bill so much as a publisher-preservation bill," the *New Yorker* said in "The Talk of the Town" in its January 31, 1970, issue. "Any newspaper that has to be preserved this way might as well be preserved in formaldehyde. . . . The public is better served by a dead paper than by one mortally sick and given a semblance of health through the connivance of the competition that its voice should continually challenge and of the government about which it is duty-bound to speak the truth." The individual citizen wishing to protect his First Amendment freedom of speech, Nicholas Johnson has said, is advised not to look for support to the broadcasting industry. The citizen wishing to protect his freedom of the press might be just as well advised not to look to the great majority of publishers who supported the newspaper bill. In many cases, the broadcasters and the publishers are one and the same.

But let us turn to the hearings held by Senator Hart. One should inquire whether they were newsworthy before complaining that coverage was inadequate. One day, David J. Leonard, a Tucson, Arizona, lawyer testifying against the bill, produced—and it is part of the record—the "Pig Document." This was a fifteen-page paper which the *Arizona Daily Star* had prepared in support of an application to the Internal Revenue Service. The purpose was to obtain relief from excess profit taxes for the World War II years 1941 through 1945. The *Star*'s argument was that its large profits in those years were wholly attributable not to the wartime boom, but to its coming together, in 1940, with the *Tucson Daily Citizen*. The "new, non-competitive arrangement," the *Star* said emphatically, did *"eliminate all competition."* The name "Pig Document" evolved naturally from an illustration which the *Star* itself thoughtfully included for the sake of clarity. At the top, under the heading "1939," the year before the papers joined, were two pigs. One was labeled, or self-labeled, "STAR." It was tugging leftward toward a trough labeled "ADV." but was held back by reason of being chained to the hind legs of a second pig tugging in the opposite direction. The second pig, labeled "CITIZEN," was trying, also unsuccessfully, to reach a trough marked "CIRC." Below this scene there was a portrayal of the profitable post-acquisition years. There were two troughs, "CIRCULATION" and "ADV." At each were two contented swine, one named "STAR" and the other named "CITIZEN."[13]

On another hearing day, Albert C. Kihn, a former television cameraman at KRON–TV, the *San Francisco Chronicle* station, provided evidence that the station repeatedly had slanted the news. In consequence he wrote to the FCC to urge that the station's license not be renewed. Soon thereafter he was menacingly followed and harassed by private detectives. Under a pretext one of them interviewed his former wife and the ex-husband of his present wife. Among the questions asked: Did Kihn "belong to any organizations espousing the overthrow of the establishment?" "What are his political leanings?" "What about marijuana?"[14] Subsequently, in a paper filed with the FCC, the Chronicle Publishing Company admitted that, through its law firm, it had engaged in the activities alleged by Kihn, claiming that it was entitled to defend itself against possible loss of its license.[15]

On yet another day, Wes Gallagher, general manager of the Associated Press, denied to the subcommittee counsel that the AP had a cartel arrangement in France under which it did not distribute news occurring in that country to its French clients. The counsel then put into the record a letter to the contrary from William B. Macomber, Jr., Assistant Secretary of State for Congressional Relations. "According to the information available to the Department both the Associated Press and the United Press International provide extensive French language services to clients in France," the letter said. "While these reports cover international events, especially American news, they do not include news and events occuring in France." Gallagher, whose counsel was William P. Rogers, now Secretary of State, insisted that Macomber's statement was "absolutely ridiculous."[16] But he never documented his denial. This is less striking than the coverage given the matter by the wire services. The AP not only did not find it newsworthy, but delayed moving a story on other aspects of the hearing for six hours. And the story was transmitted not from Washington, but from New York. Neither did the *Citizen* in Tucson find the "Pig Document" disclosure newsworthy. With few exceptions, of course, newspapers (and other media) ignored or played down not only the substantive news on what the hearings were all about, but also such choice developments as the "Pig Document" and the harassment of Albert Kihn. Meanwhile, reams of copy were sent out on the self-serving statements of publishers and editors. All in all, a depressing, dismal performance.

The lobbying campaign for the newspaper bill was intense. William T. Chapman of the *Washington Post,* in a revealing account on June 27, 1969, said that the campaign dated back more than a year and included these techniques:

> Hearst newspaper publishers in several cities wrote and called their Senators on behalf of the bill . . .
>
> A Utah publisher, representing a committee of affected newspapers, openly worked for the bill out of the offices of the two Senators from his state.
>
> House sponsors . . . formed a committee to enlist other . . . Congressmen and urged their support at a breakfast with hometown editors present.

Although there was counter-lobbying by the editors of suburban papers and weeklies, these forces were no match for the media giants.

The newspaper committee consisted of Jack Gallivan, publisher of the *Salt Lake Tribune,* Byron Boone, publisher of the *Tulsa World* in Oklahoma, and Amon Carter Evans, publisher of the *Nashville Tennessean.* Chapman wrote:

> Gallivan said yesterday he had worked for several days, during frequent visits in Washington, from the offices of Sens. Wallace Bennett (R) and Frank Moss (D) of Utah. Both, he said, had helped greatly with the bill.
>
> Gallivan's *Tribune* has an operating arrangement with the *Deseret News.* The papers exert considerable influence in Utah.
>
> Gallivan was asked if he thought enlisting support for his paper from Senators involved an editorial conflict of interest.
>
> "No," he said. "Newspapers every day are trying to persuade Congressmen and Senators to do something.". . .
>
> The Hearst newspaper chain has been especially active, and its local publishers have sought the support of their states' Senators. For example, executives of Hearst's Boston paper, the *Record-American,* contacted both Massachusetts Senators, Edward M. Kennedy (D) and Edward W. Brooke (R). . . .
>
> One particularly pressing interest for the Hearst chain is the fact that its San Francisco newspaper, the *Examiner,* has been involved in a joint operating arrangement with the *Chronicle.* The *Examiner* is being sued by private plaintiffs in four treble-damage actions charging price fixing, profit and market division. [As a practical matter, the bill would eliminate such suits.]
>
> Trying to influence the Tennessee delegation were Evans of the *Nashville Tennessean* and James Stahlman, publisher of the *Nashville Banner.* The two papers have a joint operating agreement.
>
> Evans said yesterday he and Stahlman "talked to the people (in the Congressional delegation) whom we knew best." Evans is a moderately liberal Democrat and Stahlman is a conservative. John Seigenthaler, editor of the *Tennessean,* helped organize and addressed a breakfast meeting in Washington where the importance of the bill was explained.

"The lobbying for this bill may well have set new records," Senator Thomas McIntyre said on February 7, 1970, in a speech in Chicago. "I tried, without any luck, to get some idea when the bill would come up to the floor. Then, two days before it did come up [on January 30], representatives from all the large newspaper chains in the country descended on Washington." Although McIntyre did not mention it, some senators acknowledged privately that certain powerful publishers had given them crude ultimatums: support the bill or the publishers would oppose them the next time they were up for reelection. McIntyre, continuing his account of the descent of the newspaper lobbyists on Washington, said, "Just as they departed, the bill came to the floor, brought up so suddenly I had to cancel several events I'd planned in New Hampshire." McIntyre was one of the few senators whom the unleashed supposed watchdogs of government could not intimidate. Others included Gaylord Nelson, who resisted great pressure from the *Madison Capital Times* in his home state of Wisconsin (the paper's editor promptly attacked Nelson in a front-page column), and Charles H. Percy of Illinois.[17]

In the House, Representative Emanuel Celler (D–N.Y.), chairman of the Judiciary Committee and its Antitrust Subcommittee, delayed action on the ground that more than half of the forty-four papers in joint operating agreements had failed to submit financial reports. "It's like pulling teeth," he told the *Washington Post.* That is to say, these advocates of the people's right to know and these enemies of secrecy in government were unwilling to provide the Congress with the information it would need if it were not to legislate in the dark.

Meanwhile, as in the Senate, members of the House—liberals and conservatives, Democrats and Republicans—were getting terrific heat from the publishers and, in large numbers, they melted. "The agencies of mass communication are big business, and their owners are big businessmen," the Commission on Freedom of the Press had said two decades earlier. Knowing this, many congressmen did not need to have it spelled out for them that to oppose the publishers could mean being blacked out or otherwise vengefully treated by media with pervasive newspaper and, often, television and radio holdings. Other representatives wanted to "collect IOU's" that publishers would repay in the form of endorsements in future campaigns, the *National Journal* quoted an opponent, Representative Abner J. Mikva (D–Ill.), as saying in a report on lobbying for the bill. In a few cases the lobbying was so brazen and heavy-handed that it backfired. The *Journal* report, published on July 25, 1970, said:

> One California Member, who asked not to be identified, said the heavy vote against the bill by Los Angeles Democrats was partly due to "the way the *San Francisco Chronicle* treated Jeff Cohelan." Rep. Jeffery

Cohelan, D, who has represented the California 7th District for six terms, was defeated in the June 2 primary.

The Member said Cohelan told Democratic Members of the California delegation at one of their weekend meetings that he had been called by the executive editor of the *Chronicle*, Scott Newhall, who wanted Cohelan to be a co-sponsor of the newspaper bill.

"Jeff said he told Newhall he wanted to read over the bill. Well, he didn't get a word in the *Chronicle* all through his campaign and they had supported him editorially and covered his other campaigns.

"So some of the guys just decided if it was that kind of operation, they didn't want any part of it."

To get the bill moving in the House Judiciary Committee, the publishers who had refused to disclose financial data finally provided the information under a highly questionable agreement that it forever would be kept secret. One needs a minimal imagination to envisage the outcry from the publishers, had a congressional committee made a similar deal with anyone else. When the committee reported the bill by a vote of 13 to 8, the minority, which was believed to include Celler, said in its report, "The public will never know whether any of the newspapers were failing at the time the arrangements were created, or whether the financial condition of the newspapers today justifies this exemption."

The bill came before the House on July 8. If there was to be a real fight against the bill, Celler, as the dean of the House and chairman of Judiciary, had to lead it. He didn't. He sat silent. Representative Clark MacGregor, a Minnesota Republican, led the opposition, such as it was. Another white-hat was Representative Clarence J. Brown, a Republican who himself is a newspaper publisher in Urbana, Ohio. "We ask for no special exemption," he told the House. "I do not want to be a part of seeking a special exemption for any portion of the industry in which I am involved . . . or for any other industry." The House passed the bill 292 to 87 and sent it for President Richard Nixon to sign into law. It will be remembered that after a visit from president Richard Berlin of the Hearst Corporation, Nixon repudiated his own Justice Department and endorsed the measure. Which Richard was President that day was less of a puzzle than it may seem.

In December 1968 the National Commission on Product Safety held a hearing in Boston. A couple of days later, struck by a consistent oddity in the coverage, the chairman, Arnold B. Elkind, issued a statement in which he said that "evidence was presented concerning a Pride-Trimble 'Kiddie Koop' which allegedly was involved in the death of babies. Three Boston newspapers and the TV stations reported the testimony. Not one paper in the area or one TV station mentioned the name of the manufacturer." This would have come as no great surprise to readers of the extensive report carried by the *Wall Street Journal* on July 25, 1967, on how pressures, sometimes exerted by advertisers, cause censorship, distortion and withholding of important information. The article found "considerable evidence" that press ethics in the United States are higher than they have been anywhere heretofore, and that certain newspapers, including the *New York Times* and the *Washington Post*, impose strict ethical standards. But the *Journal* nonetheless recounted a series of episodes that not only are highly disturbing in themselves, but also serve to underscore, albeit indirectly, the expanded potentials for abuse in further concentration of ownership.

The article told of an investigation into "suspected hanky-panky" that was aborted at the *Boston Herald,* where a subject of the inquiry turned out to be a stockholder in the Herald-Traveler Corporation and a friend of publisher George E. Akerson. At the *Chicago Tribune,* another investigation was halted when it threatened "to embarrass" Paul Powell, Secretary of State of Illinois, "who could help the paper in a building project." In Jackson, Mississippi, the jointly owned *Clarion-Ledger* and *Daily News* printed not a word of a case in which they were charged in Federal Court with violations of laws governing overtime pay; "staffers were even ordered to stay away from the court, and they did." While reporting maritime affairs for the *Baltimore Sun,* Helen Delich Bentley, since named by President Nixon as chairman of the Federal Maritime Commission, was paid by the American Association of Port Authorities, Inc., to run the press room at its annual convention. In California, the *Journal* said, "a batch of small newspapers run editorials endorsing the Detroit position on auto safety. All are worded similarly. An incredible coincidence, this identity not only of opinion, but of phrasing? Hardly, for all the articles are drawn from a single 'canned' editorial emanating from an advertising agency in San Francisco."

A few months before the *Journal* article was published, Harry Karafin, a prizewinning investigative reporter for the *Philadelphia Inquirer,* was arrested on charges of blackmail and extortion. The first blast at Karafin was printed by no local newspaper—not the *Bulletin,* not the *Inquirer* and not the *Inquirer*'s afternoon sister, the *Daily News* (the *Inquirer* and the *Daily News* then were owned by Walter H. Annenberg, whom President Nixon sent to the Court of St. James's, but since have been sold for the great sum of $55 million). The honors for exposing Karafin go to *Philadelphia,* a magazine fortunately independent of the papers. From the time *Philadelphia* broke the story in its April 1967 issue until the arrest of Karafin in early July, the *Journal* said, "the rival Philadelphia *Bulletin* carried not a word on the case—even though the *Inquirer* itself . . . fired him shortly after the magazine exposé and carried the whole story afterward."

It is not merely to be symmetrically impartial that we turn to magazines. It is necessary also to cite some abuses in this field of communications so as to show, in broader dimension than heretofore, the hazardous potential in multimedia ownership. In 1961, then as a member of the Senate Subcommittee on Antitrust and Monopoly, Senator Philip A. Hart began hearings on the deceptive, chaotic, and exploitative packaging, labeling, and pricing of foods and other products in the supermarkets. One could find in a single store, for example, a bewildering array of packages and prices of rice—14 ounces for 29 cents, 12 ounces for 25 cents, 1 pound 8 ounces for 47 cents. Powerful lobbies, the giant food and soap companies mainly, became busy on several fronts. When Hart sent out background materials on what ultimately became the Fair Packaging and Labeling Act a total of thirty-five women's and home magazines failed to detect a story, pro or con.

A few months before Hart was set to open a second round of hearings, Paul Willis, then president of the Grocery Manufacturers' Association (now Grocery Manufacturers of America) addressed the annual convention of the Television Bureau of Advertising. He had, he said, met with sixteen top management people from national magazines, including *Look, Reader's Digest, Life, Ladies' Home Journal,* and *Good Housekeeping.* "We wanted to discuss with them the facts of life concerning advertising-media relationships," he said. "He reported that he had suggested to the publishers 'that the day was here when their editorial department and business department might better understand their interdependency relationships as they affect the operating results of their company; and as their operations affect the advertiser—their bread and butter.' " *Consumer Reports,* source for the foregoing, went on to say:

> The magazine people, he continued, had understood. They had begun to run articles to create "a favorable public attitude" toward food advertisers. . . . In the January 26, 1965, issue, *Look*'s editorial pages displayed the byline of an advertiser, Charles G. Mortimer, chairman of General Foods Corp., as the author of an article, "Let's Keep Politics Out of the Pantry.". . . (Recorded against his own company, incidentally, are 28 violations in the last 25 years against . . . the Federal Food, Drug, and Cosmetic Act.) . . .
>
> After the article appeared, Senator Hart wrote to *Look*'s publisher and editor-in-chief, Gardner Cowles, pointing out that the legislation had been inaccurately described, suggesting that there was another side to the packaging issue, and asking whether he (Senator Hart) might not be given the opportunity to clarify some of these matters for the readers of *Look*.[18]

Cowles gave the Senator a polite brush-off. Meanwhile, *Look* took full-page ads in trade journals read by members of the Grocery Manufacturers' Association and in magazines to publicize its sponsorship of the Mortimer article.

In recent years dozens of mergers have made previously independent book publishers subsidiaries of much larger conglomerates. "Atheneum Publishers, one of the most prestigious of the dwindling group of independent publishing houses, has agreed to sell to the Raytheon Company, an expanding electronics conglomerate," Henry Raymont reported in the *New York Times* on May 2, 1970. The Radio Corporation of America owns NBC, is a leading defense and space contractor, and is an important manufacturer of appliances and other consumer goods. RCA's book-publishing acquisition was the large (in publishing) Random House, which itself previously had acquired Pantheon and Alfred A. Knopf. CBS is another conglomerate with military-industrial involvements. In addition to the New York Yankees, its interests range very widely, from Creative Playthings (toys) to television stations in Bermuda, the West Indies, and South America. In 1965 CBS invested $21 million in the credit affiliates of General Motors, Ford, and Chrysler. Its move into books brought it Holt, Rinehart & Winston. The Times Mirror Company— owner of the *Los Angeles Times,* the *Times Herald* in Dallas, and as of April 1970 *Newsday,* the prosperous Long Island paper—acquired World

Publishing Company, New American Library, and Harry N. Abrams, Inc. Downe Communications (*Ladies' Home Journal, Family Weekly, American Home,* CATV systems) acquired Bartell Media, thus getting control of two book publishing enterprises, McFadden-Bartell and Bartholomew House, and eighteen confession, fan, and sport magazines.

Time, Inc., was already a giant multimedia power when, in 1968, it acquired for $17 million Little, Brown and Company of Boston, a distinguished 131-year-old, and hitherto independent, publisher. It went on to take over the Book Find Club and Seven Arts Book Society. These were surely useful supplemental enterprises to Time-Life Books. Time, Inc., is best known as the publisher of magazines: the internationally influential and pervasive weeklies *Time* and *Life,* as well as the monthly *Fortune.* It also operates thirty-one weekly newspapers in the Chicago suburbs. It owned VHF television and AM and FM radio stations in four cities—Denver, Grand Rapids, Indianapolis, and San Diego—and a UHF station in a fifth, Bakersfield, California. (In October 1970 Time and McGraw-Hill, Inc., announced an agreement in principle for the sale of the stations, thirteen in all, for $80.1 million. McGraw-Hill, a diversified multinational publishing house, was already the holder of a 3 per cent interest in the Taft Broadcasting Company of Cincinnati. McGraw-Hill said it intended to sell the radio stations to be acquired from Time.) Time once came close to acquiring the *Newark Evening News,* an effort with a potential to fulfill the acknowledged ambition of the late Henry R. Luce "eventually to own a daily newspaper in New York."[19] With General Electric (itself a group owner of radio and television stations), Time owns the General Learning Corporation, which produces electronic teaching equipment for the schools. Time owns Time-Life Films. Its stockholdings in Metro-Goldwyn-Mayer are second only to those of Seagram Distillers, the largest advertiser of alcoholic beverages in *Time* and *Life.*

May the reader pardon a lapse into a *Time*-style now fortunately abandoned by what John Kenneth Galbraith would call the mature corporation. Mind-boggling are the interconnections, bottomless is the pit of opportunities for corporate back-scratching, numbing is the imagining of the range of possibilities for non-reporting by self-servers in Time media anxious not to risk offense to Time-related enterprises, frightening is the concentration of power over what the public reads, hears, views, learns, imbibes. Backward reels the mind to 1936, to the late, great Wolcott Gibbs writing prophetically of "future plans impossible to imagine, staggering to contemplate."[20]

"Where it all will end, knows God!" Gibbs said of Time, Inc.[21] Where it all *can* end, knows Funk & Wagnalls. The Reader's Digest Association acquired it in 1965. The merger put into the hands of the owner of the world's largest magazine (worldwide circulation of 29.6 million) an eighty-eight-year-old independent book publisher. There soon followed the first known episode of corporate book censorship of its kind. In May 1967 Funk & Wagnalls contracted to publish a critical study of the advertising business entitled *The Permissible Lie.* The author was Samm Sinclair Baker, who had written seventeen other books and numerous articles. On the basis of his thirty-year experience as an ad agency executive, he urged in the book that a cleanup of bad practices in the business be undertaken voluntarily. Before the date set for publication, June 30, 1968, Funk & Wagnalls routinely circulated advance copies. There was a vitriolic response in advertising trade journals. One editorial called Baker an "ungrateful dog." Funk & Wagnalls went ahead and printed five thousand copies. After it had done so Baker was told that *Reader's Digest,* which has estimated ad revenues of $60 million a year, had forbidden publication of the book. Baker was given the printing plates so he could sell the book elsewhere. He found a taker in World Publishing, a Times Mirror Company subsidiary, which, Robert Lewis Shayon said in the *Saturday Review,* "enthusiastically promised full-page ads with the headline, THE BOOK THAT READER'S DIGEST SUPPRESSED." This "horrified" an unidentified top Times Mirror executive, Shayon said. Although publication of *The Permissible Lie* was permitted, the *Digest's* suppression was not publicized. The reason given to author Baker was "bad taste." Baker's own interpretation was "bad business," because "World sells reprint rights to its publications to the magazine in Pleasantville, New York," Shayon said.

Earlier, when the *Digest's* censorship became known, Perry H. Knowlton, president of Collins-Knowlton-Wing, Inc., Baker's literary agency, said, "This is the only incident of this kind I have ever heard of." Hobart Lewis, president of the Digest Association and editor in chief of the magazine, told the *New York Times* that the book "doesn't jibe with the philosophy of the *Reader's Digest*," but declined to tell a reporter what that philosophy is. *Time,* however, attributed to Lewis a statement that "advertising is good for business, and business is good for the country." "We will begin reviewing all manuscripts," *Time* quoted Lewis as saying. "Reader's Digest will exert tighter quality control over Funk & Wagnalls."[22] Ultimately this took an unusual form: on March 1, 1970, the *New York Times Book Review* reported that Funk & Wagnalls "recently fired its entire editorial staff." That accomplished, the firm proceeded with plans to publish two books about Richard M. Nixon. No one expected them to fall far short of adulation. The *Digest* had carried eleven of his articles and sponsored some of his foreign travels during the 1960s while he was out of office, thus giving an invaluable assist to his return to office—the highest office.

Social note from the media-political complex: A news story about President Nixon's "inner circle" identified Hobart Lewis of the *Reader's Digest* as one of "a small group of intimate friends, men with whom he dined, shared his deepest thoughts . . ."[23] "Mr. Nixon does have some confidants out beyond the bureaucracy," Stuart H. Loory said in the *Washingtonian.* "Franklin Murphy, the board chairman of the Times Mirror Corporation, is one. (Murphy serves on the Foreign Intelligence Advisory Board, a little-known, high-level group that oversees all the American intelligence gathering operations as well as covert funny business.)"[24]

Concentration in certain industries is easy to describe. When one says that a few companies dominate automobile manufacturing one says the essential fact. Regrettably, simplicity is not an attribute of concentration in news media. Let us begin with an initial focus principally on newspapers.

Media tycoons contend that the trend toward concentration we shall describe is the result of natural economic forces which can no more be resisted than rain and snow. This is not so. To the contrary, modern production technologies long have made practicable more competition, not less. Why, then, has the potential for more daily newspaper voices gone unfulfilled? At Senator Philip Hart's hearings the answers were provided by a series of expert witnesses, including John R. Malone, a consultant on newspaper economics and technology; Bryce W. Rucker, professor of journalism at Southern Illinois University; Philip Hochstein, who for almost forty years was chief editorial executive of the giant Newhouse Newspapers chain; and J. Hart Clinton, editor and publisher of the *San Mateo Times* in California. They showed that the trend toward concentration had been set in motion and then speeded by such critically important catalysts as tax favoritism; chronic non-enforcement of the antitrust laws against predatory practices, including the sale of advertising and subscriptions below cost, and discrimination in the availability and sale of popular comics, columns, and other syndicated materials.[26]

An important measure of media concentration is the proportion of cities and towns with daily newspapers under two or more separate ownerships. In 1910 the figure was 57.1 per cent, in 1930 it was 21.5 per cent, and in 1970 it had dropped to 4.13 per cent. Today there are 1,483 cities with monopoly ownerships, compared with 64 with competing ownerships. Of the 64, almost half (29) are in cities with populations of under 100,000, and almost one-third (20) are in cities of under 50,000.[25] Of the competitive cities only New York, Boston, and Washington each has three separately owned dailies. Chicago, Los Angeles, Detroit, Philadelphia, San Francisco, Dallas, Houston, Cleveland, Pittsburgh, Newark, Miami, Denver, and Seattle are among the major cities with two ownerships. Des Moines, Minneapolis, San Diego, Louisville, and Portland, Oregon, are important cities with newspaper monopolies.

Whether a city has single or multiple newspaper ownerships, one or all of the proprietors may be Newhouse, Scripps-Howard, the Hearst Corporation, or another of the newspaper chains. These, Senator Thomas J. McIntyre, the New Hampshire Democrat, has pointed out, have achieved "startling growth."[27] In 1960 they controlled 560 dailies. In each of the seven succeeding years chains acquired an average of 40 more. As of 1967 they controlled 871, an increase of 56 per cent over 1960. The 871 dailies were 49.3 per cent of the nation's total. They accounted for 61.8 per cent of the aggregate circulation and for 19 of the 25 largest papers.

Again, there should be no casual assumption of inevitability. There have been synthetic stimuli. For example, the tax laws have given special incentives to acquisitions by making it possible for chains with excess cash to avoid income taxes by buying still more communications media.

A brief look at the chains. Newhouse, said to be worth at least $300 million, has twenty-two newspapers in cities including St. Louis, New Orleans, Cleveland, Newark, Harrisburg, and Portland, Oregon, an interest in the *Denver Post,* and shared ownership (with Scripps-Howard) of the Birmingham papers. The company owns seven television stations, three AM and four FM radio stations, and nine CATV (community antenna television) systems. In Portland and in Syracuse, New York, Newhouse owns the two newspapers and a TV-AM-FM complex; and elsewhere in Northern New York it owns seven of the nine CATV systems. The chain owns twenty nationally distributed magazines, including *Vogue, Mademoiselle, House & Garden,* and *Glamour;* the Newhouse News Service; and newsprint and rotogravure printing plants. Arthur J. Goldberg, a former Justice of the Supreme Court, has said that S. I. Newhouse, the elderly founder, has "the greatest concentration of power over the dissemination of news, ideas and advertising which has ever been placed in the hands of one person in the United States."[28] For this situation significant blame attaches to the Federal Communications Commission. The FCC was concerned when a newspaper owner came to it seeking a broadcast license. It was not concerned when an entrepreneur such as Newhouse had the wit to reverse the sequence, that is, to get the licenses first and then the newspapers.[29] Indeed, the FCC was shown by Senator Hart to have failed to require leading broadcasting interests—CBS, Westinghouse, General Tire, Corinthian (John Hay Whitney), Hearst, Scripps-Howard, the Church of Jesus Christ of Latter-Day Saints—to comply with the FCC's own rules for disclosure of additional business ties. Thus the Commission cannot claim to have known, or known fully, what it was doing when, every three years, it rubber-stamped license renewals for such interests.[30]

Scripps-Howard operates seventeen daily newspapers in cities including Washington, Denver, Columbus, Ohio, Albuquerque, Pittsburgh, El Paso, Fort Worth, and San Juan. It operates seven of these papers under joint agreements, thus alone accounting for almost one-third of the total. In Cincinnati, Cleveland, and Memphis it is the dominant newspaper and television voice. It shares ownership of United Press International with Hearst.

Hearst's eight newspapers are in Albany (two), Boston, Baltimore, (where it also owns TV, AM and FM stations), San Antonio, Los Angeles, San Francisco (where it is in a joint operating agreement with the *Chronicle*), and Seattle. It owns thirteen magazines, including *Cosmopolitan* and *Good Housekeeping,* and Avon Books.

Other important chains are the Gannett Company, which owns thirty-four daily newspapers and thirteen weeklies, two TV stations and a CATV, and which said in January 1970 that it was holding acquisition discussions for more newspapers and at least three more TV stations; Knight Newspapers (Detroit, Philadelphia, Miami, Akron, Charlotte, and Macon, Georgia), Copley Newspapers (ten in California, five in Illinois), Media General (Richmond, Winston-Salem, Tampa, and Newark), Cox Newspapers (Dayton, Ohio, Atlanta, and Miami), and Ridder Publications (just two of whose twenty-four papers, the *San Jose Mercury* and *San Jose News* in California, ranked in 1968, respectively, sixth largest in morning newspaper advertising linage and third largest in evening paper linage).

In October 1970 the New York Times Company announced that it was acquiring from Cowles Communications, Incorporated, three small Florida dailies (in Lakeland, Gainesville, and Ocala); *Family Circle,* which with a circulation of more than 7 million ranked third among all women's magazines in 1969 (and fifth in advertising volume); the leading television station in Memphis, WREC–TV, a CBS affiliate; the Cambridge Book Company, a publisher of high school textbooks (4 million hardcover and paperback copies annually); and seven professional magazines, principally *Modern Medicine,* which derives almost all of its revenues from pharmaceutical industry advertising. In exchange, the Times Company agreed to give Cowles Communication 2.6 million shares of its stock, valued at more than $50 million, and to assume $15 million of Cowles's debts. Cowles will continue to own and operate *Look* and *Venture* magazines, among other enterprises. The Times Company already owned several educational and publishing subsidiaries and WQXR–AM-FM in New York City. Along with the Washington Post Company, it held a substantial interest in the *International Herald Tribune.* A trust established under the will of Adolph S. Ochs, former publisher of the *Times* and founder of the *Chattanooga Times* in Tennessee, owned a majority of the stock of the Southern newspaper.

It is time now to shift our focus to broadcasting, although newspapers and other media necessarily will be involved. FCC rules allow a single party to hold broadcast licenses for up to seven television stations, no more than five of which may be VHF (very high frequency), seven FM stations and five AM stations. Each of the great networks owns and operates the maximum allowable number of VHF stations, which, because of their greater range and because every set can pick them up, are more highly prized than UHF (ultra high frequency) stations. All fifteen of the network VHF stations are in the nation's twenty-five largest markets, including New York, Chicago and Los Angeles. The eleven largest cities do not have even one VHF station that is not in the hands of a network, a newspaper, a newspaper chain, an owner of a group of stations or an industrial or financial conglomerate.

There are 7,350 radio and television stations. There are 1,547 cities with daily newspapers. Such figures suggest a great diversity. This is a delusion. There is no stronger supporting evidence than that dealing with the intense concentration existing in certain states, regions, and cities.

In the twenty-five top markets there are a total of ninety-seven VHF stations. In addition to the fifteen owned and operated by CBS, NBC, and ABC, newspapers as of early 1970 were operating thirty-four. Of the thirty-four, twenty-six are affiliates of one of the networks. At the request of Senator Hart the FCC provided further data bearing on media concentration as of late 1967.[31] As a starter consider communities which are outside of metropolitan areas and which have populations of between 5,000 and 50,000. In each of sixty-eight such communities where there is one daily newspaper and one AM station the paper has an interest in the station. In twenty-eight similar communities where there are two stations the single newspaper has an interest in one of them.

Now consider communities in metropolitan areas with populations of 175,000 to 2 million or more. In eight such communities a newspaper owns 50 to 100 per cent of the only radio station. In six similar communities where there are two stations the paper owns a majority interest in one of them.

The Commission data also tell of the links between commercial television stations and the ownerships of daily newspapers. In twenty-nine communities with one station and one daily the paper has a majority or, in three cases, a minority interest. In twelve communities, or markets, where there is one newspaper and two TV stations the daily has holdings in one of the stations. Single-newspaper ownerships also have majority interests in a TV station in the seventeen communities (or markets) where there are three or more TV stations.

Commissioners Kenneth A. Cox and Nicholas Johnson made a unique case study of news media ownership in Oklahoma, which in this regard they called a typical state.[32] The results were "extremely disquieting."

One finding was "that in spite of the numbers of newspapers and broadcast outlets the control of the greatest share of audience, profit and *political power* lies in the hands of very few." [Emphasis supplied.] There are in Oklahoma ninety-three commercial stations, eighty-three of them radio and ten of them television. They have seventy-three separate owners. But in 1966 four of the owners accounted for 56 per cent of the total revenue and 88 per cent of the total income. "Political candidates for statewide office in Oklahoma will have to be cognizant of the influence of these few firms and stations," Johnson and Cox said.

Oklahoma has fifty daily newspapers. Two of them, the *Oklahoman* and *Times* in Oklahoma City, account for 35 per cent of the total daily circulation in the entire state. Three other newspaper firms account for another 34 per cent.

The Oklahoma Publishing Company, owner of the Oklahoma City papers, is also the proprietor of the very large TV-AM complex in that metropolis. Of the forty-nine other communities with broadcasting stations there are twelve with media monopolies—all the stations and daily papers, where there are any, are jointly owned.

In seven Oklahoma cities newspapers are owned by Donald W. Reynolds (Donrey Media Group). In Arkansas, adjoining Oklahoma to the east, Donrey owns the two newspapers and the one TV station in Fort Smith and the AM station in Springdale.

In Wisconsin the Journal Company of Milwaukee owns both daily newspapers and the leading TV, AM, and FM stations. In Madison the *Wisconsin State Journal* is owned by Lee Enterprises. Lee also owns the *Journal-Times* in Racine and the *Tribune* and TV and AM stations in La Crosse. In Minnesota, Lee owns TV and FM stations in Mankato; in Iowa, the *Globe-Gazette* and TV and AM stations in Mason City and newspapers in Clinton, Davenport, Muscatine, and Ottumwa; in Illinois, a paper in Kewanee and AM and FM stations in Quincy; in Missouri, a newspaper and a TV station in Hannibal; in Nebraska, an AM and an FM station in Omaha and a piece of a newspaper joint operating agreement in Lincoln; and in Montana, six newspapers.

In Illinois, Lindsay-Schaub Newspapers owns the dailies and a TV-AM-FM complex in each of four cities, as well as dailies serving two additional markets in the state.

In the forty-county area of southern Michigan there is a single owner of the daily newspapers in eight substantial cities, Ann Arbor, Bay City,

Flint, Grand Rapids, Jackson, Kalamazoo, Muskegon, and Saginaw. Although six of the papers have a circulation of 30,000 to 60,000 each, Flint's is 110,000 and Grand Rapids's 130,000. The aggregate circulation is well over a half-million. The single owner is Booth Newspapers, Inc.

In the same forty-county area and across the Ohio border in Toledo and across the Indiana border in South Bend are ten radio stations whose single owner also controls four additional stations in Cleveland, Ohio, and Kokomo, Indiana. The owner is the Booth American Company. This enterprise also has CATV networks in Michigan. The owners of Booth American are John L. Booth, his wife, and their two sons. The family holds more than 8 per cent of the stock in Booth Newspapers and has a seat on the board of directors. Control of Booth Newspapers, however, is in four cousins of John Booth. One of them, Warren S. Booth, owns 2.18 per cent of the *Detroit News,* the giant of Michigan newspapers, and is chairman of its board. Another cousin is a director of the *News,* and he and the two others own 6.23 per cent of it. In turn, the *News* owns the NBC affiliates in Detroit, WWJ–TV, which has an estimated "weekly circulation" of 5 million persons, and WWJ–AM and FM.[33] "One fundamental American moral premise is that any power over the destinies of others is always subject to question and that excessive power is evil," Peter T. Clark has said. It should comfort the reader to know that Clark is publisher of the *Detroit News.*[34]

Senator Philip Hart has justly protested that although mergers have been the principal instrument for the trend toward concentration in ownership of communications neither the Justice Department nor the FCC "has distinguished itself by vigorous action to slow down the trend. Indeed, we have seen, on occasion, an Alphonse and Gaston act, leaving both agencies nodding to each other while the elevator doors close before them."[35]

Over a quarter of a century, under a succession of Attorneys General, the Justice Department presented no serious obstacles to newspaper joint operating agreements which were built upon *per se* violations of the antitrust laws. They grew in number until there were twenty-two. Newspaper ownerships were not always above using strategies and tactics which they did not yearn to have fairly reported in their own news columns. The mere existence of a profit-pooling arrangement in St. Louis, disclosed in 1967 in Senator Hart's hearings on the newspaper bill, came as a complete shock even to certain top managers in the *Globe-Democrat,* owned by Newhouse, and the *Post-Dispatch,* owned by the Pulitzer Publishing Company.

In San Francisco a joint operating agreement took effect in September 1965. One of the parties was the Chronicle Publishing Company, which has acknowledged that it had used profits from its television station, KRON–TV, to "sustain the operation" of the morning *Chronicle* in its competition with the *Examiner.*[36] The second party was the Hearst Corporation, owner of the evening *Examiner.* Note should be taken of the fact that Hearst, one of the most influential advocates of the newspaper bill whose rationale was that it would preserve the separate editorial voices of "failing" newspapers, had, since 1958, merged International News Service with United Press, closed the *New York Daily Mirror* and (in a transaction with the Times Mirror Company) the *Herald Express* in Los Angeles, helped to silence, through purchase, the voice of Scripps-Howard in San Francisco, and sold the *Chicago American* to the *Tribune,* the *Detroit Times* to the *News,* the *Milwaukee Sentinel* to the *Journal,* and the *Pittsburgh Sun* to the Paul Block chain.

On July 27, 1967, appearing before Senator Hart, Charles de Young Thieriot, president of Chronicle Publishing, testified that the operating agreement was preceded by advice from the Attorney General, then Nicholas de B. Katzenbach, "that it was not the Department's intent to institute an antitrust action."[37] More, "the Justice Department gave us a clearance letter."[38] Testifying on the same day, Charles L. Gould, publisher of the *Examiner,* agreed. "The Department advised us that it would not sue to block the proposed joint arrangement," he assured Hart.[39]

Nine months later the Justice Department contradicted this testimony. Donald F. Turner, Assistant Attorney General in charge of the Antitrust Division, testified that the arrangement was "not cleared." He offered for the hearing record a statement made by the Department at the time the joint agreement was announced. The statement said that Justice had "decided not to institute antitrust action *at this time.*" [Emphasis supplied.] The statement concluded:

> The Department of Justice is carefully reviewing the difficult antitrust problems involved in joint newspaper production agreements. The reality of one such agreement [in Tucson] is now the subject of litigation, and others may well come before the courts in the future.

Attorneys for the papers involved in the San Francisco joint production agreement have been advised that the Department's decision not to sue is subject to reconsideration in the light of future court decisions and the Department's continuing review of such arrangements.[40]

In 1965, in a move of critical importance, the Justice Department filed a civil antitrust suit against the Citizen Publishing Company, the Tucson firm which will be remembered as the author of the unique confession called the "Pig Document." The complaint was that the provisions for profit-pooling and price-fixing in the joint agreement with the *Arizona Daily Star* violated the antitrust laws. The Department won in District Court, was challenged, and in March 1969 was upheld by the Supreme Court. The vote was 7 to 1. Divestiture of the *Star,* ordered by District Judge James A. Walsh, would have been a certainty, and the twenty-one other operating agreements would have been imperiled, had it not been, of course, for the legislation which the newspaper industry had designed to meet the contingency of a court defeat.

Also in 1965, the Department filed a civil antitrust suit by which it forced the Times Mirror Company, publisher of the *Los Angeles Times,* the largest daily newspaper in southern California, to sell the Sun Company, which had been the largest independent daily newspaper publisher in southern California. Times Mirror had acquired it in 1964. In another important action, in Cincinnati, the Department obtained a consent agreement from Scripps-Howard to sell its controlling interest in the *Inquirer.* The chain continues to own the *Post and Times-Star* there.

There is an imperfect but nonetheless substantial potential for competition among newspapers, radio stations, and TV stations. All can disseminate most news and most advertising. These assumptions were verified in 1968 by a Justice Department study which showed that in each of fifty major urban markets a single owner controlled two or more broadcast media and/or at least one TV station plus one daily newspaper. In several such markets a newspaper chain or dominant newspaper owned network-affiliated TV, AM, and FM stations.

After assembling the data, the Department, in the first challenge of its kind, filed a civil antitrust suit against the Gannett chain. The purpose was to compel Gannett to sell either the dominant TV station in Rockford, Illinois, or the company that publishes the morning and one of the two afternoon newspapers in Rockford. Gannett found the case so compelling that it agreed to a consent judgment which was filed simultaneously with the suit. Later it chose to sell the television station. This decision is but one of the signals that a man need not regard himself as heartless if he turns away from the cries of poverty so often heard from newspaper proprietors.

Meanwhile, thanks in good part to Nicholas Johnson and Kenneth Cox, concentration of ownership of news media actually came to be taken seriously by the Federal Communications Commission. In March 1969, on this primary ground, the Commission voted to hold hearings before renewing the licenses of KRON–TV, the Chronicle Publishing station in San Francisco, and WCCO and WCCO–TV, the CBS affiliates in Minneapolis–St. Paul, whose licensee is Midwest Radio-Television, Inc. Midwest is 47 per cent owned by the Minneapolis Star and Tribune Company, which publishes the daily papers in Minneapolis and several papers in South Dakota and Montana, owns a CATV system in Nebraska, and also owns *Harper's Magazine*. The reader who is resolute and who enjoys weaving in and out of corporate warps and woofs may nonetheless find the next paragraph a challenge.

The 53 per cent owner of Midwest Radio-Television is Mid-Continent Radio-Television, Inc. It has two owners. One, MTC Properties, Inc., also owns 14.7 per cent of the Minneapolis Star and Tribune Company. The second owner of Mid-Continent is Northwest Publications, Inc. This is the instrument of the Ridder family that publishes the daily newspapers in St. Paul, seventeen papers on the West Coast (sixteen in California and the *Seattle Times*), one on the East Coast (the *Journal of Commerce* in New York), and four in between, in the Dakotas and Colorado.

Now: Garfield Clark, manager of KSTP Radio in St. Paul, in a statement filed in 1968 with the Senate antitrust subcommittee, protested that WCCO, the newspapers' station, had full or partial rights to broadcast the games of the Minnesota Twins (baseball), Vikings (football), and North Stars (hockey). But the Ridder family, owner of the St. Paul papers, is also part owner of the Vikings and North Stars. Not surprisingly, "an acceptable bid" by KSTP for radio broadcast of the Vikings' games, in 1967, 1968 and 1969, was turned down in favor of WCCO. "The primary reason . . . was that its newspaper ownership offered greater opportunities for newspaper publicity," Clark declared. But by a vote of 4 to 3, the FCC voted on July 16, 1970, to renew the WCCO licenses.

HEAR NO EVIL, SEE NO EVIL, SPEAK NO EVIL

In March 1970, a year after setting down the WCCO and KRON cases for hearings, the FCC announced that it would block any new efforts to acquire ownership of more than one station—TV, AM, or FM—in the same urban market. By this time, of course, combined ownerships had proliferated. According to a Commission staff study that preceded the announcement by a few days, there are 256 daily newspapers in joint ownership with holders of broadcast licenses in their respective cities. Much more boldly, the Commission floated a proposal to require mass divestitures, over a five-year period. The result would be that in any urban market a single ownership could have a newspaper, a television station, *or* an AM-FM radio combination. The proposal aroused massive and powerful opposition. Its ultimate fate is doubtful. The four Democrats then on the Commission voted to approve both actions. Among the Republicans, Chairman Dean Burch and Robert E. Lee voted against the immediate freeze but for the inquiry into the possibility of breaking up existing media combinations. Commissioner Robert Wells opposed both actions.

Special attention is owed the hazards in ownership of communications media by conglomerate industrial and business corporations. "The resolution of most urgent issues—war and peace, the growing chasm between rich nations and poor, decay of cities, inadequacy of schools, race relations, contamination of environment—depend on allocation of national wealth, which means both social policy and taxes," Ben H. Bagdikian has said. "If the news and its interpretation are increasingly merely a byproduct of huge corporations whose primary concern must be conventional gain then this is not a minor matter in public information or in the development of social and fiscal policies."[41]

The daily newspapers in Wilmington, Delaware, the *Morning News* and the *Evening Journal,* are properties of Christiana Securities, a multi-billion-dollar holding company that owns 27 per cent of the stock in E. I. du Pont de Nemours & Company, Inc. "When Shell Oil wanted to build a refinery in Delaware, the owners ordered the papers to stop commenting on the issue," Bagdikian reported in *Columbia Journalism Review*.[42] "When Congress was considering legislation for relief of the du Ponts in selling their General Motors stock under court order, the papers were told not to criticize Senator Byrd [the late Harry F. Byrd of Virginia], chairman of the Senate Finance Committee." In May 1964

Creed Black, executive editor of the papers, resigned after being told that Charles M. Hackett, executive assistant in the public relations department of du Pont, was to be his boss. "The depressing quality of the Wilmington episode is that it is not unusual," Bagdikian wrote. "Few families are so powerful, organized or dominant in their state as are the du Ponts, but newspaperdom is filled with owners whose assumptions of their responsibilities are based on their non-newspaper businesses and whose journalistic enterprises are peripheral both to their personal experience and their daily attention."

Later in the *Atlantic Monthly,* Bagdikian told a story about the *Houston Chronicle* that, if anything, was even more depressing than the Wilmington episode.[43] The sole owner of the *Chronicle,* the largest newspaper in Texas, was Houston Endowment, Incorporated. Although set up as a tax-free charitable foundation, the Endowment was a "tightly-held corporate force." It had, Bagdikian said, important interests "in thirty-two corporations, a majority interest in twenty-five, including a half-dozen banks, three hotels, several downtown office buildings, real estate, and the Mayfair House Hotel on Park Avenue, New York." In 1960 John T. Jones, Jr., titular head of the *Chronicle,* brought in, to lead a badly needed rejuvenation, William P. Steven, a respected professional editor and a moderate Republican. By standards common in Houston, however, he was, Bagdikian said, "pretty radical: he supported higher education, Lyndon Johnson and civil rights."

At about eleven thirty on the night of September 2, 1965, Jones phoned Steven to say he was coming over to see him. The editor assumed that Jones wanted to talk about a highly volatile development in local race relations that had preoccupied him most of the day. He and his wife were in bathrobes when Jones and his wife arrived at the Steven home. There was a drink and some friendly small talk. "Then Jones blurted out: 'This is the hardest thing I ever had to do,' " Bagdikian reported. " 'Bill, they had a meeting today, and they got you.' As Bill and Lucy Steven reconstruct it, the conversation went like this:

"Steven: Who is 'they'? And what do you mean, they got me?
"Jones: You know. The Endowment.
"Lucy: Who?
"Jones: The trustees.
"Lucy: What do you mean, they got Bill?

"Jones: You're all through, Bill.

"Lucy: Why? Why?

"There was no direct answer. Much later that night, Jones said: 'Bill, you had a vision. They don't want a vision; they want a voice.' "

On February 8, 1969, the Federal Communications Commission announced its intention to make a study of the problems posed "by ownership of broadcast stations by any other person or entity with large-scale business interests." The subjects listed for inquiry included "possible hazards to free and fair presentation of materials by conglomerate-owned stations." All in all, the inquiry "would cover all possible social, economic and political aspects of conglomerate activity in the broadcasting field."

Two points about this extremely belated official recognition of the problem need to be made. First, not until ten months later did the FCC get around even to agreeing to send out questionnaires to a half-dozen conglomerate owners (the vote was 4 to 3, with the minority composed of the Republican members, Dean Burch, the chairman, and Robert Wells, the initial appointees of President Nixon, and Robert E. Lee, whose original appointment, in the 1950s, has been almost universally attributed to his friendship with the late Senator Joseph R. McCarthy). Second, the Commission manipulated the timing and release of the announcement so as to conceal from most of the press and public its *simultaneous* approval of transfers of broadcast licenses to three giant industrial corporations. "The last time this Commission issued a general inquiry into ownership matters and the same day approved a case seemingly contrary to the standards newly proposed it was reversed by the U.S. Court of Appeals," Commissioner Nicholas Johnson, who dissented from the transfers, said. But in any of the instant cases a reversal in the courts, assuming the possibility of a legal challenge, would be many years away; and in the interim there would be no inhibition whatever on the profit-making potential of the corporations blessed by the Commission majority.

In transferring the broadcast licenses the majority decided not to hold hearings at which there would be a burden on the applicants to show that the public interest, convenience, and necessity were being served. That is to say, the Commission, on the very day it approved an inquiry into conglomerate involvements in broadcasting, was able to find it unnecessary even to have a public discussion of the implications of three transfers to conglomerates. A look at these cases is rewarding.

With FCC approval, a conglomerate called Fuqua Industries acquired the licenses for two television stations by taking control of the previous holder, a firm which operates 140 movie theaters in six states. One license was for WTVM–TV in Columbus, Georgia, and the other for WTVC in Chattanooga, Tennessee. Fuqua was already the owner of one of the eleven TV stations in Georgia, WJBF–TV in Augusta. The company also has holdings in TV stations in Evansville, Indiana, and Fargo, North Dakota, and in radio stations in Evansville, Flint, Michigan, and Sacramento, California. Its other interests are as diverse as power lawn mowers, mobile homes, and trucking.

The case has clear-cut political-industrial-media complex implications. The board chairman of the firm, J. B. Fuqua, was former chairman of the Georgia state Democratic party. Carl E. Sanders, a director, is a former governor of Georgia. Frank W. Hulse, is on the boards of Southern Airlines and Southern Airways as well as of Fuqua Industries. Surely, as Nicholas Johnson said in dissenting from the transfer, media ownership by a conglomerate "imposes an added burden, and an unnecessary risk, upon the integrity of the information presented to the American people. It creates a situation in which the incentives are almost irresistible for the holding company to view the mass media subsidiary as but a part of its advertising, public relations, and public information program for its more predominant and profitable industrial subsidiaries."

In the second case, the Commission transferred the license of WRTH, an AM radio station near St. Louis in Wood River, Illinois, from Madison County Broadcasting Company, Inc., to Avco Broadcasting of California. This is an Avco Broadcasting Corporation subsidiary which, in turn, is a subsidiary of Avco Corporation. Among other things, Avco was getting $500 million a year in defense contracts and ranked as the twelfth largest defense contractor in the country.

In addition to its defense business, Avco sells space products, industrial engines, aircraft frame components, farm equipment, abrasives, and financial services. It owns television and radio stations in Cincinnati and San Antonio, TV stations in Columbus and Dayton and Indianapolis, and radio stations in San Francisco and Washington, D.C.

It was appropriate for Commissioner Johnson to recall a passage from a majority FCC opinion in 1945, a quarter-century earlier, in a case involving the company that was to become Avco: "If to this concentration of economic power there is added the tremendous power of major broadcasting facilities, . . . the result is the creation of a repository of power able to challenge the sovereignty of government."

Avco was one of the half-dozen conglomerates to which the FCC, over the opposition of its Republican members, sent questionnaires about "possible hazards to free and fair presentation of materials." The Commission staff summarized the results of the pilot study in a thirty-five-page confidential report which was obtained by the *Wall Street Journal*. The results were embarrassing to Avco (and by implication to the FCC for having approved the firm's acquisition of a radio station without a hearing).

In Avco's case, Wayne E. Green reported in the *Journal* on August 11, 1970, "the FCC staff questions methods it says were used in trying to convince certain nonbroadcast Avco subsidiaries to channel their advertising exclusively to Avco's radio and television stations instead of to competing outlets." Specifically, the staff was

> primarily critical of certain aspects of a promotional effort in which the Avco Broadcasting Corp. unit tried to persuade Avco's consumer finance subsidiaries to place their advertising with Avco stations instead of with competing newspapers. It focuses heavily on correspondence in which, the report says, Avco Broadcasting executives stress the Avco family relationships and the financial interests of the conglomerate in making their pitch.

Properly, advertising is placed on the basis of price, quality, and service. Avco's injection of "family ties" and self-interest obviously made it harder for media rivals of Avco stations to compete for Avco advertising. Green said the Commission staff found this inappropriate and suggested "that the FCC consult the Justice Department for its views on the question whether in-house dealings by broadcast conglomerates is a form of restraint of competition that might violate antitrust laws." Moreover, the staff "wonders whether the stressing of corporate family ties to attract advertising is in keeping with the public interest standards demanded of broadcasters." Green added:

> The report contends there's evidence of Avco family considerations in its sports news programing too. It centers mainly on correspondence in which an Avco Broadcasting official is explaining to another Avco sub-

sidiary that because of a late-arriving press release Avco's San Francisco radio stations weren't aware that two Avco-sponsored hockey teams were playing in a tournament there, and as a result, the stations didn't give them news coverage.

As the FCC staff sees it, the letter was indicating that the stations hadn't considered the tournament newsworthy but that they might have had they known about Avco's interest. *The letter clashes with Avco's declared policy prohibiting the use of Avco stations to promote other corporate interests, the study contends.* [Emphasis supplied.]

The third of the license transfers announced by the FCC on February 8, 1969, may in many ways be the most interesting. It involves a political-industrial-media-religious complex. The FCC here approved the sale (by John Poole Broadcasting Company, Inc.) of two radio stations in Los Angeles, KBIG–AM and FM, to the Bonneville International Corporation. Bonneville is a wholly owned property of the Deseret Management Corporation, a wholly owned subsidiary of the Church of Jesus Christ of Latter-Day Saints (Mormon). The holdings of the Church are far-reaching. Here is an incomplete list:

Industrial and other non-media holdings: Drawing from sources cited in his dissent, Nicholas Johnson named these:

. . . a 50% interest in the Utah Idaho Sugar Company (beet sugar) . . . a 25% interest in Zion's Cooperative Mercantile Institution (a Salt Lake City department store); Hotel Utah and Hotel Temple Square in Salt Lake City; Beneficial Life Insurance Company (insurance in force $535,000,000); Home Fire Insurance Company; Deseret Farms, Inc.; Deseret Farms of Florida, Inc.; Zion's Securities Corporation (real estate management); a trucking company; a pineapple plantation; three large ranches in Canada; a total of 600 farms, 40 mills, factories, and salvage stores; a 6,500 acre sugar plantation in Hawaii; and 360,000 acres (another source indicates 700,000 acres) in Florida.

Newspapers: Until almost two decades ago in Salt Lake City the Mormon Church owned the evening and Sunday *Deseret News.* Their influence extended not only throughout Utah, but far into the entire Rocky Mountain region—into southern Idaho, eastern Nevada, western Colorado, and western Wyoming. The Kearns-Tribune Corporation also exerted major influence as publisher of the morning *Salt Lake Tribune* and the evening *Telegram.* In 1952 the two companies entered into a joint operating agreement which combined all commerical activities and fixed advertising and subscription prices. The *Deseret News* gave up its Sunday edition but emerged with a monopoly in the evening field. The *Tribune* dropped its evening paper but came out with a monopoly of the morning and Sunday fields. In Los Angeles, where in 1969 it acquired the AM and FM stations, it already had a 5.12 per cent ($20 million) interest in the Times Mirror Company, publisher of the *Los Angeles Times*.

Broadcasting: In Salt Lake City the Mormon Church owns and operates KSL–TV–AM–FM, the CBS outlets. Either directly or through devices known as translators, which extend the range of electronic signals, KSL–TV reaches thirty-five of the thirty-nine communities in Utah, one county in Colorado, and three counties each in Idaho, Nevada, and Wyoming. The Church operates Brigham Young University in Provo, Utah, which is the licensee for educational TV and FM stations. The Church also owns an AM and an FM station in Kansas City, Missouri, and, in New York City, an FM station and one of the three privately owned international shortwave stations in the United States. In Boise, Idaho, the Church owns 6.2 per cent of a TV-AM-FM group.

Media interlocks: Kearns-Tribune Corporation, the partner of the Church in the newspaper operating agreement, owns 35 per cent of KUTV–TV, the NBC affiliate in Salt Lake City (plus substantial mining, real estate, and financial interests in Utah). The balance of the stock in KUTV–TV is owned by A. L. Glassman and his son-in-law, George C. Hatch. The Glassman-Hatch interests own the only daily newspaper in Ogden, which is Utah's second largest city and is thirty-five miles from Salt Lake City; seven additional TV and radio stations in Utah, Idaho, Montana, and Hawaii; and several CATV systems. There are only three commerical TV stations in Utah, all of them in Salt Lake City. The third station, an ABC affiliate, is owned by a subsidiary of Columbia Pictures. This station has joined with the CBS affiliate (Mormon Church) and the NBC outlet (Kearns-Tribune and Glassman-Hatch) in a CATV venture.

"To put it mildly, Utah is under the control of a communications cartel with external resources and holdings elsewhere in the United States," Phil L. Hansen, Attorney General of Utah, testified at the hearings on the Failing Newspaper Bill held by the Senate Subcommittee on Antitrust and Monopoly. He called the joint operating agreement in Salt Lake City "patently illegal."[44]

111

The Commission's approval of the transfer of the Los Angeles stations, which was opposed by commissioners Robert Bartley and Kenneth Cox as well as Nicholas Johnson, was predictable. Only two weeks earlier the FCC—again without a hearing—had voted 4 to 3 to renew the television license of KSL, the Mormon Church station in Salt Lake City. Formally, the action was a denial of a petition for reconsideration of the initial approval given in October 1968. The challengers were a highly educated and a highly unusual Salt Lake couple, W. Paul Wharton, a taxi driver, and his wife, Ethel C. Hale, a social worker. They had made a citizens' protest to the FCC in which they raised serious questions about the fairness of KSL in handling controversial issues and about the corporate interrelationships at issue. To discourage the couple, and possibly other members of the public concerned about the public's airwaves, the Commission engaged in a series of shabby bureaucratic tricks to stop them from poaching in bureaucratic-corporate preserves. For example, the FCC once notified the couple that they had failed to comply with regulations by sending in a letter that was not on "double-spaced typewritten pages." Rejecting the FCC's refusal to hold a hearing on the KSL renewal, the couple, generously aided by Robert N. Levin, a young Washington lawyer, took the case to the United States Court of Appeals in Washington. While the case was pending, the Commission took an action which was difficult to reconcile with its position in the KSL matter.

The action involved the Frontier Broadcasting Company, controlled by the McCracken family (Robert and William and their mother, widow of the founder, Tracy McCracken). Entirely through internal growth, not acquisition, in a relatively small and isolated area, Frontier owned KFBC–TV, the only television station in Cheyenne, Wyoming. In addition, Frontier controlled the only full-time operation among the four AM stations in Cheyenne, and the only CATV system there. It published the only two daily newspapers in the area (and five others elsewhere in Wyoming), had a construction permit for the city's second FM station, and operated a satellite television station in Colorado and another in Nebraska. On February 12, 1970, the FCC became so exercised about the situation in Cheyenne that it held up renewal of KFBC–TV's license for hearings, which were set for the fall of 1970. Four days later, the Court of Appeals affirmed the Commission's refusal to hold hearings on the vastly more serious KSL renewal, not on the merits, but because the FCC then was reviewing its doctrines on media concentration. The fact is, the Commission's position on the Cheyenne case could not be squared with its position on the Salt Lake case. And the "undue concentration of control" that justified hearings in Minneapolis–St. Paul and San Francisco also justified a hearing in Salt Lake.

But there is a consistency, of sorts, in the FCC. Having voted in February 1969 to approve the transfer of the Los Angeles radio stations to the Mormon Church, it could, a month later, vote to renew the licenses of four additional California radio stations licensed to a conglomerate —even one, which, at that very moment, was being sued by the United States of America. The stations were KHJ–AM and FM in Los Angeles and KFRC–AM and KFMS–FM in San Francisco. The conglomerate was RKO General, a subsidiary of the General Tire and Rubber Company which, Commissioner Johnson said, is "one of the most politically powerful group owners."

In Los Angeles, in addition to the radio stations, General owns KHJ–TV, a station whose performance was so poor that an FCC examiner voted against renewal of its license; and the Commission voted to hold a hearing in *that* case. In New York, Boston, and Detroit, General owns TV-AM-FM combinations. In Washington it owns AM and FM stations, in Memphis a TV-AM combination, and in Hartford a TV station. In Schenectady it had owned, until late 1969, the *Union-Star*, but sold the paper to the Hearst Corporation (which, in yet another demonstration of its determination to preserve the voices of failing newspapers, converted it into a Schenectady edition of its papers in Albany). Its CATV properties serve about thirty communities.

General also owns Aerojet General Corporation, which is sustained almost entirely by a very large volume of defense contracts; 57.9 per cent of Frontier Airlines, Inc., of Nevada; the Variety Club Beverage Company of Ohio, and about 125 movie houses. It owns or has interests in approximately eighty other diverse enterprises.

The lawsuit, filed by the Justice Department in 1967 in Federal Court in Cleveland, Ohio, charged General Tire and three subsidiaries, including RKO General, with having conspired to violate the antitrust laws. Particularly, the defendants were accused of having engaged in reciprocal dealings in which they used their purchasing power "to coerce and persuade certain actual and potential suppliers of the defendants" to buy tires, advertising time on RKO General stations, and other products and services. On August 24, 1970, the Justice Department announced a proposed consent agreement in which General Tire and the three subsidiaries promised not to engage in such violations.

In the case of the four RKO General stations in California, the Commission once again renewed the licenses automatically, without requiring a hearing at which the conglomerate would have to show that renewal would serve the public interest.

In all five of the conglomerate merger cases—Fuqua Industries, Avco Corporation, the two Mormon Church proceedings, and General Tire—the performance of the Commission majority surely enhanced the credibility in such matters of Milton Friedman, the conservative economist. He has said that a governmental system cannot be devised "which will not be taken over by vested economic interests and exploited for the preservation and enhancement of their own wealth."[45]

The National Traffic and Motor Vehicle Safety Act of 1966 requires manufacturers of motor vehicles and of components to certify that their products meet applicable safety standards. In the case of tires the initial safety standards adopted by the National Highway Safety Bureau were those previously set by the tire industry itself. On a scale which is pathetically small because of a tiny budget, the Bureau contracts with testing laboratories to determine if tires which have been certified to meet safety standards actually do so. It was found that certain tires, including two particular models and sizes manufactured in a particular time period by General Tire and Rubber, blew out or otherwise failed compliance tests. In October 1969 General Tire avoided a possible civil action by paying an unprecedented penalty of $50,000. We do not pretend to know how the nineteen RKO General stations handled this news, but that is not, we believe, the essential point. A larger question is whether it is prudent to entrust decisions over news that can be so deeply involved with human life to the very corporations responsible for the hazard.

Ownership of communications media by giant diversified corporations raises problems that do not end with them, because they often are entwined with banks and other financial interests. In a report in 1968, the staff of the House Subcommittee on Domestic Finance cited numerous cases in which the trust departments of commercial banks hold (but do not own) large blocks of media stock.[46] Bank holdings were found in eighteen companies which together publish thirty-one newspapers and seventeen magazines while operating seventeen television and radio stations.

As of 1967, the staff found, there were director interlocks between a media owner and a bank in these cases, among others: Time, Inc.— Chemical Bank New York Trust and First National Bank of Chicago; Copley Press, Inc.—First National Bank of Chicago; Dow Jones Company, Inc. (*Wall Street Journal,* the *National Observer* and *Barron's*) —Morgan Guaranty Trust: A. S. Abell Company (*Baltimore Sun*)—Mercantile-Safe Deposit Company and Maryland National Bank; the *Hartford Courant*—Hartford National Bank and Connecticut Bank & Trust.

The staff listed cases in which a bank held sole or partial voting rights in the stock of media companies. In Baltimore, for example, Mercantile-Safe Deposit held sole voting rights in 27 per cent of the stock in A. S. Abell. In New York Morgan Guaranty held 4.1 per cent of the sole voting rights in Time, Inc., and 8 per cent in Dow Jones.

On the day the subcommittee staff report was issued, Thomas S. Gates, chairman of Morgan Guaranty Trust, said that his bank makes investment decisions "solely to achieve the best investment results for our trusts." If his bank's trust department "should confuse its investment decisions with other considerations," Gates added, "our punishment would be swift and sure. Our investment record would deteriorate. Our trust customers . . . would desert us. And our ranking . . . would slide from No. 1 toward the cellar."[47] Surely Morgan Guaranty has weighty responsibilities. As of 1967, its trust department assets totaled more than $16.8 billion, it held 5 per cent or more of the common stock in no fewer than seventy-two major corporations, and it had interlocking directorships with more than one hundred major corporations.[48] Surely, too, Gates was expressing sound fiduciary doctrine. But he was not necessarily expressing sound public doctrine about the First Amendment responsibilities of communications media in which his bank—or any other financial institution—has interests.

The dilemma can be readily illustrated. A bank has a director and stock interlock with a newspaper and with an airline. A story in the paper on airline safety might have an adverse result on the airline and a life-saving result for the public. Another bank has a similar interlock with a news magazine and a manufacturer of oral contraceptives. A story pointing out that the safety of the Pill was not demonstrated before marketing or, for that matter, long afterward, could lower the value of the drug company's stock while protecting women from avoidable blood clotting diseases. A third bank has a director interlock with a television network and with a large insurance company. A documentary on abuses in the field of auto insurance, again, could be adverse to the carrier but beneficial to motorists. One can produce long lists of examples of stories to show that a newspaper's or a magazine's or a network's connections with banks could not possibly have had any effect. Yet the situation is not one to produce tranquility. Such lists do not deal with the less tangible matter of stories that have *not* been done. And some may have noticed, as did the *Guild Reporter,* how various media handled the report of the subcommittee staff:

> The Baltimore Sunpapers, mentioned in the report, ran it on the financial page. The rival *News-American,* which was not involved, carried a banner headline on Page 1.
> The *Chicago Tribune,* also mentioned, carried it on the financial page. The uninvolved *Sun-Times* ran it near the front of the paper.
> *Time* magazine, another target, ran nothing. Newsweek, not mentioned, gave it a column.[49]

The *News-American,* a Hearst paper, may have overplayed the story, possibly for self-serving reasons. But stories of this sort are rare, and good exposure even rarer. Surely the zeal of the *News-American* was less deserving of criticism than the suppression by *Time,* or, for that matter, an underplay of absurd proportions in the *New York Times.*

Commissioner Nicholas Johnson of the FCC discussed the problem of bank involvement with communications media in testimony before the House Banking and Currency Committee. He told of the Taft Broadcasting Company, owner of sixteen radio and television stations many of which are in the nation's largest markets. The Bank of America in California held approximately 6.6 per cent of Taft's stock, and Bankers Trust Company in New York held 3.7 per cent. David Ingalls, chairman of the board of Taft, also is a director of the First National Bank of Cincinnati, the First Ohio Savings Association, the Ohio Valley Financial Corporation, and the Inter-Ocean Insurance Company in Cincinnati. Roger Drackett, another Taft director, is on the board of the Union Trust Company and the Equitable Insurance Company, both Cincinnati institutions.[50] The potentials here for investigative reporting of the banking, savings and loan, and insurance businesses may be apparent. They may be even more evident where a one-bank holding company *owns* news media. This is the case in Rocky Ford, Colorado, where the Rocky Ford Investment Corporation owns the Rocky Ford National Bank, a quarter interest in a trailer manufacturing firm, and the only two radio stations in town. In his testimony, Johnson noted that the licenses of the stations were recently routinely renewed at staff level in the FCC "with no mention of the bank ownership question."

Apart from involvements in media through ownership, trust holdings, director interlocks, and voting rights in stock, banks also have a potential to exert influence through loans which, the Commissioner testified, "may carry significant restrictions on the broadcaster getting the loan." The bank-owned media "may get very favorable credit," giving them an advantage over competitors. Johnson went on to say:

> Now, these are the types of potential abuses that give one pause in assessing bank control of mass media. The basic question is whether we as a society need or should permit the risk of these abuses. Those who argue that until abundant evidence of abuse is shown no action is needed really miss the point. Abuse is very hard to show—and there is no institution in our society that regularly examines the functioning of the mass media to determine whether these abuses occur. The line between "All the News That's Fit to Print" [the *New York Times* motto which, if the Fair Packaging and Labeling Act reached newspapers, would be outlawed] and "all the news that fits we print" is thin indeed; legitimate editorial judgment to include, alter or omit information is almost impossible to distinguish from similar decisions motivated by corporate economic self-interest.[51]

"It is difficult to believe that it is fear of government regulation which keeps broadcasting so sterile of opinion," Robert MacNeil, a former NBC newsman who now represents the British Broadcasting Corporation in Washington, said a couple of years ago. "Government regulation by the FCC does not appear to be nearly so effective in bringing broadcasters to heel as is the occasional direct interference of an elected official or the general awareness of being part of a business community with a large stake in the economy."[52]

In late 1969 an elected official, Vice-President Spiro T. Agnew, made speeches on the media in Des Moines, Iowa, and Montgomery, Alabama. Although the Vice President and President Nixon denied it, many in the media believed that the speeches were something very much like a

117

"direct interference" and were intimidating, especially to broadcast media dependent upon licensing by the FCC. Such suspicions were reinforced when Dean Burch, newly installed by Mr. Nixon as chairman of the Commission, called the network presidents to ask for transcripts of the commentaries on President Nixon's speech of November 3 on Vietnam. Burch, denying any intimidation was intended, said he simply wanted to get the transcripts swiftly. Although the Republicans did not yet have control of the FCC, it was noted that they would after mid-1970, when the term of Kenneth Cox, a strong friend of the public interest and, secondarily, a Democrat, expired. No one could prove that the purpose of the Agnew speeches was to scare broadcasters into behaving the way the Nixon Administration wanted them to behave, or, if you prefer, to make them, through public pressure, be fair.

In Des Moines on November 13 Agnew said that the networks have "a concentration of power over American public opinion unknown in history," that "we'd never trust such power . . . in the hands of an elected government," and that "it's time we questioned it in the hands of a small and unelected elite." There is, the Vice President said, "a tiny, enclosed fraternity of privileged men [network commentators] elected by no one" which uses a government-licensed monopoly to exercise inordinate power, sometimes unfairly and unwisely.

The foregoing is sufficient to indicate the nature of Mr. Agnew's complaints. There was of course some merit in them. But on balance they must be judged intimidating. In *The Selling of the President 1968* Joe McGinnis tells about a conversation during the presidential campaign with Frank Shakespeare, then a top adviser to Richard Nixon. The candidate was "down on NBC," Shakespeare said, especially because it used Frank Mankiewicz, press secretary to the late Senator Robert F. Kennedy, as a commentator at the Republican National Convention. Shakespeare said, "Do you know that at one point during the convention Mankiewicz made the comment that Nixon was 'half scared to death'? Half-scared to death. Can you imagine that? And then he compared Nixon to Harold Stassen." After a bit more conversation Shakespeare "began to smile" and said:

> "Now. Now listen to this. Here's what I thought I'd do. I thought I'd go to Walter Scott, the NBC board chairman—this would be in private, of course—and say, 'Here are the instances. Here are the instances where we feel you've been guilty of bias in your coverage of Nixon. We are going

to monitor every minute of your broadcast news, and if this kind of bias continues, and if we are elected, then you just might find yourself in Washington next year answering a few questions. And you just might find yourself having a little trouble getting some of your licenses renewed.' "

McGinnis said that "Shakespeare paused and smiled. 'I'm not going to do it because I'm afraid of the reaction. The press would band together and clobber us. But goddammit, I'd love to."[53] Mr. Nixon *was* elected. Agnew *did* make the speeches. Dean Burch *did* phone the networks.

But the press did not "band together and clobber us," even allowing generously for the protests that were made. What Agnew really was suggesting, as Nicholas Johnson said, was something very dangerous, a transfer of power "from a handful of men in New York to a handful of men in the White House."[54] The networks could have "clobbered" Agnew, but did not, had they called forceful attention to a simple fact: that it was *impossible* for the Vice President to reconcile his professed concerns about concentration of media power with his failure, and Mr. Nixon's failure, to stand up against the Pastore bill, then pending, which as has been noted would have guaranteed in perpetuity the triennial renewal of licenses held by the very networks the Vice President had savaged.

In Montgomery on November 20, Agnew commendably said, "And the American people should be made aware of the trend toward the monopolization of the great public information vehicles and the concentration of more and more power over public opinion in fewer and fewer hands." At the time, we were working on this book and that subject, and, we must say, nothing could have surprised us more than the discovery that the Vice President shared our concern. Agnew went on to mourn, as do we, the death of independent newspapers across the country and the fact that some survivors have "grown fat and irresponsible." He was not, clearly, alluding to those newspapers that, say, failed to report the hearings on the Failing Newspaper Bill at which the facts on media concentration were developed and laid out on the public record. He did not mention Copley Newspapers, whence came Herbert G. Klein, Director of Communications at the White House, or any of the newspaper chains which the Nixon Administration counts as allies. Instead he went after the *New York Times*. He made some specific criticisms which were so wildly inaccurate that the president and publisher of the *Times,* Arthur

Ochs Sulzberger, easily demolished them in the *Times* of November 21, 1969. For example, Agnew said that the *Times* "did not carry a word" the morning after three hundred congressmen and fifty senators signed a letter endorsing the President's policy in Vietnam. Actually, the *Times* *did* carry the story, in a later edition than the one home-delivered in Washington; and thereafter it cited the development in four separate stories published in a nine-day period before Agnew spoke in Montgomery.

The Vice President also attacked the Washington Post Company, saying it "holds control of the largest newspaper in Washington, D.C., and one of the four major television stations, and an all-news radio station, and one of the three major national news magazines (*Newsweek*) —all grinding out the same editorial line—and this is not a subject you have seen debated on the editorial pages of the *Washington Post* or the *New York Times*." Agnew was no more accurate about this—*any* of it— than he was about the *Times* and its handling of the letter from the legislators.

Washington, New York, and Boston are the only cities in the United States where there remain three daily newspapers each under separate ownership, as has been noted. In each city there is also a diversity of broadcast media—in Washington, four VHF and three UHF television stations and thirty-five radio stations. For Agnew to go to Alabama to attack the *Times* and the Post Company was "like going to Cairo to attack Arthur Goldberg," Senator Hart commented.[55] Agnew, in his speech, did not note that in Montgomery there is a newspaper monopoly. Neither did he acknowledge any of the examples of concentration that were surrounding him. In Alabama, Newhouse owns the dailies in Huntsville and Mobile, a TV-AM-FM group in Birmingham, and a CATV in Anniston. Not far away, Newhouse owns the dailies in New Orleans and Pasagoula, Mississippi. In Memphis, Scripps-Howard owns the dailies and a TV station. In Birmingham, Alabama's largest city, Scripps-Howard and Newhouse jointly operate the two daily papers.

It is not to be wondered that an audience in Montgomery, Alabama, had not seen the subject of monopoly journalism debated in the editorial pages of papers in Washington and New York which they do not read. But readers of the *Washington Post* saw the subject debated on August 22, 1967, in an editorial concluding that the Failing Newspaper Bill would "make the press beholden to the Government, and a beholden press is one whose freedom is surely imperiled." Readers of the *Times* saw the subject debated on March 13, 1969, in an editorial which said that the First Amendment "provides the press with no warrant for seeking exemption from the laws prohibiting monopoly." Thus Agnew happened to misrepresent the position of two of the extremely few newspapers that had the editorial guts to oppose the newspaper bill (so far as we could determine, the only others were the *Wall Street Journal,* the *New York Post,* and the *Louisville Courier-Journal*).

It was *impossible* to reconcile the concern Agnew professed over media concentration with his silence on the bill and the President's endorsement of it in the face of opposition from Mr. Nixon's own Justice Department. Not only, as noted in the Prologue, did the Department protest that the measure would shield "absolute monopoly," "flout the basic principles of free enterprise" and impair the "watchdog" relation of newspapers to government, but it would also, Justice said, invite applications from magazine and book publishers, movie producers, and others (who reasonably could expect newspapers not to criticize their efforts).[56] But news media ignored or blacked out these stunning inconsistencies.

The Agnew speeches, at best the product of carelessness and ignorance, did not produce genuine or constructive concern with the serious problems of concentration we have discussed here. The speeches did add to the popularity of the Nixon Administration by subtracting from the popularity of George C. Wallace, and by restraining robust media criticism of the President, especially as to the war in Vietnam. Rather than aiding the cause of diversity in the media, the Agnew speeches injured that cause, directly by intimidation and indirectly by ignoring the genuine threats to diversity in the broadcast and newspaper bills which then were pending. By failing to relate the speeches to the legislation, the media, made vulnerable by the elements among them that were seeking special favors on Capitol Hill, became accomplices of Agnew. The newspaper bill could become "the first step toward affirmative Government regulation of and interference with the press despite the First Amendment," Professor John J. Flynn, of the University of Utah College of Law, has said. "For the public will not tolerate the existence of such an important force in our society free of regulation."[57]

From a "Newsmakers" items in *Newsweek,* March 2, 1970:

"The Vice President is incredible," Tricia Nixon told UPI. "I feel I should write him a letter. He's amazing, what he has done to the media, helping it to reform itself. I'm a close watcher of newspapers and TV. I think they've taken a second look. You can't underestimate the power of fear. They're afraid if they don't shape up . . ."

What of the future? Senator Hart, in 1968, said that "the electronic laboratories of the nation will make it possible to have instantly available the collected wisdom of the world. There is no question in my mind that the home of the future will be connected to this vast supply of information either by wire or by microwave in some form of CATV system. Each house will have a unit capable of receiving an electronic display or print-out of the document. The pipeline to the home will be the method by which the printed and electronic forms of communication will be delivered." Hart went on to sound this warning:

> This technology can be handled so that new competitive voices can be created and material can be available at low cost, or it can lead to monopolization and high prices. Today there is great effort by media corporations to gain control of this means of transmission.
>
> The many newspapers which are buying CATV systems in their markets seem convinced that by controlling this distribution system they can make it impossible for anyone to start a competing newspaper.
>
> Related congressional developments are the attempts to extend the duration of copyrights and to have the computer storage of a book or other material considered a "use" within the meaning of the copyright law. This might make it possible to insist that to get a book you use the hardware of the electronic company which has the copyright.[58]

Hart also warned that telephone companies were trying to gain control of the CATV pipeline. Early in 1970 the FCC took a couple of useful preventive steps. The Commission ruled that phone companies cannot own CATV systems in areas in which they provide local phone service. Except in rural or sparsely populated areas, phone companies presently supplying CATV service, whether directly or through an affiliate, in their own phone-service areas must cease doing so within four years. Three months later, on June 25, the Commission commendably went much further. It ordered the networks to dispose of any CATV systems they may own within three years and ordered television stations to dispose of any cable systems they may own in the same locality. These orders affected at least CBS and NBC and the numerous station ownerships that have an interest in an estimated 38.7 per cent of existing

CATV systems. At the end of 1969 these numbered about 2,400. In addition, the FCC proposed that newspapers and radio stations be barred from owning CATV systems in the areas they serve.

A staff report to the National Commission on the Causes and Prevention of Violence said, "If the ultimate in concentration of media control ever arrives, there is no reason to believe that government control would not be better. At least the government is apt to be more responsive than a self-perpetuating corporate management with such tremendous power. Today we are moving in that direction and one thing seems clear: the policies of the First Amendment can no longer be secured simply by keeping the government out."[59]

3 TOLLS ALONG THE HIGHWAY

Consumers in an economy moving swiftly down the road of concentration must pay numerous tolls. One of the reasons is that concentration frustrates traditional tools for fighting inflation. The attempts to halt the escalating inflation of the late 1960s clearly show this.

One of the conventional anti-inflation tools is "fiscal policy." The government brought it into play with the 1968 income tax hike and the surtax. The desired result was a drop in consumer demand, and that result was achieved. Another traditional tool is "monetary policy." The Federal Reserve resorted to this when it tightened the credit supply. Again, the desired result was achieved: interest rates went up and the amount of money available for loans was curtailed, at least for small borrowers.

And so, the economy was "cooled off." By May 1970, "fiscal policy" and "monetary policy" had worked so effectively that hundreds of thousands of workers were newly unemployed, industrial production was below 1969 levels, and corporate profits were down.

But something was grotesquely wrong: the conventional tools were not having the desired effect on prices. The theory was that slackening demand would force prices down. But they were going up. Thus the consumer found himself in the worst of all possible worlds. His taxes were higher. His interest rates, for a home mortgage or other credit, were out of sight. Jobs were hard to find. His savings were declining. The stock market was down. And yet prices were up.

Why? Because, simply, conventional wisdom is useful only in a truly competitive economy. However, our economy is significantly concentrated. In such an economy a lessening of demand may have the paradoxical effect of forcing prices upward.

Many basic industries, such as steel, use "target pricing." The corporation may set a profit goal, say a 15 per cent return on investment. As demand falls, the corporation may raise prices in order to maintain the target profit. At the same time, companies may cut back production. By thus reducing supply to meet demand, supply and demand are kept in equilibrium—without cutting prices. Generally, this kind of behavior can take place only in highly concentrated industries, which, as we have seen, include many basic ones. These industries also utilize follow-the-leader pricing. One company sets the price and the rest follow in lock-step fashion. Smaller companies either go along or face destruction by the giants.

The techniques of administered pricing—pricing by industry rather than market forces—have been well documented, particularly in twenty-four volumes of hearings by the Senate Subcommittee on Antitrust and Monopoly under the leadership of the late Senator Estes Kefauver. Nevertheless, our government leaders have refused to acknowledge very basic facts of life: traditional methods of dealing with high prices will not work in a highly concentrated economy. Indeed, they may lead instead to higher unemployment, higher taxes, higher interest rates, and higher prices—all under the banner of fighting inflation. Stefan H. Robock, Professor of International Business at Columbia University's Graduate School of Business, summed up the problem:

> The Nixon Administration is assuming greater structural flexibility in the economy than actually exists. Overall demand is being reduced, but in many key industries that are quasi-monopolistic, the reaction has been to increase prices and try to maintain profits through increased sales.[1]

President Nixon would have been well advised to heed the final report of his predecessor's Council of Economic Advisors:

> Furthermore, concentrated industries often maintain prices in the face of declining demand, reducing output instead. As demand fluctuates among products over time, prices may rise where demand increases but fail to decline when demand decreases. This results in an inflationary bias, which might be substantially reduced by greater competition.[2]

But a concentrated economy tends to insulate giant corporations from true competition. The staff of the Cabinet Committee on Price Stability, in its report of January 1969, used the term "discretionary power" to describe the ability of concentrated industries and firms to escape the signaling of the forces of supply and demand. It said:

A free market economy relies on private decision makers who are constrained by market forces to translate the forces of supply and demand into the "appropriate" prices. We cannot be certain, however, that appropriate price behavior will occur if firms have considerable discretion in setting their prices. . . . Discretionary power enables firms to raise prices in order to pass along increases in costs. Sometimes firms charge higher mark-ups than the long run structural characteristics of an industry allow. Although ultimately such mark-ups will be eroded, this can be delayed if the industry leaders are content to operate with excess capacity. Firms with discretionary power may also increase prices even when industry demand is falling.[3]

Testifying in September 1969 before a House subcommittee, Joseph A. Califano, Jr., who was an assistant to President Johnson, provided stark examples of how concentrated industries have used "discretionary power" to raise prices. Since January of that year, he said, copper producers had increased prices no fewer than four times, for a total increase of 24 per cent. In the same eight-month period, zinc producers raised prices three times, for a total increase of 11 per cent. In the first six months of 1969, the price of gasoline went up 5.3 points on the Consumer Price Index, an annual rate of increase of 9.4 per cent. In the first seven months of 1969 the price of steel mill products went up 4.5 points on the Wholesale Price Index, an annual increase of 7.1 per cent. This was about equal to the percentage increase during the entire eight-year period from 1961 through 1968. In 1969, there was a 4.8 per cent increase in the price of rolled steel sheets—the steel which goes into every automobile and virtually every appliance Americans buy. Califano testified:

> With this latest whopping hike, steel price increases for 1969 will far outstrip the increase during the past eight years. In the first seven months of 1969 aluminum ingot has increased 4 points on the wholesale price index, an annual rate of increase of 7% . . . The examples are taken from basic industries with administered prices, *where price increases fan out across thousands of products that the individual buys* and where the basic industries are so concentrated that even large corporate purchasers have virtually no control over the price they pay.[4]

Califano suggested a return to "jawboning," or, more realistically, threats (yet another phrase, more sophisticated but less descriptive, is "incomes policy"). Presidents Kennedy and Johnson had brought such pressures to hold down prices. Obviously they recognized, at least intuitively, that concentrated markets don't work the way competitive ones do. As already noted, President Nixon, at the very outset of his administration, made it clear—with immediate and calamitous consequences—that he opposed "jawboning." Eventually even some of Mr. Nixon's supporters in the media became disenchanted. In an editorial appearing in the spring of 1970, the *Washington Evening Star* said:

> Pressures are increasing for the Nixon administration to take a more active role in achieving the goal of an economy combining non-inflationary growth with high employment. At the moment there is no real growth, joblessness is rising, corporate profits are falling and inflation continues at a canter if not a gallop. The original ailment, inflation is the focus of several proposals for more direct government action. The most influential backing for some form of "incomes policy" to discourage excessive price and wage increases came recently from Arthur F. Burns, Chairman of the Federal Reserve Board. . . .
>
> "Incomes policies" include the wage-price guideposts of the Kennedy-Johnson years, presidential "jawboning" against inflationary actions and government watchdog activities to point the finger at erring industries and labor organizations. Such measures are gaining adherents in and out of the government as inflation continues strong despite slowing business and rising joblessness. . . .
>
> President Nixon and his chief economic advisers oppose "jawboning" and similar efforts on philosophical and practical grounds. Such policies intrude on the free market, they feel, and are not effective on a long-term basis.

President Nixon and his economic advisers are correct that such policies would intrude on a "free market." These policy-makers are correct also that they are not effective on a long-term basis. But the point is that the basic assumption is wrong. There is no "free market" in many of our basic industries.

Finally, in June 1970, President Nixon acknowledged for all practical purposes that many markets are not "free" when he announced his own toothless version of "jawboning," the "inflation alerts" with which he would try to hold prices in line. The best measure of his success came with the announcement of Bethlehem Steel on January 11, 1971, of increases of 12.5 per cent in the prices of plates, structural shapes and other items which together comprise almost 18 per cent of shipments by the steel industry as a whole. With this, the administration tried to devise something more intimidating than an "inflation alert."

The "something" proved to be a meeting five days later between Mr. Nixon's economic advisers and representatives of the largest firm in the steel industry, United States Steel. The result was an announcement by that corporation that it would limit its price increases on the same items to 6.8 per cent. Within three days the predictable follow-the-leader syndrome set in. The other steel makers dutifully raised *their* prices by 6.8 per cent, and Bethlehem dutifully cut back its increases to 6.8 per cent. The administration then praised the industrial statesmanship of United States Steel—as if an increase of 6.8 per cent somehow represented a sacrifice in the public interest. The entire episode served to reinforce a fundamental point: government pressures cannot adequately cope with price increases by concentrated industries, significantly because they cannot replace authentic competition.

Assume that a company actually incurs higher costs. A new union contract, say, has raised wages more than they will be offset by increased productivity. Or the prices for raw materials or credit have gone up. Even so, the company cannot automatically pass along the higher costs to consumers—provided it has authentic price competition from other firms. In such a situation, the company must be concerned with what its rivals will do about their own higher costs. Some competitors, for example, may decide that greater sales volume will overcome the cost increases and therefore will hold prices steady, in hopes of getting a larger share of the market. Further, manufacturers' costs are never exactly the same. Some have more efficient management, others have greater productivity, still others have introduced more efficient new technology.

However, even though the costs of all manufacturers in an industry are not the same, they must all meet the same market price. "Meeting the competition" in a competitive industry means precisely that—if your competitor cuts his price, you cut yours in order to stay in business.

In concentrated industries, for all practical purposes, prices also may be identical. But companies in concentrated industries do not compete on prices; they simply match them. When your competitor raises his price, you raise yours by the same amount, explaining your action as "meeting the competition." When this was explained to the Senate Antitrust and Monopoly Subcommittee in 1957 by Roger Blough, then head of U.S. Steel, it was reported by *Time* magazine as a definition of competition which would delight all lovers of *Alice in Wonderland.* Alice, as we know, is ageless. Ford Motor Company in October 1970, a time of declining demand and increasing foreign imports, announced it was raising its prices another $14.00 to "match" General Motors. In a competitive industry, GM would have been likely to respond by cutting prices. But, of course, GM did no such thing.

Cost increases therefore are less likely to be absorbed in a concentrated industry than in an industry where price competition exists. Indeed, in times of inflation, prices in concentrated industries may rise more slowly than in competitive industries. The distortion occurs as demand declines. Then prices will drop in the competitive industries. But in the concentrated industries, prices generally will not respond to changes in demand. Rather, they will keep going inexorably upward with the participants' matching each upward movement of the others—unless, of course, a serious recession occurs, in which case even firms in a concentrated industry may start shading prices. Firms in concentrated industries prefer instead to engage in non-price competition—in advertising or other areas where the benefit to consumers is negligible.

One need not pursue the excellent academic studies of lockstep pricing in many concentrated industries to see how it works.[5] The *Wall Street Journal* is easier reading and makes the point. Articles in the *Journal* for the years 1964 through 1969 describing price changes, most of which the paper faithfully reports in the major industries, show that in copper, steel, aluminum, chemicals, containers—in one concentrated industry after another—the pattern is depressingly repetitive.

First, one company announces that because of rising costs and other factors it is raising its price, say, 4.2 per cent. The *Journal's* story then reports that other manufacturers are sympathetic and are studying the move. Within a week all other members of the industry will have raised their prices. The percentage of increase will be the same. The stated reasons also will be the same.

Two examples should make the point. The *Journal* had this headline on a story on April 9, 1970:

> KAISER ALUMINUM TO BOOST PRICES ONE CENT A POUND
> RISE SECOND SINCE OCTOBER; FIRM CITES HIGHER COSTS;
> MOVE STUDIED BY OTHERS
> "INCREDIBLE," SAYS ONE BUYER

The story:

> Kaiser Aluminum & Chemical Corporation, which led the last successful
> round of aluminum price boosts, announced that it again will increase the
> price of primary aluminum ingots and its fabricated aluminum products
> one cent a pound. . . . In Pittsburgh, Aluminum Company of America, the
> country's biggest producer, said it would have no immediate comment on
> the Kaiser move. In Richmond, Virginia, second-ranked Reynolds Metals
> Co. said Kaiser's move is "eminently justified." The company added, how-
> ever, that it would study the increase before making any announcement
> of its own prices. . . . "The upward moves are necessary to help offset the
> effects of continuing inflation and rising costs that are putting an increasing
> pressure on adequate profit levels." Mr. Ready [T. J. Ready, Jr., Kaiser's
> president] said yesterday in announcing the price increase. . . . Against these
> factors, it is not possible for the industry to produce an appropriate return
> for its stockholders without compensating price increases which are
> realistically related to the existing economic situation, Mr. Ready said.

Mr. Ready, you will note, said that "industry" is not able to produce
an appropriate return for its stockholders, rather than "Kaiser Aluminum." This also is a common pattern. Company executives tend to think
not in terms of individual firms, but in terms of their common "industry."

The story said further that in commenting on the price situation in
the industry, a top executive of one of the country's largest independent
aluminum fabricating operations described Kaiser's price move as "incredible, just amazing." He said: "Kaiser's fabricating business is very
bad right now, it will be interesting to see if Alcoa follows, because their
mills are down too." His interest was short-lived. On April 13, just four
days later, a *Journal* headline read: "Six Producers Follow Boosts in List
Prices on Primary Aluminum." The story:

> Six more producers raised list prices on primary aluminum ingots and
> products fabricated from aluminum, following similar moves by the three
> largest U.S. aluminum companies and the U.S. subsidiary of the biggest
> Canadian producer.

After reporting the amount of the boost, the story continued:

> That's the same as the boost initiated by Kaiser Aluminum & Chemical
> Co. last Wednesday, and followed Thursday by Aluminum Co. of America,
> Reynolds Metal Co. and Alcan, Aluminium Ltd.'s U.S. subsidiary.

TOLLS ALONG THE HIGHWAY

The second example involves the steel industry. If it raises prices, other industries soon do so, too. This is because steel is a component of so many basic products.

On April 6, 1970, this headline appeared in the *Wall Street Journal*:

STEEL MILLS SEE SLUGGISH SECOND QUARTER;
SHIPMENTS PUT AT 5%–10% BELOW YEAR AGO

Directly below was a story with this headline:

FIRMS FOLLOW PRICE BOOSTS

The story said in part:

> More steel companies joined in price increases.
>
> National Steel Corporation, the fourth biggest mill, said it will raise prices $9 a ton, effective April 15, on hot rolled bars. . . . This is in line with other producers.
>
> Youngstown Sheet & Tube Co., a subsidiary of Lykes-Youngstown Corp. . . . posted increases of from $4 to $14 a ton on various continuous weld, seamless and electroweld standard and line pipe. The increases are similar to one made on Thursday by U.S. Steel Corp. and are effective with shipments May 1.

The magnitude of these increases could be traced in the Bureau of Labor Statistics Wholesale Price Index for "Steel Mill Products." The index showed steel wholesale prices moving up in fifteen of eighteen months beginning at the end of 1968.

One aspect of this inflation in steel prices illustrates the political muscle of important concentrated industries. From 1959 through 1968 the lack of competition in the domestic industry was offset to some extent by price competition from foreign producers; the power of the price leaders to raise prices was tempered by the fact that every attempt to exercise this power turned more customers to foreign sources. The industry, however, was able to persuade its friends in government to negotiate a pair of agreements effective January 1, 1969—with the Japanese and the European Coal and Steel Community—by which shipments to the U.S. were cut by 20 per cent in 1969 and limited as to growth in 1970 and 1971. With foreign competition controlled in this way, the industry was free to effect greater price increases between January 1969

131

and June 1970 than it had in the entire preceding decade. Of course, the January 1971 increases made the situation much worse.

The *Wall Street Journal* might have had its own pages in mind when Lindley H. Clark, Jr., asked on March 20, 1970, "Why Don't Companies Start Cutting Prices?"

> In recent testimony before a Senate Banking Subcommittee Leif H. Olson, Senior Vice President and Economist of New York's First National City Bank, pointed to a steady drop of industrial production, a slowdown in orders, slackening in inventory accumulation, a decline in corporate profits, along with a reduction in demand for labor since last October. "I can assure you," he said, "that the conditions which give rise to price increases are being significantly eroded and many manufacturers and retailers have become keenly aware of the fact in the past few months."

In the face of this kind of situation, the headline "Why Don't Companies Start Cutting Prices?" is indeed fair. The story continued:

> Progress on the price front is always uneven in an economy that is both large and largely free. When sales slow down or decline some businessmen will at first try to raise prices to preserve profit levels, others hold prices to keep their share of the market, while still others cut prices to try to expand their sale. Given a continuation of a reasonable amount of financial restraint, however, a growing number of businessmen will come around to price concessions.

The point, of course, is that in a concentrated industry—where firms price as an industry unit rather than individually—it may take a deep recession to produce those "price concessions."

It was fashionable, in the *Wall Street Journal* articles surveyed, for industry leaders to blame increasing prices on labor costs. Dr. Willard F. Mueller, former chief economist of the Federal Trade Commission, has explained the problem this way:

> Organized labor also may cause seller inflation if it is successful in demanding wage increases that exceed increases in productivity [generally technological advances which reduce the number of labor hours needed to do a particular job]. This is usually called "cost push inflation," pushing up of production costs by labor. While this kind of labor-originated cost push

inflation could theoretically occur in any industry with powerful labor unions, it most often occurs in those industries in which strong labor unions bargain with concerns having substantial market power. First the large profits of such firms entice labor to ask for a bigger piece of the pie, second, labor believes that management of these concerns has sufficient pricing discretion to pass on higher wage costs to consumers. Moreover, because concerns with significant market power do in fact have the discretion to pass on wage increases, they are more likely to grant wage demands exceeding productivity increases than are the concerns which do not have this power.[6]

It may well be that the role of this cost-push inflation has been greatly exaggerated. Senator Philip A. Hart, in a prescient speech in January 1967, pointed out that after-tax corporate profits had jumped by $20 billion yearly, or 88 per cent, over the base years of 1957 to 1959. Consumer prices had risen 14 per cent. However, manufacturing labor costs, which take productivity into consideration, had gone up less than 2.5 per cent. Hart said:

> This indicated clearly enough that higher prices have little relationship to higher costs and prices also no longer bear a clear relationship to demand. . . . Competition in many of the nation's basic industries has diminished to the point where one corporation sets prices to meet a target profit and others follow along. This lock-step pricing means that price competition is not at work to force the sharing of high profits with the consumer in the form of lower prices. American industry is riding the crest of the greatest profit boom in history. At one time, a 10% return on net worth was considered good, now 20% is not uncommon. Yet prices go up very often in industries that are operating far below productive capacities, indicating the price hike is not in response to an overwhelming demand exceeding an insufficient supply.

More than three years later, on October 14, 1970, the *Wall Street Journal* reported: "Labor costs, far from soaring, are only inching upwards nowadays. Some analysts, in fact, predict labor costs may soon begin to decline."

A study by Victor B. Fuchs, an economist at the National Bureau of Economic Research, confirmed the less-than-vital role labor unions play in increasing prices in most industries. As reported in the *Wall Street Journal*:

The stereotype of big unions commanding big pay increases and causing ultimately big wage boosts just doesn't jibe with the facts.

The story, under the headline "Analysts Say Prices Rise Fastest in Fields Lacking Labor Unions," continued:

. . . Instead, the economic record shows that the biggest price increases are coming where highly skilled professionals are needed to meet sharply rising demand, or where it's difficult to offset higher wage gains with automated equipment, or where factors are involved that have little at all to do with labor costs.[7]

Monetary policy—making credit harder to get and raising interest rates—also can lead to higher prices. Medium-sized or smaller firms may not be able to pay the higher interest rate even if they could get the tight money. This group includes most builders of residential homes. However, the big corporations, because of their tie-ins and links with the big lenders, are able to get first crack at the high-priced money. In addition, they often can pass on the charges in the form of higher prices. One especially onerous result of higher interest rates, of course, is the increased cost of mortgage money, so that a consumer must pay more in order to own a house, if he can buy one at all. High interest rates also have cut back the number of housing starts, a sector of the economy where demand does indeed outstrip supply, thus raising the cost of owning a home. To some people, this may be "cooling off the economy." But to the consumer, it means increasing the price for a basic necessity.

Indeed, in regulated industries, which account for 15 per cent of the nation's income, monetary and fiscal policies intended to be anti-inflationary almost insure that prices will go up, not down.

In 1969 and 1970, the Interstate Commerce Commission allowed three increases in railroad shipping rates in order to offset higher taxes and credit costs, among other factors. This, of course, will be reflected in the ultimate price of the goods shipped.

The Civil Aeronautics Board allowed hikes in air fares while passenger travel fell off. In other words, as demand dropped—in keeping with the purpose of monetary-fiscal policies—prices rose.

And utilities, regulated by either state or federal authorities, were seeking to raise their rates to offset the 10 per cent surtax Congress imposed in 1968. The additional costs go into the rate base, and, generally, friendly utility regulators grant higher rates to absorb the higher costs.

TOLLS ALONG THE HIGHWAY

Senator Lee Metcalf, (D–Mont.) as reported in the *Congressional Record* of June 1, 1970 said:

> Electric, gas, and telephone utilities are trying to add another inflationary $2 billion onto utility bills before the public learns how well the companies did last year, and how well they could do this year without rate increases.
>
> None of the Nixonomists at the White House, Budget Bureau, or Council of Economic Advisers mentioned the inflationary impact of high utility bills and the pending requests for another $2 billion.
>
> Current utility reports indicate profits will stay at their record, inflationary level, or even increase, unless the facts are disclosed and publicized promptly, and lax regulators are forced by the public to do their job.

The antitrust laws were passed for the purpose of compelling firms to act competitively instead of monopolistically. They have fallen short of complete success. This reflects not on the laws but rather on lack of enforcement. If the Constitution is a charter for political freedom, the Sherman Act, our basic antitrust law, is a charter for economic freedom. One knowledgeable commentator has said:

> The principle of the Sherman Act is as endearing and fundamental as the notion of due process of law. It speaks to the perpetual problem in the organization of all societies, namely, how shall power be distributed and controlled. As the Constitution of the United States concerns itself with the distribution and control of political power, the Sherman Act addresses itself to economic power. In principle, both documents seek a maximum dispersion of power consistent with the marshalling of our spiritual and material resources.[8]

Toward the end of the nineteenth century, vast business combinations known as trusts had come to dominate much of the nation's economic life—and much of its political and social life, as well. There were trusts in oil, in steel and lead, in salt and sugar, in meat and whiskey. The public became intensely hostile. Great outcries were heard against the evil practices associated with vast business combinations, such as fixing prices, dividing markets, restricting production, eliminating competitors, and restraining and monopolizing trade. Concern grew in Congress about the rapidly increasing concentration of economic power in the trusts and the consequent rapidly diminishing freedom of economic opportunity available to smaller enterpreneurs. Finally, in 1890, Congress adopted the Sherman Act, the original antitrust law.

Section 1 of the Sherman Act makes it unlawful for two or more persons to restrain trade by such means as price-fixing, group boycotts, or division of markets. Section 2 makes it unlawful for any person, alone or with others, to monopolize or conspire to monopolize any part of the country's interstate commerce. Under certain circumstances, even attempts to monopolize are proscribed.

One section, then, prohibits the means by which trade is monopolized and the other prohibits the end result, monopoly.

The Clayton Act, another antitrust law, as passed in 1914 and amended in 1936 and 1950, deals with rather precise business practices, such as price discrimination, exclusive dealing and tie-in arrangements, mergers, and interlocking directorates. Generally, by restraining mergers and predatory conduct, it seeks to nip monopoly in the bud.

Thus, the Clayton Act speaks in terms of practices the effect of which *"may be"* to substantially lessen competition or "tend" to create a monopoly, while the Sherman Act deals with the ultimate result of such practices.

The antitrust laws are the basic weapons against concentration of industrial and political power. But, in an economy that has been allowed to become highly concentrated—in good part through non-use of those laws—they also are potential weapons against inflation. They are designed to create the competitive markets without which monetary or fiscal policy cannot be effective, as we have attempted to demonstrate. They also avoid the large bureaucracy and other problems inherent in wage and price controls.

In 1966, the *Economic Report* of the Congressional Joint Economic Committee stated:

> Achieving full employment without inflation necessarily centers attention primarily on monetary and fiscal policy. It is easy to overemphasize the overall approach and neglect the promotion of competition and the prevention of monopoly. In this endeavor our antitrust laws play a key role. . . . Antitrust policy can also play a key role in implementing the wage-price guideline program for preventing inflationary price increases. It is no coincidence that the most serious problem areas in achieving these goals have been the concentrated industries where prices are administered and do not respond freely to the forces of supply and demand.

The phenomenal growth of conglomerates has intensified the difficulties of fighting inflation. If companies in particular concentrated industries can partially insulate themselves from the marketplace, what happens when these same companies meet each other in *scores* of industries? The power that such companies exert in one industry may then be exerted in several. Their ability to isolate themselves from supply and demand factors thus increases.

The economic report on conglomerate mergers prepared by the Bureau of Economics of the Federal Trade Commission describes at length the methods by which conglomerates insulate themselves from the marketplace. They may engage in business reciprocity. This means simply that instead of a decision to buy the best product at the lowest price, a decision is made on the basis of "I'll scratch your back if you'll scratch mine." The larger the corporation and the more diverse its products, the greater the opportunity to engage in reciprocity. It was such a possibility that led *Fortune* magazine, in a 1965 story entitled "A Customer Is a Company's Best Friend," to raise the possibility of a United States economy completely dominated by conglomerates happily trading with each other in a new kind of cartel system.

The Federal Trade Commission report on corporate mergers describes another method by which conglomerates dictate competition: "conglomerate inter-dependence and forbearance." This means that if one conglomerate meets another in many markets, each takes it easy as far as competition is concerned, lest the other retaliate. According to the report:

> The simplest form of conglomerate interdependence probably involves pricing decisions. Firms that meet as competitors in many markets are likely to regard each other with greater deference than if their decisions were constrained solely by what happened in a particular market. The resulting mutual forbearance in making pricing decisions results because conglomerate rivals may hesitate to gain an advantage in one market by price cutting lest their conglomerate rivals retaliate in others.[9]

Further, a conglomerate with large profits in one industry, where it may be in a monopoly position, is able to subsidize a less profitable operation in another industry. Thus, it further protects itself from market forces.

In addition, the follow-the-leader pricing which we have seen in highly concentrated markets is also likely to occur even in less concentrated markets where the same firms continuously meet each other. Be-

137

cause a firm powerful in one market may be less influential in another, it must be judicious about any pricing activity that would stir a competitor to react adversely.

Consumers have paid a staggering price for the general failure to apply the antitrust laws to conglomerates, concentrated industries, and the anticompetitive practices in which they engage. Price-fixing for many years was almost as common in major industries as lockstep pricing is now. The significance of this cannot be overstated: During price-fixing periods, it has been estimated that prices tend to be at least 35 per cent higher than in periods when prices are not rigged; and costs tend to be artificially raised.[10]

The antitrust laws condemn price-fixing out of hand. Yet administered pricing and lockstep pricing have the same effect on consumers. By simply playing follow-the-leader, rather than conspiring in the traditional sense, the firms that engage in administered pricing and lockstep pricing get around the antitrust laws.

One authoritative source, writing in 1964, placed the resulting loss to consumers at approximately 6 per cent of national income.[11]

The editors of *Antitrust Law and Economics Review* have written:

> The economic costs—and the social costs that go hand in hand with it—of maintaining the industrial status quo in this country have now reached intolerable proportions. Various estimates have been made, for example, as to the annual cost of monopoly and related industrial crimes to the American consumer, including Senator Hart's recent estimate that "easily 30 percent of all consumer spending is wasted. And, I would not say 'nay' if someone theorized that the percent was as high as 40." In other words, $174 to $231 billion consumers spend each year may buy no product value. Monopoly pricing in one form or another accounts for the bulk of this consumer loss, particularly price-fixing conspiracies and the economic collusion or non-independence inherent in the high concentration ratios found in certain segments of American manufacturing.

The editors pointed out further:

> Empirical studies by economists have copiously demonstrated that, beyond a certain point on the concentration scale—generally, when the 4 largest hold 50% or more of the market—competition ceases to function effectively and the price paid by the consumer tends to rise higher and higher above

the level that would have prevailed had that market been competitively structured.[12]

Fully 25 per cent of American manufacturing fits these criteria.

The magnitude of these monopoly costs, whether they be $174 billion or $231 billion, best can be appreciated when comparative figures are used. For instance, the country's total crime bill, according to the FBI, came to $32 billion in 1969. The Vietnam war's total price tag, according to the Defense Department, was $27 billion in 1969. Eliminating poverty in the United States ($3,000 minimum income for all families) would cost $11 billion per year.[13]

In 1970 a Federal Trade Commission staff report, entitled *The Influence of Market Structure on the Profit Performance of Food Market Manufacturing Companies,* concluded:

> Profit rates are significantly higher in food manufacturing industries where the top four firms account for more than 40% of the total shipments as compared to industries with lower levels of concentration. Industry profit rates tend to be still higher when significant advertising barriers to entry exist. Extensive diversification has a negative effect on profitability and the absolute size of a firm has no significant independent influence on firm profitability.

Where such high levels of concentration exist, therefore, the lack of true price competition removes pressures on management to translate high profits into lower prices.

One anticompetitive device forbidden by the antitrust laws is the tie-in sale—if you want *one* of my products, you have to take another. Many of the 76 million consumers who have purchased $76 billion in credit life insurance in this country do not even know they have done so. But almost any time a loan is made by a bank, an insurance company, or other lending agency, the borrower is asked to sign a form insuring the loan, so that if he dies, the bank or other lending institution is assured that it will get its money. While there are incidental benefits to the borrower, he is in fact paying for an insurance policy to protect the lender. It would be a rash borrower indeed who would say to the lender, "I'll take the loan, but I'll get my credit insurance elsewhere." Hearings by the Senate Antitrust and Monopoly Subcommittee demonstrate only too clearly that unless the borrower takes insurance from the lender, he will not get a loan.[14] The annual cost of anticompetitive practices in the sale of credit life insurance has been estimated at $216 million.[15]

The consumer who takes out such a loan usually does not know that generally the insurance carrier gives back to the lender a portion of the premium. This may amount to 60 per cent. As a result, a reverse form of competition in the industry has become standard: instead of seeking out the lowest-priced insurance for the borrower, the lender seeks out the highest-priced. The more money the borrower pays, the larger the rebate to the lender.

Even the Bank of America, the nation's largest, has engaged in such practices. Prior to 1965, the Bank of America was selling such insurance to its customers at thirty-nine cents per hundred dollars of coverage. This reflected the fact that the Prudential Insurance Company was willing to sell such insurance to the Bank of America at thirty-seven cents per hundred. This premium rate produced a satisfactory profit for Prudential and a sufficient markup for the administrative expenses of the bank. However, at the bank's behest, Prudential raised its price to sixty-one cents per hundred. The result was that in 1965, on premiums of $2,247,000, Prudential paid back to the bank, as dividends, $1,340,000. And in 1966, of about $2,500,000 in premiums, Prudential's dividends to the bank amounted to about $1,200,000. This was approximately 45 per cent of the actual premiums collected. It is an example of how competition can be turned upside down when one party has the power to tie in the sale of its product—in this case, credit—to another party who needs the service.

It is also one more example of how the consumer pays when competition is thwarted and antitrust laws are not vigorously enforced.

Economic power tends to overwhelm the smaller producer and business man and to present them as victims of inexorable progress. Indeed, it has become fashionable in some academic circles to treat derisively the activities of the small producer by stating that the "days of the Mom and Pop store and the backyard foundry are gone forever."

The backyard foundry may be a relic of the past. But small manufacturers in plastics, reinforced concrete, electronics, metal fabrication— nails, wire, etc.—and hundreds of other products should be the wave of the future. Given a fair competitive chance, their vigor will increase.

Those who argue that the smaller producer no longer has a place in the modern complex economic structure are thinking in the obsolete context of the first industrial revolution which burst upon the Western world in the late eighteenth century. The factory system then began to replace the skilled craftsman, and there were the beginnings of mass production. But, the *new* industrial revolution, now upon us, has resulted from the development of the new breakthrough technologies, such as the computer.

These technologies make the smaller producer not merely relevant, but also an important factor in any industrial complex. If the smaller producer has not been able to secure a greater share of the market, it is not because of any inherent disability, but because concentrated power stands in the way of his success.

Competition, after all, requires competitors, and in sufficient numbers. And it is the smaller competitors that may keep the larger ones competitive. Nevertheless, smaller manufacturers tend to be absorbed or cowed by the large conglomerate, not because they lack efficiency, but because they lack power.

The vital difference between power and efficiency sometimes becomes blurred.

The difference can be illustrated by the following example. Suppose a group of law graduates at the State Capitol for bar examinations are handed boxing gloves and told to slug it out, with the understanding that only the 60 per cent left standing at the end will be licensed to practice law. The strongest, of course, would become lawyers. And, in a sense, that would be an efficiency—but not a useful one. Physical power, not ability, would decide who enters the ranks of the legal profession. This is comparable to what has happened to many smaller, efficient producers in our society.

The same techniques of power which insulate the conglomerate from the marketplace also can destroy the smaller enterprise as a competitor, or make it an ineffectual competitor.

Advertising discounts for the conglomerate make success in consumer goods industries a rarity for the smaller, single-line company. Its product may be superior, but its dollar buys only a whisper; the conglomerate's dollar buys a shout.

Reciprocity—I'll scratch your back if you scratch mine—also devastates the smaller producer.

The aforementioned *Fortune* article concluded:

Trade relations [reciprocity], while helping big companies can hurt little ones. A big company, after all, constitutes in itself an important market for a great many products. Between giants, the awkward danger that one company or the other will come to depend too much on reciprocity is lessened. General Tire's Trade Relations man, for example, says frankly that his work moves most smoothly when he deals with companies as large and as diversified as his own. Thus, trade relations between giant conglomerates tend to close a business circle. Left out are the firms with narrow product lines. As patterns of trade and trading partners emerge between particular groups of companies, entry by newcomers becomes more difficult.[16]

The practices have been examined and condemned in the Federal Trade Commission's *Economic Report on Conglomerate Mergers* in congressional hearings and in antitrust cases. Apparently, however, giant companies are willing to accept the antitrust risk because of the benefits available to them from such practices. But this provides no solace for the smaller producer who can't understand why his lower price for a good product gets no takers from the giant corporation.

How reciprocity works was described in Senate Antitrust and Monopoly Subcommittee testimony involving the Bank of America's excursion into the credit life insurance business. As noted earlier, Prudential Life was the underwriter. In turn, Prudential reinsured a portion of the business. Reinsurance is usually undertaken to spread a risk. Prudential, however, has assets of over $26 billion. On the face of it, it would seem that a $26 billion company could cover the credit life sales of the Bank of America amounting to approximately $2 million or $2½ million a year.

At an Antitrust Subcommittee hearing, Kenneth C. Nichols, senior vice president of Prudential, was asked why his $26 billion company reinsured with Aetna Life and Casualty, Metropolitan, and Occidental Life, which are much smaller companies. He replied, "Because the Bank of America instructed us to do that. Including percentage." When asked what motivated the instruction, Nichols replied, "You will have to ask the Bank of America."[17]

Kenneth V. Larkin, vice president of the Bank of America, at a later hearing,[18] was asked just that question. The colloquy with the subcommittee counsel, one of the authors, follows:

142

MR. COHEN. One last question. In discussing re-insurance, you state "these carriers have given us good service and have established business relationships with us over the years."

By "these carriers," I assume you mean the ones that you directed Prudential to re-insure with, is that correct?

MR. LARKIN. Yes.

MR. COHEN. This was no lack of confidence in Prudential?

MR. LARKIN. Oh, certainly not. Certainly not.

MR. COHEN. What kind of business relations are you talking about?

MR. LARKIN. Well, I guess the relationship between banks and insurance companies covers a wide range. They carry deposit balances [interest free] with us. We on the other hand will sell off real estate loans to them. In fact, California I would say was built as much on moneys that were poured in by insurance companies, you might say foreign imports from the East and other States, into California as was generated by our own savings and loans and banks. We have an active mortgage selling activity of the banks so that we make real estate loans and then sell them to long-term investors so that we may use those dollars over and over again, else we might get frozen in. So quite often with certain of the large insurance companies, we have programs whereby on occasion, if they like what they see, and this is purely optional, they will buy an attractive loan or buy one large loan that covers an office building. So there are just a great variety of services that flow back and forth. And then, too, a bank as large as ours with some 30,000 employees has a number of insurance requirements, such as the benefits program of the bank. It covers many types of insurance, accidents, casualty, loss insurance, all the things that a bank does with an insurance company. These create relationships between banks [and insurance companies] . . .

MR. COHEN. Would you say, then, you are using your re-insurance program in a way that as you say "will not offend these other insurance companies with whom you have some mutual business relations"?

MR. LARKIN. I would say we do it to keep friends in the insurance industry.

The point is clear; only the largest banks can afford to direct the large flow of reinsurance money to insurance companies that, in turn, will cause them to favor the bank with deposits and other business.

Another club over the smaller producer's head is the ability of the conglomerate to subsidize its operations in one industry where it faces his competition from its profits in another where it does not.

This is a tactic against which the smaller producer, generally limited to one industry, cannot compete. Subsidization in less elegant form was practiced by most of the early robber barons—the Jay Cookes, Jay Goulds, Andrew Carnegies, J. Pierpont Morgans, the Astors, the Vanderbilts, and others. When faced with competition, they slashed prices to the bone. They either bought up a beaten competitor or ran him out of business.[19] They thus won the market for themselves—and were free to raise prices to monopoly levels.

Here is how it operates almost a century and a half later. Roy E. Kumm, chairman of the board of the G. Heilemann Brewing Company, La Crosse, Wisconsin, described the tactics being used to destroy one efficient, small-sized brewery after another. He told the Senate Antitrust and Monopoly Subcommittee in 1966 that within several years, five brewers would sell most of the beer in this country, not because they are more efficient, but as he put it, "because they have a ruthless disregard for honest competition."[20]

This colloquy in hearings of the subcommittee summed up the problem:

MR. COHEN. Based on your experience in the industry, when the big breweries go into say five counties and they cut this price to the bone—or as you have, I think, expressed it, below their cost or whatever it might be—and they have driven out these other [independent] breweries, do they still maintain the price after their competition is gone from that area or does it go back up again?

MR. KUMM. It will go back up. . . .

MR. COHEN. Your suggestion is based on what has happened in other areas that you have observed—that after the big breweries have gone in with these unreasonably low prices—below cost prices—and have driven out the small competitors, the price then goes back up primarily to where it was before; is that right?

MR. KUMM. Yes.

MR. COHEN. This is the kind of economic power that you are primarily objecting to.

MR. KUMM. If they would not move area by area, if they would move all over, I think that they would find themselves with economic problems themselves. It is the concentration here and there. By that I mean in an area, off, and then another area. This moving around is the dangerous part.

MR. COHEN. In other words, picking areas where there are smaller competitors or regional competitors, going into that area, cutting the prices to the bone, driving out these competitors, then raising the prices again and going to another area and repeating the same pattern; is that what you are saying?

Mr. Kumm. Right.

M. H. Robineau, president of the Frontier Refining Company, supplied the subcommittee with this example of subsidization or predatory pricing:

Let's take Continental out in our territory. In supplying Utah, they supply from refineries in Billings, Montana. Between there and Utah geographically is the Yellowstone National Park. It is a much shorter haul to the Park than it is to Salt Lake and it costs money to haul those products. Yet the price in the Yellowstone National Park stands alone where they have an exclusive with the Department of the Interior. There is no independent, or anybody else, and at times, when the same gasoline was being sold to the consumer in the Salt Lake market at 22.9 and 23.9 cents a gallon [where they have competition] it was being sold at a shorter haul basis, lower delivery cost basis in Yellowstone Park for as high as 40 cents a gallon, and that is what happens when competition is eliminated, and that is not good for the consumer in the long run.[21]

Francisco Fernandez, President of the Puerto Rico Atlas Yeast Corporation, attempted to enter the market in Puerto Rico for baker's yeast, which is used in all bread produced in this country. He told the subcommittee that the yeast business in the United States has since 1900 been a *de facto* monopoly dominated by Standard Brands, Inc., and since 1927, Anheuser-Busch. (Technology is not a factor in the yeast industry. The entry costs are low.) Fernandez said that countless small yeast manufacturers have been put out of business after a series of maneuvers which were a disgrace to the industry. He stated:

Although there had been no increase in yeast prices in Puerto Rico for 5 years and all costs of yeast manufacturing had risen considerably, one month before we started to produce yeast Standard Brands cut the price of yeast to the largest consumer about 14 percent (in Puerto Rico only). About one month later Standard Brands increased the price of yeast one cent per pound, in the entire continental United States, this despite the fact that the yeast sold in Puerto Rico and the eastern U.S. continental seaboard was produced in the same factory in New York. . . . Standard Brands cut the price of yeast to not all, but to all of certain classes of quantity use consumers in Puerto Rico. They "gerrymandered" their price so as to hurt us.[22]

145

The same tactics have been used to drive independents out of the food industry, petroleum industry, fabricating industries and a host of others. Thousands of pages of Congressional hearings document this.[23]

The smaller businessman who has competitors that also are his suppliers faces a situation known as dual distribution. It is yet another weapon available to economic power when it wants to squeeze out any one of less than giant size.

Dual distribution exists in the petroleum and fuel oil industries, copper and steel fabricating and a host of others. An independent steel fabricator, say, buys steel from a giant producer and processes it into fencing or nails. However, the giant also processes steel into fencing or nails. If the giant decides to squeeze the independent, he has but to raise the price of the steel and drop the price at which he sells the finished products. Generally his total profit remains the same, because he is taking money from one pocket and putting it into another. This may go on until the independent fabricator is driven to the wall. Then the company—in control with competition disciplined—is freer to charge the prices it wants.

The testimony of David Coleman, president of the Coleman Cable & Wire Company of River Grove, Illinois, at the Hart Subcommittee hearings tells how dual distribution has worked among the 320 manufacturers of wire and cable:

> They range in size from small businesses, who do less than $1 million per year, to large manufacturers who do as much as $250 million per year. They are all dependent upon the copper producers, who consist mainly of Phelps Dodge and Anaconda and Kennecott. These 3 same companies also manufacture wire and cable in competition with the remaining 317 manufacturers and in essence control the destiny and the power of life and death over the entire industry. In times when the supply is tight they control and allocate the supply as they are presently doing, using a climate of "shortage" and "tight supply" in order to improve their own position and to eliminate competition to their manufacturing facilities. When the supply is plentiful, they have been known to sell some finished products merely for the price of copper contained therein plus the bare cost of fabrication, thereby precluding the independent manufacturer from participating in those particular areas of the business.
>
> In the present market they have cut back the copper supply to the independent fabricator to practically zero as in our case, and in other cases

to varying degrees, while at the same time they have increased their own productivity and profits by approximately 60 percent.

By controlling copper manufacturing, they have the ability to capture certain markets almost at will.[24]

We now have completed our review of some of the methods the powerful use to discipline the weak. These tactics, it should be emphasized, enable the big to get bigger by frustrating genuine competition. Competitors are either driven out or become afraid to compete. Thus economic power strangles economic freedom. The consumer is the principal loser. His options are narrowed. He is forced to pay prices that are set at monopoly rather than competitive levels.

Labor unions also feel the heel of the giant conglomerates. But, unlike smaller producers, they may have enough power to react in kind.

The meaning of the conglomerate merger movement to the labor unions has been well expressed by Joseph P. Molony, Vice President of the United Steelworkers of America, AFL-CIO:

> Our members suddenly find established rights threatened in these mergers. Their unions are faced with concrete, day-to-day problems of protecting the transfer rights, job security rights, and pension rights of our members and a host of other administrative problems. We are also faced with the disturbance of established bargaining relationships when, for example, an employer with whom we have dealt for years suddenly finds itself gobbled up by a conglomerate and must adopt the labor policies of the new parent company which are totally different from the policies to which both parties have become accustomed and with which both have learned to live.

The heart of the labor movement, of course, is collective bargaining. Yet how does one collectively bargain with a conglomerate?

> We find we are no longer bargaining with valve manufacturers or pump manufacturers. Instead, we are bargaining with banks, utilities, railroads, and above all, with multi-plant, multi-product, multi-union conglomerate companies.
>
> Our concern with large conglomerate corporations is not merely that they are large. We are also concerned with the social and economic aspects of conglomerates as they affect our union. It is the effects of such mergers on our Union members and on the communities in which they live that are

147

our gravest concern. We know from our own experience with conglomerates that they pose serious threats to our collective bargaining structure and to the welfare and jobs of our members.

A union's ultimate leverage is the strike. But how does one strike a company which manufactures a wide variety of products that cut across many industries, particularly when many different unions may hold bargaining rights at different plants of the corporation?

These industrial empires are spread over such a broad spectrum of different industries that it is hard to hurt them with a strike in any one segment. If a union shuts down one industry line, the conglomerate can continue to make vast profits in another division. If there are related facilities at widely-scattered plants, even in the same industry, operations can be shifted to another operating plant in an effort to weaken the union at a struck plant.

If we are to bargain successfully, and if our picket lines are to be effective, we must coordinate, bargain together and, if need be, strike together, whether it involves several locals of the same international union or locals of several international unions. How can we effectively strike at the Huntingdon Machine Division of Bonney Forge and Foundry, a subsidiary of the Miller Mfg. Company, which in turn, is a subsidiary of Gulf and Western Industries; or at the Joan Bean Division of the FMC Corporation in Tipton, Indiana where we have 104 employees? We cannot. The big conglomerates here involved could take a strike at these or any other single plant of the company indefinitely and the parent company would not feel any real economic pressure.[25]

The union, in the face of the new problems resulting from conglomerate mergers, could not be expected to sit idly by. It has not. Molony said: "If the companies we deal with expand into many product areas, the obvious answer is for unions to move with them. This we are doing."

These efforts have acquired the descriptive name of "coordinated bargaining," a phrase that Jack T. Conway, while director of the AFL-CIO's Industrial Union Department, illuminated when he asserted a need for

the formation of a new "superstructure" connecting individual unions into a single unit for negotiating with a conglomerate corporation or industry. While this wouldn't require actual merger of the unions, it would provide a structure with its own revenue and its own strike fund, designed to balance the power held by giant corporations.

He saw this, however, as but the first step toward conglomerate unions: "What we may need is the creation of *conglomerate unions* to deal with the power of the conglomerate corporation today."[26] [Emphasis supplied.]

And so we may face labor conglomerates as well as industrial conglomerates. One is reminded of the prophetic words of Senator Estes Kefauver:

> The increased concentration of economic power is dooming free enterprise. The present trend of great corporations to increase their economic power is the antithesis of meritorious competitive development. It is no accident that we now have big government, big labor unions and big business. The concentration of great economic power in a few corporations necessarily leads to big bureaus in the government to deal with them.[27]

The Economic Report on Corporate Mergers of the Federal Trade Commission commented:

> Although the future and ultimate implications of coalition or coordinated bargaining are not yet clear this reaction to the growing conglomeration in American industry demonstrates again that the impact of centralized economic power, as the Congress feared in 1950, can reach beyond product markets to affect more general and wide-reaching economic relationships.

The question is, how does the general public fare in an economy dominated by big business, big government, and big labor? How can it fare well if, as we have shown, power attracts what it cannot run over? Power seldom countervails. Instead, those who have it tend to work out mutually acceptable accommodations.

We do know that unions tend to think more and more in the same terms as the large corporations with which they deal so closely. Thus, when the Federal Communications Commission announced in 1968 that it was going to examine the rate structure of the American Telephone and Telegraph Company, it was the Communication Workers Union that took out a full-page advertisement condemning the FCC proposal.

The Steel Workers Union has stood shoulder to shoulder with the industry on preventing foreign imports, as have the Textile Workers with the textile industry. Yet, when imports are limited, competition is lessened, and the consumer again is the one who must pay the price.

The specter of a single "establishment" dominated by giant government, giant business, and giant labor is moving closer to reality. It is a structure in which the consumer will have to pay more and more for less and less. At the same time he will lose more of the ability to improve his own economic and political condition.

4 THE POLITICIAN AS AN INVESTMENT

The concentration of economic power, opinion power and political power creates a sort of closed loop. Politicians must raise money from corporations in order to pay the networks the enormous cost of television time. Corporate advertisers call the network tune. And the networks must curry favor with the successful politicians to assure their franchise. The open society seems to be closing—not by conspiracy, but by this mutual dependence.

—KINGMAN BREWSTER, JR., president of Yale University, December 6, 1969.[1]

This chapter and the three that follow develop a few political-economic facts. It costs money, more all the time, to seek elective public office. The money is obtained from where it's at, which is primarily large corporations and financial institutions. Their campaign "contributions" are really not that at all; they are investments in licenses to govern the government, or, if you prefer, to translate economic power into political power. Being prudent, the investors take out insurance by, for example, investing in both political parties at once. The investors get all that money can buy from candidates and parties, which is not to say they get *everything* they want. As compared with corporations, those who cannot afford such investments, or who are unorganized to make them—the poor, the blacks, Puerto Ricans, Spanish-speaking and Spanish-surnamed Americans, Indians, workers displaced by advancing technology and retreating resources, much of the middle class, even professional men —generally get bad deals. "Under the circumstances, it is utterly amazing that the public makes out as well as it does," Senator Russell B. Long (D–La.) once said. "Even so, the Government pays out many billions of dollars in unnecessarily high interest charges; it permits private monopoly patents on over $12 billion of Government research money annually; it permits billions of dollars of Government money to remain on deposit in banks without collecting interest; it permits overcharging by many concerns selling services to Government; it tolerates all sorts of tax favoritism; it fails to move to protect public health from a number of obvious hazards; it permits monopolies to victimize the public in a number of inexcusable ways. It provides for too much tariff protection to some industries and too little to others."[2]

To concentrate economic power is to magnify the power of giant corporations to make government behave in ways such as those deplored by Senator Long—to make a bad situation worse. One has but to think of the major oil companies, which have so rigged the tax structure as to pay federal income taxes at a rate comparable with that paid by a laundry worker. In the five years 1963 to 1967, for example, Standard Oil of New Jersey paid at an average rate of 5.2 per cent, Texaco 2 per cent, Gulf 8.4 per cent, Mobil 5.2 per cent, and Standard of California 2.5 per cent. In all, they paid $1 billion, or 4.9 per cent on before-tax net profits of $21 billion. "They paid foreign governments more than five times as much," Ronnie Dugger has pointed out.[3]

And partly through acquisitions the power of such oil companies—possibly the power to go on forever taxing almost everyone else—has increased. The thirteen years ending in 1969 saw 20 oil companies acquire 226 other companies and 18,737 filling stations. The chemical division of Standard Oil of New Jersey grew to be one-third as large as E. I. du Pont de Nemours.[4]

Senator Albert Gore (D–Tenn.), who lost his bid for reelection in 1970, and Representative Sam M. Gibbons (D–Fla.) called attention to the acquisition by Continental Oil Company of Consolidation Coal, which sells more coal than any other company in the world. Internal Revenue Service rulings bore decisively on this merger. In the article already quoted, Ronnie Dugger said the net effect of the rulings

> was that the oil company paid no income taxes at all on its $460 million of profits from operating the coal company—profits with which it was buying the company—but *was* permitted to deduct its $128 million in coal-mining costs. The coal company paid no taxes on its income from the sale because it was liquidated under a certain section of the tax code. "I can foresee a situation, not far off," Gore warned, "when we will no longer have

an independent coal industry. We may well have all major energy sources—petroleum, coal, uranium—under the control of a very few powerful corporations."[5]

In a later review, one of the authors and Robert K. Warner demonstrated that interfuel competition in the energy field, which is vital to long-term consumer protection, was being swiftly eroded. For example, they said in a *Washington Post* article on August 23, 1970, Standard Oil of New Jersey had become one of the two largest holders of coal reserves and, at the same time, a principal operator in uranium, the newest competitor to coal and oil. Of the twenty-five largest oil companies, all have interests in natural gas, which may be inevitable, but at least eleven have significant interests in coal as well; and the industry as a whole acounts for at least 25 per cent of coal production. Six of the ten largest oil companies have interests in *every* other fuel.

The *Post* article was especially concerned about uranium, because nuclear fuel is expected to produce more than half of all electricity by about 1990. Obviously, if oil companies control uranium as well as rival fuels used to generate power, they can set prices so as to make Americans pay billions of dollars more for electricity. The article reported that at least eighteen oil companies have invested in the production and processing of uranium; that the petroleum industry holds 45 per cent of all known uranium reserves, makes more than half of the new discoveries, and already accounts for one-sixth of uranium production, and that two firms, Kerr-McGee (which owns 23 per cent of total uranium milling capacity) and Atlantic Richfield, do all of the conversion of "yellow cake," the uranium concentrate that results from milling. The conversion produces UF6, a compound used in enriching uranium for use as nuclear fuel.

In the production of atomic power, however, neither the oil companies nor any other private enterprise can control one crucial process: the enrichment of uranium by increasing its content of the fissionable isotope U–235. This work is done at government-owned gaseous diffusion plants at Oak Ridge, Tennessee, Paducah, Kentucky, and Portsmouth, Ohio. In November 1969 President Nixon announced that he intends to sell the plants, which cost the taxpayers $2.3 billion, "at such time as various national interests will best be served." Senator George D. Aiken, the Vermont Republican, saw only Mr. Nixon's and the oil industry's interests being served. "The President probably feels indebted to those who helped elect him," he told the *Post* in a brutally candid interview. Thus, economic power was translated into political power which, in turn, worked to expand economic power still more. Even before the major oil companies reached out for all energy sources they could make Presidents feel, in Aiken's word, "indebted." Where do they go from there?

Senator Aiken, who said he believes that sale of the gaseous diffusion plants would be "the most advanced step toward private control of the nation that has ever occurred," is one of the few men on Capitol Hill who has spoken out on the political dangers of concentration. Another is Representative Henry S. Reuss, a Wisconsin Democrat who is a senior member of the Joint Economic Committee. After the Federal Trade Commission announced in July 1968 that it was going to make an in-depth investigation of the effects of conglomerate mergers, Reuss asked the FTC to consider their political implications. Let the Commission try to determine the extent to which mergers that concentrate economic power also concentrate political power, he proposed. In a letter to FTC Chairman Paul Rand Dixon, Reuss also said:

> If, for example, a conglomerate (or any large corporation) has significant holdings in a majority of the congressional districts in this country, is it likely to have an inordinate influence over congressional action?
>
> I realize that this will not be an easy question to answer. However, you might begin by determining how many corporations have significant hold-ings in more than 35-40% of the congressional districts in the country. You might then pick out certain legislative issues which are of direct importance to these corporations and try to determine whether there is any correlation between a Congressman's favorable vote in committee or on the floor and a corporation's holdings in his district. I am sure that additional approaches will suggest themselves as the investigation proceeds.[6]

Reuss was not a man lacking the imagination necessary to sug-gest some instant additional approaches, such as a study to establish whether there is any correlation between the interests of presidential campaign contributors and actions affecting those interests taken by the White House and Executive agencies. Neither was he a man to be sur-prised when Dixon, while granting "that increasing concentration of economic power . . . may also lead to concentration of political power," ruled out a study of the problem. The chairman was regretful about this, but said that the FTC had, to begin with, "very limited resources" to make a conglomerate merger study and had no additional appropriation for the one it had decided to make; tactfully, he did not add how wildly implausible it would be to expect Congress to appropriate money for a Commission investigation with such an explosive potential.

Reuss replied with a press release, which was one of his own very limited resources. Warning against "a nationalization of parochialism," he gave an example of the kind of question that troubled him. "If a conglomerate owns a small radio manufacturing firm on the West Coast, as well as a great number of unrelated businesses throughout the country, is it likely to pressure Congressmen in every district where it has substantial holdings to vote for high tariffs on Japanese radios?" The word "pressure" may be lacking a bit in subtlety. In a congressional district in which jobs are scarce, for example, a plant might be built—but then again it might be built elsewhere. A contribution may be made to the campaign of an incumbent—but possibly to his challenger. A company airplane might just be flying from National Airport in Washington to a congressman's district most weekends—but it might have to be used on more urgent business.

Former President Dwight D. Eisenhower, troubled about election financing, said in 1968 that

> we have put a dollar sign on public service, and today many capable men who would like to run for office simply can't afford to do so. Many believe that politics in our country is already a game exclusively for the affluent. This is not strictly true; yet the fact that we may be approaching that state of affairs is a sad reflection on our elective system.[7]

In 1968, the same year in which the General expressed his concern, $100 million was spent to elect a President, by estimate of the nonprofit, nonpartisan Citizens' Research Foundation of Princeton, New Jersey. An additional $200 million was estimated to have been spent by all other candidates and committees at all levels of government. The grand total, $300 million, was half again as much as was presumed to have been spent in 1964.[8]

The $100 million presidential estimate included the pre-convention expenses of all candidates for nomination for the Presidency, as well as the cost of the conventions to party organizations and delegates. The various committees which worked for the election of Richard M. Nixon,

Hubert H. Humphrey, and George C. Wallace and their respective running mates actually reported expenditures of about half as much, or $50.4 million. The acknowledged expenditures for congressional candidates came to $19.7 million. Such figures grossly understate the reality, porosity having been built deliberately into the reporting laws. They do not, for example, deal at all with the cost of primaries for federal elective offices, although these often are of pivotal importance and incite bigger spending than the general elections. Neither do they reflect spending by campaign committees operating within a single state.

After the 1970 congressional elections a team of nine *Washington Post* reporters went to ten states to investigate campaign spending, with especial attention to the costs of television. In a roundup story on November 22, they offered abundant evidence that new spending peaks had been reached. In North Dakota, for example, Representative Thomas S. Kleppe (R) spent $300,000 in a losing effort to unseat Senator Quentin N. Burdick (D), who spent about $150,000. But Kleppe's spending was *five times* as large as it had been in 1964, when he had made his first attempt to defeat Burdick. "These campaigns are just too expensive," Burdick told reporter Nick Kotz. And Kleppe said, "This whole thing is getting completely out of hand."

In Tennessee, Don Oberdorfer reported, Senator Albert Gore's campaign organization in the primary and general elections spent in excess of $500,000—"more than *five times as much* as in either of Gore's 1958 or 1964 campaigns for re-election." [Emphasis supplied.] Gore lost to Representative William E. Brock III, a Republican whose reported spending of more than $1 million was twice that of the incumbent and at least triple that of any previous GOP candidate in Tennessee.

In New York State, estimated spending in the senatorial races totaled $5.3 million. Of that, James L. Buckley, who was elected on the Conservative Party ticket, reported about $2 million, Richard L. Ottinger, the Democrat, $2 million, and Charles E. Goodell, the Republican incumbent, $1.3 million. Goodell told reporter Haynes Johnson that he had been outspent from all sides and was left with debts of $400,000. "We were always on the verge of a blackout because of lack of money," he said. Johnson said that Goodell "candidly describes how he raised his money. An executive finance committee of fifteen wealthy, influential men was able to call other wealthy men able to give from $1,000 to $10,000 apiece."

156

But lest one be awestruck by the combined spending by these senate candidates of $5.3 million, although it is doubtless a tidy sum, a couple of points need to be taken into account. One is that Governor Nelson A. Rockefeller reported that he alone had spent $1.5 million more, or $6,794,627, in winning reelection. A second is that actual spending exceeds reported spending by uncertain but sometimes vast amounts. Thus estimates of Rockefeller's spending, Johnson reported, "range from $10 million up to $20 million." And Ottinger, who also was able to draw upon a family fortune, actually spent about $4 million—double the estimated sum—in his losing effort, Johnson said.

Whether the grand total of spending was $300 million or $900 million in 1968, and whatever it was in 1970, neither adds nor detracts significantly from the essential point, that politics is largely a game for those who are affluent, who want to become affluent, or who, at the expense of the public interest, are prepared to use the affluence of special interests to obtain and perpetuate themselves in elective office. "A vote in the U.S. Senate," former Senator Albert Gore has said, "is of such great effect and influence that any person who is willing to sell his soul can have handsome financing for his campaigns."[9] By eliminating political payoffs to contributors, true reform would achieve economy in government on an almost unimaginable scale. Yet, Senator Long has observed, such reform is what "the robber barons will oppose the most. . . . Investments in this area can often be viewed as monetary bread cast upon the water to be returned 1,000-fold."[10]

Few men in public life could claim better credentials to discuss investors in government than Russell Long. He is not only a senator, and not only a former Majority Whip, but he is also chairman of the Senate Finance Committee, which writes the tax laws. In an interview with one of the authors, he volunteered the remark that he is referred to as "the darling of the oil and gas industry."[11] This was generally known, but it was refreshing to hear Russell Long himself say it. On Capitol Hill his relentless determination to protect the oil industry from fair taxation and fair competition, such as removal of the oil import quota system would help bring, is unsurpassed. Long receives a large income from his own oil and gas interests. In the years 1964 through 1969 this included almost $330,000 which was tax-free by reason of the oil depletion

157

allowance.[12] That allowance he at all times, as chairman of Senate Finance, has tried to protect. He denies there is a conflict of interest with the rather curious argument that his financial interests are "completely parallel" with those of the state of Louisiana—as if the interests of millions of Louisiana consumers are identical to those of a relative handful of gas and oil producers.

At the same time, Long has shown a sustained and commendable concern about the generic problem of campaign financing. Some of his statements on the subject have been so abrasive and bold as to infuriate Senate establishmentarians. When he was a lonely defender of Senator Thomas J. Dodd (D–Conn.) against a censure resolution for the misuse of campaign funds, for example, Long charged that half the members of the Senate Ethics Committee "couldn't stand the investigation Senator Dodd went through." Going further, he suggested the same would be true of "half the Senate."[13] Later, he proffered a formal apology. He described the members of the Ethics Committee, headed by Senator John Stennis (D–Miss.), as "six of the finest members who have ever served in this body." The faint ambiguity which a cynic might see in that was not diminished by an unusual burst of iffiness: "If I made a mistake and if I did wrong by saying what I said, I am here to offer them a public apology. If I have any complaint of this body it is that their standards are too high."[14] In the same year in which all of this happened, 1967, Long made a highly revealing speech on the Senate floor about campaign financing. Here are excerpts:

> Most campaign money comes from businessmen. Labor contributions have been greatly exaggerated. It would be my guess that about 95 percent of campaign funds at the congressional level are derived from businessmen. At least 80 percent of this comes from men who could sign a net worth statement exceeding a quarter of a million dollars. Businessmen contribute because the Federal Corrupt Practices Act prohibits businesses from contributing. . . .
>
> A great number of businessmen contribute to legislators who have voted for laws to reduce the power of labor unions. . . .
>
> Many businessmen contribute to legislators who have voted to exempt their businesses from the minimum wage.
>
> Businessmen contribute to legislators who have fought against taxes that would have been burdensome to their businesses, whether the tax increase was proposed as a so-called reform, a loophole closer, or just an effort to balance the Federal budget.[15]

THE POLITICIAN AS AN INVESTMENT

In October 1966, there was a tax measure which became so loaded down with special-interest riders that it became known as the "Christmas Tree" bill. For the benefit of the processers of clam and oyster shells that are used in cement and chicken feed, Long tripled the depletion allowance, to 15 per cent. Senator Vance Hartke (D–Ind.) undertook to provide, in the mordant phrase that came close to being included in the report of the Senate Finance Committee on the bill, "vital aid for a dying industry." This was the manufacture of hearses which, George Lardner, Jr., reported in the *Washington Post,* is concentrated in Indiana and Ohio.[16]

> Power company officials [Long continued] contribute to legislators who vote against public power. . . .
>
> Bankers, insurance company executives, big moneylenders generally contribute to legislators who vote for policies that lead to high interest rates.
>
> Many large companies benefit from research and development contracts which carry a guaranteed profit, a so-called fixed fee of about 7 percent of the amount of the contract. Executives of such companies contribute to those who help them get the contracts or who help make the money available. . . . Research contractors contribute to legislators who vote to permit them to have private patent rights on government research expenditures.
>
> Drug companies are often able to sell brand-name drug products at anywhere from twice to 50 times the price of identical nonbranded products for welfare and Medicare patients if the companies can prevail upon government to permit their drugs to be prescribed and dispensed by their private brand names rather than by the official or generic name of the product. Executives of drug companies will contribute to legislators who vote to permit or bring about such a result.
>
> Many industries are regulated. This includes the railroads, the truckers, the airlines, the power companies, the pipelines, to name but a few. Executives of regulated companies contribute to legislators who vote to go easy on the regulation, and ask no more questions than are necessary about their rates.
>
> Companies facing threat of ruinous competition from foreign sources have executives who contribute to those who help protect them from competition by means of tariffs and quotas.
>
> Many industries are subsidized . . . the merchant marine, the shipbuilders, the sugar producers, the copper producers and a host of others. Executives in such industries contribute to those who help keep them in business.
>
> This list is merely illustrative. . . . Merely by assiduously tending to the

159

problems of business interests located in one's own state, a legislator can generally assure himself of enough financial support to campaign effectively for re-election.

The Corrupt Practices Act of 1925 makes it "unlawful for any national bank, or any corporation . . . to make a contribution or expenditure in connection with any election to any political office." In no way does this deal with root causes—mainly, the desire and need of candidates for money, and the desire and need of the sources of money to make sound political investments. That being so, Senator Long has argued, the law may well have made "the conditions which lead to corruption worse rather than better."[17]

The law permits a donor to give up to $5,000 to one political campaign committee—but puts no limit on the number of committees that can receive contributions. This is but one item in a catalogue of subterfuges which the law was designed to permit while assuring the unwary that all is well. In 1968, Howfield, Incorporated, a Los Angeles advertising agency then under investigation by the Internal Revenue Service, disclosed several practices used by corporations to contribute indirectly to political campaigns. Here is a summary of the practices:

●Corporate payments of cash bonuses to employees with the understanding that a portion of the funds will be used as a political contribution to a selected candidate and the remainder for payment of taxes on the entire "bonus."

●Corporate salary payments with the understanding that a specified portion of the salary is to be used for political contributions at the direction of the corporation.

●Corporations loaning employees to work in political campaigns while still paying their salaries.

●Corporations paying professional fees to attorneys with the understanding a portion of the fee is to be contributed by the attorney to a specified political candidate.

●Corporations which rent billboard space on a yearly basis turn space over to candidates without charge during the month preceding an election.

●Corporations purchasing copies of non-political books . . . the profits for which go to a party or candidate.[18]

Later, Randolph W. Thrower, commissioner of IRS, listed some additional evasive devices. These included arrangements by corporations to pay fake invoices that are supplied by a candidate's advertising agency, to pay for phony consultations, to let a candidate use company airplanes, credit cards, and hotel suites, and to give sometimes genuine legal business to law firms solely because of their associations with office-seekers and officeholders.

Senator Eugene R. McCarthy failed to pay in full some of the substantial bills he ran up during his bid in 1968 for the Democratic presidential nomination. "Various McCarthy committees owed A.T.&T. $305,000 for telephone service, but wound up paying only $75,000," two political financing experts, Herbert Alexander, director of the Citizens' Research Foundation, and Harold B. Meyers have pointed out. "American Airlines, which was owed $285,459, got $141,903." They correctly said that a corporation which settles a politician's bills for less than value "is in effect making an indirect campaign contribution."[19]

Now and then, the use of a subterfuge is detected and exposed. One case involved the Chrysler Corporation and T. E. Metevier, whose disarming title is manager of legislative relations. He once mailed eight hundred dollars in checks, signed by Chrysler executives stationed around the country, from company offices in Highland Park, Michigan, to the chairman of the Georgia State Democratic Committee. Another batch of checks, in about the same total amount, went out to the Georgia State Republican Committee. The practice was disclosed when the checks intended for Democrats inadvertently were addressed to Republicans, and vice versa.[20]

Another subterfuge is the appeal for contributions to political slush funds made by executives of a corporation rather than by the corporation itself, in order to stay within the letter of the Corrupt Practices Act. On rare occasions a resentful subordinate, taking care to be sure that he cannot be traced as the source, puts a letter of appeal into the hands of someone who will make it public. Such letters have certain common characteristics. They are marked, for example, by an emphasis on the "voluntary" nature of the operation. There are pious assurances that a refusal to give will not impede one's climb up the executive ladder— no, not even for one second. The amount of the suggested gift is based on income. There are Olympian disclaimers of narrow partisanship: the money will be disbursed evenhandedly to Democrats as well as Republicans. However, the recipients, candidates for state as well as federal offices, are never identified; neither are the sums the candidates get divulged. Above all, there is a pervasive unctuousness in which the private interest of a company, and of the industry of which it is a part, is presented as inseparable from the public interest.

On August 7, 1970, two vice presidents of Sterling Drug, Inc., J. N. Cooke and J. H. Luther, sent a letter to the 525 executives of the firm earning fifteen thousand dollars or more. They asked for donations of a half of one per cent of salary but with a top of two hundred dollars; the indicated minimum was thirty dollars. "Please make your personal contributions payable to 'cash' and send it along in the attached 'Personal & Confidential' envelope," they said. "Our many *personal* thanks." Cooke, on whose personal letterhead the appeal was made, told one of the authors, "We have nothing to hide." That being the case, would he then identify the legislators who are getting the money? No, he wouldn't. "We don't tell our employees that," Cooke said. Were the donors not entitled to know where their money went? "We are in a much better position to judge," he said. In a separate conversation with a reporter for the *Washington Post,* Luther, who is Sterling's associate general counsel, had something else to hide: he refused to discuss whether a filing for the fund had been made with the Clerk of the House of Representatives under the Corrupt Practices Act (none had been). He termed the question "irrelevant," saying that all applicable laws had been complied with.

Cooke did allow that he considered a particular piece of legislation "unsound" and made it clear that no candidate who supported it could expect help from his unnamed committee. That bill would provide federal payments for drugs prescribed and dispensed under Medicare and Medicaid so long as they are within a reasonable price range; but if the medicines are in a higher-than-normal range, as is often the case with trade-named drugs, payment would be made only if the products are demonstrated to be therapeutically superior to less expensive rivals. The sponsor of the bill was Senator Russell Long, who, it will be remembered, said in the 1967 speech on political financing that pharmaceutical executives "will contribute to legislators who vote to permit or bring about" an environment in which they can sell "brand-name drug products at anywhere from twice to 50 times the price of identical nonbranded products." Sterling Drug, it happens, is a leading supplier of trade-named prescription drugs, as well as over-the-counter medications (including Bayer aspirin), toiletries, cosmetics, and household products. In

1969, with sales of $546.8 million, it ranked two hundredth on *Fortune's* list of the five hundred largest corporations. Here are excerpts from the Cooke-Luther letter, which was disclosed in the *Washington Post* on October 8, 1970:

> In the "political arena" (both Federal and State), we have *many* friends of *both* parties—important to industry in general and *very* important to the advancement of our industry and through it to the advancement of public welfare. In the Fall elections this year, these legislators have a right to receive help from their supporters and friends. . . . Sterling . . . *may not,* under the law, contribute to political campaigns. So, the choice is difficult:—either we disregard our very important political friends when they *need* funds for campaign purposes, or we do what most other major corporations do,—go to the key members of the corporate *team* for help. . . .
>
> Specifically, we're asking for a *voluntary* contribution from you for a political fund to be allocated to those legislators at the Federal and State level, be they Democrats *or* Republicans, whose re-election or election is *important* to our industry and to *Sterling Drug Inc.* [Emphasis in the original.]

The letter went on to say, with appropriate awe, that "what happens in Washington and in the 50 state capitols" deeply affects "the success of *Sterling* as well as your success and mine," that " 'Sterling's Business is Everybody's Health,' " and that, as always, "allocations from this fund are not made by me [Cooke] alone but instead are made by Mr. J. H. Luther . . . and me together with a group of qualified objective individuals both within and outside our company who have the best interest of our industry at heart." And, of course, there was the standard blessing for those who may find it better not to give: "We will certainly understand and can *assure* you that your non-participation will in no way ever prejudice your standing with our company." What a lovely nuance: "your" standing, "our" company.

The same *Washington Post* story also told of a "Dear Friend" letter, dated January 8, 1970, that Kerryn King, vice president of Texaco for public relations and personnel, sent out. As in the Sterling case, the letterhead was his own—and the address his company's. King told one of the authors that about 250 persons, some of them colleagues at Texaco, but all "friends," annually participate in his project, which he had undertaken to offset a morally atrocious situation in which a deserving candidate can run into "a lot of trouble finding financial support without selling his soul." Surely, no right-thinker could countenance *that*. In the letter, King said his purpose was to discuss "our mutual efforts to support financially deserving candidates . . . particularly those who represent us in the Congress and as Governors of the several states." He went on to say:

> There are far too many representatives in the Congress who are simply anti-business and anti-oil industry, regardless of the merits of our position. It is almost incredible that many Congressmen are willing to sacrifice the national security of this country to the siren song of low cost foreign oil. Those of us in the oil industry know that the strength of our nation is dependent upon an adequate supply of energy that cannot be cut off. . . . We must as individual citizens support those candidates who understand and appreciate the validity of our position.
>
> As you will recall, in 1968 each participant was asked to contribute $10 a month, or $120 a year. In 1969, this was reduced to $5 a month, or $60 for the entire year. . . .

King said that at least tentatively the lower rate, five dollars a month, would suffice in 1970, because the number of participants in his effort to save the souls of candidates had increased. He asked that checks be "made out to Cash."

In 1960, J. T. Naylor, then vice president and chief executive for telecommunications operations of the International Telephone and Telegraph Corporation, was among a group of ITT executives who, he said in a sworn affidavit, were enlisted in an effort "to 'butter' both sides so we'll be in a good position whoever wins."[21] Naylor attributed the quoted phrase to William T. Marx, another former ITT executive who later denied ever having solicited campaign contributions for anyone. According to Naylor, Marx said that "Hal [Harold S. Geneen, president and board chairman] and the board have a program that is very important to political protection and business development. Hal has given me a selected list of top executives to contribute to the election campaign. You are down for $1,200. This can be financed for you by the company if necessary. . . . You will be expected to recover the amount by covering it up in your traveling expense account." Naylor balked. Several days later, on October 18, the affidavit said, Marx introduced him to Robert G. (Bobby) Baker, then secretary to the Senate majority, and left him with Baker and M. R. Mitchell, then vice president and counsel. Naylor said Mitchell told him, "Please make out your check in favor of the 'Texas Business and Professional Men's Committee for Johnson for Vice President.'" Naylor resisted but finally wrote a check for $1,200. The check was deposited on November 10, two days after the election. In March 1961, Naylor said, he had a bitter confrontation with Harold Geneen in which he said that he had never tried to recover the $1,200, and in which the ITT chief told him, "Everybody does it and the board wanted it this way. It is 'paying off big in Washington.'" Soon thereafter, Naylor resigned. In December 1966, when the ITT's proposed acquisition of the American Broadcasting Companies was pending before the Federal Communications Commission, Senator Wayne Morse (D–Ore.) said that Naylor had made his affidavit available to the Senate Rules Committee and the Justice Department, both of which investigated Baker. The Department said that the FBI and a grand jury in Washington had investigated but found no basis for a prosecution.

Until 1969, there had been only two prosecutions of corporations for violation of federal election laws. But in that year and in the first seven months of 1970 there were sixteen—the product of a major investigation initiated in 1966, during the Johnson Administration, by Sheldon S. Cohen, then Commissioner of the IRS. Some of the more important cases in which guilty pleas were entered and fines imposed were:

The Fluor Corporation of Los Angeles admitted having made illegal contributions of $30,000 to an unnamed presidential candidate in 1964 and to congressional candidates in 1966. The presidential candidate was presumed to have been Barry Goldwater, since the honorary chairman of the company, John Simon Fluor, was chairman of the United Republican Finance Committee of Los Angeles County in 1964 and Maurice H. Stans was a director of the firm from 1963 until early 1969, when he became Secretary of Commerce in the Nixon Administration. The office of the late Senator Richard B. Russell, the Georgia Democrat, acknowledged having received a $1,500 contribution from a "J. S. Fluor."[22]

Howfield, the ad agency, formerly known as Galaxy, Incorporated, and three savings and loan associations owned by the late Los Angeles tycoon Howard F. Ahmanson (Arrowhead, Continental, and Home), admitted contributing $50,026 to a 1964 presidential candidate and fraudulently deducting $177,469 from tax returns. The presidential contribution was for Lyndon B. Johnson, although a decade earlier Ahmanson raised more than $400,000 for the campaign for Governor Goodwin J. Knight, the California Republican.[23]

Rossmoor Corporation, developer of the Leisure World retirement communities, admitted making an illegal $5,000 contribution to the 1964 senatorial campaign of Pierre Salinger, who had been President Kennedy's press secretary. The money was in the form of a check to the Walter Leftwich Organization, the Beverly Hills ad agency that handled his campaign.[24] In Baltimore, the National Brewing Company, owner of the Baltimore Orioles professional baseball team, admitted making a donation in the same amount through the same agency.[25] Salinger defeated Alan Cranston in the 1964 primary but lost the general election to George Murphy. In 1968 Cranston was elected to the Senate.

Two shipping companies, American President Lines and Pacific Far East Lines, pleaded guilty and were fined for having made contributions totaling $8,200 to unnamed House and Senate candidates of both parties in 1966 and 1968.[26]

International Latex Corporation pleaded no contest to a charge that it made an illegal contribution of $8,000 to the 1964 campaign of Senator Thomas J. Dodd (D–Conn.) and was fined $5,000.[27]

"When the Republic was founded," Senator Daniel K. Inouye of Hawaii, chairman of the Democratic Senatorial Campaign Committee, has said, "the majority of architects were quite intent on ridding themselves of an aristocracy. I am afraid that realities and practicalities of the election process have, to some extent, developed a new aristocracy of wealth and power."[28] One of these realities is the high cost of television time. Without the "bigger contributor" to provide "big chunks of money," Senator Charles McC. Mathias (R–Md.) has said, "you couldn't make the commitments for various media contracts."[29] His 1968 campaign, which was not notably lavish, cost an estimated $500,000.

The media, mainly television, is where much of the money goes because that is where so many of the voters are, watching the tube. The Twentieth Century Fund's Commission on Campaign Costs in the Electronic Era has summed up the total broadcasting charges for presidential and vice presidential candidates.[30] These increased from $4.6 million in 1956 to $11 million in 1964 and to $20.4 million in 1968.

Television has so increased the cost per vote that it was three times as high in 1968 as it was in 1952, when TV for the first time was a dominant force in a presidential election. Specifically, the cost per vote was 19 cents in 1952, 29 cents in 1960, 35 cents in 1964 and 60 cents in 1968. In 1968 a half-hour of prime television time on the National Broadcasting Company network cost $83,200 and a one-minute spot commercial $26,000.

In all of 1964, all candidates and parties spent $34.6 million for television and radio broadcasting, according to Federal Communications Commission figures. In 1968 they spent almost $25 million more, or $59.2 million, the FCC data indicate. "If production and other costs are added, the total bill for putting political messages on the air in 1968 was about $90 million—nearly a third of all the money spent on campaigning in that year," Herbert Alexander and Harold Meyers calculated. "Unfortunately for underfinanced candidates, television and radio time has to be paid for in advance. All indications are that television will become even more important in the future."[31]

The team of *Washington Post* reporters that looked at campaign spending immediately after the 1970 midterm elections found from television station records that vast amounts had been spent to buy time on the tube. In California, Leroy F. Aarons reported, Representative John V. Tunney (D) spent an estimated $800,000 in his successful race against incumbent Senator George Murphy (R), whose TV spending was about $500,000. In Indiana's senatorial race, George Lardner, Jr., estimated, Senator Vance Hartke (D) spent $246,000, well under the $441,000 spent for TV by his unsuccessful challenger, Representative Richard L. Roudebush (R). One of the authors found that at just five major television stations in Dallas and Houston, $115,540 was spent by Lloyd M. Bentsen, Jr. (D), in winning a Senate seat from Texas. Bentsen defeated Representative George Bush (R), now Ambassador to the United Nations, who spent $184,000, or about $68,000 more, at the same five stations.

In New York City, files at the six major television stations showed that in the senatorial races James L. Buckley, the Conservative and the winner, had spent $310,557, Charles E. Goodell, the incumbent, $463,854, and Richard L. Ottinger, the Democrat, $544,740. Reporter Haynes Johnson estimated that together the three candidates spent an additional $881,000 for television elsewhere in New York State, for a grand total of $2.3 million.

Soon after he became chairman of the Democratic National Committee, Lawrence F. O'Brien looked ahead, grimly, to 1972. In an interview with R. W. Apple, Jr., in the *New York Times* on March 28, 1970, O'Brien was said to consider it "doubtful that his party will financially be able to made an effective contest for the Presidency in 1972." A healthy skepticism always should be brought to such claims. The possibility of overstatement and self-serving aspects cannot casually be discounted. It suffices to point out that O'Brien was speaking before the November elections which, as David S. Broder of the *Washington Post* put it, gave the Democrats "a massive infusion of strength in the state capitols and a revival of support from both Dixie and the union halls." It is reasonable to assume that if in 1972 business should make a judgment that the Democratic ticket is a good investment (because it appears likely to win) and the Republican ticket a bad investment, money will flow to the Democrats. Yet the possibility that O'Brien spoke a prophetic truth also should not be lightly discarded. Thus fortified, let us pick up Apple's story:

> Mr. O'Brien, who took office three weeks ago, said in an interview this week that the Democrats were almost certain to be "completely priced out of the market" by the enormous costs of television advertising and the Republicans' far greater access to large sums of money.
>
> Two years from now, he said, the Republicans will be able to spend close to $50-million for their national campaign, as opposed to about $10-million for the Democrats.
>
> "Outspent 5 to 1," he said. "Is that a two-party system? I don't think so. It's just impossible. It would mean that no matter how good an organizing job we do, how good our candidates are, we could not make our case.
>
> "The question is a basic one—*do we have to abide by the decisions of the private sector as to whether we have a chance to present the views of our candidates effectively to the public?*"
>
> Mr. O'Brien, who managed former Vice President Hubert H. Humphrey's campaign for the Presidency in 1968, said that President Nixon's supporters had spent almost three times as much as he had been able to spend. At a crucial stage of the campaign, he added, he was obliged to trim $3 million from the television budget, because the networks insisted on being paid cash before selling air-time.
>
> "I'm not crying crocodile tears," said the sandy-haired, deep-voiced party leader. "But it cost us the election. It's really as simple as that." [Emphasis supplied.]

O'Brien's forebodings could only have been justly increased by disclosures of White House financing of the 1970 congressional campaigns—although one should bear in mind that many Republican candidates thus enriched did poorly at the polls. In the *Washington Post* campaign financing roundup of November 22, Nick Kotz reported from Fargo, North Dakota:

> "The President asked me 'what do you need?'" explains Rep. Thomas Kleppe of the crucial step of the most expensive political campaign in North Dakota history. "I told him I needed a professional campaign manager, a professional media man, and substantial financing from outside the state. These things were deliverable and they were delivered."
>
> Kleppe's entire campaign was, in fact, planned, financed and directed from Washington, D.C., by a team of professionals assembled by the White House.

Senator Quentin N. Burdick, who defeated Kleppe, received most of his campaign financing from liberal antiwar groups and labor unions, also from outside of North Dakota. But, as noted earlier, Kleppe outspent the incumbent Democrat two to one. Kotz wrote:

> Throughout the campaign the postman walked into Anderson's Bismarck law office [Harold Anderson, Kleppe's finance chairman] with letters containing checks from wealthy individuals all over the country. Thirteen of the letters contained $5,000 campaign gifts and another 50 letters brought gifts of from $1,000 to $4,000. When money ran short, Anderson said he would talk to Republican officials in Washington and more checks soon would arrive. . . .
>
> "I got the money because of White House help," said Kleppe of about $200,000 he received from individuals outside North Dakota.

The White House helper was disclosed by Jack W. Germond of the Gannett News Service and Jules J. Witcover of the *Los Angeles Times* to have been Jack A. Gleason, an aide to Harry Dent, the President's political adviser. Witcover, in a story on November 26, 1970, said that Gleason had been detached from Dent's office to run a "behind-the-scenes" fund-raising operation that "funneled millions of dollars into the 1970 campaigns of selected GOP candidates this fall, beyond the substantial amounts raised by the Republican National Committee and congressional campaign committees." The story continued:

Important contributors were contacted directly and arrangements made to channel money on short notice to the favored candidates. . . .

Centralization within a White House-connected structure gave the President and his political strategists a closer hold on each campaign that was aided. . . .

According to one Republican politician importantly involved in a campaign favored by the special White House operation, Gleason boasted after the election that more than $12 million had been raised for GOP candidates through it.

After defeating Albert Gore in Tennessee, Representative William E. Brock III, a conservative heir to a candy company fortune who received an estimated $1,000,000 to $1,250,000 in contributions, told the *Washington Post,* "I have no idea where the money came from . . ." That need not be taken seriously. He added, ". . . and I don't want to know." It is more important that the people of Tennessee seem not to want to know, because they have no state law to require senatorial candidates to disclose sources of campaign funds; and it is also more important that the people of the United States seem not to want to know, because they have no federal law to require similar disclosure. On Capitol Hill, all a candidate needs to do in order to conceal his campaign income and expenditures is to own up only to that collected and disbursed with his "knowledge and consent." Among the 1970 senatorial candidates, several, including all four from Illinois and Indiana, admitted to no financing at all—with, of course, their "knowledge and consent."

Despite the campaign financing laws and non-laws, there are a few clues which point to the ultimate sources of the millions of dollars that Jack Gleason was funneling out, surely to Brock, among other favorites of President Nixon and Vice President Agnew, from a small back-room office in the basement of a building at 1310 19th Street N.W. in downtown Washington.

Some of these sources had donated heavily to President Nixon's 1968 presidential campaign. One was W. Clement Stone, a Chicago insurance tycoon who was the biggest backer of Ralph T. Smith, the Illinois Republican who lost his bid to remain in the Senate to Adlai Stevenson III. In addition, Stone made numerous donations to other Republicans around the country. In Texas, Paul W. Eggers, running for governor, and Representative George Bush, running for the Senate, each reported gifts of $2,500 from Stone. Each also listed $3,000 from Thomas A. Pappas of Boston, who is one of the leading supporters of the ruling military junta in Greece and has oil, petrochemical, steel, and Coca-Cola ventures in that country. Eggers and Bush lost. New York State's new senator, James L. Buckley, listed $2,500 from Stone.

As an advocate of what he calls "Success Through a Positive Mental Attitude," Stone would be right to console himself with the thought that even if some of the candidates he backed failed of election, he can count on sympathetic treatment in Washington of problems affecting the insurance business.

The most thorough congressional study of campaign financing involved the 1956 general elections for the Presidency, the House and the Senate. It is valuable even if in many respects outdated. For one thing, the investigators, led by Senator Albert Gore as chairman of a subcommittee of the Senate Committee on Rules and Administration, obtained otherwise unavailable records with subpoenas. Some of the comparative figures on contributions to the two parties speak well enough for themselves.[32]

For example, contributions of $500 or more yielded to the Republicans $8,064,907, and of $5,000 or more $2,894,309, compared with $2,820,655 and $860,380, respectively, for the Democrats. Twelve selected families gave the Republicans $1,040,526 (with the du Ponts accounting for $248,423, the Pews $216,800, the Rockefellers $152,604 and the Mellons $100,150) and the Democrats $107,109. Officials of the 225 largest corporations gave the Republicans $1,816,597, the Democrats $103,725. For officials of the 100 largest military prime contractors the figures were $1,133,882 versus $40,975; for officials of the 29 largest oil companies, $344,997 versus $14,650; for officials of the 10 leading radio and television station licensees, $37,800 versus $1,000; for officials of 17 certificated airlines, $132,150 versus $31,609; for officials of 37 leading advertising agencies, $51,600 versus $0; for officials of 47 leading underwriters of investment bonds, $237,800 versus $2,000; for officials of 13 professional, business and other selected groups, $741,189 versus $8,000, and for officials of 88 corporations participating in the atomic energy program, $387,342 versus $34,700.

Weight should be given to the fact that in the 1956 election, for reasons including some that had nothing to do with campaign contributions, General Eisenhower was a shoo-in and Adlai E. Stevenson was doomed from the start. In 1964 it was Lyndon B. Johnson who was certain to be elected and Barry Goldwater defeated. But that was only part of the explanation why, for example, things were so turned around that of all contributions received by the national Democratic campaign committees, 69 per cent were in amount of $500 or more, compared with only 28 per cent for the Republicans. Now the Democrats had became "the party of the 'fat cats,' " as Herbert E. Alexander put it.[33] A good many of the "fat cats" were of a relatively new breed of space and defense contractors who contributed $1,000 or more each to gain admission to Mr. Johnson's "President's Club." Henry Ford II and John T. Connor, then president of Merck, the big pharmaceutical firm, were cochairmen of the National Independent Committee for Johnson and Humphrey, an organization for raising funds among businessmen for which there was no Democratic predecessor in 1956.

In 1968 the situation again was reversed. Richard Nixon held none of the terrors for the business community that Barry Goldwater had in 1964, and Hubert Humphrey, gravely disadvantaged by such developments as the violence at the Democratic National Convention in Chicago, had to fight a decidedly uphill battle. All of this was reflected in expenditures for general election campaigns at the national level. According to *Congressional Quarterly*, major Republican committees reported having spent $29.4 million, or 53.4 per cent more than in 1964, while their Democratic equivalents reported $13.6 million, an increase of a mere 1.7 per cent.[34] By estimate of Herbert Alexander, spending by the Nixon-Agnew organizations alone, including late bills paid in 1969, came to $25 million, compared with $10.6 million for the Humphrey-Muskie groups. The Wallace-LeMay committees reported spending, $6,985,455.[35]

As of early 1970 the Democratic National Committee was about $9 million in debt. If the party should be unable to get out of the hole except by resorting to traditional money sources, the debt will prove to be a national disaster of sorts, although it will not generally be recognized as such. The reason, of course, is that some of those traditional sources will make a business judgment that something of value may be had at giveaway prices in Washington.

Thanks to the skilled and tenacious reporting of Walter H. Pincus, Herbert Alexander, and *Congressional Quarterly*, it is possible to get some idea of who were the principal *recorded* givers in the 1968 campaigns. Insofar as presidential candidates are concerned, the focus here will be on Richard Nixon because he won, collected more money, is in the best possible position to express his appreciation, and may with his donors repeat the scenario in 1972.

The Business Council's members are an elite who run the nation's major enterprises. In 1964 they gave more to Lyndon Johnson than to Barry Goldwater. But in 1968, the Citizens' Research Foundation determined, sixty-six members (and their wives, whose contributions of $500 or more were lumped with those of their husbands) gave $257,925 to the Nixon-Agnew groups, while only two others, along with three of the sixty-six who gave to the Republicans, contributed to Humphrey-Muskie. The sum of the five donations to the Democrats was $83,000.[36]

In *Fortune,* Alexander and coauthor Harold Meyers also told of the $500-or-more contributions made by 354 of the 2,129 officers and directors of the twenty-five largest industrial corporations and the seventy-five largest government contractors, twenty-five each for defense, space and atomic energy (duplications reduced the total number of firms from one hundred to seventy).[37] Of the 354 contributors, 315 gave Republican causes $1,153,559, and 46, plus 12 who gave to both parties, gave the Democrats $221,201. None of the 354 gave anything to Wallace. The GOP-Democratic division of over-$500 gifts was substantially a reenactment of 1956.

This was also true of the pattern of giving by "centimillionaires," the term used by Alexander and Meyers for persons with fortunes of at least $100 million (*Fortune,* in an article in April 1968, listed sixty-six of the "richest of the rich": persons with an estimated worth of $150 million to $1.5 billion). By their estimate, forty-six "centimillionaires" contributed $1,105,000, of which all but $132,000 went to the GOP.

As of the eve of the November 1968 election, the various Nixon-Agnew committees, in their reports to the Clerk of the House, had listed contributions from W. Clement Stone, of Chicago, president of the Combined Insurance Company of America, of $22,000. As of November 18, which was thirteen days after the election, the committees were listing Stone's gifts at $100,000, or almost five times as much. But by his own estimate, made in an interview with Bernard Nossiter of the *Washington Post,* he actually gave more than $500,000. Yet, in theory, the intent of the Corrupt Practices Act was to enable the voters to know *before* an election the essential facts about a candidate's receipts and expenditures.

Stone, who charges up his 3,500 insurance salesmen by making them stand and chant in unison, "I feel happy, I feel healthy, I feel terrific," told Nossiter that in 1970 he gave $250,000 in Illinois and almost $750,000 elsewhere, all, of course, to supporters of the President (whom he admires for having "PMA—a Positive Mental Attitude"). "If a family has wealth in the neighborhood of $400 million," he asks plausibly, "what's a million in gifts?"[38]

In a period of approximately three months preceding the 1968 Republican National Convention in Miami, the generosity of Clement Stone was surpassed by Mrs. John D. Rockefeller, Jr., step-mother of Governor Nelson A. Rockefeller, Jr., of New York. Her giving was of a different caste, however, because it was for a member of the family who was seeking a chance to work his way through the Electoral College. She gave $1,482,-625 to the Rockefeller for President (New York) Committee. This sum presumably was subject to gift taxes of as much as $900,000, bringing the total contribution to about $2,382,000, Alexander and Meyers said.[39]

Jack J. Dreyfus, Jr., then chairman of the Dreyfus Fund, made recorded gifts of $76,000 to Republicans and $63,000 to Democrats. Max M. Fisher, Detroit oil man and industrialist, was listed for $105,000 to the GOP. Henry Salvatori, of Los Angles, who also made a fortune in oil, gave $95,000 to Republicans. Officers and directors of Litton Industries, including chairman Charles B. Thornton and president Roy L. Ash, were listed for $61,000 in gifts to the GOP. While President-elect, Nixon picked Ash to lead a study of the need to reorganize the Executive Branch, although Litton Industries (of which, by the way, Salvatori is a director) makes extensive sales to Federal agencies, and although the merger activities of this conglomerate require examination by the Department of Justice and the Federal Trade Commission.

The late Richard King Mellon, then honorary chairman of Mellon National Bank and Trust Company and a director of General Motors; Richard Mellon Scaife, a director of the same bank; and two other members of the Mellon family (whose interests include Gulf Oil and Aluminum Company of America), Mrs. Ailsa Mellon Bruce and Mrs. Cordelia Scaife May, together gave a recorded $198,462 to the GOP.

Twenty-eight directors and officers of GM, excluding Richard King Mellon, were listed for $50,000, all to Nixon groups. Henry Ford II gave $30,000 to Humphrey (and $9,450 to Republicans); but his brother Benson gave the GOP $41,000, and John S. Bugas, another Ford Motor executive, was listed for $20,000. While Thomas J. Watson, Jr., president of IBM, was giving $21,000 to Democrats (and $2,000 to Republicans), his brother, Arthur K., chairman of IBM's international subsidiary, was giving $49,000 to Nixon.

In March 1970 President Nixon named Arthur Watson Ambassador to France. Kingdon Gould, Jr., a Washington parking lot tycoon, was listed for $22,000 in donations to the GOP. He became Ambassador to Luxembourg. The President's choice for Ambassador to Malta was John C. Pritzlaff, former board chairman of Republic Properties in Arizona. He had given $22,000; but his step-father and uncle, Spencer T. Olin and John M. Olin, of the giant chemical corporation bearing their name, had given $47,500 more.

"Serving in the Caribbean," one of the authors wrote in the *Washington Post* of January 31, 1971, "is Vincent de Roulet, who headed a marketing research firm in New York. His wife's parents . . . gave an additional $28,000. The in-laws are Charles S. Payson, board chairman of Vitro Corp., and Joan Whitney Payson, president of the New York Mets. De Roulet is now ambassador to Jamaica."

At least for the of sake diversity, a few other contributors might be noted. Elmer H. Bobst, who is extremely close to the Nixon family, was listed for gifts of $63,000 to the GOP. William S. Lasdon, a director of Warner-Lambert Pharmaceutical, of which Bobst is honorary chairman, and of Capital Cities Broadcasting, gave a recorded $27,000 to the GOP. The Democrats, meanwhile, received $69,400 from Mary Lasker, widow of Albert D. Lasker, an advertising magnate; $58,000 from Norman Cousins, president of the *Saturday Review;* $56,000 from Herbert A. Allen, a New York investment banker, and $54,906 from Lew R. Wasserman, president of Music Corporation of America. John M. King of Denver, then chairman of King Resources Company, an oil, gas, and minerals enterprise, was listed for $42,500, although confusion and obscurities in the records indicated he may have given almost twice that sum. On January 25, 1971, a Federal grand jury indicted him on charges that he illegally diverted money from his company to Investors Overseas Services, Incorporated, the mutual-fund complex based in Geneva. The founder of IOS, Bernard Cornfeld, was listed as a $25,000 donor to the Democrats.

De Witt and Lila Wallace, co-chairmen of the Reader's Digest Association, were listed for gifts of $49,851 to the GOP, and Hobart Lewis, president, for $3,000. Six top executives of Bethlehem Steel gave at least $15,000, nine top officers of Goodyear Tire & Rubber Company at least $9,000, and two officials of the International Mining Corporation at least $22,500.

W. Pat Jennings, clerk of the House of Representatives, took an unprecedented step to facilitate enforcement of the Corrupt Practices Act of 1925. After the 1968 election, he referred to the Justice Department lists of politicians and organizations that had failed to comply with one or more provisions of the law.

One list named twenty of the twenty-one committees that raised $21 million to elect Richard Nixon and Spiro Agnew, but had failed to meet the deadlines prescribed in the law for filing of preelection reports on receipts and expenditures. Ramsey Clark, then in his final weeks as Attorney General, initiated an FBI investigation which was inherited by his successor, John N. Mitchell—who had been Mr. Nixon's campaign manager.

A second list consisted of 107 congressional candidates, some of whom were elected or reelected. Of these candidates, 65 had failed to file required campaign spending reports, and 42 had filed after the specified deadlines. A later check by the *Washington Post* showed that 23 incumbent members of Congress and 129 candidates for the House had failed to meet the deadlines, and that more than 100 unsuccessful candidates had failed to report the source and use of political contributions, as required by law.

Mitchell let the whole opportunity—golden opportunity might be closer to the mark—fade away. This was wholly predictable, but such things ought to be noticed by those who would watch what the nation's chief law enforcement officer does about "law 'n' order," rather than what he says about it.

The soliciting of massive campaign funds from investors who call themselves contributors, the "centimillionaires," and the directors and officers of corporations; the concealment of these sources and the bloated scale of their giving from the voters *until after the election* by the simple lawless act of missing the filing deadlines; and the nonenforcement of the law by the campaign manager–become–Attorney General—all of this may mean many things, but one of them certainly is a translation of economic power into political power.

176

Other examples demonstrating the translation of economic power into political power are presented in succeeding chapters on the Executive, the Congress and the regulatory agencies. The complexity of the regulatory process warrants a prefatory word.

Regulation takes different forms. It is important to discriminate among them. Some regulatory operations, such as the Food and Drug Administration, are directly under the control of the executive branch. The Federal Trade Commission is closely aligned with Congress. Major areas of the economy are regulated by numerous "independent agencies," bodies theoretically free of substantial political interference by the executive or legislative branches of government. Examples of this type of agency are the Interstate Commerce Commission, the Federal Communications Commission, the Civil Aeronautics Board, the Federal Maritime Commission, and the Federal Power Commission. Still other bodies, usually in the form of government-chartered corporations with significant regulatory authority, spin around in their own orbits. In this category is the Federal Reserve Board.

Confusion is compounded because most regulatory bodies were conceived for an *ad hoc* purpose and were delivered in individually unique historical circumstances. For example the ICC was conceived in the rural Populist furor of the late nineteenth century and born in the 1887 legal climate of *laissez-faire*. The Securities and Exchange Commission was created to curb the speculative abuses of the 1920s and came into being during the depression. The Federal Communications Commission found its parents to be the technological limitations of the radio spectrum and the uncontrolled access to the airwaves that gave rise to a Tower of Babel in the late 1920s and early 1930s.

The scope of regulation also differs. Natural-monopoly regulation usually involves control of entry, exit, and mergers; regulation of rates; and the prevention of unjustified rate and service discrimination. The scope of regulation turns on the presumed or accepted need for it. For example, the basis of regulation may be health or safety, as in the case of the Food and Drug Administration, and may require powers of inspection, testing, labeling, and removal of a product from the market. Or the need may be to prevent fraud and deception in the marketplace, and regulation may take the form of cease and desist orders, as is the case with FTC enforcement, or full disclosure before entering the market, as is the case with SEC regulation. In still other cases, regulation may be predicated on the need to promote or contract the supply of credit. In these cases, regulation may take the form of federal insurance, control of interest rates, inspection of financial books and records, and civil sanctions or criminal fines and jail sentences.

However diverse their origins and responsibilities, and their places in the structure of government, each regulatory mechanism tends to build up a common set of characteristics:

1. A strong sense of self-preservation.
2. A special constituency.
3. A jargon understood only by those immersed in the affairs regulated.
4. A set of highly complicated procedural rules.
5. An ethical value system peculiarly applicable to itself.

Moreover, there is always what Commissioner Nicholas Johnson of the FCC has called a "sub-government," whether regulation is in the executive branch or in an independent agency. In any specialized private interest–government relationship, Johnson said, the

> sub-government is self-perpetuating and endures over a long period of time, unaffected by the tides of opinion and efforts for reform. It is made up of spokesmen for the largest regulated corporations, the specialized law firms and a bar association, the trade press, trade associations, public relations and management consulting firms, and various other hangers-on. . . . It also includes the permanent government staff—regulatory, executive and congressional—which is concerned with day-to-day activities of the private interests in question. People in this sub-government typically spend their lives moving from one organization to another in the sub-government. People who pursue the course of protecting the public interest are rarely admitted to this club.[40]

Rather than treat regulatory activities in a unitary way, we will parcel them out among the chapters on the Executive, the Congress and the regulatory agencies, as dictated by the particular history and nature of each activity.

5 THE EXECUTIVE

Economic power has been translating regularly into power at the White House for a long time, in Democratic administrations and in Republican administrations. The examples that follow primarily involve Richard M. Nixon, for an arbitrary but sufficient reason: he occupies the White House today and will continue to do so at least until January 1973. The examples that follow involve several industries, including securities, mining and shipping. But the strongest and most consistent emphasis is on oil. Ample reasons for this were provided by Robert Engler in the introduction to his richly documented *The Politics of Oil: A Study of Private Power and Democratic Directions.*[1] The oil industry "has harnessed public law, governmental machinery, and opinion to ends that directly challenge public rule," Engler said. He added:

> In the name of prosperity and technology, the industry has been able to destroy competition and limit abundance. In the name of national interest it has received privileges beyond those accorded to other industries. In the name of national security, oil has influenced and profited from a foreign policy that has supported the chauvinism of a few rather than generosity to the aspirations of the many in underdeveloped areas. In the name of private enterprise, it has contributed to the attenuation of vital portions of democratic life, from education to civic morality. In the name of the right of representation, it has so entrenched itself within the political processes that it becomes impossible to distinguish public from private actions. In the name of freedom, the oil industry has received substantial immunity from public accountability.[2]

On September 18, 1952, the *New York Post* and the *Los Angeles Daily News,* which is now defunct, disclosed that Senator Richard Nixon, the Republican candidate for Vice President, had an $18,000 fund intended to help defray his personal expenses as a legislator. The contribu-

179

tors were seventy-six millionaires, including fifteen oil executives, eleven real estate executives, and bankers, government contractors, and others with significant interests on which Mr. Nixon voted. His votes were the votes the contributors wanted. For example, he voted to reduce the availability of public housing and to hasten the end of wartime rent controls; and some would say that on these and other matters he voted his conscience. The oil industry was pleased that he voted against reducing the 27½ per cent depletion allowance, but his position on these and other legislative issues of concern to the industry was the same as that of, say, Senator Lyndon B. Johnson, who would become his immediate predecessor in the White House.

Certain similarities existed between the case of the fund for Senator Nixon in the 1950s and the fund for Senator Thomas J. Dodd, the Connecticut Democrat, in the 1960s. Few in Washington were better qualified to make a comparison than the late Drew Pearson and Jack Anderson, who exposed the improper uses Dodd made of campaign funds. In *The Case Against Congress: A Compelling Indictment of Corruption on Capitol Hill*, the columnists said:

> More money was contributed to Dodd's personal fund between 1958 and 1967 than to Nixon's while he was running for Vice President in 1952, but the principle involved was similar. The punishment, however, was not. Dodd was censured by the Senate despite an emotional appeal to his peers. Nixon made a similar emotional appeal to the American people on television, and was elected Vice President of the United States. Probably the basic reason for the differing outcomes to the cases was the way the press reported the stories. . . .
>
> With the exception of the St. Louis *Post-Dispatch* . . . no newspaper subsequently dug into the ramifications of the Nixon fund and demonstrated the benefits that had been received by those who secretly contributed to it.[3]

Pearson and Anderson cited the case of Dana Smith, who had collected the $18,000 for Senator Nixon, and who "earlier had a personal tax case before the Justice Department involving a $500,000 tax refund that he was demanding from the Government. Nixon sent a member of his office staff to apply pressure on Smith's behalf." The columnists commented:

> Under the rules of Congress, a member is at liberty to help his constituents but at no time is he entitled to received remuneration for that help. On

the contrary, there is a clear-cut statute making it a criminal offense for him to receive any remuneration for any representation he makes before the United States Government. . . . But the Nixon case was marked by gratitude expressed in the form of campaign contributions for favors done and votes cast while he served in Congress.[4]

On February 3, 1956, the late Senator Francis Case, a South Dakota Republican, told the Senate that an attempt had been made to buy his vote for a bill to lift federal price controls on natural gas. With astonishing crudeness, Case said, a lawyer had turned over to his election fund in his home state an envelope containing twenty-five $100 bills—"the largest single contribution I could remember for any campaign of mine." The lawyer was John M. Neff, a dispenser of political monies for the Superior Oil Company. Neff was under the direction of Elmer Patman, who in turn had been retained by Howard B. Keck, president of Superior, to disburse campaign contributions at his discretion.[5]

The disclosure cried out for a sweeping investigation, but the cry was heeded neither by Lyndon Johnson, the Majority Leader; other powers in the Senate; nor the presiding officer of the Senate, Vice President Richard Nixon. Together they blocked any searching inquiry.[6]

In the same year, as noted in the preceding chapter, three families with heavy interests in oil, the Rockefellers, Pews and Mellons, together gave almost a half-million dollars to the Republican campaign forces, led by General Eisenhower and Richard Nixon, and nothing to the Democrats.

In 1960 Mr. Nixon was the Republican nominee for President. On October 25, in the final phase of his campaign against John F. Kennedy, Pearson and Anderson disclosed in their column, "Washington Merry-Go-Round," facts about a $205,000 loan which had been made to the candidate's brother, Don Nixon. They identified the lender as Howard Hughes, the sequestered multimillionaire who at the time of the transaction, December 1956, was the principal stockholder in Trans World Airlines. "The loan, secured by a mortgage on Lot 10 on Whittier Boulevard in Whittier, California—a piece of real estate that no bank would have accepted as security for a loan of that size—was apparently never repaid," the columnists said in their book. "The Hughes Tool Company was an important defense contractor. TWA had applied for an extension of its route from the Philippines to Japan. Hughes himself faced an antitrust suit. And he had other problems, none of which were likely to become aggravated by the fact that the family of Richard Nixon, a man who might become President of the United States, was beholden to him financially." Again, the press minimized the potential for embarrassment. In New England, for example, among forty-three newspapers that normally run "Washington Merry-Go-Round" only three carried the column.[7]

In the Kennedy-Nixon campaign, officers and directors of the American Petroleum Institute, which is regarded as first of all the spokesman for the "Big Seven" (the Standard Oil companies of New Jersey, Indiana, and California, Mobil, Shell, Gulf, and Texaco) gave the Republicans a reported $113,700 and the Democrats $6,000.[8]

In 1962 Richard Nixon ran for governor of California but was defeated. He then joined a Wall Street law firm whose principal clients were Warner-Lambert Pharmaceutical Corporation and PepsiCo, Incorporated. The arrangements were facilitated by two old friends, Elmer H. Bobst, honorary chairman of the drug firm, and Donald M. Kendall, now president of PepsiCo, of which Pepsi-Cola, the soft-drink outfit, is a subsidiary. The law firm, which was renamed Nixon, Mudge, Rose, Guthrie, Alexander & Mitchell (John N. Mitchell now Attorney General), has several clients which are subject to government regulation and which have substantial stakes in actions or (non-actions) of the White House and Congress, including mutual funds and oil and gas interests. There was, for example, John Shaheen, a New York City financier. In 1967 he retained Mr. Nixon to negotiate a tax-exempt status for an oil refinery in Newfoundland, Canada. At one point, Mr. Nixon appeared at the Interior Department to plead for an import quota for Shaheen.[9] In November 1968 Shaheen was reported by Nixon-Agnew committees to have given $7,000. Other GOP groups listed him for an additional $9,500.[10]

After the 1968 election Mr. Nixon and Mr. Mitchell resigned from the law firm, which became Mudge, Rose, Guthrie, & Alexander. Warner-Lambert remained a principal client. That firm decided it wanted to merge with another pharmaceutical house, Parke, Davis & Company. Richard W. McLaren, the Assistant Attorney General for antitrust, opposed the merger, on the ground that it could tend substantially to lessen competition. Indeed, he said publicly that he wanted the Justice Department to go to court for a temporary restraining order and then for a temporary injunction, as the *Washington Post* reported on November 26, 1970.

Mitchell disqualified himself "in order to avoid any possibility of or appearance of a conflict of interest." But, on the eve of consummation of the merger, in a move that stunned antitrust lawyers, Richard G. Kleindienst, the Deputy Attorney General, overruled McLaren, refusing even to let him seek to delay the merger for a few days.

It was a nice victory for the law firm of Mudge, Rose, Guthrie & Alexander and for Warner-Lambert. Kleindienst, a long-time political operator whose appointment to a post of high trust was never claimed to be related to his record in the administration of justice, did not need to be told about the special identities of the law firm, its client, its client's honorary chairman, and the chairman's friends in Washington.

During the 1968 campaign, contributions of at least $48,000 were made to Republican committees by Robert O. Anderson, chairman of Atlantic Richfield.[11] In the years 1964 to 1967, this oil company earned profits of $465 million—while making no federal tax payments whatever and, incredible as it may seem, accumulating a tax credit of $629,000.[12] "Personal" contributions of $90,000 were acknowledged by Harold M. McClure, the Republican National Committeeman from Michigan and immediate past president of the Independent Petroleum Association of America. The destination of part of the money makes one curious whether oil is less adept than politics at making strange bedfellows. A check for $2,000, Stephen D. Isaacs and Leonard Downie, Jr., disclosed in the *Washington Post* on September 5, 1969, went to the reelection campaign of a Democratic senator, Daniel B. Brewster of Maryland. The explanation given by McClure was that he had given money to Senator Russell B. Long, a Democrat but an oilman, and that it was Long who selected the recipients—which may prove that oil is thicker than blood. McClure, Erwin Knoll (who is Washington correspondent of the *Progressive*) wrote in March 1970, "recently testified before a Federal grand jury investigating allegations of political bribery."[13] On Capitol Hill, no one expected anything to come of it, and as of early 1971, nothing had.

Soon after the tumultuous Democratic National Convention in August 1968, top fund-raisers for Vice President Hubert Humphrey flew to Houston. "They were desperate to get a quick million-dollar loan so that the Humphrey presidential campaign could start off with a splash of national television advertising," Murray A. Seeger reported in the *Los Angeles Times*. His story, which appeared three months after the election, went on to say that the Humphrey aides, going logically to men capable of making million-dollar loans,

> sat down with a group of oil millionaires in the Houston Petroleum Club.
>
> When the Humphrey men made their bid for cash, the oil men asked what the Vice President was prepared to do about percentage depletion allowances, the special tax loophole given to oil, gas and hard mineral investors. Humphrey was known as an opponent of depletion allowances. [In fact, he was, with former Senator Paul H. Douglas (D-Ill.), an early fighter for reform; in 1951, for example, he sponsored an amendment to reduce depletion for oil to 15 per cent.]
>
> "We told them the Vice President would not promise them a thing," Jeno Paulucci of Duluth, a millionaire businessman and long a Humphrey friend, recalled recently. "We told them he would not be a political prostitute. The oil men wouldn't give us a dime."[14]

Subsequently, a group of Texas oilmen went to Humphrey's summer home in Waverly, Minnesota. Sitting around the swimming pool with the candidate, they offered several million dollars for his campaign if he would guarantee that, as President, he would not recommend or support a cut in the oil depletion allowance. Humphrey, who disclosed the incident, through an aide, to one of the authors, recalled telling the oilmen, "We need tax reform and no President can offer a tax reform bill without a cut in the oil depletion allowance." The result, again, was that they gave him nothing.

In the *Los Angeles Times* story on the earlier unreported meeting in Houston, Seeger recalled that while campaigning through Texas, the Republican candidate had pointed out that Humphrey opposed $27\frac{1}{2}$ per cent. "As President," Mr. Nixon said in Lubbock, Texas, "I will maintain it." His position, Ronnie Dugger said in "Oil and Politics" in the *Atlantic,* was shared by "a substantial majority of Republicans in Congress, and his campaign was funded accordingly. Preliminary reports indicate that the Mellons gave the Nixon campaign $215,000 and the Pews, of Sun Oil, contributed $84,000."[15] Few investments could have offered more promise, since Mr. Nixon had been proving his soundness in these matters at least since 1952.

"The tax gifts from politicians are given back to them, in part, as political contributions," Dugger said. The writer, who is publisher and editor-at-large of the *Texas Observer*, a brave and independent fortnightly of high editorial quality, added, "Legal or not, this is a kickback to politicians. 'I'll give you tax money assuming that you'll give me some of it back for my career in politics.' That, making due allowance for every principled exception, is the truth of it."[16]

Dillon, Read & Company, the big New York investment banking house, is the firm of C. Douglas Dillon, Under Secretary of State in the Eisenhower Administration and Secretary of the Treasury under President Kennedy and President Johnson. In 1960, when John Kennedy was elected, Dillon gave nothing to the Democrats and $26,550 to the Republicans, which put him among the ten most generous contributors of record to the GOP in that year. In 1964 Dillon gave the Democrats $42,000 and the Republicans nothing, but in 1968 he contributed $9,000 to the Republicans and nothing to the Democrats.[17]

The 1968 election brought to the fore a vice president of Dillon, Read, Peter M. Flanigan, who was a fund-raiser for Richard Nixon. He also was president and managing director of the Barracuda Tanker Corporation, owner of the tanker *Sansinena*. Because it had flown the Liberian flag since 1957, it was ineligible under maritime law to engage in coastal shipping, that is, in shipping between United States ports. This ineligibility severely depressed its market value. By estimate of then Senator Joseph D. Tydings (D–Md.), the *Sansinena* was worth $4.5 million under the Liberian flag but would be worth $11 million, or $6.5 million more, if it could be used in coastal shipping.

Barracuda Tanker, in which Flanigan was a 3.9 per cent stockholder, had been organized solely to charter tankers at least until 1985 to a client of Dillon, Read, the Union Oil Company of California. In speeches on the Senate floor on March 9, 10, and 11, 1970, Senator Tydings disclosed that Fred Hartley, president of Union Oil, had been trying since 1967 to get a waiver of the law which limited the usefulness of the *Sansinena* and depressed its value. Since 1950, the law had authorized such a waiver if this could be shown to be essential to the national defense. But, Tydings said, documentary evidence showed that Hartley was consistently rebuffed on the ground that tankers of American registry were available.

Peter Flanigan became an assistant to the President in April 1969. He was assigned special responsibility for financial affairs, and he became the author of a White House code of ethics warning members of the staff against attempts to influence regulatory agencies. Flanigan also became the President's staff expert on oil.

In the Senate speeches, Tydings said that as of early 1970 four American tankers were vainly seeking oil cargo but finally had to turn to the grain trade. In addition, there were indications that the Defense Department did not support, if it did not oppose, a waiver for the *Sansinena*. On February 25, Flanigan's 308 shares of stock in Barracuda, which had been held in trust by his father, Horace C. Flanigan, were sold to others in the Barracuda venture. On March 2, the Treasury Department granted not merely a special-purpose waiver for the 66,883-ton tanker, but an unprecedently broad one, on the ground that the national security required increased tanker capacity in coastal shipping. Tydings told the Senate that merely "by the stroke of a pen," Treasury had added $6.5 million to the value of the *Sansinena*. On Capitol Hill, it became apparent that unless the waiver were withdrawn there would be investigations in the House, the Senate, or both. The night of March 9, following the first Tydings speech, the White House summoned Treasury officials to a meeting. The next day, David M. Kennedy, Secretary of the Treasury, announced cancellation of the waiver. In effect, he was saying that what was essential to the national security on March 9 was inessential on March 10. Ronald L. Ziegler, the President's press secretary, said that Peter Flanigan had been "unaware" of the waiver. Although Secretary Kennedy was said by a spokesman to take "full responsibility for the waiver decision," it was believed to have been made, or, at least, heavily influenced, by Paul W. Eggers, the Department's general counsel. About three weeks after the waiver was canceled, Eggers resigned—to campaign for the Republican nomination for governor of Texas.[18]

After the election, one of the authors, as a member of a team of reporters who looked into campaign financing, went to Texas where he examined the income and expenditures statements filed in the primary and general elections by six candidates: Lloyd M. Bentsen, Jr. (D); incumbent Senator Ralph W. Yarborough, whom Bentsen defeated in the primary; Representative George Bush (R), defeated by Bentsen in the November election; Bill Archer, who was elected to Bush's seat in Congress from Houston; Governor Preston Smith (D); and Eggers, who lost to Smith.

The examination of records, a story in the *Washington Post* disclosed on December 6, 1970, "indicates that oilmen accounted for almost 46 per cent of the individual contributions of $5,000 or more listed for this year's elections." Among a grand total of almost $4 million in listed gifts, those of at least $5,000 each—exclusive of loans (which legally are contributions) and committees—amounted to at least $550,155, of which oilmen gave $250,775. Bankers, investors, mutual fund managers, and others in the financial world were listed for an additional $103,900. Thus, the story said, oil and financial contributors "alone accounted for slightly less than 65 percent of the $550,155." Yarborough, whose support of humane and liberal causes antagonized powerful Texas interests, received but a few gifts of $5,000; and his total reported income for his race in the primary was a relatively trivial $247,652. But gifts of $5,000 and more, the *Post* story said, "seemed to fall like confetti" on Bentsen, a banking, insurance, and mutual fund multimillionaire, and on Bush, an oil multimillionaire, as well as on Archer, Smith, and Eggers. Bush, Bentsen, and Smith each reported combined primary and general election income of about $1 million, Eggers $611,000, and Archer—in the general election—$145,000.

The generosity of at least a few of the dozens of donors named in the story is worth recording. Patrick R. Rutherford, a Houston oil producer, was listed by Bentsen for $12,500. His son and business associate, Mike G. Rutherford, was down for $5,000. Together, they also gave Smith $7,500, according to the Governor's filing. The Rutherfords' grand total: $25,000.

Bush listed Edgar W. Brown, Jr., a seventy-six-year-old Orange, Texas, oil, timber, and banking entrepreneur, for $17,500 which was more than double the sum recorded by Yarborough from labor groups even though he was known as a friend of labor and was chairman of the Senate Committee on Labor and Public Health. Eggers reported that Brown gave him $3,500 and loaned him $2,500. The grand total from Brown to the two candidates: $23,500.

Oil operators J. R. Butler, Sr., and J. R. Butler, Jr., were listed by Bush, Eggers, and Archer for aggregate gifts of $16,650 plus a $4,500 loan to Eggers. The same candidates listed A. B. Fay, another oil operator and former GOP National Committeeman, for a combined total of $16,135.

Bentsen listed oil operator William B. Blakemore for $10,000, and Governor Smith listed him as well, for $3,000. The two Democrats listed yet another oilman, Paul F. Barnhart, for $5,000 each.

Eggers listed an Abilene, Texas, rancher and his wife, Mr. and Mrs. John A. Matthews, for $10,000 and Bush also listed them, for $6,000. Eggers also recorded combined gifts of $8,000 from oil operators H. W. Bass, Jr., and Richard D. Bass, his son; these Dallas men were also listed by Bush, for $8,500.

"The spotlight here belongs more on lawmakers and respectable businessmen with bulging brown briefcases than on lawbreakers and furtive men with little black bags using side entrances of hotels," Robert Engler said in *The Politics of Oil.* "Government policy on oil has increasingly become indistinguishable from the private policies of oil."[19]

The 27½ per cent depletion allowance—which has been regarded as a sacred rate even though it was the product of a compromise between those who would not accept 25 and those who would not accept 30—has made government and private policies indistinguishable, one from the other, since it was enacted in 1926. It was but one of several gimmicks by which the private government of oil—an *international* private government—has operated through the public government of Presidents, senators and representatives to shift an enormous tax burden to ordinary citizens and other industries. Counting lesser allowances which came to be provided for other minerals and clam and oyster shells, depletion allowances by 1969 would have depleted the Treasury by about $1.3 billion a year, had the pocketbooks of others not been depleted to make up the loss. In "The Oil Lobby Is Not Depleted," published in the *New York Times Magazine,* Erwin Knoll pointed out that $1.3 billion was a sum comparable to the "inflationary" spending increments that President Nixon used in justifying his veto of the appropriations bill for fiscal 1970 for the Department of Health, Education, and Welfare and the Department of Labor.[20]

The 27½ per cent depletion allowance—reduced in 1969 to 22 per cent, thanks to the sustained efforts of men such as former Senator Paul Douglas (D–Ill.), Senator John J. Williams (R–Del.), and Senator William Proxmire (D–Wis.)—classically illustrated taxation of the many because of representation of the few. In procuring enactment of the allowance, such senators as David Reed of Pennsylvania and Reed Smoot of Utah prevailed over men such as Senator William King, also of Utah, who said, "I cannot understand this great solicitude for the Standard Oil Company, the Shell Oil Company, the Sinclair Company, and the other great organizations, whose annual profits are many hundreds of millions of dollars."[21]

The depletion allowance involves some dizzy economic notions. For tax (or non-tax) purposes it bases the valuation of capital, which in this case is discovered oil, not on the sensible and traditional base, investment, but on selling price. If an investor in other fields realizes a capital gain he is taxed for a capital gain—but not if he invests in an oil well. The oil in the well is a wasting asset. That is, the supply eventually will be depleted and the well eventually will be worthless. But a machine is also a wasting asset. That is, it too, eventually will wear out and be worthless. But the $27\frac{1}{2}$ per cent depletion allowance has been roughly 90 per cent more generous to the investor in the oil well than the depreciation allowance has been to the owner of the machine, even though the issue in both cases, the erosion of an economic asset, is similar. Further, the depletion allowance pumps tax benefits for the well owner so long as the well pumps oil, long after the investment has been fully recovered, in many cases, while depreciation bears some relation to the actual cost of the machine. Finally, a couple of simple points: The sum invested in any capital asset logically relates to its worth. Granting that an oil well someday will be exhausted, the investment in that asset will reflect this— at one level if depreciation applies, and at a much higher one if a depletion allowance applies. And income dollars pumped by oil look exactly like the income dollars produced by other businesses. They should not be taxed differently.

But logic is seldom potent when deployed against an array of money power and legislative power. The $27\frac{1}{2}$ per cent allowance remained on the books unchanged, as if it were sacred, and no matter who attacked it. In the 1930s Senator Huey Long, father of Senator Russell Long, said the allowance should be eliminated. President Roosevelt said its purpose was "to dodge the payment of taxes." Ronnie Dugger, to whom we are grateful for an assemblage of such piquant quotations, found that Senator Robert A. Taft, who was known as "Mr. Republican," had said the allowance was "to a large extent a gift . . . a special privilege beyond what anyone else can get." In 1950 President Truman said, "I know of no loophole . . . so inequitable." But in the 1968 campaign Richard Nixon said, "As President, I will maintain it."[22]

The tax laws allow oil and gas producers to get special tax breaks from so-called intangible costs for exploration, drilling and development, even when such activities are engaged in off foreign shores. This is not all: they are allowed to apply most of the amounts they pay to various sheiks of Araby and other foreign powers as dollar-for-dollar offsets for taxes which otherwise they would owe the government of the United States. Over the years, these offsets have saved the oil companies billions of dollars in taxes which, of course, the rest of the taxpayers have made up. One should not be quick to assume that the companies have shown gratitude to the taxpayers. Between 1965 and the spring of 1969, for example, Standard of New Jersey raised the price of gasoline four or five cents a gallon. During the same period it *lowered* the price to its Japanese affiliates for Arabian crude 10 to 12 per cent. This was brought out during a hearing of the Senate Subcommittee on Antitrust and Monopoly by its then chief economist, Dr. John M. Blair.

Citing calculations by the Treasury Department, Erwin Knoll said that the special tax privileges given to oil and gas companies have saved in taxes nineteen times as much as the original investment in an average well. In 1968, he said,

> American oil companies paid less than 8 per cent of their income in taxes, compared with more than 40 per cent for all corporations.
> Clearly, the tax laws have played an important part in making the oil industry the formidable economic and political force it is. The industry's annual sales total more than $60 billion. Among the 2,250 largest American companies surveyed last April [1969] by the Economic Newsletter of the First National City Bank of New York, the 99 oil companies alone accounted for more than 25 per cent of the total profits.[23]

But a mere twelve oil companies accounted for 19 per cent of the $6,127,814,000 in after-tax profits earned in 1968 by the 2,250 largest American companies. The top seven oil companies accounted for 16 per cent of the grand total of earnings, and the top three among the seven—Standard of New Jersey, Texaco, and Gulf—alone accounted for 10 per cent. Knoll went on to say:

> The industry's average profit of 9 per cent (based on net sales) is about double the average for all manufacturing companies; only one other industry—drugs—maintains a higher profit level.

The oil industry is believed by specialists in campaign financing to outspend all other industries in political contributions. No one knows

190

how much has been given, but no one doubts that the payoff in the tax laws has made the investment extremely worthwhile. Apart from such contributions, oil governs through other techniques, including lobbying and propaganda campaigns, through always managing to have more friends than enemies on the tax-writing committees of Congress, and through legislators such as Senator Russell Long who themselves have very large interests in oil and gas. In his article on the oil lobby, Erwin Knoll said:

> Few of his colleagues can match Senator Long's holdings, but many share his concern for the industry's welfare. Among those on whom the oil moguls can generally count for unstinting support are Senators John G. Tower of Texas, Gordon Allott of Colorado, Clifford P. Hansen of Wyoming, Henry L. Bellmon of Oklahoma, Roman L. Hruska of Nebraska, Robert J. Dole of Kansas, Peter H. Dominick of Colorado, Allen J. Ellender of Louisiana, Theodore F. Stevens of Alaska, George Murphy of California and Karl E. Mundt of South Dakota.[24]

The 1970 elections struck Murphy from the list, but surely Lloyd M. Bentsen, Jr., of Texas will ably fill the vacancy.

By 1969 the oil import quota was costing the public $7.2 billion a year by the estimate of John Blair. He further calculated that in the decade ended in 1969 the quotas in the aggregate had cost the public between $40 billion and $70 billion. Even if a more conservative estimate for 1969 of $5.2 billion were to be accepted, the cost to, or private tax on, a family of four in New York State was $102.32 added to bills for gasoline and home heating oil.[25]

President Eisenhower established the system on March 10, 1959, by executive order. By restricting imports of cheap foreign crude, including that from Libya which is low in sulphur content and therefore in air-pollution potential, it assured a market for expensive domestic crude. Specifically, as of the summer of 1969, by Blair's calculations, a barrel of crude from the Middle East could be laid down in New York for $2.00, compared with $3.75 for a barrel of domestic crude from the Gulf Coast.

Mr. Eisenhower's justification for the order—a truly massive interference with the market mechanism by a Republican Administration—was "national security." Sherman Adams, who in the early Eisenhower years was "deputy President," acknowledged in his memoirs that "the imposing of import quotas on oil was primarily an economic decision brought about by an economic emergency." The "emergency" was

191

created by the importation of foreign oil "at such a rate that the American oil-producing centers were being forced into desperate straits." But, Adams said, General Eisenhower based his executive order "upon security considerations in accordance with the law."[26]

Neither explanation—"economic emergency" or "security considerations"—suffices. In establishing a mandatory system of import quotas, Mr. Eisenhower issued an order that was, almost word for word, the text of a report recommending such a system. Six Cabinet members, acting collectively as the Special Committee to Investigate Crude Oil Imports, had prepared the report. One of them was Robert B. Anderson (not to be confused with Robert O. Anderson, president of Atlantic Richfield). He was widely considered the most powerful figure in Mr. Eisenhower's second-term Cabinet insofar as domestic affairs—especially oil—were concerned. Anderson had, Bernard D. Nossiter disclosed in the *Washington Post*, "a direct personal interest in the price of domestic oil." And this price was protected by the quota system because it limits imports of low-cost foreign oil.

The Senate confirmed Anderson as Secretary of the Treasury on July 2, 1957. Eighteen days earlier, Nossiter said in a copyrighted story on July 16, 1970, he had "completed a deal with some oil men designed to pay him nearly $1 million. Of this amount, $270,000 was scheduled to be paid during his term in office. His chances of receiving some $450,000 of the rest depended in part on the price of oil." As it turned out, Anderson apparently received, through 1963, less than $300,000. In any event, he told Nossiter, "it never crossed my mind" that he had as Secretary a direct interest in oil prices. "I think anybody who comes into these things tries to think of the national interest," he told the reporter.

The deal Anderson made shortly before becoming Secretary, which he described to Nossiter as "ordinary, normal," involved some properties, chiefly in Texas. For a time, Sid W. Richardson, the late, enormously wealthy oil operator, had leased the Texas property; but at the time of the deal the leaseholder was the Stanolind subsidiary of the Standard Oil Company of Indiana. It was for finding a driller to drill for oil for Stanolind that Anderson was to get the ("ordinary, normal"?) sum of $1 million. The driller he found, who at the time held the bulk of the surrounding property, was none other than his friend Sid Richardson. How Richardson could have been so hard to find as to warrant a $1 million finder's fee is not easy to see. In Midland, Texas, for example,

Stanolind could have found Richardson's office only one block away from its own; and in Fort Worth both had offices, too.

Nossiter cited an explanation that he brought up in an interview with Anderson, but that Anderson refused to discuss. It concerned a purported effort by President Eisenhower to have Anderson, whom Ike greatly admired, replace Richard M. Nixon as his running mate in 1956. According to this wholly credible report, for which Nossiter found independent support, Anderson was willing but told Mr. Eisenhower that he would need $1 million to afford this. The President, the story goes, told Richardson of the problem; and Richardson devised the $1 million finder's fee to offset the loss of income that Anderson would have suffered as Vice President. But Mr. Nixon had influential friends, including Republican National Chairman Leonard Hall. The upshot was that Mr. Nixon remained on the ticket and General Eisenhower managed to keep his esteemed friend Anderson close at hand by making him Secretary of the Treasury. Nossiter wrote:

> The Cabinet Committee on which Anderson sat recommended, and Mr. Eisenhower approved, a special kind of quota system. It assigned quotas to all refiners, including those in the nation's interior, regardless of whether they had ever imported oil before. . . . One of the biggest inland refiners is the Standard Oil Co. of Indiana. Its subsidiary, Stanolind, held the lease on the Texas property for which Anderson served as a broker. Since its birth in 1959, the quota system has given Standard of Indiana what amounts to a windfall estimated at $193 million.

But even if there had been an "economic emergency," as Sherman Adams claimed, there was no need to give an advantage to an inland refiner such as Standard of Indiana or to any special class of companies. Equitable remedies were available. A tariff could have been imposed; this would have produced revenue for the taxpayers rather than for particular oil companies. A similar benefit would have come from an auctioning off of quota assignments. Limits on imports hurt the traditional importers of foreign oil, the coastal refineries; quotas could have been assigned to them. But the Cabinet committee of which Anderson was a member rejected all such alternatives. Instead, it not only recommended that quotas go to all refiners, but also voted to allow those with quota assignments ("tickets") to "exchange" them for domestic oil. This made the "tickets" very valuable, because of the cost differential between domestic and Middle Eastern oil laid down on the East Coast. During much of the 1960s the price of a "ticket" was $1.25 per barrel. Standard of Indiana alone got quotas for 155 million barrels. Thus Mr. Eisenhower, rubber-stamping the report of Anderson and his fellow Cabinet members on the Special Committee, gave this company rights worth almost $200 million.

Even apart from such windfalls and their resultant immense private taxation of the public, the quota system produced a wide range of deleterious and strange effects. Here are some of them, as established in hearings which Senator Philip Hart's Subcommittee on Antitrust and Monopoly held in 1969 on "Governmental Intervention in the Market Mechanism":

In Hawaii there is but one refinery. The operator is Standard Oil of California. Also in Hawaii are four other international oil companies which sell premium and regular gasoline to motorists, under their own brand names. But all of this gasoline is Standard Oil's. The five companies would have Hawaiians believe that they compete. Alone among the companies, Standard has "tickets" to bring in foreign crude. The rationale for the quota system for Hawaii was that it was getting its crude from the West Coast—a fiction. Indeed, at a shipping cost of one cent a gallon Standard was carrying 20 to 37 per cent of the gasoline it refined in Hawaii to Seattle. There, presumably because of a measure of competition, Standard was selling the gasoline for three cents a gallon *less* than in Hawaii. Were the quota system to be removed and competition allowed, Congresswoman Patsy T. Mink told Senator Hart, the average Hawaiian car owner would save at least thirty-nine dollars a year.

Governor Kenneth M. Curtis of Maine testified that because of the Mandatory Oil Import Program, to use the formal name, foreign crude is imported at Portland, is transported by pipeline 230 miles to Montreal, and is there refined into home heating oil. But the oil sells in Canada for 3.59 cents a gallon less than New Englanders must pay, because of the quota system.

The "feedstocks" for petrochemicals—which ultimately reach every consumer in a multitude of forms, including plastics, paints and fiberglass—are two. One is natural gas, the supply of which is expanding only half as fast as the demand for raw materials, and which by 1975 is expected no longer to be competitive in price on the world market with crude oil, the second "feedstock." Unless the import quota system is lifted

194

to give the petrochemical industry access to foreign crude, it will be forced by world competition—by foreign companies that *do* have free access to that crude—to build plants abroad, rather than in the United States, at a rate of $2.5 billion a year. This warning was given to the Subcommittee by the Chemco Group, an informal alliance of nine companies (Union Carbide, Celanese, Dow Chemical, Monsanto, E. I. du Pont, Eastman Kodak, Olin Mathieson, National Distillers and Publicker Industries). At the time, American crude, as noted above, cost $1.75 more per barrel than foreign crude. The Chemco Group's reason for seeking a swift decision was the "lead time" problem—it takes five years to design and build a petrochemical complex, whether in this country or abroad.

The oil import quota system was under heavy attack when the Nixon Administration took office. There was the "tax revolt" in which the oil industry was a prime target. Senators from states that were particularly victimized by the system, including Edward M. Kennedy of Massachusetts, Edmund S. Muskie of Maine, and Thomas J. McIntyre of New Hampshire, were on the offensive in behalf of enraged and exploited constituents. Senator William Proxmire of Wisconsin was battling frequently on the Senate floor with Senator Russell Long. Additional heat was generated by a proposal to build a refinery in a foreign-trade zone at Machiasport, Maine, that would be permitted to process 100,000 barrels of imported crude a day—in excess of the imports allowed under the quota system. And, of course, there were the Senate antitrust hearings.

Apparently with the intention of blocking the Machiasport proposal, Michael L. Haider, retired board chairman of Jersey Standard and chairman of the American Petroleum Institute, and Frank N. Ikard, a former Texas congressman who is president of the institute, proposed on February 5, 1969—only thirty-six days after the Inauguration—the creation of a White House task force to review the quota system. The President accepted the proposal. He formed a unit composed of the secretaries of State, Treasury, Defense, Commerce, Interior, and Labor and the director of the Office of Emergency Preparedness, and named Labor Secretary George P. Schultz chairman. Professor Phillip Areeda of the Harvard Law School, was chosen to head the staff. Probably to the chagrin of the big oil companies, the staff did a fair and thorough job and resolutely resisted pressures from, among others, Chairman Wilbur

J. Mills of the House Ways and Means Committee. And certainly the industry had not counted on an attack on quotas from the Justice Department. But one came, from Assistant Attorney General Richard W. McLaren's Antitrust Division. "The import quotas themselves do nothing to preserve this nation's domestic oil reserves," the Division told the task force. In addition, it said, the program "intensifies the effect of the existing lack of competitive vigor in various domestic oil markets."

On November 6, 1969, Erwin Knoll has reported, Frank Ikard met over a quiet dinner with three governors.[27] The next day, they and a fourth governor met at the White House office of Peter M. Flanigan, the top presidential assistant. The four governors were Preston Smith of Texas, Robert B. Docking of Kansas, Stanley K. Hathaway of Wyoming, and Richard D. Ogilvie of Illinois. Which one of the four had not met with Ikard has not been established. In any case, they were acting in behalf of the Interstate Oil Compact Commission which, Knoll said, "has nothing to do with the oil-import program, but . . . has engaged in heavy lobbying for retention of the quota system." Assembled to hear their views, which were supported by the governors of thirteen other states in telegrams that were of strikingly similar phrasing, were Secretary Shultz and three other members of the Cabinet Task Force on Oil Import Control.

At about the same time, Michael Haider, the retired Standard Oil chairman, had a private audience with President Nixon. *Oil Daily,* a trade journal, said he emerged "feeling more optimistic" after "a very good conversation." The paper said Haider "believes Nixon has a good grasp of the problems surrounding oil-import controls and is more confident that the outcome will be favorable."

When the Cabinet task force held its last full meeting in December, Attorney General John N. Mitchell was present for the first time. This was significant for several reasons, apart from the fact that he took a position out of line with that of his own Antitrust Division. He is the President's closest adviser and his former law partner, and, as the manager of Mr. Nixon's 1968 campaign, must be presumed to have a good idea of where campaign contributions come from. Mitchell "emphatically told Shultz, 'Don't box the President in,' " Erwin Knoll reported. "Some of those present interpreted the remark as a Presidential request for retention of quotas"—a position strongly urged by Secretary of the Interior Walter J. Hickel and Secretary of Commerce Maurice H. Stans.

The White House released the task force report on February 20,

1970. A five-member majority, led by George Shultz, recommended abolishing the quota system and putting in its place a tariff that would let oil prices fall a very moderate thirty cents a barrel—at a saving to the public of billions of dollars. The majority analyzed and decisively rejected every defense of the system made by the industry, the governors, secretaries Hickel and Stans, and John N. Nassikas, chairman of the Federal Power Commission, who was a task force observer.[28] Later, in testimony before Senator Hart, Shultz said the import quota system "does not reflect national security needs, present or future, and is no longer acceptable."[29] His estimate, more conservative than John Blair's, was that the system cost consumers $5 billion a year but would cost $8.4 billion annually by 1980. Apart from this, he testified, "the quotas have caused inefficiencies in the marketplace, have led to undue government intervention and are riddled with exceptions unrelated to national security."

When the report was made public, President Nixon did not so much as mention the recommendation of five of his own top officials, including four members of the Cabinet, for the crucial switch from quotas to a tariff. Instead, he called attention to the divergence of views, as if that were of greater significance, and postponed action indefinitely. To keep the ball in the air, he appointed a new Oil Policy Committee headed by George A. Lincoln, head of the Office of Emergency Preparedness. The members included all of the Cabinet members who served on the task force but one—George Shultz. His replacement was John N. Mitchell.

Newsmen were briefed on the report—while Shultz was on the West Coast, and Areeda was teaching a class at Harvard—by Peter Flanigan. He "sought to give the impression that Mr. Nixon was doing exactly what his task force had recommended, which was untrue," William K. Wyant said in the *New Republic*.[30]

The oil industry's reaction to Mr. Nixon's treatment of the report was not merely favorable, but joyous.[31] This was to be expected when, as Senator Proxmire put it, "The consumers have been sacrificed once again to the interests of big oil." A *New York Times* editorial expressed revulsion at the hypocrisy of "an Administration that prides itself on being a great inflation fighter when it comes to trimming outlays for health, education and welfare [but] does not mind letting consumers pay out more than $60 billion in extra oil bills over the coming decade."[32]

The new Oil Policy Committee that Mr. Nixon set up to give him the recommendation he wanted made its report six months later. It reached its decision to retain the oil import quota system "without any formal discussions or working papers by the responsible officials involved," Bernard Nossiter reported in the *Washington Post* on August 19, 1970. He said that George Lincoln, the committee chairman, acknowledged this at a press conference the day before. The story continued:

> In response to reporters' questions, Lincoln said that his fellow Oil Policy Committee members only discussed the issue "now and then, casually" and "my staff didn't prepare written papers on this."
> Lincoln also disclosed that Peter Flanigan, a White House aide, sits in regularly on the committee's meetings and was present at the crucial "principals only" session last Thursday when the Lincoln letter [a letter bearing Lincoln's signature urging that there be no relaxation of the quota system; the White House released the letter on August 17] was adopted. Lincoln, however, denied reports that Flanigan had dictated the letter's essence. Lincoln acknowledged that he had discussed it in advance with White House figures whom he declined to name.

The industry gushed out welcomes to this rigged oil deal as soon as Mr. Nixon announced his acceptance of the committee's recommendation. The timing was such that the oil companies could show their gratitude in the form of campaign support in time for the congressional elections of 1970, when the President was trying his best to help Republicans take control of the Senate, and, of course, again in 1972, when Mr. Nixon is expected to seek reelection. On the same day that the Oil Policy Committee's recommendation was made and accepted, at a cost to the public of up to $20 million a day, Mr. Nixon attacked the Democratic Congress for failing to act on certain economy proposals he had made, at a cost to the public—if the President's claims for them were to be taken at face value—of $2 million a day. But such discrepancies rarely have troubled Richard M. Nixon, who always has managed, somehow, to pay the bills for his political campaigns.

During the 1968 presidential campaign, executives of numerous investment firms and funds and brokerage houses recorded substantial contributions to Nixon-Agnew committees. In the *Washington Post,* Walter Pincus reported, for example, contributions of at least $60,000 from Jack J. Dreyfus, Jr., chairman of the Dreyfus Fund; $32,600 from Frederick Ehrman, partner in Lehman Brothers; $19,000 from David

Van Alstyne, Jr., partner in the Noel Van Alstyne securities firm and board chairman of New Idria Mining & Chemical Company; $15,000 from Richard J. Buck, vice president of Bache & Company, and then a fellow director of Mr. Nixon's on the board of Harsco Corporation, a maker of steel products; $1,000 each from five partners of White, Weld & Company and from five partners of Goldman Sachs & Company; $2,400 from two partners of Lazard Frères, and $1,600 from the Wall Street partnership itself. (Contributions by partnerships are permitted under the law. It should also be noted that donations to Nixon-Agnew committees were by no means the end of the matter. Thus Jack Dreyfus later was reported to have given GOP groups of all kinds a total of at least $76,000.)

On September 27, 1968, a letter went out from Mr. Nixon to leaders of the securities industry. The letter was not made public by the Nixon organization but was disclosed by Eileen Shanahan in the *New York Times* of October 2. In the letter, the Republican leader promised that if elected President he would end the "heavy-handed bureaucratic regulatory schemes" of the Johnson Administration. He denounced proposed legislation, which mutual funds strongly opposed, to compel such funds to limit their charges to investors, who frequently were unaware of the size and nature of the fees. In addition, the letter attacked moves made by the Securities and Exchange Commission and the Justice Department aimed at reducing the commission rates on sales of stock listed on the New York Stock Exchange. Early in 1971 Mr. Nixon announced his intention to nominate as chairman of the SEC William J. Casey, a tax lawyer who was listed for $17,750 in gifts to the GOP in 1968.

Some who invest in political campaigns do so in hopes of being able to influence presidential appointments to the independent regulatory commissions. "The test of competence for each candidate consists of the submission by the White House of his or her name to industry executives before sending it on to the Senate for confirmation," Louis M. Kohlmeier, Jr., author of *The Regulators,* has said.[33] He continued: "Every President in recent history has run some sort of check with industry before appointing or reappointing a regulator. . . . The appointment machinery apparently works well enough, for example, to satisfy one bank executive, who said of the banking regulators: 'This system works best if there's a blob in every job.' "

During the 1968 presidential campaign Jack Gould, the broadcasting columnist of the *New York Times*, said, "Yet if the next President should pick a broadcaster for an F.C.C. post, it would represent a reverse in the executive traffic flow that has been the general pattern since 1944."[34] One of President Nixon's first two appointments to the Federal Communications Commission was Robert Wells, a broadcaster.

Here is a concise summary of the regulatory climate in the Nixon Administration, as seen by the *Wall Street Journal* on November 21, 1969, just ten months after Mr. Nixon entered the White House:

> Nixon appointees to regulatory agencies swing their weight, mostly pro-industry.
>
> [Federal Communications Commission Chairman Dean] Burch, three weeks on the job, starts giving specific instructions to the staff, runs meetings with a firm hand. Burch promptly took part in a phone-rate decision considered pro-business, though he's been critical of TV networks. Maritime Commission skipper [Helen Delich] Bentley calls for her staff to help the shipping industry, not harass it.
>
> CAB Chairman [Secor] Browne appears to encourage airline mergers, as well as fare boosts. He even favors airline marriages with other transportation companies, requiring a law change. Power Commission chief [John] Nassikas pleases gas producers with hints of price rises. A gas consumer representative calls the commission "far more industry-oriented than in the past."
>
> *One sign of FPC change: A Texas Republican comes in as general counsel, succeeding an advocate of low gas prices.* [Emphasis in the original.]

The "mere appointment of quiet conservatives" such as Nassikas, Christopher Lydon reported on January 14, 1970, in the *New York Times,* "has already been enough to slacken the pace of agency activity and re-establish the traditional Republican preference for invisible regulation."

To run the Federal Aviation Administration the President chose John H. Shaffer. The *New York Times* said that "according to those who know the industry, [this was] a result, in part, of his lifelong Republican affiliation and of the fact that the choice was acceptable to the two opposing factions of the airline industry—the major airlines and the 'general aviation' sector."[35]

The Federal Aviation Administration is a unit of the Department of Transportation. It is one of numerous units of the executive branch that have regulatory powers of one kind or another. Others include the National Highway Safety Bureau, which in March 1970 was removed from the Federal Highway Administration but remains in the Department of Transportation; the Oil Import Program and the Bureau of Mines, both in the Department of Interior; and the Food and Drug Administration in the Department of Health, Education, and Welfare.

Unlike members of independent regulatory agencies who are appointed to terms of a duration fixed by law, the administrators of the dependent agencies serve at the pleasure of the President or a Cabinet member. Thus a campaign contributor who wishes to influence a dependent agency has more reason to apply leverage at the White House than he would in the case of an independent agency.

A month after Richard Nixon was elected President, T. C. (Tom) Snedeker sent a letter to executives of major oil firms. The text is self-explanatory:

> The position of Administrator of the Oil Import Program will be vacated by Mr. Elmer Hoehn when the Administration changes.
>
> As you know, I have been Assistant Administrator since the program's inception in 1958. My own beliefs, with regard to the fundamental philosophy of the program, have been uniform from the beginning. I believe the program is necessary to the purpose for which it was established (our national security) and the most equitable program is one of strict controls without the all too numerous exceptions which have been granted in recent years. In many instances, I alone objected to the granting of these exceptions. Now, I would like very much to return the program to the basic principles upon which it was founded.
>
> Any support you may give me in this behalf, either through Members of Congress or through other individuals, will be greatly appreciated. For your information, both my wife and I have been registered Republicans for many years.
>
> I am enclosing a brief outline of my experiential background. Thank you.
>
> Sincerely yours,
> T. C. SNEDEKER
>
> P.S. Any support should be sent to:
>
> Mr. Harry Fleming [sic]
> Office of the President-elect
> % The White House
> Washington, D. C. 20500

A copy of the letter found its way into the hands of Frank C. Porter of the *Washintgon Post,* and Snedeker did not become Administrator of the Oil Import Program. But a do-it-yourself approach is often less rewarding than more orthodox intercessions by, say, a giver or receiver of a large campaign contribution who has a friend at 20500, the nation's most exclusive ZIP code.

No implication is intended that able and dedicated men are rarely appointed. Presidents Kennedy and Johnson on many occasions appointed such men and promoted others. To name a few: Philip Elman at the Federal Trade Commission, Nicholas Johnson at the Federal Communications Commission, Joseph Swidler and Lee C. White at the Federal Power Commission, and Manuel F. Cohen at the Securities and Exchange Commission. President Nixon has made extremely few appointments that merit praise from public-interest advocates.

Because the Food and Drug Administration literally exercises a life-and-death responsibility for all of us, it warrants a special note. For years it had been a captive of industries it supposedly was regulating. The late George P. Larrick, who was commissioner from 1954 to 1966, once proudly received an award from the Pharmaceutical Manufacturers Association for "devoted service to the public welfare" and for his "understanding of mutual problems."[36] The most pungent comment on that kind of thing probably was made by Peter Lyon in *To Hell in a Day Coach*: "When the chairmen of the boards of railroad companies start talking about the public interest, it is time to count the spoons."[37]

A hopeful new era began in 1966 when John W. Gardner, Secretary of Health, Education, and Welfare, appointed Dr. James L. Goddard to succeed Larrick. The Secretary once told one of the authors:

> I have backed Dr. Goddard very strongly and have never faltered in that, even when I thought he had done something not fully wise. I have looked at a lot of regulatory operations, including the FCC and the FAA. I know what I want in a man to head such an operation. I want a man with a driving determination to get the job done. In any regulatory activity, the forces tending to produce inaction are overwhelming. Interested parties can produce a thousand reasons why you should do nothing. You need a man who has a real bite to him, and a zest for action. You pray that he has impeccable judgment, but very few of us have that. I'd rather have a man I have to slow down than a man I have to wake up.[38]

But for the most part the man who has to be slowed down rather than wakened up is seldom picked to begin with, is seldom backed by a John Gardner if he is chosen, is nibbled to death while he holds office, and doesn't stay very long. First Gardner quit and then, after two and a half years, Goddard.

Within a few months after taking office as Secretary of HEW, Robert H. Finch demonstrated that he was not of a mind to emulate Gardner. The case involved the combination of antibiotics known as Panalba, which the National Academy of Sciences–National Research Council said has "no place in rational therapeutics." In December 1968 the FDA made a preliminary move to take it off the market. Having grossed $16.8 million from Panalba in 1968 alone, the manufacturer, the Upjohn Company, obviously had a good deal at stake. The firm is a corporate constituent of Representative Garry E. Brown (R–Mich.). He arranged a meeting of company officials with Finch and Under Secretary John G. Veneman, at which Upjohn made several requests intended to overcome the FDA's plans. The same day, May 5, Veneman instructed the FDA to "consider" resolving the issue with certain actions that, it turned out, were the very ones Upjohn had proposed. For this interference with the judgment of an FDA Commissioner about a hazardous drug there was no known precedent.

Commissioner Herbert L. Ley, Jr., protested bitterly to Finch that he could not go on certifying Panalba as safe and effective when it was neither. Asking the Secretary for support, he said in a memo: "The basic question is whether the government is prepared to move promptly and effectively to stop the use of a hazardous drug when the available facts and the national drug law dictate such action."

Three days later, after access to FDA files had been demanded by the House Intergovernmental Relations Subcommittee, Finch backed down and supported Dr. Ley. Ironically—and to the detriment of very large numbers of patients (Dr. Ley has estimated that each year Panalba injured, needlessly, hundreds of thousands of persons)—the Commissioner himself procrastinated.[39] Not until March 1970, after the FDA had won a final victory in the Supreme Court, did Upjohn finally withdraw Panalba from the domestic market (but not the $10 million-per-year foreign market, where the product is sold as Albamycin-T). By this time the FDA had had a new commissioner, Dr. Charles C. Edwards, for four months. In several areas of crucial importance to the public health, including the handling of cyclamates, the artificial sweeteners; the oral contraceptives; and combination antibiotics, Finch gave no indication of taking the approach to his own appointee that John Gardner had taken to Dr. Goddard—to back him very strongly and never falter. On June 6 a new cycle, probably somewhat for the better, began when the President announced that Elliot L. Richardson, Under Secretary of State, would replace Finch.

On January 4, 1969, more than two hundred coal miners gathered at a rally in Logan, West Virginia. Many of them were "disabled and dying from 'black lung,' " Hank Burchard reported the next day in the *Washington Post.* The purpose of the rally was to push for proposed state legislation and for federal standards for coal mine health and safety that would limit dust in the mines to three milligrams per cubic meter. High standards had been adopted decades ago in other countries, including England and Czechoslovakia, with a resulting massive avoidance of preventable death, disease and injury. Burchard reported that Dr. Hawley Wells, a crusader against black lung, told the miners, "You breathe coal dust every working day, at levels of 3000 milligrams per cubic meter of air"—a thousand times the maximum level that should be tolerated. Burchard wrote:

> Dr. Wells, holding aloft a dried slice of diseased lung tissue, said, "This is what I find in your lungs when your bodies pass through my shop." He crumbled it and let it sift through his fingers to the table before him. "Dust, dust, dust. Coal dust," he said. "The tissues are full of it. So are yours."

Here is the way Ben A. Franklin, of the Washington Bureau of the *Times,* began four successive stories in 1970 and a fifth in 1971:

February 23: "After more than a year of unsuccessful efforts to oust John F. O'Leary, the Director of the Bureau of Mines, the Nixon Administration is making another attempt to replace him with a man more acceptable to the mining industry and the Republican party."

February 28: "The Nixon Administration, reacting to criticism of John F. O'Leary's aggressive conduct from the mining industry, today ousted him as director of the Bureau of Mines, a safety agency recently given greater enforcement powers."

March 4: "The Interior Department abruptly interrupted today a series of mine-safety briefings for the coal industry that had been under way across the country under plans drawn up by John F. O'Leary, who was dismissed four days ago as director of the United States Bureau of Mines."

March 23: "Three Democratic members of the House of Representatives joined a coal miner today in a suit to compel the Administration to publish immediately overdue Federal health and safety regulations for mine owners."

January 17, 1971: "A lawyer and former city judge who has worked as a Republican party fund raiser, a campaign consultant and a lobbyist for the Iowa Association of Coin Operated Laundries, is being given the $30,000-a-year job of 'enforcer' of Federal coal mine safety standards in the Bureau of Mines."

The Administration's performance makes sense, of a kind, if one is aware that coal companies increasingly have come to be owned by oil companies.

⑥ THE CONGRESS

"It is the third branch of government, the legislative, where things have gone awry," Joseph S. Clark said in *Congress: The Sapless Branch*. Clark was highly qualified to speak on the point, having been a senator from Pennsylvania for twelve years, until 1969, and, before that, mayor of Philadelphia. He went on to say:

> Whether we look at city councils, the state legislatures or the Congress of the United States, we react to what we see with scarcely concealed contempt. This is the area where democratic government is breaking down. This is where the vested-interest lobbies tend to run riot, where conflict of interest is concealed from the public. . . . I have no hesitation in stating my deep conviction that the legislatures of America, local, state and national, are presently the greatest menace in our country to the successful operation of the democratic process.[1]

If the legislatures are in fact "the greatest menace," or just a great menace, one of the principal reasons is that so many of their members are excellent business investments. Clark did not put it quite that way, but he put it pretty strongly. Talking about the four Democratic and Republican congressional campaign committees—two in the House and two in the Senate—for example, he said that they "are to a substantial extent prisoners of the lobbies." Thus, he pointed out,

> the conservative oil and gas lobbies, which contribute so heavily to the Democratic Senatorial Campaign Committee, had not the slightest interest in the re-election of Senator Paul Douglas of Illinois in 1960, he having been a staunch advocate of cutting the depletion allowance. But they were vitally interested in the re-election of the late Senator Bob [Robert S.] Kerr of Oklahoma, who was the most articulate spokesman for the oil interests in the Senate. Quite naturally Senator Kerr received a very much larger contribution from the Senatorial Campaign Committee than Senator Douglas.

The lobbies quietly earmarked their contribution to the committee for Senator Kerr, and the committee, as an implicit condition for receiving the money, sent it to Oklahoma, where it wasn't needed, rather than to Illinois, where it was.[2]

Kerr was the archetype of the most direct, undisguised form of government by business. He was himself big business—oil, gas, uranium, beryllium, boron, helium, potash—and in the Senate he unabashedly furthered the interests of Kerr-McGee Industries, Incorporated, of which he owned 22 per cent. But rather than focus on Kerr, who died in 1963, let our emphasis be on current and recent examples of business governing the Congress.

In 1969, for the first time, the House of Representatives began to require its members to file statements with a new House Committee on Standards of Conduct in which certain financial disclosures are made. The rules for disclosure are so loose that, for example, Representative Alonzo Bell (R–Calif.), a millionaire, said he was filing "a negative report" because the questionnaire to which he had to respond did not cover his interest in the Bell Petroleum Company. Nevertheless some interesting data were produced. These were analyzed for the *Washington Post* by William Greider and Jan Krause. Here are excerpts from their stories of May 7 and 8, 1969:

About two-thirds of the 435 House members have significant outside interests, either shares in private businesses or fees paid for services rendered away from their Capitol Hill jobs.

The banking industry is, by far, the most popular. In fact, a study of the reports showed that one in every five Congressmen has a personal stake in financial institutions, usually one of his hometown banks.

According to the reports, 90 members own stock in banks or savings and loan associations. Of these, 37 Congressmen held a large enough interest to be elected to the board of directors or, in a few cases, chairman of the board.

Beyond banking, the most important provider of extra income is the legal profession. However, House members also reported investments or income in virtually every important segment of the economy—from airlines to insurance companies to oil fields. In all, 275 Congressmen have reported private investments or income-producing activities.

Fifty-six members reported that their names are still on the doors of law firms where they were partners before entering Congress. Another 19 lawyer-Congressmen said they practice individually or by referral from other firms. Ten others said they have terminated or are "on leave" from private practice back home.

Congressional stock-market investments covered the spectrum from mutual funds to the major American corporations. Oil and gas interests are held by at least 41 Congressmen; communications, airlines and railroads, and insurance followed closely behind.

Fourteen members reported stock held in radio and television corporations and another six said they are the owners or principal investors in radio or TV stations.

The reporters found numerous cases in which members had interests in enterprises which are subject to laws written by the committees of which the congressmen were members. Representative Clarence J. Brown (R–Ohio), for example, was president of a radio station in Urbana, Ohio, and a member of the House Committee on Interstate and Foreign Commerce, which writes laws regulating the communications industry. Representative William E. Brock III (R–Tenn.) owned stock in major defense manufacturers, and was a member of the Joint Committee on Defense Production. Representative Emanuel Celler (D–N.Y.), who has served in the House since 1923, longer than any other member, was senior partner in a law firm in Brooklyn and chairman of the House Judiciary Committee.

With the Senate Finance Committee, the House Ways and Means Committee writes the tax laws. Greider and Miss Krause said that six members of Ways and Means, or about a quarter of the total, reported banking relationships, and a seventh, Representative Herman T. Schneebeli (R–Pa.), had such a relation but did not report it. A similar situation, on a larger scale, existed in the House Banking and Currency Committee, which has broad authority over the lending industry. Twelve of its members, more than a third of the total, disclosed interests in banks or savings and loan associations. Representative Del Clawson (R–Calif.), had such an interest but did not list it.

"The banking lobby is the single most potent lobby that operates year-round in Washington," Representative Wright Patman (D–Tex.), chairman of Banking and Currency, has said. Patman, a tough, battling populist who reached his present eminence thanks to the seniority system, addressed the National Press Club on July 31, 1969. This was two days after the *Wall Street Journal*, in a story by Jerry Landauer, made some startling disclosures about Representative Seymour Halpern of New York, the third-ranking Republican on the committee. Halpern was more than $100,000 in debt to banks and other creditors. This burden included a loan of $40,000 made by the First National City Bank of New York—without security and at the prime interest rate, that is, the rate usually reserved for a lender's largest and most reliable corporate customers. First National City was the first of the ten largest banks to set up a one-bank holding company under which, it will be recalled, other businesses of all kinds can be owned and operated free of the restrictions applying directly to banks. Not long before Landauer's story appeared, the Banking and Currency Committee had acted on bills to restrict one-bank holding companies. Patman favored strong legislation. But the committee majority—five Southern Democrats and all of the fifteen Republicans—voted for a loophole measure which would allow such companies not only to engage in other businesses "functionally related to banking," but also to remain in such businesses if they had been initiated before February 17, 1969. First National City, which was "grandfathered in" by the loophole bill, and Halpern, who had voted for that bill, denied any impropriety. Bankers hailed the committee vote as "a signal victory," the *New York Times* reported.

Patman, in his speech, did not mention Halpern by name, but referred to the revelation in the *Wall Street Journal* as "tragic." Promising an investigation of "the banking lobby," which the committee majority later was able to block, Patman said that it has offered large amounts of bank stocks and bank directorships to committee members, immediate loan service to freshman congressmen on their arrival in Washington, campaign contributions, and mass mailings to stockholders in behalf of certain political candidates. "I leave it to you," Patman told his audience, "to judge what these contributions and campaign assistance might mean on a crucial vote on banking legislation."

Lacking hard evidence, we must leave it to the reader to judge what contributions and campaign assistance might have meant in the treatment the Senate Banking and Currency Committee gave one-bank holding company legislation. This was the sequence of events:

After the "signal victory" in the House Banking and Currency Committee, an opposition coalition, including threatened insurance and travel agents, mustered support for a strong bill. They prevailed; and in November 1969 the House passed a measure that promised to revitalize the wise American tradition of fostering separation of banking and commerce in order to inhibit the creation of blocs of overwhelming economic power. The House bill not only prohibited one-bank holding companies from entering certain specified business activities, but required the more than eleven hundred existing companies of this kind to spin off functionally unrelated operations acquired after May 9, 1956— thirteen and a half years earlier. Of course, this would have been a near-fatal blow at the one-bank holding companies set up by First National City and other giant banks in the late 1960s.

The bill went to the Senate, which referred it to the Banking and Currency Committee. Meanwhile, the big banks regrouped. They had strong allies, mainly about twenty-five conglomerate corporations each of which had acquired, and was determined to keep, a bank of its own. The formidable nature of the stakes—and, hence, of the power— is suggested by a stark statistic: By the end of 1969 one-bank holding companies had come to hold no less than about 43 per cent of all bank deposits in the United States.

A sense of urgency on the part of Senator John J. Sparkman (D– Ala.), chairman of Senate Banking, surely would have been appropriate; but it surely was utterly lacking. Sparkman let the bill languish for months—another "signal victory" for the giant banks and conglomerates, and an especially pleasant one because it slipped by almost unnoticed, with none of the uproar that attended the Congressman Halpern affair. Finally, in May 1970, the committee began hearings. The spectators usually were "an enraptured throng of lobbyists—many of them former employees of the legislators," Jan Nugent Pearce said in a *Washington Post* news analysis on August 9, 1970. "In this atmosphere of good fellowship," she continued, the committee produced a measure of its own which would protect all of the big banks and conglomerates with a cutoff date for functionally unrelated operations of March 24, 1969. This date, as fresh and crisp as a new dollar bill, was five weeks later than that in the original bill, the one approved by House Banking; and if that bill had been a "signal victory," the Senate measure would have to be classed as a "signal super-victory," or something of the sort. Indeed, Mrs. Pearce wrote, the Senate bill would reach only about 19 per cent of the one-bank holding companies. Among those excluded were twenty-six controlled by conglomerates. Mrs. Pearce continued: "Sen. Harrison Williams (D–N.J.) , up for re-election this year, sponsored a "grab bag" amendment that exempted at least 899 companies—including some controlled by the nation's biggest conglomerates."

The committee approved its bill in July 1970. The Williams amendment was part of it. There was no record vote. This made it difficult for the press (although possibly not for lobbyists who had been committee employees) to find out who voted how. But it was not difficult to see that the legislation was in truth being written not by a committee of the United States Senate, but by the Capitol Hill branch offices of giant banks and giant conglomerates. On September 16 the Senate passed the bill 77 to 1, Senator William Proxmire (D–Wis.) being the lone dissenter. The bill was inadequate, because it "grandfathered in" most of the major one-bank holding company acquisitions that already had occurred. As reported by the Banking and Currency Committee, the cutoff date for such acquisitions without government approval was March 24, 1969. On the Senate floor, Proxmire, aided by Edward W. Brooke (R–Mass.) and Charles E. Goodell (R–N.Y.) did manage to set the date back nine months, to June 30, 1968.

The Senate and House bills then went to a conference to be reconciled. On balance, the result must be considered a victory for the banking industry, because the conferees agreed to a law—enacted in December 1970—that left untouched the great concentrations of banking power with which this very legislation supposedly was to deal. True, the law provides that the Federal Reserve Board investigate all large one-bank holding companies formed before June 30, 1968; and in special circumstances it may require divestiture of holdings that fail to meet certain "public benefits" tests. This provision figured in Congressman Patman's description of the law as a "strong" measure that "will firmly separate banking from non-banking businesses."

His may be an optimistic appraisal, in the light of the close relationship that often has prevailed between the Fed and the banking industry.

Could contributions to, or, more accurately, investments in, political campaigns possibly have figured in the efforts to make this legislation pro-bank, pro-conglomerate, and anti-public?

There are bits of evidence on this. On May 14, 1970, for example, one of the authors disclosed in the *Washington Post* that for years some of the largest banks in the country—including Manufacturers Hanover

Trust in New York, Union Bank of California, National Bank of Commerce in Seattle, and Central National Bank of Cleveland, Ohio—had "invited" all of their officers to "contribute" systematically, on the basis of income, to the particular bank's own "good government league." Each such "league" made contributions to candidates favoring federal and state legislation favored by the banks, a point made perfectly clear in the dunning letters. A few of the bankers interviewed for the newspaper story said defensively that they were engaging in a practice in which all, or almost all, other large banks also engaged. But not one of the bankers would specify how much money they raised or identify the candidates to whom they donated, or in whom they invested. Representative Patman, in a letter to Attorney General Mitchell, said that a large segment of the banking industry was engaged in "massive political fund-raising" in possible violation of the law.

Until the spring of 1970 the bankers said they did not have an organization with the specific purpose of coordinating their political contributions on a national basis. This lack was remedied with the creation of the Bankers Political Action Committee, or BankPAC. It set a fund-raising goal of $520,000. Lewis K. McKee, chairman of the National Bank of Commerce of Memphis, Tennessee, became chairman of Bank-PAC, and Ralph L. Stickle, former executive director of the Michigan Bankers Association, became executive director. On October 22, 1970, which was eleven days before the congressional elections, the *American Banker,* "The Only Daily Banking Newspaper," reported that BankPAC "will begin within the next five days disbursing more than $200,000 in campaign contributions to some 40 members of key committees in Congress who are up for re-election." The story, which was indicated by later events to have been an overstatement, was based on an interview with Stickle on October 21; yet, two days later, BankPAC filed a financial report with the clerk of the House of Representatives listing contributions of $93,609 but no expenditures at all for candidates for the House and Senate. The reporter, James S. Byrne, said Stickle told him "that the contributions would go solely to incumbents the bankers favor and who need financial assistance, and not to challengers of incumbents bankers oppose." Byrne also said: "The candidates who will receive help from BankPAC will be selected members of the House Banking and Currency, Ways and Means and Rules Committees, and the Senate Banking and Currency and Finance Committees."

The Corrupt Practices Act requires that the final preelection report be mailed from an established post office five days before the election. BankPAC's reached the House clerk on October 31, or three days before the election. It disclosed contributions of $100 or more totaling $149,641 as of October 29; but contributions and, as well, expenditures could be made after that date free of a legal requirement to disclose them until two months after the election. In any event, BankPAC said it had spent $11,482 on miscellaneous expenses and $55,500 on congressional candidates, leaving $82,659, at a minimum, to be spent before election day, if the organization cared to do so.

BankPAC said that it gave one of its two $5,000 contributions to Senator Harry F. Byrd, Jr., of Virginia, which was about as natural as it was for the AFL-CIO to pay a salary to George Meany, and the other to Senator Harrison A. Williams, which also was quite natural, Williams having put through the "grab bag" amendment to the one-bank holding company bill. BankPAC also recorded gifts of $35,000 to twenty-one of the thirty-five members of House Banking and Currency, including $2,500 to each of three Republicans who were to join Williams after the election on the House-Senate conference committee on the differing versions of the one-bank legislation. These Republicans were William B. Widnall (N.J.), the ranking minority member; Albert W. Johnson (Pa.); and J. William Stanton (Ohio). BankPAC even gave $2,500 to a Democrat on House Banking who was unopposed for reelection, Robert G. Stephens, Jr. (Ga.). Another $2,500 went to a Maine committee for Senator Edmund S. Muskie, who by this time was in truth seeking the 1972 Democratic presidential nomination while running for reelection to the Senate. BankPAC's contributions were intended, Congressman Patman said, "to weaken the holding-company bill. Now is the time to spread the money around if they want to influence it."

Preelection publicity about BankPAC and about a request by Patman for a Justice Department investigation set off something akin to panic among the candidates the organization had listed as beneficiaries. In a report filed with the clerk of the House in December 1970, BankPAC said that thirteen of twenty-six recipients had returned checks for $27,000 almost half of the sum donated. Among those returning the gifts were Senator Williams, Representative Widnall, Representative Johnson, and Representative Stanton.

Banking legislation immediately involves money. Trucking legislation has an immediate potential to involve human life as well as money. The trucking industry, principally through the American Trucking Associations, Incorporated, has long been pushing a bill under which the states could authorize bigger trucks on federally financed interstate highways. The maximum permissible width would be increased from 8 to 8½ feet, for example. Total weight could be 69 tons, compared with the present limit of 36. The leading opponent of the measure, Representative Fred Schwengel (R–Iowa), has warned that it would not only make driving more hazardous for ordinary motorists, but would so add to the strains on the roads that they would require renovation at a cost of at least $3 billion.

In the *Des Moines Register* of July 25, 1968, Nick Kotz, a Pulitzer Prize-winning reporter, disclosed that the trucking industry had in 1966 and 1968 contributed at least $29,000 to members of congressional committees concerned with the bill. The largest single reported contribution, $3,000, went to Representative John C. Kluczynski (D–Ill.), who introduced the bill in February 1968. He was the fourth-ranking Democrat on the Public Works Committee and chairman of the Roads Subcommittee to which the bill was referred. A majority of the thirteen members of the full committee who received contributions sat on the subcommittee. Contributions of $1,000 each were listed for George H. Fallon (D–Md.), the committee chairman, the second- and third-ranking Democrats, John A. Blatnik (Minn.) and Robert E. Jones (Ala.), and the second-ranking Republican, William H. Harsha (Ohio). Contributions of $500 each were listed for the seven other ranking Democrats and the third-ranking Republican. The committee approved the bill.

The bill went to the House Rules Committee. Kotz reported that in 1966 and 1968 the truckers had contributed $500 to each of six of the nine ranking members and $2,500 to a seventh, B. F. Sisk (D–Calif.). The Rules Committee cleared the bill after a perfunctory hearing.

In the Senate, the Public Works Committee also approved the measure. Kotz said that contributions of $1,000 each were recorded for two Republican members, Howard H. Baker (Tenn.) and J. Caleb Boggs (Del.) and in 1966, before he left the committee, for a third, Jack Miller (Iowa).

The contributions were made through the Truck Operators' Nonpartisan Committee. Its treasurer, Frank Grimm, told the reporter, "We do what we can for those on the committees who might help us. It's as simple as that."

The Johnson Administration supported the bill, on the stated ground that it would permit greater efficiency and economy in freight hauling. Despite all the jackpot politics, the measure died in the Ninetieth Congress. The measure was pending again in 1970 but was opposed by the Nixon Administration and given little chance, thanks largely to Congressman Schwengel. But it may be assumed that the trucking industry will try again, as soon as the political climate becomes more favorable.

Candidates from many states have found a wondrous vacuum in the District of Columbia. It has no law requiring reporting of campaign contributions or expenditures. When the Bankers Political Action Committee sent a check for $5,000 to Senator Harrison Williams, it did not mail it to his home state of New Jersey, but to the "Harrison A. Williams D.C. Committee" at Suite 352, Old Senate Office Building, Washington, D.C.—his legislative office. In view of the fact that financial reporting is not required by the District, it is understandable that an aide to the Senator, told of the BankPAC donation, could say he had no record of such a contribution. Why should he have?

A campaign committee in the District is often nothing more than a bank account with a label on it—say, "Ecologists for Jones." Jones may be a legislator who wishes to conceal from the voters back home that he is getting $1,000 each from the presidents of Air Pollution, Inc., and Water Degradation, Ltd. So the contributions are funneled into "Ecologists for Jones," which then draws a check for $2,000 and mails it to "Anti-Polluters for Jones" in his home state. Dutifully, that group files a report which records—what? Why, a $2,000 gift from "Ecologists for Jones" in Washington. No one knows the original source of the cash. Lest any of this be thought whimsical, here is what a Capitol Hill aide told Haynes Johnson of the *Washington Post*: "So then you set up a D.C. bank account, so that way you wouldn't have to report what labor union or what corporation gave how much, and then send that money back home for the 'Citizens for ———— Account.' "[3]

But an award for candor about District of Columbia committees ought to go to Senator James L. Buckley, the New York Conservative, and David R. Jones, who managed his election campaign. In a voluntary postelection report to the secretary of the Senate, Buckley said he had received more than $400,000 through more than fifty D.C. committees with names such as "League of Middle American Women," "Scientists for Sensible Solutions to Pollution," and "Town Meeting Preservation Society." James R. Polk, an Associated Press reporter who disclosed all of this in a story on December 28, 1970, said that Jones told him, "We made a game out of it."

The "only reason" for setting up the D.C. committees was to hide the names of the donors, who included Republicans among Wall Street bankers who wanted to avoid antagonizing the New York State GOP organization, Jones told the reporter. The D.C. committees, Polk said, were the sole contributors to "100 other Buckley committees set up in New York. These 100 passed on the money the same day to Buckley's campaign." All of the New York committees, bearing such names as "Chenango County Friends of Buckley," had the same treasurer, K. Ross Jordan, an executive in Buckley's family firm. Jones, saying reforms were needed to make such devices unnecessary, told Polk, "I think it's absurd. But you have to do it this way."

The Johnson Administration proposed in 1967 that the postal rate for third-class bulk mail—mainly advertising materials—be raised from 2.7 to 3.8 cents per piece. This would have cost the bulk mailers more than $150 million a year—or, in the alternative, would have kept a lot of "junk mail" out of our mailboxes. The bulk mailers wanted to slow down the proposed increases with an amendment which was supported by, among others, then Senator Daniel B. Brewster, a Maryland Democrat who was defeated for relection in 1968. Congress resolved the issue in December 1967 by setting a rate of four cents per piece for each piece in excess of 250,000.

On December 1, 1969, following an investigation ably led by Stephen H. Sachs, then United States Attorney for Maryland, a grand jury in Baltimore returned a rare bribery indictment. Named defendants were Brewster, who by then was ill in Ireland; Spiegel, Incorporated, a huge mail-order house in Chicago; and Cyrus T. Anderson, Spiegel's Washington lobbyist. The indictment charged that in a period of slightly more than two years starting in January 1966, Spiegel and Anderson made five payments, totaling $24,500, to Brewster to influence his "action, vote and decision on postage rate legislation" while he was a senator and a member of the Senate Post Office and Civil Service Committee. Three

216

payments totaling $14,500 were made through the "D.C. Committee for Maryland Education." Spiegel denied wrongdoing while acknowledging having made contributions "openly and legally" to "various committees in Washington, D.C."[4]

In a pretrial proceeding, Norman P. Ramsey, counsel for Brewster, argued for dismissal of the indictment on the ground that the Constitution, in Article I, Section 6, immunizes members of the Senate and House "from arrest . . . for any speech or debate in either House [and says that] they shall not be questioned in any other place." All that Brewster had done in connection with postage-rate legislation, in other words, was legislative "speech" and consequently privileged. Alan I. Baron, a special prosecutor, disagreed. "I can't believe that election to the Congress of the United States amounts to a license to steal," he said. On October 9 in Federal Court in Washington, Judge George L. Hart, in a brief oral opinion, held that the Constitution *does* shield Brewster "from any prosecution for alleged bribery to perform a legislative act." With that, Hart dismissed the indictment against the former senator. The Justice Department appealed to the Supreme Court. The indictment against the other defendants was left standing.

Most stock brokerage firms are partnerships. Unlike corporations, banks, and unions, they are free under the Corrupt Practices Act to contribute their own funds directly to congressional (and presidential) campaigns. Naturally, there is in such firms an interest in regulating the regulators and in shaping and blocking legislation. During 1968 there was a fair amount of activity in this area. A bill to regulate the fees and cost to the public of mutual funds was before the Senate and, in July, was passed, only to die in the House. The Securities and Exchange Commission was seeking lower commissions for brokers on volume purchases and sales of stock. In May 1968 there was formed the Exchange Firms Campaign Committee. Richard O. Scribner, general counsel of the Association of Stock Exchange Firms, was named treasurer. He said the purpose of the committee was to involve "many individuals in political giving" to congressmen and senators on a bipartisan basis—"on the basis of merit." The appeal to merit was strong enough to produce $125,000 within a few months. A list of contributors filed with the clerk of the House in September included such well-known brokers as the following, each of which was down for $5,000: White Weld & Company; Carl M.

Loeb Rhoades & Company; Hornblower & Weeks–Hemphill, Noyes; Eastman Dillon, Union Securities & Company; Carlisle & Jacquelin; Reynolds & Company; Paine, Webber, Jackson & Curtis, and DeCoppet & Doremus. In the *Washington Post,* Walter Pincus said the contributors also included individuals associated with brokers around the country. "For example, more than 30 persons listed as giving $100 to $800 work for Dean Witter & Co.," Pincus said. "This securities firm—unlike the partnerships . . . was recently incorporated and thus is barred by Federal law from contributing its own funds to the campaign committee."[5]

Also in May 1968, Merrill Lynch, Pierce, Fenner & Smith, Incorporated, the biggest stock broker in the country, set up its own Effective Government Association. By September 1, in a disclosure unique for a corporation, it reported contributions of $44,775. Checking the list of donors, Walter Pincus found that nineteen of Merrill Lynch's twenty-nine directors were down for $500 each, lesser officials were listed at $200 or $300 each, and salesmen $100 each. The number of contributors exceeded a hundred and fifty, including a few outsiders, according to William J. La Fleur, treasurer of the Association and assistant general counsel of Merrill Lynch. Until Pincus's story was published in the *Washington Post* on October 18, the Association worked for its proclaimed goal of "effective government" by contributing to individual candidates. One of these was Representative W. S. Stuckey (D–Ga.), who got $500 even though he had no opponent. He did, however, have something else to commend him, Eileen Shanahan reported in the *New York Times*—his membership on a House Commerce subcommittee with jurisdiction over legislation affecting the securities industry. In 1969, after the Senate passed some fairly tough mutual-fund legislation which the industry opposed, the bill reached the subcommittee where "a watered-down substitute," in the phrase of Clem Morgello of *Newsweek,* was offered.[6] The author was Stuckey.

After the Pincus story was published in 1968, an event that Merrill Lynch made clear it did not welcome, the firm stopped giving to individual candidates. Adopting a new policy, it began donating in equal amounts to Democratic and Republican fund-raising committees. "We're not out to influence candidates," La Fleur told Pincus. "I don't think we could."

Taken literally, LaFleur was saying that the money was being raised and spent to non-influence candidates and to non-achieve "effective government." This is of course absurd. But there are some subtleties in all of this to which we must attend. Much of the time, it is idle to try to establish a cause-effect relation between a campaign contribution and the vote of a congressman or senator. When such a relation exists it is most difficult to prove. Sometimes no such relation exists: the legislator may behave as he does for any of several reasons—habit, prejudice, principle, to please his constituency—contribution or no contribution. It should be noted that Congressman Stuckey is a wealthy man to whom a $500 contribution, even if for a non-campaign in which he was unopposed, possibly meant little, if anything.

There is no Newtonian Law of politics in which every campaign contribution always produces an equal and apposite reaction in the form of a desired vote. "Each Senator is a bundle of principles, areas of concern, viewpoints, fields of expertise and publicly stated positions," one of the authors wrote in the *George Washington Law Review*. He continued:

> Based on past positions, votes and public utterances, he has projected an image which he values. That image is more important to him than the arguments of any and all Washington lawyers urging an inconsistent position. The head of the antitrust subcommittee seldom can be expected to support exemptions from the antitrust laws. A free trader generally will not support greater import restrictions. On the other hand, you don't need much influence to convince an oil state Senator that oil quotas make good sense or a western state Senator that water conservation legislation should be supported. These are facts of political life.[7]

The Merrill Lynch episode is perhaps most useful in serving to remind us that those with economic power have, and are willing to use, a capacity to reward their friends in government. Ordinary citizens lack such a capacity. This places them at an enormous disadvantage. The Merrill Lynch episode also provides an opportunity to point out that legislators can show appreciation to the economic powers who benefit them in ways that are difficult to detect, in contrast with a recorded vote on the floor of the House or Senate.

A great deal of the activity of the committees of the Congress is conducted in secret. This enables some legislators to pay debts to various contributors with no public awareness of what is happening. Envision, if you will, a closed session of a subcommittee in which no transcript of the proceeding is to be made. Imagine also that the chairman is pressing for action on a bill which is adverse to company X. He needs a quorum. A member who has been given a contribution by company X might simply choose not to come, thus preventing a quorum and pleasing his benefactor. Or he might go to the meeting feeling that he should vote for the bill, but that he doesn't want to be hard on company X. And so he tells the chairman that he wants a single word changed: instead of saying that a regulatory agency "shall" require firms such as company X to do something or other, he wants to say "may" require. The chairman knows this change of one word may eviscerate the bill, but without the member's vote he will be able to report no bill at all. And so he yields. The member had taken a contribution from company X. No strings were attached. If he is a decent man he feels obliged to show his gratitude; if he doesn't he is an ingrate.

Another thought may cross the mind of the member. The trade association of which company X is a member invites selected congressmen to be speakers or panelists at its annual meetings. The "honorarium" for this chore is $5,000. If he is an ingrate he will not be invited. He will not get the $5,000—which, incidentally, is a real, not a fanciful, figure.

Giving practical tips to its members in its *Political Handbook for Bankers,* the California Bankers Association described the nature of the "overnight accommodations" that should be offered a legislator invited to a bankers' cocktail party and dinner:

> They should be complimentary and very pleasant without being pretentious. Further thoughtfulness can be displayed by having a basket of fresh fruit or another appropriate gift delivered to his room before his arrival. Flowers should be sent if his wife accompanies him. . . . The news media should not be invited to these functions, but it is possible they will show up. . . . It should be made clear to them that the legislator's remarks are strictly "off the record."

The twenty-six-page handbook, whose useful advice was given broader circulation by the *Washington Post* on May 14, 1970, made an astute observation in the following passage in which, we note in advance, the emphasis was in the original:

> Mere volume of mail alone, rarely—if ever—sways a politician. Pressure groups have become so proficient in running off "canned letters" and

flooding legislators with them, that this technique is no longer effective. *The legislator is very sophisticated today and it's what's inside the envelope that influences his thinking.*

Some legislators arrange things so that they are not told of specific contributions; not knowing, they can swear in campaign financing reports that they were made without their "knowledge and consent." Yet even a lawmaker who leaves these matters to aides knows in general that certain legislative behavior on his part is likely to produce contributions from certain companies, organizations, and unions, and that different behavior can dry up these sources—quite possibly without new sources becoming available. One legislative assistant described his role to Haynes Johnson of the *Washington Post:*

> "I'd always tell the Old Man, 'you don't want to know where it (the money) comes from, but if I tell you to see a guy, you'd better damn well see him. But I don't want you to know what he gave or how. If he's going to get sore at anyone, he'll get sore at me, not you.'"

The aide, who was not identified, told Johnson that by the time a campaign was at hand he already had drawn up a list of potential major contributors:

> "It would be a list that covers everything from steamship companies to gas companies to—well, Christ, you name it. And you'd set a quota. How much you're going to raise from each group. Then you'd get alone with them in private, without any witnesses, and you'd say, 'This is what I want, and this is how I want it.' In cash, or whatever.
>
> "Cash was always desirable, because by the time election day came around there was always money to spend—hiring poll watchers, renting cars, getting additional office help. I have made many, many trips back to my state with a briefcase full of money—in 20 or 100-dollar bills, as much as $23,000 at a time. Or, if it wasn't a cash payment that you got, you might want the contributor to pick up a certain sizable bill.
>
> "I always felt the only way to operate was to talk frankly, but I was capable of being tough, of saying either they did this or they were out, of telling them if they didn't contribute they weren't going to get in this office again because I was going to be here until ———'s in his grave.
>
> "And, of course, I always said I knew they were going to play the other side of the street (by contributing to the opponent) and that was okay with me. All we wanted was our fair shake."[8]

221

Another aide, also unnamed, told Johnson of having raised considerable sums of money for political candidates and of having flown across the country delivering cash payments. The aide said:

> "It's the prostitution of the political system, there's no question about that . . . but how else are you going to do it under the present situation?"[9]

"Most Congressmen are elected only with the active assistance of two or three giant economic forces in their districts," Larry L. King, who for more than a decade was an administrative assistant in the House, has said.[10] But, as the following example indicates, the generosity of a large corporation in one district can reach out to most other districts in the state.

On March 22, 1969, the "D.C. Nine," a group of antiwar militants, broke into the Washington offices of the Dow Chemical Company, the Midland, Michigan, firm which has been a special target of the peace movement because it produced napalm, defoliants, and other chemicals for the military in Vietnam. The Dow offices were vandalized, and, in the process, certain files were stolen. In February 1970, shortly before the "D.C. Nine" went to trial (and were convicted) on charges of burglary and destruction of property, members of the group distributed copies to newsmen. One of the papers was a list of contributions made to fifteen members of the Michigan congressional delegation, for their 1968 campaigns, by Myles McGrail, Dow's governmental affairs representative in Washington. He told Saul Friedman, of the Washington bureau of Knight Newspapers, that the contributions were "my personal money," and that Dow does not make contributions because that would be "illicit." Later, McGrail being ill, Friedman asked his wife where the money came from. "It's none of your business," she said.

In a story in the *Detroit Free Press* on February 5, Friedman said that nine Republicans and three Democrats were down for $100 each, one Democrat was down for $300 and two Republicans for $500 each. Another Democrat sold McGrail two $50 tickets to a fund-raising dinner. The only Michigan representatives not on the list were Gerald R. Ford, Jr., the House GOP leader, and Democrats Charles C. Diggs and John Conyers, both Negroes. Congressman William Broomfield, a Republican from Royal Oak, said that the representative whose district includes Midland, Republican E. A. Cederberg, on occasion received money from Dow officials to distribute to other members of the Michigan delegation. Broomfield also said, "I know you can't take a corporate check, but it's all right if it comes from McGrail or another officer or employe. This is the way many companies contribute." The interesting thing here is not the amounts of money, which were small, but the mechanism that was exposed—"the way many companies contribute."

An important but little-perceived reason for the 1969 reforms in the tax laws affecting foundations goes back to a speech of July 1, 1968, by Congressman John J. Rooney (D–N.Y.), who has represented a Brooklyn district since mid-1944. He told his colleagues—one of whom said afterward that he had "listened with amazement"—"To put it bluntly—and I address myself to every Member of this Congress—unless you are a wealthy person or unless you have wealthy supporters who can help you fight back, you may find yourself in some future election being overwhelmed by a deluge of tax-exempt money."[11]

During the 1968 primary Rooney's only significant opponent was Frederick W. Richmond, a wealthy businessman and coffin manufacturer. "Mr. Richmond does not dispute reports that he has spent $250,000 in this campaign," the New York Times said on June 12, 1968. "That is a lot of money," Rooney commented. "It is, in fact, as much as any member of this House will earn from politics in eight years."

Rooney's speech dealt mainly with how the money was gathered and spent. In 1962 Richmond set up the Fredrick W. Richmond Foundation. Politically, at least, it was inactive until late 1967, a matter of months before the primary on June 18, 1968. Then the Walco American Corporation, controlled by the candidate-to-be, contributed $113,500 to the foundation. Another firm whose directors include Richmond gave $1,000. "Although it is against the law for a corporation to contribute to a political campaign, here is an easy way to get around that law," Rooney told the House. "The corporation simply makes a donation to a tax-exempt foundation which in turn supports the candidate."

The Fourteenth Congressional District (in which, Rooney charged, Richmond did not actually reside) has a number of minority groups. Starting in late 1967 their organizations began to be blessed by the Richmond Foundation. The United Talmudical Academy, for example, got six separate donations totaling $4,000. A month before the primary, the Sacred Heart Day Care Child Center got $5,000. Puerto Rican and black institutions were not forgotten. These gifts of taxpayers' money—

which is what tax-exempt money is in part—were politically exploited. One Richmond campaign leaflet told of the gifts to the Talmudists. Another showed the candidate talking with a Catholic pastor and, Rooney said, "apparently handing him a $5,000 check to help the Sacred Heart Day Care Child Center." The foundation also put $43,000 into a group of Neighborhood Study Clubs for which a tax exemption had been obtained—but which, Rooney said, were created "to publicize Mr. Richmond on a neighborhood basis, like the old ward clubs."

Rooney won the primary and went on to easy reelection to his fourteenth term. Other congressmen, not anxious to be fought by challengers with tax-exempt foundation funds, enacted reforms to prevent reenactments of the Richmond episode. There is, however, an ironic footnote, as will be seen in the following excerpt from a story in the *Washington Post* soon after the 1968 election:

> NEW YORK, Nov. 23—Fourteen officials from the State Department and U.S. Disarmament Agency or their wives made contributions ranging from $25 to $1000 to the re-election campaign this year of Rep. John J. Rooney (D–N.Y.), the man on Capitol Hill who for years has exercised almost dictatorial control over the spending of both agencies.

The donations were unusual. Not only does the law prohibit congressmen from soliciting federal employees, but it also prohibits the employees from making campaign contributions, directly or indirectly, to congressmen. However, the Civil Service Commission has conveniently interpreted the law to mean that such donations can be made if they are entirely voluntary. But there are more conventional situations in which legislators and businessmen tie themselves to each other.

There are, first of all, the legislators—more than 300 out of 535 members of the House and Senate—who are lawyers. Drew Pearson and Jack Anderson made a study of fifty typical law firms with partners on Capitol Hill. "These have a remarkable similarity of clients," they said in *The Case Against Congress: A Compelling Indictment of Corruption on Capitol Hill.* "They represent the vested interests of America: the banks, insurance companies, gas and oil interests, great corporations." The columnists gave these further details:

> Of the 50 law firms in the survey, 40 represent banks, 31 represent insurance companies, 11 represent gas and oil companies, 10 represent real

estate firms. Some of the biggest corporate names in America are listed as clients of Congressmen's law firms in such out-of-the-way places, say, as Nicholasville, Kentucky. . . . The Travelers Corporation, for one, has retained legal counsel in such unlikely places as Piqua and Findlay, Ohio, where the company's political radar led them straight to the law firms of Representatives William McCulloch and Jackson Betts, respectively. The same insurance company was also guided unerringly to the law firms of Representatives James Harvey in Saginaw, Michigan, and Wendell Wyatt in Astoria, Oregon. Solid Republicans all, the four have always managed to find in their hearts an extraordinary sympathy for the corporate view on insurance problems. Betts has been particularly effective as a champion of the insurance industry on the tax-writing Ways and Means Committee.[12]

The Panhandle Eastern Pipeline Company of Texas is another notable example of an outsize client attracted to out-of-the-way law firms. In East Lansing, Michigan, Panhandle retained a firm with which Representative Charles E. Chamberlain (R) is affiliated. In Peoria, Illinois, it retained Morgan, Davis & Witherell. This firm had an agreement to pay Senator Everett M. Dirksen (R–Ill.), the late Minority Leader, undisclosed amounts for referring clients.[13]

"Many in Washington are curious about why such major companies as International Paper Company and Panhandle Eastern . . . have retained the law firm as local counsel in Peoria," William J. Eaton and Robert Gruenberg said in the *Chicago Daily News.* They added:

> Former Sen. Paul H. Douglas (D–Ill.), writing on ethical problems of politicians, discussed this, saying, "The potential evils of this practice are obvious."
>
> But Dirksen insists he does not see any possible conflict of interest in sending "non-Federal" clients to Morgan, Davis & Witherell. ("And if they want to remunerate me for it, why not?")[14]

The law firm of Senator Jacob K. Javits (R–N.Y.), Javits, Trubin, Edelman and Purcell, "is known to represent some of the nation's greatest real estate trusts, including the First National Real Estate Trust of New York and the Crown Zellerbach Corporation," Pearson and Anderson said. "This does not seem to have inhibited Javits from voting on real-estate legislation."[15]

In Portsmouth, Ohio, there is a law firm known as Kimble, Schapiro, Stevens, Harsha and Harsha. One of the two Harshas is Representative

William H. Harsha (R). The columnists said that he introduced legislation to limit imports of fuel oil, which presumably pleased two corporate clients of the firm, Phillips Petroleum and Ashland Oil and Refining. They also recalled that on June 22, 1964, he led a fight in the House against the Mass Transportation Act. He denounced the measure as "nothing more than a tool to drive private transportation systems out of existence." He did not say that the law client which had left the legislative driving to him was Greyhound Bus Lines.[16]

Apart from the cases in the Pearson-Anderson book, of which the foregoing were merely illustrative, one more may be cited. It involved a New York City law firm, Weisman, Celler, Allan, Spett & Sheinberg, and the Penn Central merger. "Celler" is Representative Emanuel Celler (D–N.Y.), dean of the House, chairman of its Judiciary Committee, and chairman, as well, of Judiciary's antitrust subcommittee. Many times over many years, Celler has vigorously served the antitrust cause; and, with Senator Estes Kefauver, he cosponsored the 1950 legislation which had the purpose of tightening the merger provisions of the antitrust laws. And so it was of especial interest that reports filed with the Interstate Commerce Commission show that the Penn Central retained the law firm before as well as after the merger, which was formally completed in February 1968. Reporting this in the *Washington Post,* Ronald Kessler said that the railroad's filings with the Commission showed that the Celler firm

> received $51,664 for legal services in 1968 and $37,799 in 1967 . . . [and] a $47,462 payment in 1965.
>
> Celler said yesterday [September 15, 1970] the payments were for legal services performed by his firm, which was chosen by Penn Central because it is a specialist in "containerized types of railroad cars." He said no conflict of interest was involved. . . . "We haven't been paid (for 1969), and don't forget to get that in your story," Celler said.

The Congressman told Kessler that he had never discussed the Penn Central merger with the Justice Department, over which, as chairman of House Judiciary, he has jurisdiction.

The fund-raising dinner is so common and tedious a phenomenon as to seem unworthy of renewed attention. But here are two that were unusual. They were held within a few days of each other in September

1969. The site was Chicago—although neither of the beneficiaries was from Illinois. One of them, Republican Senator Roman L. Hruska of Nebraska, is possibly the most unabashed supporter of big business in the Senate. Even before his reelection in 1970 he was the ranking minority member of the Senate Committee on the Judiciary and of its very important Subcommittee on Antitrust and Monopoly, and, as well, a ranking member of the powerful Appropriations Committee. The other banquet was for a Democrat, Senator Vance Hartke of Indiana. He was an influential member of two committees in which business manifests a continuing and profound interest: Commerce, where he ranked third, and Finance, where he ranked sixth.

Each of the dinners was a $100-a-plate affair, with Hruska's drawing 175 guests and Hartke's 600. Only a handful of the guests were from Nebraska or Indiana, Richard T. Cooper said in a thorough report in the *Los Angeles Times*.[17] "Virtually all who bought tickets were men who spend their days directing major business corporations. How they came to attend the costly dinners for two senators from other states illustrates some significant aspects of the marriage between politics and wealth."

> Why, specifically [Cooper wrote], were politicians from Nebraska and Indiana seeking funds in Illinois? A matter of conveninence, dinner sponsors said: This is where the market is for $100 dinner tickets.
>
> Also a matter of discretion, others might say: This is where the voters of Indiana and Nebraska are not. Some might misunderstand or become alarmed at the sight of their elected representatives sitting down with the heads of corporations and labor unions.

Cooper found "patterns in the lists of guests and sponsors." Among those on the Hartke dinner committee were top executives of three steel companies, Youngstown Sheet & Tube, United States Steel, and Inland. A guest speaker at the dinner assured them that if import quotas to protect the domestic steel industry should become necessary, "Vance Hartke will provide the leadership." The guest speaker was Senator Russell Long, chairman of the Senate Finance Committee.

Another member of the Hartke committee was the president of Mead Johnson & Company, a drug manufacturing subsidiary of Bristol-Myers, Incorporated, in Evansville, Indiana, where Hartke had been mayor. But on the Hruska dinner committee were executives of three drug companies, G. D. Searle, Baxter Laboratories, and Abbott Laboratories. Among the Indiana firms represented at the Hruska dinner were Standard Oil, the Guarantee Reserve Life Insurance Company, and several banks. Entertainment at the Hruska dinner was provided by Senator Clifford P. Hansen (R–Wyo.), who said his colleague "knows that if we are going to have jobs, we have to have businesses that make a profit. We all live better when profits abound and exist."

Farmers naturally gravitate to agriculture committees and lawyers to judiciary committees. Such examples prove nothing except that simplistic, uninformed judgments on the ethical questions involved in matters of this kind may be hazardous. But there was no undue risk in assuming that there was a question about the propriety of an arrangement that Senator George Murphy had with Technicolor, Incorporated, starting five weeks after he entered the Senate on January 3, 1965. The firm, which then was dominated by Patrick J. Frawley, Jr., a wealthy supporter of right-wing causes, retained Frawley's friend Murphy, a California Republican, as a consultant. The contract guaranteed Murphy $20,000 a year, a $260-a-month subsidy for rental of an apartment in Washington's plush Watergate complex, and free use of a Technicolor air-travel credit card. In return, Murphy was to advise the company on public relations; he had been a Technicolor vice president before his election to the Senate.

Jack Anderson, who broke the story in his newspaper column, raised the question of propriety. It turned out that at Murphy's request, Senator John C. Stennis (D–Miss.), chairman of the Senate Select Committee on Standards, had screened the Technicolor contract. The Mississippian found it "reasonable and not a conflict of interest," Murphy said.[18]

Because he was a director of Technicolor and therefore an "insider," Murphy was required under regulations of the Securities and Exchange Commission to file reports on his transactions involving company stock. He filed such reports from the time he took his oath as a senator until March 1967. Then he stopped, failing to report twelve separate transactions, covering 21,700 shares, over the next three years. On June 2, 1970 he defeated industrialist Norton Simon in the primary contest for the GOP senatorial nomination. The next day, the SEC received a letter from Murphy in which he said he had been delinquent and in which he said he intended to return to the company $12,616 in

228

illegal profits, plus accrued interest. In a story disclosing Murphy's neatly timed admission, reporters Robert L. Jackson and Ronald J. Ostrow of the *Los Angeles Times* said on June 5 that Murphy purported to have written the letter four days before the primary and to have mailed it three or four days before that election.

Governor Ronald Reagan fervently defended Murphy, saying, "I would swear by his integrity." But Representative John V. Tunney, Murphy's successful Democratic challenger in the November elections, made a prime campaign issue out of the Technicolor arrangement. The voters of California apparently thought an impropriety may have been involved even if Senator Stennis did not; and even though President Nixon, Mrs. Nixon, Tricia Nixon, and Vice President Agnew came to California to campaign for Murphy he lost.

An effort must be made not to conclude that Capitol Hill, in Haynes Johnson's words, "is a vast seedbed for graft and influence peddling, a place where lobbyists are constantly waving big bills in return for something else." The effort must be made because Capitol Hill is, as we have seen, more complicated than that, and also better. There are men and women—senators, representatives, staff—of great (may the word be said) virtue—meaning courage, integrity, honor, acceptance of a numbing workload, zealous dedication to the public interest. There are too few such men and women, and maybe there always will be. But the situation will remain worse than it need be, and will deteriorate, unless and until ways are found to lessen the dependence of those who seek and hold public office on those who have money to invest and favors to bestow.

The crippling of a regulatory operation can begin at the root, with the way in which the law to be enforced is written. The Food, Drug, and Cosmetic Act of 1938, for example, has "a whole multitude of loophole situations," Congresswoman Leonor K. Sullivan (D–Mo.), has said. Most of the loopholes were "deliberately written into that law," she charged,

> in order to appease one or another powerful industry. Senator Royal S. Copeland of New York, a physician who handled the bill on the Senate floor, frankly acknowledged in the debate that soap was exempted from the law because the soap manufacturers, who were the biggest advertisers in the country, would otherwise join other big industries to fight the whole bill.

So soap was officially declared in the law not to be a cosmetic. . . . The railroads and truckers got a special loophole, too; so did the dairy industry; so did many others. These loopholes are still in the law. . . .

The hair dye manufacturers were given a license to market *known dangerous products,* just so long as they placed a specified warning on the label—but what woman in a beauty parlor ever sees the label on the bulk container in which the hair dye was shipped? Occasionally a customer loses her hair. Too bad; the law can't help her, or prevent recurrences. Other cosmetics items can be *taken off* the market if dangerous, but there is no power to prevent their marketing *before* they do harm.[19] [Emphasis in the original.]

There has been unusually broad support for the charge that under the chairmanship of Paul Rand Dixon in the 1960s the Federal Trade Commission did not fully use its resources in the field of consumer protection.

This charge entered the realm of conventional wisdom in 1969 when it was embraced by a study group appointed by the American Bar Association at the request of President Nixon.[20] The chairman of the study group was Miles W. Kirkpatrick, who later would succeed Caspar Weinberger as chairman of the FTC. The Commission often had preoccupied itself with trivia, such as whether to require labeling disclosure of foreign origin of a piece of watchband representing less than 1 per cent of its value. This and similar complaints were among those made earlier, in January 1969, by the first group of "Nader's Raiders" to make a report on a federal agency, and by Commissioner Philip Elman.[21] And there was some reason for Elman to say, in reply to a questionnaire from a Senate subcommittee, that a larger budget "would simply buy more unimportant cases, more inefficiency, more aimlessness, and, unless the spoils system is ended, more incompetent personnel at the higher staff levels. It should be clear that more money, alone, is the path not to reform but to decay."[22]

Yet Dixon had some justifiable complaints of his own against Congress. The FTC is, after all, its creature. In 1962, for example, the Commission started a study of intercompany relations among the one thousand largest corporations. Funds for the study, which Dixon said would have better equipped the Commission to deal with the conglomerate merger wave, were approved by the Bureau of the Budget. But, he told the Senate Subcommittee on Executive Reorganization,

Congress not only refused to appropriate funds for the study, but for three years in a row tacked a rider on the FTC's money bill to forbid spending of any agency funds for the inquiry. In 1965, Dixon told Senator Abraham A. Ribicoff (D–Conn.), the subcommittee chairman, the FTC tried to "do something about the massacre that goes . . . under the name of cigarette smoking." The agency proposed a rule to require disclosure of the health hazards of smoking in cigarette advertising. Before the rule could take effect, he testified, "Congress intervened, passing a bill that expressly prohibited us from doing anything about cigarette advertising."[23]

In theory, the deficiencies of the independent regulatory agencies and of units of the executive branch with regulatory powers would be alleviated and on occasion maybe even corrected if Congress reliably and seriously exercised its responsibility to oversee their performance. The unhappy truth is that reliable, serious, and sustained oversight is the exception rather than the rule on Capitol Hill. Not even in remote degree have the oversight mechanisms of Congress kept pace with the enormous growth of the Executive. Thus vast bureaucracies can bumble on for years, with hardly anyone noticing or caring. The point has been proved each time competent Capitol Hill investigators have been told to turn over the rocks at the Department of Defense, the Department of Health, Education, and Welfare, the Department of Interior—you name it.

One case suffices to make the point. It involved a very important law, the Insecticide, Fungicide, and Rodenticide Act, and the agency—probably one most Americans have never heard of, the Pesticides Regulation Division of the Agricultural Research Service of the Department of Agriculture—that was supposed to enforce it. The act says that until the Department registers a pesticide it cannot be shipped in interstate commerce. The law directs the Department not to register a pesticide product unless it has adequate evidence that the product is safe and effective when used as directed. More than 45,000 products, involving one or another form or trade name of 900 different chemical compounds, are registered.

In late 1968 the General Accounting Office, an investigative arm of Congress, made a report disclosing serious deficiencies in the way the law was being administered. The House Intergovernmental Relations Subcommittee then began a staff investigation, led by James R. Naughton, the counsel. The GAO assigned Morton A. Myers and Richard E. Chervenak to help him. Later, the subcommittee, headed by Representative L. H. Fountain (D–N.C.), held two days of hearings and, on November 17, 1969, its report was issued by the parent Committee on Government Operations.[24]

In general, the report concluded that the Pesticides Regulation Division had "failed almost completely" to enforce provisions of the law intended to protect the public. This failure lasted from 1947, when the law was enacted, until mid-1967, when the division got a new assistant director for enforcement, Lowell E. Miller. Even after Miller's debut serious deficiencies persisted. Here are some specific findings in the report:

Under an agreement made in 1964 between the Department of Agriculture and the Department of Health, Education, and Welfare, representatives of the departments were to confer in the event of a disagreement about whether a pesticide product should be registered. If either department objected to a proposed registration, and if an agreement could not be reached within two weeks after the objection was made, the issue was to be referred to the Secretary of Agriculture for a final decision. At a subcommittee hearing, Dr. Harry W. Hays, who was director of the Pesticides Division for four years until his demotion in May 1970, estimated that a mere half-dozen products had been approved over HEW objections. Actually, the subcommittee showed, in a five-year period ending June 30, 1969, HEW had objected to 1,633 proposed registrations, or about 275 times as many as Hays had acknowledged. Further, not one of the 1,633 cases was referred to the Secretary of Agriculture, as required by the interdepartmental agreement.

In 1953, the Food and Drug Administration made a study of vaporizers that continuously emit lindane, a pesticide, and have been widely used in restaurants. The study, which the FDA gave to the Agriculture Department, warned that the vaporizers contaminate food in the vicinity not only if it is uncovered, but if it is packaged in anything but metal. Although this was a significant health hazard, the Pesticides Regulation Division continued to register and reregister lindane vaporizers for use in restaurants. The excuse was that scientific data showing a hazard were lacking. The division's own medical advisers provided precisely such data in 1967, to no effect. Then came the critical GAO report. The division, which for sixteen years had failed to contract for or undertake tests of its own to establish whether the vaporizers deposited residues on food, finally, in 1969, had such tests performed. The tests, which the division's own laboratories did in five days, proved that the FDA had been correct in 1953. Finally, a few days before the subcommittee hearings were to begin, the Agriculture Department canceled the registrations for lindane vaporizers. (As opposed to a finding of an "imminent hazard" to the public followed by a suspension of registration, which actually stops sales, a cancellation permits sales to continue during the protracted period during which affected manufacturers may be expected to contest the action in elaborate administrative and possibly court proceedings. On June 14, 1970, which was fourteen months after registrations for the vaporizers had been canceled, James Risser reported in the *Des Moines Sunday Register* that nine companies which had invoked the appeal mechanisms "still are producing and selling lindane vaporizers.")

A similar case involved the Shell Chemical Company, a division of Shell Oil, and its widely sold "No-Pest Strip." This is a strip of plastic impregnated with a pesticide called vapona, which is continuously released for about three months. In 1963 the Pesticides Division registered vapona for use in restaurants and other places where food is left uncovered. This was done even though tests made by Shell showed that the strips left residues of pesticide on exposed food, and even though the hazards were serious enough that the Agriculture Department's meat inspection officials refused to permit use of the strips in meat-processing plants. The Food and Drug Administration was not consulted by the Pesticides Regulation Division, and in any event there is serious doubt whether the law would have permitted the FDA to set any tolerance level for pesticide residues on food.

Starting at least as early as 1965, the Public Health Service had protested registration of the strips, on the ground that they subjected humans to continued exposure to a pesticide. In late 1967 PHS officials agreed to withdraw their objection provided a warning were added to the labeling against use of the strips in rooms occupied by infants and aged and infirm persons. Shell Chemical agreed to inclusion of such a warning in January 1969, did not actually start including it until mid-April 1969, and did nothing to add the warning to already marketed strips until June 1969. Even then, Shell did not act until forced to do so by the Pesticides Division; and the division did not move until a few days after its own nonfeasance and misfeasance had been exposed in the second subcommittee hearing on June 24.

The subcommittee uncovered three cases of possible violation of the conflict-of-interest laws. All involved Shell Chemical, one of the leading pesticide producers. All of the cases were referred by the Agriculture Department to the Justice Department, which declined to prosecute.

One of the cases concerned Dr. T. Roy Hansberry, of Modesto, California, an executive of Shell Chemical's research subsidiary, Shell Development. In 1965 the Agriculture Department named Hansberry as the industry representative on a seven-member task force to study pesticide registration procedures. Although this obviously deeply concerned Shell Chemical, which by then had registered 162 pesticide products (plus 94 more from 1965 through June 1969) Hansberry's personnel clearance carried a typed, unsigned note saying, "The Agricultural Research Service does not have, or know of, any official business with the persons, firms, or institutions with which Dr. Hansberry has other financial interests . . . which might constitute a conflict of interest." Efforts to discover the origins of this notation failed.

The second case concerned Dr. Mitchell R. Zavon, assistant health commissioner for Cincinnati and an official of the Kettering Laboratory of the University of Cincinnati College of Medicine. He held stock in a Shell Oil affiliate and was a consultant to Shell Chemical. For a period of about six years, he was simultaneously a consultant to the Pesticide Regulation Division. While he was counseling the regulatory agency and the regulated company, Zavon was issuing reports on tests which purportedly showed vapona strips to be so safe as to require no warning for infants and old and sick persons. At one point he attended a meeting, sponsored by the Public Health Service, at which vapona strips were discussed. The subcommittee said he "presumably" was there as a consultant to Shell—but implied that he may have created the impression he was there as a consultant to the Pesticides Regulation Division. For one thing, he charged his travel expenses to the government. PHS files contain numerous letters from state and local health officers objecting to or opposing the use of vapona strips. However, the subcommittee said, a letter from Zavon "is the only instance known . . . in which a health officer wrote PHS to endorse the use of [vapona] strips."

The third case involved John S. Leary, Jr., who as the Pesticide Division's chief staff officer for pharmacology, overruled a subordinate's objection to the original Shell registration of vapona in 1963. In November 1965 an ad hoc committee of eight scientists met at the request of the PHS to study safety questions relating to vapona strips (and insecticides, including lindane, used in vaporizers). Six members opposed the strips (all eight opposed lindane). The director of the division, Harry Hays, received the committee report in September 1966. He then called a meeting of three medical consultants to consider the same safety questions the PHS committee had studied. Instead of giving the consultants the report of the PHS committee, he gave them a memorandum which did not oppose use of vaporized pesticides. The writer of the memo was John Leary.

On November 14, 1966, Leary submitted his resignation, effective December 31, to join Shell Chemical. A few weeks before leaving he sent a second memo to Hays saying the PHS report "serves no useful purpose." In 1967 and 1968, when the Pesticides Division finally was insisting on a warning in the labeling against use of vapona strips in the presence of infants and the elderly and sick, John Leary, as a member of a Shell delegation, "took an active part" in resisting such a step, the subcommittee said.

Dr. Hays assured the subcommittee that the labeling of pesticide products was carefully screened before approval. The subcommittee then produced a label, approved in May 1969, for a concentrated fly and roach spray made by Hysan Products Company of Chicago. On one part of the label was a warning:

> Use in well ventilated rooms or areas only. Always spray away from you. Do not stay in room that has been heavily treated. Avoid inhalation.

Elsewhere on the label were ridiculously contradictory directions for use:

> Close all doors, windows, and transoms. Spray with a fine mist sprayer freely upwards in all directions so the room is filled with the vapor. If the insects have not dropped to the floor in 3 minutes repeat spraying, as quantity sprayed was insufficient. After 10 minutes doors and windows may be opened.

Dr. Hays assured the subcommittee that the division's arrangements for obtaining information on pesticide poisonings was working well. In 1968 the division received reports on 52 incidents involving 163 persons. "Other Federal agencies," the subcommittee said, "received about 5,000 such reports and the total number of pesticide poisonings is estimated to be as high as 40 or 50 thousand annually."

If Agriculture inspectors found a potentially hazardous or ineffective pesticide, the Pesticide Division's practice was to seize the product at the outlet where it was discovered—but not to seize the same product at other outlets where it was being sold.

Despite evidence of repeated violations by some shippers—242 in 1966 alone—the division did not initiate a single criminal prosecution for thirteen years.

Under an amendment to the law enacted in May 1964, the division was given specific authority to cancel the registration of pesticides found not to be in compliance. But the division never canceled a registration in a contested case. Until late 1969, it did not even have procedures for conducting hearings in cancellation cases. "When registrants receiving cancellation notices requested hearings," the subcommittee said, "cancellation action was halted indefinitely and the product left on the market."

The division had no procedures for warning householders about newly discovered hazards of pesticide products that already were in their homes.

Products containing the chemical element thallium long were used to control insects and rats. The products were unsafe because to be effective they had to be put in places that were as accessible to children as they were to insects and rats. In 1962 and 1963, according to the Public Health Service, about four hundred children were reported to have been poisoned by products containing thallium. In August 1965 the division canceled registrations for such products, theoretically removing them from the market. But more than two years later the General Accounting Office reported that thallium products were on sale in six of twenty-two retail establishments spot-checked in the Washington, D.C., area.

The entire pesticides case serves to warn us not only of the need for greater congressional oversight of agencies with regulatory responsibilities, but, more importantly, of the dangerous potential in corporate power over Congress. The pesticides law was slow in being enacted, to begin with, and weak in part because of corporate power. Once the law was passed, enforcement was ineffective, again, in part, because of corporate power. The chemical firms could not have neutralized the House Intergovernmental Relations Subcommittee had they tried. But there are very few such oversight units on Capitol Hill, and very few legislators such as Congressman Fountain to run them. And even when such subcommittees do their job, economic power seeks to have Congress frustrate or ignore their recommendations, and it often succeeds.

7 THE REGULATORY AGENCIES

The public provides public utilities, through rates, with such experts as the public utilities may require to protect the utilities' rights, but the public, through taxes, does not provide adequate funds for its own protection.

FLORIDA PUBLIC SERVICE COMMISSION, quoted in *Washington Post*, April 13, 1969

After John F. Kennedy was elected President in 1960 he asked an old friend of the family, the late James M. Landis, to write what would become the *Report on Regulatory Agencies to the President-Elect*. A former dean of the Harvard Law School, Landis was extraordinarily qualified, having been chairman of the Securities and Exchange Commission in the 1930s and chairman of the Civil Aeronautics Board in 1947. His report dealt concisely with a fundamental problem, the relationships an agency has with the industries it regulates and with the public.

Direct contacts by industry representatives "of necessity . . . are frequent and generally productive of intelligent ideas," Landis said. At the same time, "Contacts with the public are rare and generally unproductive of anything except complaint." The following key sentence contained a warning which is as valid today as it was in 1960:

> Irrespective of the absence of social contacts and the acceptance of undue hospitality, it is the daily machine-gun-like impact on both agency and its staff of industry representation that makes for industry orientation on the part of many honest and capable agency members as well as agency staffs.

Public participation in the regulatory process is minimal. The citizen comes to be regarded as an intruder, if he should attempt to participate at all. Over and over again, regulatory agencies have been discovered using secrecy as a device to make it impossible for representatives of the public to defend their interests, or even to know that their interests need to be defended. At the Interstate Commerce Commission, for example, secrecy played a role in the merger trend in transportation. Staff experts made a report warning the ICC to assert new authority to meet the growing trend among railroads to reorganize as conglomerate corporations. On July 6, 1970, Murray Seeger wrote in the *Los Angeles Times:*

> The report was made in March, 1969, just as the Penn Central Railroad was preparing to transform itself into a holding company. Fifteen months later, when the railroad was bankrupt, the study was still marked "administratively confidential" and was "under study" by the ICC.
>
> Since the ICC did not exert wider authority when it was urged to do so, the new breed of transportation conglomerates are not effectively monitored by government, in the view of many Washington experts. . . .
>
> "More specifically" [the suppressed staff report said], "the conglomerate holding company provides a convenient means for the transfer to other industries of assets now devoted to transportation."
>
> In the view of several congressional investigators, the warnings contained in last year's ICC study have come to reality in the 1970 bankruptcy of the nation's largest railroad.

In the Federal Communications Commission, Nicholas Johnson has said, citizen participation in the decision-making process "is virtually non-existent," with the "necessary but unhappy result . . . that the FCC is a 'captive' of the very industry it is purportedly attempting to regulate." Replying to a questionnaire from a subcommittee of the Senate Committee on the Judiciary, Johnson recalled the case of a Jackson, Mississippi, television station, WLBT. Renewal of its license was opposed by the United Church of Christ, on the ground that WLBT had systematically promoted segregationist views, refused to present opposing views, and excluded Negroes. A favorite technique at WLBT was to flash a "Sorry, Cable Trouble" sign on the screen whenever a network program was presenting somebody or something the station management didn't like. What made the case noteworthy, however, was the refusal of the FCC over a period of years to recognize that the United Church had "standing" to appear and present its arguments. "Petitioners were told, in effect, that they were not even entitled to be heard so far as the FCC

was concerned," Johnson said. The issue of "standing" finally was re-
solved by the United States Court of Appeals for the District of Columbia.
In a decision that slapped down the Commission, Judge Warren E.
Burger, now Chief Justice of the United States, said:

> The broadcast industry does not seem to have grasped the simple fact that
> a broadcast license is a public trust subject to termination for breach of
> duty. . . .
>
> We cannot believe that the Congressional mandate of public participa-
> tion which the Commission says it seeks to fulfill was meant to be limited
> to writing letters to the Commission, to inspection of records, to the Com-
> mission's grace in considering listener claims, or to mere non-participating
> appearance at hearings.[1]

The passive approach to public participation is so ingrained in
regulatory bodies that almost never do they go out into the community
to seek the views of affected citizens—say, the blacks who comprised 47
per cent of the population in WLBT's viewer area.

Nicholas Johnson gave several additional examples in testimony
in July 1970 before Senator Edward M. Kennedy (D–Mass.). One case
involved the issue whether, in bald terms, the FCC as a matter of course
will renew existing broadcast licenses each three years in perpetuity.
Senator John O. Pastore sponsored legislation to grant just such a bounty
to the broadcasters, as we noted in an earlier chapter. When his bill
failed the FCC rushed into the breach. Johnson testified:

> In January 1970 the Commission, working with White House approval,
> adopted a "policy statement" which inhibits community groups and other
> private citizens from competing for broadcast licenses. Under the new policy
> a potential competitor must show that the existing licensee has not "sub-
> stantially" served his community in the previous three years. Since the
> Commission has no standards whatsoever as to what constitutes substantial
> service, competitors have nothing to go on in determining what licenses to
> challenge. The Commission, with its traditional preference for the powerful
> and the status quo, will not say what these standards are. Since the policy
> statement, not one competing application has been filed for a television
> station license—which would tend to indicate that the policy statement has
> served its intended purpose. This statement was adopted without any op-
> portunity for public comment. In fact, the Commission *rejected* such com-
> ments before the policy was adopted.[2]

Johnson emphasized that rather than being unique, the FCC "is but a microcosm of what passes for governmental representation of the public generally." Here is a microcosm of what passes for public representation at the Interstate Commerce Commission:

On February 26, 1970, the Southern Railway System filed an application to abolish discounts on all round-trip tickets and to establish a minimum one-dollar fare. The effect on commuters between Washington, D.C., and suburban Alexandria, Virginia, would have been almost to double the price of a round-trip ticket, which then was fifty-five cents. Neither the ICC nor the railway took any step to notify the commuters, and the fare changes were ordered into effect on April 1. On March 30, however, a friendly ticket agent tipped off one of the commuters. A protest to the ICC followed. The next day, the Commission reversed itself, postponed the increases for seven months, and promised an investigation and a public hearing.[3]

The Civil Aeronautics Board has shown similar disdain for air travelers, even those who happen to be congressmen. Under the law either the CAB or an air carrier may set fares. However rates are set, an airline must incorporate them in a tariff filed with the Board. A carrier that charges rates other than the filed ones violates the law. The Board may change the rates on its own initiative or on receipt of a complaint —but only after serving notice and holding a hearing. Over the years, however, *ex parte,* informal meetings between the CAB and officials of airlines seeking fare increases have undermined the ritual prescribed in law.

Several times, Representative John E. Moss (D–Calif.), a determined fighter for public and consumer causes, protested to the Board about the *ex parte* meetings and, as well, about the Board's lack of standards for testing the reasonableness of fares. His protests went unheeded, and the *ex parte* meetings continued into the summer of 1969. At that time United Airlines filed new fare increases. In early August several carriers followed United's lead. While the proposed increases were pending, CAB members and officials of the airlines scheduled an *ex parte* meeting for August 14.

Moss learned of the meeting. He requested but was denied permission to attend; it goes without saying that an ordinary airline passenger would not have been admitted, either.

Following the closed August 14 meeting with the airlines, the Board issued an order calling for oral argument on whether it should exercise its power to investigate and suspend the new rates before they could become effective. Nowhere in the order did the Board suggest that it might propose a fare formula of its own.

Moss, by now joined by thirty-one other congressmen, not only renewed the complaints about the *ex parte* meetings, but also urged the Board to suspend the new rates, to undertake a general investigation aimed at defining with greater precision the standards of reasonableness for fares, and, finally, to use the more precise standards to set fares.

The CAB went ahead and heard oral arguments. Moss and his associates refused to participate, on the ground that the Board had made up its mind in advance and that the proceeding was *pro forma*. Eight days later, on September 12, 1969, the Board ruled. It declared the increases proposed by the airlines possibly unjust or unreasonable and suspended them. But it gave the airlines, which had pleaded their cause in secret, no cause to weep, and the public, which had been excluded from the *ex parte* meetings, no cause to cheer. After all, the Board asserted, the carriers had demonstrated a need for "some additional revenue." And so it held that a 6 per cent fare increase, which, to be sure, was a lesser one than the airlines had formally filed, was necessary. It will be remembered that the Board had not publicly hinted at the possibility that it would outline a fare formula of its own. Yet the CAB not only set out such a formula, but also took the regulatory steps required to make the formula effective almost immediately. The cooperation of the airlines was essential; having met in secret with the CAB, it is not surprising that their cooperation was forthcoming.

Representative Moss and his colleagues then appealed to the Court of Appeals in Washington. A three-judge panel gave them an unprecedented victory. "This appeal," Judge J. Skelly Wright said for the court on July 9, 1970, "presents the recurring question which has plagued public regulation of industry: whether the regulatory agency is unduly oriented toward the interests of the industry it is designed to regulate, rather than the public interest it is designed to protect." Answering the recurring question by sending the case back to the CAB for further proceedings, the court said:

> We hold that the procedure used by the Board is contrary to the statutory rate-making plan in that it fences the public out of the rate-making process. . . . While we recognize that . . . the Board has an obligation to afford

the carriers sufficient revenues, that obligation cannot become a *carte blanche* allowing the Board to deal only with the carriers and disregard the other factors, such as the traveling public's interest in the lowest possible fares and high standards of service . . . we emphatically reject any intimation by the Board that its responsibilities to the carriers are more important than its responsibilities to the public.

Although our focus in this chapter is on the independent regulatory agencies, it is well to point out that regulatory operations of all kinds have suffered from the lack of public participation. The Federal Trade Commission provided a memorable example in 1963 when it proposed to make the Flammable Fabrics Act applicable to blankets used principally to wrap or clothe infants. "A public hearing was held but there was no government agency or individual who could appear to represent and defend the consumer interest," Commissioner Philip Elman has said. "Incredibly, despite evidence that the fabric used in baby blankets was dangerously flammable and could not legally be used in making clothing for children and adults, and despite the obvious and conceded fact that receiving blankets are worn by infants as clothing, serving essentially the same purpose as a bathrobe or dressing gown, the Commission ruled that baby blankets were not articles of clothing and thus not protected by the Flammable Fabrics Act."[4] Later the law was amended to include baby blankets.

Issues of arcane complexity but substantial importance are commonplace in the regulatory agencies and in units of the Executive with regulatory powers. Whether an antibiotics producer is permitted in the prescribing instructions for physicians to recommend use in particular infections may determine whether a particular product will be a money-maker or a money-loser—and, if that use is ill advised, whether it will create needless hazards by displacing safer alternative therapy. Whether flammable or fume-producing fabrics and carpeting are permitted in airliners is a matter of money for the airlines—and possibly a matter of asphyxiation for passengers in a plane in which fire occurs. Whether standards are set, and *what* standards are set, for dust levels in the coal mines and for radiation in the uranium mines, determines whether men live or die. Whether the Federal Trade Commission, in measuring tar and nicotine in various cigarette brands, used a butt length favored by the tobacco industry or a length favored by public health groups involved a difference of seven millimeters, or 0.27559 inch. However, the butt length favored by the industry tended to make one brand pretty much like another; the length favored by the health groups disclosed large differences.[5]

How "peanut butter" is defined determines whether what is sold under that name is derived mainly from peanuts or is substantially flavored vegetable oil. Whether a bake mix for "blueberry" muffins can contain chemical pellets instead of blueberries; whether a General Foods drink concentrate called "Orange Plus" could contain less orange than orange juice; whether a Carnation Company "eggnog" could contain no eggs—such questions also are regulatory matters.

Rarely has the public been represented in agency proceedings. Never are major industries without representation, usually by platoons and battalions of Washington lawyers—products of the very best law schools.

In 1892, Richard S. Olney, a railroad attorney who became Attorney General under President Grover Cleveland, told the president of the Burlington Railroad that the Interstate Commerce Commission "can be of great use to the railroads. It satisfies the popular clamor for a government supervision of railroads, at the same time that supervision is almost entirely minimal. The part of wisdom is not to destroy the Commission, but to utilize it."[6]

That is really what it is all about.

Founded in 1887 to regulate railroads, the ICC is the oldest regulatory agency and, in terms of volume of cases (8,000 in 1969), the busiest. "Time and time again, the ICC has proved to be protector of the railroads rather than the public interest," Representative Richard L. Ottinger (D–N.Y.) told a House subcommittee. "Time and time again, the railroads have used the Commission as a mere extension of their corporate structures. The ICC's usual attitude is one of torpor; on occasion, it awakens long enough to authorize the discontinuance of a few more passenger trains."[7] A group of law students who, under Ralph Nader's guidance, investigated the ICC called it an "elephants' graveyard of political hacks" designed and run to protect transportation industries from consumers. In a report of more than one thousand typewritten pages, the students documented charges of incompetence, subservience to the highway, rail, and water transport industries, suppression of price competition in favor of collusion, and price-fixing and nonenforcement of safety requirements. Robert C. Fellmeth, a Harvard law student who directed the investigators, summed up by saying that the ICC has become so infested by "institutional corruption" as to be "an extension of the [transportation] industry."[8]

Once again a balancing act must be undertaken. No implication is intended that all regulatory agencies have the dismal record of the ICC. It will be recalled from the previous chapter that in May 1968 Merrill Lynch, Pierce, Fenner & Smith set up its own Effective Government Association and by September 1 had raised reported contributions of $44,775. At the time Merrill Lynch began its enterprise in open political fund-raising the firm was under investigation by the Securities and Exchange Commission, which was the most effective of the regulatory agencies until the advent of the Nixon Administration, when a process of disintegration set in. In August 1968 the SEC filed charges of securities fraud against fourteen Merrill Lynch officers and employees. In October William J. La Fleur, treasurer of the Effective Government Association and assistant general counsel of Merrill Lynch, insisted to Walter Pincus of the *Washington Post* that the SEC case had played no part in the decision to set up the association.

Subsequent events provided no basis to doubt this assertion. Merrill Lynch consented to an SEC finding that it had used advance "inside" information from the Douglas Aircraft Company for the advantage of preferred institutional clients, in the process defrauding the investing public of an estimated $4.5 million. On November 26, 1968, the SEC imposed the most severe penalties in its history for misuse of "inside" information. The Commission ordered suspension of one vice president for sixty days, and of another vice president and five salesmen for twenty-one days. The SEC also censured three vice presidents. In an action that is formally said to imply neither guilt nor innocence, the SEC dropped charges against an executive vice president, a senior vice president, and two plain vice presidents.[9]

Even a strong regulatory law, or strong sections of such a law, can be readily frustrated. Rules to implement the legislation must be drafted, adopted, and interpreted. Each step in the process affords affected industries opportunities to undercut the law and to fight delaying actions in administrative and court proceedings that sometimes seem interminable.

Those who would undertake mergers involving broadcast media are required by law to bear the burden of showing that the public interest would be served, but the law did not deter the Federal Communications Commission from approving, over opposition on antitrust grounds by the Justice Department, the acquisition by the International Telephone and Telegraph Company of the American Broadcasting Companies.

The Interstate Commerce Commission presided over the deterioration of passenger service, which pleased the railroads but was not what the law required or the public wanted. In the eleven years ending in 1969 the number of intercity passenger trains declined more than two-thirds, from 1,448 to 480, and fourteen railroads abandoned all intercity service. Finally the Commission requested authority over standards of passenger service, but, in a signal to the railroads not to worry, Commissioner Kenneth H. Tuggle said, "We do not intend to use that jurisdiction in requiring heavy investment in new passenger equipment."[10]

Now and then an internal critic comes along to tug at the Tuggleses —a Philip Elman in the Federal Trade Commission, but he left in 1970; a Nicholas Johnson in the Federal Communications Commission, but his term is up in 1972. The FCC "has performed as the ally of the broadcasters in every light skirmish with the public," Johnson said in a brutally candid article in the *New Republic*. He continued:

> The FCC once decided that a radio station with more than 30 minutes of commercials per hour was serving the public interest. It approved the renewal of a station that quite candidly reported it proposed to program no news, and no public affairs. . . . It examined the record of a station guilty of bilking advertisers out of $6000 in fraudulent transactions—while on a one-year probationary status for similar offenses earlier—and found that the station had, nonetheless, "minimally met the public interest standard." And recently the Commission showed its reluctance to enforce even its technical and business standards, when it refused to consider license revocation for a licensee who had been charged with not paying his employees, stealing news, ordering his engineer to make fraudulent entries in the station's logbook, operating with an improperly licensed engineer and 87 other technical violations over a three-year period.

But the broadcasting industry, the Commissioner noted, has to his knowledge never "complained that the kind of intellectually corrupt decisions just mentioned are as much of a disservice to the industry as to the public—as I believe to be the case. The industry has for decades deluded itself into believing, as National Association of Broadcasters Chairman Willard Walbridge put it on "Face the Nation," that "the public says that the programming is fine . . . that they like broadcasting pretty much the way it is."[11]

Many men assume regulatory responsibilities with the intention of someday leaving government to go to work for the industry or specific companies they have been regulating. Congressman Richard Ottinger discussed some examples involving the Interstate Commerce Commission before a House subcommittee. One case involved William H. Tucker, a former chairman. "Mr. Tucker left the ICC, served nine months in the 'purgatory' of his law firm, Maguire and Tucker (which virtually shares offices with the Penn Central Railroad), then became vice president for New England operations of Penn Central," Ottinger said.[12]

In 1969 Bernard F. Schmid, the ICC's managing director and top administrative official, abruptly quit to join the same law firm. The report by the team of investigators led by Ralph Nader charged that Schmid had a "close" relationship with a regulated firm in New York City, U.S. Freight Company, which has several freight forwarders as subsidiaries. The investigators said they were told by past and present ICC staff members that Schmid "frequently called U.S. Freight officials . . . to inform them of the activities of rival freight forwarders in the ICC." Schmid said the charges were "untrue."

While chairman of the Federal Communications Commission, Rosel H. Hyde provided a decisive vote in each of three decisions that staved off a challenge to the renewal of the television license of KSL, which is a cornerstone of the news media empire of the Mormon Church. This performance was consistent with Hyde's votes in similar cases. In March 1970, soon after retiring, Hyde joined Wilkinson, Cragun and Barker, the law firm which represented KSL in the FCC proceedings. On April 6 the National Association of Broadcasters presented Hyde with its Distinguished Service Award.

"The record number of FCC Commissioners and other staff who have left the agency over the years to go to work for the very industries they were supposed to be regulating is not a fact to inspire confidence in the agency's performance," Nicholas Johnson said in his July 1970 testimony before Senator Kennedy. "It is what another witness here today, Ralph Nader, has characterized as the 'deferred bribe.' But as blood curdling as the realities may be of those who are performing at an agency with one eye on their next job, it is even more frightening to find that those who *do* want to stay and serve are driven off one way or another."

While a congressman, Melvin R. Laird, the Secretary of Defense, expressed concern over the possibility that some government regulators would "so position themselves as to (1) obtain lucrative positions with the regulated enterprises and (2) open themselves and their agencies to perhaps valid accusations of conflict of interest."[13] In the case of the Food and Drug Administration, a study made at Laird's request showed that of 813 scientific, medical and technical employes who left in the four years ended December 31, 1963, 83 appeared from available records to have taken positions with FDA-regulated companies. The true figure, however, may have been higher, because data were not available on 98 persons who had left before retirement or on others who may have taken industry employment after retirement. The big exodus from the FDA to industry came after Commissioner Goddard's appointment in 1966. The most important involved Dr. Joseph F. Sadusk, Jr., who had been the agency's top doctor for two years. He was pro-industry from the start. Many of his actions and statements involving, among other things, a long-acting sulfonamide called Midicel and an antibiotic called Chloromycetin, were considered perilous to children but advantageous to Parke, Davis & Company, the supplier. After a year at Johns Hopkins Medical School Dr. Sadusk joined Parke, Davis as a vice president.

The total annual budget of the federal government is about $200 billion. All of the expenses associated with operating the Congress, the federal judicial system, and all of the major regulatory agencies—all of these expenses together come to approximately $500 million, or one-half of one per cent of the total. The 1970 budget of the independent regulatory agencies was $150 million—less, Ralph Nader has noted, "than women spent on wigs last year." Yet he is among those who say that some agencies get too much money, either because they have outlived their usefulness or because they fritter away much of the money they do get.

Caution must be taken, however, against overreaching implications. The National Highway Safety Bureau, a unit of the Department of

Transportation, offers itself as an example. It is so starved for funds that only one professional person is assigned to work with state and local officials on matters of school-bus safety. The Bureau has money for the design *but not the production* of prototype safety cars, which promise great dividends in terms of new safety features. Further, the Bureau has grossly insufficient sums to test vehicles and components, including tires, to be certain that the certifications of safety provided by manufacturers can be relied upon. The inadequate funding of the Bureau, of which more examples could be provided, should be laid alongside its mission: nothing less than to do something truly important about a highway traffic toll that, in 1969 alone, left 56,400 persons dead and 2 million with disabling injuries. On a daily basis the toll amounted to 155 deaths and 5,479 injuries, 365 days a year. The Bureau's budget for fiscal 1970 of $30.2 million could be contrasted with the profits after taxes of General Motors in 1969, $1.7 billion.

Economic concentration aggravates the already formidable difficulties of effective regulation. The point is possibly best illustrated by public utilities. As monopolies they represent concentration in its most extreme form. Efforts to regulate them in the public interest have been gross failures.

The biggest monopoly of them all, of course, is the American Telephone and Telegraph Company. It is a corporation with more assets than any other in the world, more employees than the federal government excluding only those in the Defense and Post Office departments, and more bank deposits than any other firm in the United States. It is, Joseph Goulden said in *Monopoly,* published in 1968, "a corporate state, a Super Government, if you will, whose presence in the United States is felt more keenly on a daily basis than even that of the Federal Government."[14] In addition, Goulden said, "AT&T isn't always a nice company. Indeed, its rapacious attitude toward potential competitors, its frequent contempt for government at all levels, the press and other institutions of a free society, are as disgusting, as brutal, as anything found in the robber baron era of American capitalism."[15] Is it really possible to regulate AT&T? Let us look first at some memorable examples, from Goulden's book, of the impact of AT&T's financial policies on our phone bills.

One example concerned Bell's manufacturing subsidiary, the giant Western Electric Company, and the inability of regulators to determine whether the prices paid by AT&T to Western Electric are fair. Goulden wrote:

> The California PUC [Public Utilities Commission] found a route around this problem in 1964 by deciding that Western Electric's rate of return on its equipment sales should be no more than that allowed the Pacific Telephone & Telegraph Company [which is 89.6 percent owned by AT&T] on its California operations. Had Western Electric been held to this limit during the forty-five-year period 1916–61, chosen by the PUC for study, its earnings from sales to PT&T would have been reduced by $340,746,000 (the difference between its composite earnings of 9.1 percent and the composite 6.1 percent authorized by the PUC). Not only did this $340,000,000 come from phone subscribers' pockets, but they also had to pay PT&T an annual return on it averaging 6.1 percent.[16]

Despite such policies, the Federal Communications Commission, whose jurisdiction includes interstate phone charges, did not consider them within the structure of a formal rate case until October 1965—more than three decades after the FCC was established. Until that time rates were negotiated without formal hearings. Thus in October 1953 the FCC authorized interstate rates intended to yield—by AT&T's calculations—6.5 per cent on rate base. Actually, Bell promptly began earning much more than that. The FCC's Common Carrier Bureau repeatedly pointed this out to the Commission, then headed by Rosel H. Hyde, but he would not permit the staff even to undertake informal negotiations to see if AT&T would voluntarily lower long-distance rates. Had Bell been held to 6.5 per cent in the years 1955 through 1957 alone, the staff estimated, the savings to phone users would have been about $159 million. Goulden reported:

> When the House Antitrust Subcommittee headed by Representative Emanuel Celler made growling sounds about the excess profits in the spring of 1958, the FCC busied itself finally with a negotiated reduction of $45,300,000 a year. There was scant effect on Bell. Long-distance returns were 7.9 percent in 1959; 7.8 percent the next year; 7.7 percent in 1961. Again, the FCC declined its staff's recommendation that a serious study be made of AT&T's return (By this time, according to Celler's computations, AT&T's returns for 1955–61 were $985,000,000 above the authorized 6.5 percent return—*nearly a billion dollars in excess telephone payments by the U.S. public*). [Emphasis in the original.]

The FCC finally agreed with its critics in 1961 that the difference between AT&T earnings and the permissible limit made an unsightly gap, so it moved to narrow it—by increasing its definition of an "acceptable" return from 6.5 percent to 7.5 percent.[17]

Finally, on October 27, 1965, the FCC authorized an in-depth staff study of AT&T's charges and earnings for its various interstate services. On July 5, 1967, the Commission handed down a decision in the first phase of the case. It deemed a "fair" return to be in the range of 7 to 7½ per cent, while doing nothing about the excess profits earned, say, in the preceding nineteen months when, during almost half of that period, the rate was at least 8½ per cent. Lest this be dismissed as a bit of nitpicking on our part, remember that we are dealing with a situation in which an increase of only one-tenth of one per cent costs telephone subscribers $60 million a year, or roughly $1.30 per subscriber annually. To drop AT&T's earnings thereafter into the desired percentage range, the FCC ordered interstate rates reduced so as to decrease annual revenues by $120 million. Of course, a great many subscribers found themselves paying more for *intrastate* long-distance calls, and so the actual public benefits were open to question. In addition, the FCC decided to ponder rather than rule on whether to require Bell to adopt accelerated depreciation. While it pondered, the public was forced to pay "about $500,000,000 a year extra in phone bills," Goulden said.[18]

For years, the General Services Administration had a unit called the Transportation and Public Utility Service (TPUS). It acted as counsel to the federal government as a *customer* of phone companies. Its budget was $300,000 a year. Intervening in rate cases, it won rate reductions of $16 million a year—$160 million over the ten-year life of the major contracts involved—on a defense communications system called SAGE. The success of the twelve-member TPUS team, which was headed by Frederick W. Denniston, doomed it. AT&T launched a massive, coordinated lobbying campaign to eliminate TPUS. The effort was led by Edward B. Crosland, who, Joseph Goulden said in *Monopoly,* "bore the title of AT&T vice president for regulatory matters and the unofficial rank of chief lobbyist." In 1962, during the Kennedy Administration, a battered GSA agreed to take itself out of rate cases, save in instances where "the government is being penalized by rates or services." The story of how Crosland accomplished this, told in detail by Goulden, is a classic in the annals of how corporations govern the government and regulate the regulators—even to the point of regulating them almost out of existence.[19]

Up to now we have presented an array of examples illustrating how economic power translates into economic power in regulatory agencies at the federal government level. At the same time, we cannot ignore the states. They, too, have regulatory responsibilities, and how these responsibilities are carried out is of great moment to their citizens. By and large, however, state regulation in the public interest has failed dismally.

Gladwin Hill of the *New York Times* provided a powerful example of failure in a story on December 7, 1970, about how representatives of the principal sources of air and water pollution—corporations of one kind or another—sit on and even dominate most of the state boards primarily responsible for cleaning up the air and water. "The roster of big corporations with employes on such boards reads like an abbreviated bluebook of American industry," Hill wrote.

> One Colorado state hearing on stream pollution by a brewery was presided over by the pollution control director of the brewery. For years a board member dealing with pollution of Los Angeles harbor has been an executive of an oil company that was a major harbor polluter. The Governor of Indiana recently had to dismiss a state pollution board member because both he and his company were indicted as water polluters.

But the clearest and most relevant record of inadequate state regulation with great economic impact on the citizenry is in the fields of insurance and public utilities. Here we will illustrate with the utilities, which as monopolies represent concentration in an ultimate form.

A few states, including Texas, avoid hypocrisy by not even attempting to regulate utilities. As for the states that do regulate them, thorough documentation of failure has been provided by Senator Lee Metcalf (D–Mont.) in the extensive hearings that he conducted on his proposed Utility Consumers' Counsel Act, and in *Overcharge,* the book that he wrote together with Victor Reinemer, his executive secretary.[20]

As of 1969, for example, state public utility commissioners were in general agreement on the after-tax rates of return that are reasonable for regulated monopolies—6 per cent on rate base, which is the value assigned to properties, and 9 per cent on common stock. In 1967 alone, according to Federal Power Commission figures released by Metcalf, the private power companies' earnings exceeded reasonable rates of return by $1.4 billion. Just one utility, Commonwealth Edison Company of Chicago, had an 8.8 per cent return on rate base and a 14.8 per cent return on common stock. The "overcharge" was $96.9 million—almost double the $50 million spent in the same year by all of the regulatory commissions of the states and the District of Columbia.[22]

Accurate accounting lies at the heart of effective regulation. But in opening hearings on his bill by the Senate Subcommittee on Intergovernmental Relations, Metcalf disclosed that the regulatory commissions of twenty states had only one or two accountants. More than half of the agencies had one or two lawyers—or none at all. The figures on rate analysts were similar.

Arizona's regulatory agency is the Corporation Commission. One of its members, who are elected, is Dick Herbert. Testifying in 1969 before Senator Metcalf, he said that attorneys for the Arizona Public Service Company, which provides electricity or gas or both in twelve of the state's fourteen counties, had prepared the Commission's opinion and order in its last "important rate case." Herbert, who dissented in the case, which was decided in September 1967, said that the company lawyers, going still further, put into the opinion and the order statements of fact and law which had never surfaced in the hearings—even in the company's own testimony and exhibits. A *Washington Post* account added:

> Herbert told Metcalf he recognized that the winning side in a court proceeding commonly prepares an order for the judge to sign.
>
> But, he said, the losing counsel has a chance to review the order. In a rate case in which the Commission is the "judge," however, the consumer would have to be represented to make the situation comparable. In the Arizona case there was, Herbert said, "nobody representing the consumer."
>
> The Commissioner charged that Arizona Public Service filed the opinion, a 35-page document, with "the cases and the language and the parts of the hearing that were most favorable to them," so as to appear to be "one great big benevolent charitable concern." Then, he said, the company used the opinion "as a medium to disperse company propaganda."
>
> He said that the $380,000 spent by Arizona Public Service to prepare its case was almost triple the $130,000 spent by the state.[22]

Joseph Goulden's *Monopoly* is a prime source of information about AT&T's relationships with the states. Norman L. Parks made another important contribution in a two-part article in the *Nation* entitled "Who

Will Bell the Colossus?"[23] Obviously only a few points can be touched on here, even if we limit ourselves to those bearing on state regulation. Discussing regulation by the states over the years, Parks said it has been mostly "tame." He said that the bound volumes of *Public Utility Reports* include

> numerous findings, ostensibly written by the commissions, but actually the work of Bell officials. These decisions show careful preparation; they analyze all of the state operations of the company and make elaborate and judicial-sounding findings that point by point sustain the claims of the company with respect to revenue, expense, depreciation, cost of money and rate of return.
>
> Once issued, such decisions are promptly and successfully pressed upon other commissions as precedents. Less compliant commissions could find themselves inundated with briefs, exhibits and supporting data. At one state hearing the commission was confronted with data weighing in excess of 8 tons! . . .
>
> Speaking of his eleven years of experience as a Tennessee commissioner, during which time he became known as one of the most able and fearless rate experts in the nation, [Leon] Jourolmon declared: "I do not believe it is possible to regulate a company with as much economic strength as the telephone monopoly. I do not think any commission ever has been set up with sufficient resources . . . to enable it to cope with all the different parts of the telephone system on a state-wide basis . . . on the Tennessee commission I never once saw a rate case in which the results were fair to the consuming public."

A few summary points about federal as well as state regulation by now should be clear. A genetic variation of Newtonian law operates here: each time a regulatory operation becomes effective in the public interest it generates a larger and opposite counterreaction. Because concentrated economic power sustains this counterreaction—in the executive mansions, on Capitol Hill, and in the statehouses, as well as in the agencies themselves—it usually prevails sooner or later. Thus, it is imprudent to put too much hope for enduring reform in, say, the appointment of a strong chairman or in reorganizations. Ultimately, these gains founder on the massive economic power of the regulated interests.

8 "CRIME IN THE SUITES"

"Went to Nauset Light on the back side of Cape Cod," Ralph Waldo Emerson said in his *Journal*. "Collins, the keeper, told us he found obstinate resistance to the project of building a lighthouse on this coast, as it would injure the wrecking business."[1] A century later, the world's largest industrial corporation was advertising the slogan "General Motors Is People." Both messages—that business deliberately sacrifices life for profit, and that GM is Just Folks much like, perchance, the apple grower and the peanut vendor—essentially are caricatures of reality. There is a more serious objection. It is that such oversimplifications lead us away from, rather than toward, a few truths which are indispensable to understanding corporate behavior.

Large corporations commonly engage in criminal behavior, although sustained underreporting of this fact in communications media severely limits public appreciation of it. Crime is behavior which the state regards as socially harmful and for which the law provides penalties. That is the legal definition. If an act is punishable it is criminal even if punishment is not invoked, and it is criminal regardless of the particular administrative procedures that are prescribed to deal with it. Corporate crime is socially harmful behavior by corporations for which the law provides penalties. This was the definition used by the late Edwin H. Sutherland, who made the first systematic study of corporate crime and, in 1949, published his classic *White Collar Crime*.[2] This phrase means crime committed by "persons of respectability and high social status" in the course of their occupations. He based the book on his study of the life careers of seventy of the largest manufacturing, mining, and mercantile corporations. His sources were official records of violations of laws governing restraint of trade; misrepresentation in advertising; infringement of patents, trademarks, and copyrights; fair labor practices; rebates; financial fraud; conduct in wartime; and some miscellaneous categories. The average age of the seventy companies, none of which was an oil company, and none of which, regrettably, was named, was forty-five years. The terminal date of the analysis was, generally, 1944.

"Of the seventy large corporations, 30 were either illegal in their origin or began illegal activities immediately after their origin," Sutherland said. Forty-one of the companies were convicted in criminal courts a total of 158 times, or an average of 4 times each. "In many states," he noted, "persons with four convictions are defined as 'habitual criminals.'" In addition to the convictions, a total of 822 adverse decisions were rendered against the seventy corporations, including 296 in civil courts and 129 in equity courts. The balance, 397, were orders, confiscations or settlements by one or another official commission. In all, an average of 14 adverse decisions had been rendered against each of the seventy companies, and in one case there were 50.

These figures grossly understate the reality. Not all violations are recorded. Some of the laws that were violated were not enacted until the New Deal came to power in the 1930s. In addition, Sutherland pointed out, "vigorous prosecution of corporations has been concentrated in the period since 1932." Of the grand total of 980 adverse decisions against the seventy corporations only 292, or less than one-third, were rendered in the first three decades of the twentieth century.

This chapter will present numerous specific examples of criminal and antisocial, or harmful, behavior. This will serve several precise purposes. Each example involves an impact on people that, in itself, argues for its inclusion, and, in addition, illuminates one or more aspects of a large and complex whole. The assembly of specific examples in one place will assist appreciation of the enormity and pervasiveness of corporate conduct which violates the legal and ethical codes that supposedly guide society. The presentation may also contribute to a more balanced perspective on law and order than currently prevails. Most importantly, this chapter is intended to enlarge public understanding about conscience in an entity that lacks a soul. The public depends significantly on the corporate conscience to protect their lives, health, and pocketbooks. This tends to be counterproductive. It delays the advent of the kind of mature economic and political processes which would require more corporations, more of the time, to behave *as if* they had consciences.

Rarely, an individual of conscience has found it possible to transfer his personal standards to the business under his control. That was the case with William H. Danforth, who died in 1955, and his company, Ralston Purina. Ferdinand Lundberg, who does not casually bestow compliments, said:

> As far as the record shows, Danforth (unlike many of his prominent business contemporaries) never engaged in any shady practice, was never involved in any swindles, was never the defendant on criminal charges and was never accused of exploiting his workers. Nor was he, it seems, ever seriously criticized, knocked, called to account or rebuffed in good times or bad. For a portrait of the American capitalist as an extremely good, wholesome, honestly Christian earnest outgoing do-gooder one must turn to William H. Danforth.[3]

Those who see Ralston Purina or another corporation as "good" tend to see yet other corporations as "bad." This accords with the phenomenon of "The Personification of Corporation," to use the title of a brilliant chapter in Thurman Arnold's *The Folklore of Capitalism*.[4] "The ideal that a great corporation is endowed with the rights and prerogatives of a free individual is as essential to the acceptance of corporate rule in temporal affairs as was the ideal of the divine right of kings in an earlier day," he said. Arnold, writing in New Deal days, continued:

> Men have come to believe that their own future liberties and dignity are tied up in the freedom of great industrial organizations from restraint. . . .
>
> The origin of this way of thinking . . . is the result of a pioneer civilization in which the prevailing ideal was that of the freedom and dignity of the individual engaged in the accumulation of wealth. The independence of the free man from central authority was the slogan for which men fought and died. This free man was a trader, who got ahead by accumulating money. . . . Men cheerfully accept the fact that some individuals are good and others bad. Therefore, since great industrial organizations were regarded as individuals, it was not expected that all of them would be good. Corporations could therefore violate any of the established taboos without creating any alarm about the "system" itself. Since individuals are supposed to do better if left alone, this symbolism freed industrial enterprise from regula-

tion in the interest of furthering any current morality. The *laissez faire* religion, based on a conception of society composed of competing individuals, was transferred automatically to industrial organizations with nation-wide power and dictatorial forms of government.[5]

To personify large corporations is to obscure the important fact that they must march to different tunes than William Danforth's. He was moral and they are amoral. In his special circumstances his conscience was his guide, and his conscience was Ralston Purina's guide. In the circumstances of giant corporations profit must be maximized. This may or may not accord with the individual consciences of the owners and managers. The crucial difference is that while Danforth owned Ralston Purina, had the freedom to manage it as he wished, *and* was enormously successful, a similar set of conditions does not prevail for most corporations. Ownership is separate from management. Directors and executives do not have a freedom such as Danforth's. A corporate director, Benjamin N. Cardozo, the late Associate Justice of the Supreme Court, once said, owes a "duty of constant and unqualified fidelity" to the corporation and its stockholders who, of course, are seeking the best possible return on their investment dollars—an earthly rather than a heavenly reward.[6] After researching the literature on the subject, the Library of Congress found that a director "must exercise his unbiased judgment, influenced only by considerations of what is best for the corporation. . . . Many courts have spoken of the rule as being that a director owes a loyalty that is undivided and an allegiance that is influenced in action by no consideration other than the corporation's welfare."[7]

The corporation's welfare traditionally has been defined in terms of its financial statement. And, Bernard D. Nossiter has said, "there is nothing in the logic or practice of concentrated corporate industries that guides or compels socially responsible decision-making."[8] To be even blunter about it, the rule of thumb is that if conscience is operative in a corporation it is because conscientious conduct pays, and if conscience is absent it is because *that* pays.

The point was memorably made by two titans of business in an exchange of letters that has drawn remarkably little public attention. The correspondence began four decades ago. The principals were Lammot du Pont, president of E. I. du Pont de Nemours & Company, and Alfred P. Sloan, Jr., president of General Motors Corporation. On August 5, 1929, the two executives had a conversation about the possible use in

Chevrolets of safety glass, one of the single most important protections ever devised against avoidable automotive death, disfigurement, and injury. The next day, Lammot du Pont initiated the exchange of letters. Noting that the production capacity of his company was, at that time, limited, du Pont urged Sloan to try at once "to come to a decision" as to whether it wanted safety glass, or Pyralin for making safety glass, for Chevrolets.

August 7: Sloan acknowledged that "non-shatterable glass is bound to come." But, he told du Pont, for GM "to take an advanced position" at a time when production volume is increasing "at a decelerated rate" cannot "do other than to materially offset our profits."

> We have always felt, rightly or wrongly, that it was not in the interest of the industry and to ourselves to advertise improvements in safety control through the exploitation of accidents. We all know that there are a very large number of automobile accidents. Every once in a while it looms up in such a way that it appears as if it would have more or less serious consequences. The only way I know we can bring the public to a realization that they are willing to pay a substantial amount more for a car that has non-shatterable glass as compared with one that has not, is to exploit in some form or other this general idea.

Sloan went on to point out that in the past year GM's Cadillac division had equipped La Salles as well as Cadillacs with safety glass, that Packard, a competitor, had not, and that Packard's sales had not been materially affected. "In other words, I do not think that from the stockholders' standpoint the move on Cadillac's part has been justified. I believe that when any of us are dealing with safety matters we should perhaps not be commercial yet it is hard to avoid that phase of the question."

August 9: The point of advertising about safety glass, du Pont replied, would be "not to call attention to serious accidents, but to press the minor accidents which would not count for anything more than running over a stone in the road, were it not for the fact that the glass breaks, someone gets slightly cut, or cut in such a place as to constitute a permanent disfigurement. Can't the advertising stress *that feature* rather than what [the fear] most people have of the dangers of automobiles namely serious accidents and someone getting killed."

August 13: "Accidents or no accidents, my concern in this problem is a matter of profit and loss," Sloan told du Pont. He especially feared, he said,

> that the advent of safety glass will result in both ourselves and our competitors absorbing a very considerable part of the extra cost out of our profits. You, of course, are familiar with the comparatively large return the industry enjoys and General Motors in particular. I think you will agree with me that it is a very easy thing to reduce that return. I am fighting it not only every day but practically every hour of every day.

After explaining that production costs had gone up without a proportionate increase in production volume sufficient to absorb the cost increases, at least to the same degree as in previous years, Sloan said:

> I may be all wrong, but I feel that General Motors should not adopt safety glass for its cars and raise its prices even a part of what the extra cost would be. I can only see competition being forced into the same position. Our gain would be a purely temporary one and the net result would be that both competition and ourselves would have reduced the return on our capital and the public would have obtained still more value per dollar expended. I feel that it is much better to let the thing take its logical course and do what seems necessary when the necessity arises. . . . Naturally, from your standpoint . . . it is to your interest to have safety glass go in a large way irrespective of how it may affect the profit position of the automobile manufacturers but, of course, that is not my position and it is not your position in a broader sense.

August 20: Du Pont was "inclined to agree" with Sloan "that the adoption of safety glass, as well as the adoption of other improvements, is almost sure to result in the long run in lower profits to General Motors. I have entire confidence, however, that whether General Motors adopts it now or not, safety glass will be forced upon them."

The two men then apparently stopped corresponding about the matter for almost three years. On April 11, 1932, du Pont revived the question. In a letter to Sloan, he said that GM should encourage the use of safety glass, "rather than discourage or be apathetic. I understand that the new Ford models all have safety glass in the windshield and all the sports models have it all over. I think we should keep our 'eyes open' and 'ears to the ground,' so that we won't lose out in the procession if safety glass becomes popular."

Replying four days later, Sloan said that Ford for years had used safety glass in windshields, but "that is no reason why we should do so. I am trying to protect the interest of the stockholders of General Motors and the Corporation's operating position—it is not my responsibility to sell safety glass." Instead of burdening the stockholders, Sloan said,

> I would very much rather spend the same amount of money in improving our car in other ways because I think, from the standpoint of selfish business, it would be a very much better investment. You can say, perhaps, that I am selfish, but business is selfish. We are not a charitable institution—we are trying to make a profit for our stockholders.[9]

Although Sloan's resistance to the adoption of safety glass presumably was responsible for a large number of preventable deaths and serious injuries, he violated no law and, indeed, was obeying the dictates of a conscience which did not let him forget his obligation to GM's stockholders. Yet, obviously, his conduct had harmful and antisocial results. Nothing has happened in the four decades since the safety-glass episode to diminish the point that there is no sensible relation between the harmfulness of certain corporate behavior and its legality.

Some years ago Congress passed a law making it a criminal offense to adulterate motor vehicle brake fluid, a practice with grave potential to cause brake failure without warning. This legislation was absorbed by the National Traffic and Motor Vehicle Safety Act of 1966. Before this measure was enacted, Senator Warren G. Magnuson (D–Wash.), chairman of the Senate Committee on Commerce, and Senator Vance Hartke (D–Ind.), a member of the committee, led a fight to provide criminal penalties not only for adulteration of brake fluid, but for all *willful and knowing* violations. They were defeated by the auto industry, whose principal Senate advocate on this issue was John O. Pastore (D–R.I.). Civil penalties, in the form of fines, were provided instead. The primary concern here is not with whether it was objectively and practically right to provide criminal or civil sanctions, or both, but that an act as terrible as willful and knowing adulteration of brake fluid could be, helter-skelter, a criminal violation one day and a civil violation another day—while being potentially calamitous any day.

Until the Safety Act of 1966 was adopted a manufacturer violated no law in, again knowingly and willfully, selling an automobile with safety-related defects (and, certainly, it was not an offense to sell cars, the Corvair being a classic example, which embodied what Ralph Nader has called "designed-in dangers"). Further, no law was violated by a standard industry practice, a non-action of not notifying customers when a defect was discovered. In 1959, for example, the Michigan Supreme Court ruled against General Motors in a case that was initiated by a dealer mechanic whose leg was crushed by a 1953 Buick Roadmaster which, because of a defect, had lost its braking capacity. "Defendant Buick division warned its dealers," the court said. "It did not warn those into whose hands they had placed this dangerous instrument and whose lives (along with the lives of others) depended upon defective brakes which might fail without notice."[10] If the number of repair kits distributed afterward by Buick to its dealers is a reliable guide, 54,000 of these dangerous instruments were on the highways.

In a case involving the Chrysler Corporation, a manufacturer's bulletin urged dealers to recall for inspection 30,000 already delivered 1965 Chryslers, full-size Dodges, and Plymouth Furys with particular serial numbers. The purpose of the inspection was to determine if it was necessary to reweld a mounting bracket for the steering gear. The company neither notified the owners directly nor ascertained how many of the possibly hazardous cars actually were brought in to dealers' shops.[11]

Once the Safety Act was in force automobile makers were compelled, for the first time, to notify buyers of safety-related defects. These turned out to exist on a huge scale. In less than three years, "very limited investigations" by the National Highway Safety Bureau showed, manufacturers notified purchasers of 12 million vehicles of safety-related defects, including 2 million which had been brought to the industry's attention by the Bureau, a pathetically understaffed, underfinanced unit of the Department of Transportation.

Working under a contract from the Department, a research firm reviewed 287 separate campaigns by manufacturers to notify buyers of defects. Of the 5.5 million vehicles involved in the period in question, the two years ended September 30, 1968, the number recalled for inspection and possible correction of defects was as follows:

Defects that would or could cause loss of control *without warning:* 1,177,408.

Defects that would or could cause loss of control, but *with* warning: 4,000,620.

Defects that could cause control to deteriorate: 349,021.

The component most commonly involved was the steering system, although more than one defect sometimes figured in a single notification campaign. In all, 2,859,221 vehicles were recalled for possible defects in steering systems. Other categories included service brakes, 799,831 vehicles recalled; parking brakes, 33,539; and suspension systems, 277,085.[12]

One case stands out. It involved 1960 through 1965 model Chevrolet and GMC three-quarter-ton pickup trucks—200,000 of them. Apparently as a cost-cutting measure, General Motors equipped these trucks not with standard one-piece wheels, but with three-piece disc units, in the 15 x 5.50 size, made by the Kelsey-Hayes Corporation. In September 1968 Ralph Nader submitted evidence to the Safety Bureau that a number of the wheels had collapsed without warning. Bureau engineers made an investigation that confirmed the evidence. They said the wheels had an inherent metallurgical defect that made them "prone to failure . . . at unpredictable times" even when used on "straight" pickups, i.e., those which were not equipped with "camper," van, or other heavy bodies. Consequently, the engineers warned, a hazard existed not only for occupants of the vehicles equipped with the wheels, but also for other motorists, pedestrians, and bystanders. GM, denying the existence of an inherent fault, insisted that only the use of heavy bodies and improperly inflated tires could create a safety-related defect.

Because the Bureau had not yet been separated from the Federal Highway Administration, the issue came to the administrator of that agency, Francis C. Turner, for decision. He ruled for G.M. In doing so, in October 1969, he announced in a press release that the corporation had agreed to replace without charge the wheels on 50,000 of the 200,000 trucks—those on which heavy bodies had been installed. According to unofficial Bureau estimates which GM later said were low, the cost to the company would be $5 million; but it would save triple that amount if it could avoid replacing the wheels on the 150,000 "straight" vehicles.

The Bureau engineers, in their investigation, had found fifty-six trucks—fifty-four of them equipped with special bodies—on which the three-part wheels had collapsed without warning. Serious injuries sometimes resulted. Urging Turner to require GM to notify all 200,000 owners of a safety defect, the engineers said, "There is every indication that 96 per cent of all known wheel failures have occurred *under loads which are below the design wheel strength level specified by the truck builder.*" [Emphasis supplied.] Yet Turner, in his press release, claimed there was "some doubt at this time as to whether it could be said that a safety-related defect existed." Nader, in a letter to Secretary of Transportation John A. Volpe, denounced this claim as "utterly false."

Rather than letting it go at that, Nader and some allies—the Center for Auto Safety, Physicians for Auto Safety, and Larry J. Silverman of Nader's Study for Responsive Law, all represented by the Center for Law and Social Policy and the law firm of Arnold and Porter—filed a suit in Federal Court in Washington. The action, which included Volpe and Turner as defendants, essentially sought an order to make the Department of Transportation and its subdivisions enforce the auto safety law as Congress intended it be enforced.

On June 30, 1970, Judge Joseph C. Waddy not only held that Turner had made "a mis-statement" of the findings of his own engineers in the Safety Bureau, but issued an order that was both unusual and important. The order looked behind a settlement made by a federal regulatory operation and a regulated company, and it authorized Silverman to participate in subsequent proceedings (which the Department had not allowed him to do up to that time). Most importantly, the judge ordered the Department to complete or reopen its investigation of the wheels, to take such remedial steps as the investigation should warrant, and to report back to the court *why* it was taking such actions as it would decide to take. With this, the Department began to abandon its former position and move toward requiring GM to notify the owners of 150,000 "straight" pickups of a safety-related defect (the auto safety law does not empower the government to require a manufacturer to *correct* a defect).

In a report filed with the court on September 15, Bureau engineers said that they now had learned of fifty-two wheel failures on twenty-four trucks that had not been overloaded, that as of August 29 there had been a grand total of ninety-eight failures on twenty-four "straight" pickups, that failures must be presumed to have eluded their surveillance, and that additional failures surely were occurring. In one case, they said, a wheel collapsed only one day after the owner took delivery. The truck turned over one and a half times, struck an oncoming vehicle, and was demolished. Five persons were injured. The engineers also said that contractors engaged to examine the fifty-two wheels found that ten of them failed under loads of less than 1,520 pounds each—although the claimed design strength was 2,060 pounds.

At an informal Safety Bureau hearing on September 30, GM refused to present engineering testimony but claimed the Bureau had "no evidence" of an inherent defect in the wheels. It asked that the investigation be dropped. But two Syracuse University professors who made a study of the three-piece design, engineer Martin E. Barzelay and metallurgist Volker Weiss, said that the "factor of safety" was "far below commonly accepted practice."

Finally, on November 4, Douglas W. Toms, director of the Safety Bureau, said that the wheels made the 150,000 "straight" pickups subject to "sudden and catastrophic failure resulting in an unreasonable risk of accident, death and injuries to persons using the highways." He asked GM to notify the owners that the wheels were defective. The company responded, the same day, by filing a suit to block the action in Federal Court in Wilmington, Delaware—an effort to bypass Judge Waddy, who had retained jurisdiction in the case that had been brought in Washington. Two days later, the Justice Department, in behalf of the Safety Bureau, asked the Federal Court in Washington to impose civil penalties on GM of $400,000, the maximum allowed. It was the first action of its kind. While it was pending, Judge Caleb M. Wright in Wilmington threw out GM's suit.[13] General Motors, which has spent millions of dollars to promote the claim that GM is the "Mark of Excellence," spent tens of thousands more to resist the Safety Bureau in Federal Court in Washington, while allowing the uninterrupted use on the highways of trucks with wheels subject to "catastrophic failure."

Over the decades in which manufacturers discovered defects—no one knows how many—in cars, school buses, and trucks, but failed to notify the owners because they were not forced to do so, they financed "traffic safety" campaigns. These cost relatively little. They may even have had a certain limited value. But they were also a decoy. They deflected attention from the role of quality control and of automotive design, even from dangers as obvious as the millions of knobs which needlessly protruded toward knees and skulls. There was too much emphasis on "the nut behind the wheel." There was no emphasis at all on the nut behind the system.

The news media are owed some of the blame. In 1956 Representative Kenneth A. Roberts, a conscientious Alabama Democrat who headed the health subcommittee of the House Committee on Interstate and Foreign Commerce, opened hearings on the relation of automotive designs to safety. He continued the hearings into 1963 (and the next year was defeated for reelection by a Goldwater Republican). In conducting the hearings Roberts "was surrounded by apathy and opposition in Congress and with hostility from the automobile industry and its traffic safety establishment," Ralph Nader said.[14] The apathy, opposition, and hostility would not have been so effective had the news media told the public about the hearings, but they gave them negligible attention. The price paid, as reflected in the toll of highway death and injury, can only be conjectured.

In 1970, after an investigation of new-car warranties, the Federal Trade Commission said in a report to Congress that the industry had failed "to meet its obligation to provide the public with defect-free cars." All five members of the Commission, including Caspar Weinberger, the first chairman appointed by President Nixon, approved the report. The report said that "quality control of automobiles is unsatisfactory, the warranty coverage putatively provided by manufacturers is inadequate, and the industry response to the problem insufficient to protect the public."[15]

If a thief breaks into your house and steals money the loss is obvious. But how does a manufacturer who has designed an appliance, an automobile muffler, or a light bulb to give out with all deliberate speed demonstrate moral superiority over a burglar? Questions of this kind could cause difficulties for those who overprice, impose usurious finance charges for installment buying, or inflict widespread harm, say, by polluting the biosphere, putting untested or inadequately tested additives into foods, or by loading excessive fat into 15 billion hot dogs a year, as was done until recently. But such questions pose no great difficulties for a youth who is a member of a gang and who, Robert C. Maynard said in the *Progressive*, "tends to see the world as a series of gangs, a few of them on his side but most of them arrayed against him . . . including the corporations that will not hire him into their hustle." Maynard, a reporter for the *Washington Post*, told of an afternoon in Chicago when he talked on a street corner with a dispirited member of the Black P Stone Rangers, one of the biggest gangs in the country:

> This young man wanted out of the whole business of the streets but he had no place he knew of to go.
>
> "All of the good shit," he told me, "is either staked out or played out."

To him, the law was an instrument of the rich to protect what they had for their own against the incursions of the likes of him. "They don't pay no attention to no goddamn law unless they want to. . . .

"The law," the Ranger sneered. "When last you hear of a millionaire going to the electric chair? When last you hear of the president of one of those big old corporations"—he sneered again at the sound of that word—"going to jail for fixing prices or selling people rotten meat that could kill them or even for income-tax evasion? When you hear anything like that?"

It is, unfortunately, an everyday occurrence for judges to impose brutal, even sadistic sentences—twenty years for possession of marijuana, fifteen years for stealing a Social Security check, and the like. Even an arrest for a trivial offense can imperil a man's livelihood. If convicted, a man realistically may expect to be derisively referred to thereafter as an "ex-con."

Such harshness does not attend corporations, even those that may massively steal and inflict violence. For what they like to depict as the war against crime, such men as Attorney General John N. Mitchell and Senator John L. McClellan say that wiretapping and preventive detention are essential. They are not talking about corporate crime. They do not intend to allow policemen to snoop on the phone conversations of business executives. They have no thought of detaining officers and directors of recidivist corporations in jail in order to prevent these organizations from committing new crimes. If a violation is charged a corporation can be fined, but, on the basis of ability to pay, the amounts usually are trivial. It will have the best of lawyers. Its career is not likely to be ruined or even set back. It cannot be put on a rock pile, be wrenched away from its family, be deprived of a normal sex life or be put among, as the standard phrase has it, "hardened criminals." And even if recidivist it is not called an "ex-con."

Secret, numbered bank accounts in foreign countries, mainly Switzerland, have been widely used to conceal criminal activities, including evasion of income taxes and Federal Reserve Board regulations on margins for stock trading. For violating these regulations Robert M. Morgenthau, then the United States Attorney in New York City, prosecuted Coggeshall & Hicks, a member of the New York Stock Exchange; Robert S. Keefer, Jr., a senior partner in the brokerage firm; the manager of the firm's office in Geneva; and the Arzi Bank of Zurich. All pleaded guilty to charges of having arranged for employes and customers of Coggeshall & Hicks to trade, over a five-year period, $20 million worth of stock through secret, numbered Swiss bank accounts. The firm was fined $50,-000, the maximum allowable. At the sentencing proceeding Keefer was represented by Simon H. Rifkind, who for nine years was a federal judge in the Southern District of New York. In the *New York Times* Neil Sheehan reported that before imposing sentence, the presiding judge, Irving Ben Cooper, told Rifkind, "Judge, I might as well say it now, I will say it later anyway, that they have chosen well in having you. You know you have the great respect of this Court." Sheehan went on to say:

> Mr. Rifkind compared his client's offense with breaking "a traffic regulation." Mr. Keefer, he said, was like most of the defendants he has represented, "people who have had good careers, good reputations, and who have slipped on the ice of some regulation or some emotion or something of that kind, rather than hardened criminals who make crime a way of life."
>
> In those five years of easy credit with the Arzi Bank, Mr. Keefer's firm had received $225,000 in illegal commissions, besides the profits accumulated by its customers and Mr. Keefer and his associates on their clandestine stock trading. During the grand jury investigation Mr. Keefer had repeatedly perjured himself.

Judge Cooper fined Keefer $30,000. He also gave him a suspended one-year sentence and put him on probation. This was done with "a tongue lashing," Sheehan said. The reporter drew a contrast:

> Last August, a week after Mr. Keefer's sentencing, James C. Harris, an unemployed shipping clerk, appeared before Judge Cooper. Harris is a Negro, married, with two children and has a prior record for armed robbery in 1964. He was now charged with stealing a Japanese television set worth less than $100 from an interstate shipment from a bus terminal. He got a year in jail.
>
> This disparity in punishment is not a personal quirk of Judge Cooper's. It is common to his fellow judges on New York District Court and to others in similar positions elsewhere. Judge Cooper and his colleagues regularly hand out five-year jail terms for minor Federal narcotics violations, as they are required to by law.[16]

"I will match the integrity and morality of the pharmaceutical industry with that of our accusers any time," declared Foster Whitlock, chairman of Ortho Pharmaceutical Corporation, a division of Johnson

& Johnson, in a speech to the Seventeenth Annual Rutgers Pharmaceutical Conference, May 15, 1968.

In December 1963 a federal grand jury in Washington indicted Richardson-Merrell, Inc., its William S. Merrell Company division, and three of the corporation's scientists for falsifying data it gave to the Food and Drug Administration in order to have released to the market MER/29, an anti-cholesterol drug. The indictment charged that other data unfavorable to the product, which no longer is sold, were withheld from the agency. Of the estimated 418,000 persons for whom MER/29 was prescribed in the United States, a few thousand suffered what became known as a "classical triad" of injuries—usually operable cataracts in both eyes, loss or thinning of hair, and severe skin reactions. Ultimately the defendants pleaded no contest to eight of twelve counts and, on June 4, 1964, in Federal Court in Washington, were sentenced. The corporation was fined $80,000, the maximum allowable. In the fiscal year ended a few weeks earlier, Richardson-Merrell's consolidated income on sales of $180 million was $17,790,000. This was $276,000 more than income in the previous fiscal year—not a bad indicator of how corporate virtue triumphs.

"I have taken the view," Judge Matthew F. McGuire said from the bench, "that responsibility in the background of this case is a failure . . . of proper executive, managerial and supervisional control . . . the responsibility . . . falls on the Company and its executive management." This view accorded with that of counsel for the company, Lawrence E. Walsh, a former federal judge who from 1957 to 1960 was Deputy Attorney General of the United States.

Earlier in the MER/29 proceeding Walsh had told Judge McGuire, "All I can say is there certainly was no intention by this Company or any of its employees to put on the market a dangerous drug. . . . If there must be punishment, we ask that it fall on the Company and not on them." One of the defendants, Harold Werner, was (and continued to be) vice president for research at William Merrell and, therefore, presumably was part of executive management. Nevertheless, McGuire put all three individual defendants on probation for six months. Each had faced a maximum sentence of five years in prison and a fine of $10,000.[17]

In 1966 the Justice Department, acting for FDA, filed a two-count criminal information against another leading drug manufacturer, the CIBA Pharmaceutical Company. The case involved Esidrix and Esidrix-K, two prescription products that were widely used to remove excess fluids and to lower blood pressure in patients with congestive heart failure and other diseases. The government complained that CIBA had falsely and misleadingly promoted the diuretics to physicians. A case in point was an advertisement in the *Journal of the American Medical Association* (*JAMA*) which failed to make adequate disclosure of Esidrix-K's side effects and its contraindications—the medical conditions in which a drug should not be used. After initially pleading innocent, CIBA switched its plea to no contest. In October 1968, represented by Clyde A. Szuch, the company went into Federal Court in Newark, New Jersey, to be sentenced. Judge James A. Coolahan, in a proceeding that lasted but a few minutes, agreed with Szuch that the issues "are, of course, highly complex." The maximum allowable penalty was a $1,000 fine on each of the two counts, but the judge said, "All right, a fine of $200 on each count."[18]

In 1960, Wallace Laboratories marketed a prescription product which combined meprobamate, the sedative/tranquilizer most commonly sold under the trade names Miltown and Equanil, and the diuretic hydrochlorothiazide. Literally millions of times over the next several years, the company listed contraindications for the product in the official prescribing brochure, which is in every package that goes to the pharmacist, and in the *Physicians' Desk Reference,* the prescribing guide of which approximately a half-million copies are distributed annually. On June 1, 1964, the *Journal of the American Medical Association* published the first of four successive weekly advertisements that made the stunningly false claim: "Contraindications: None Known." In addition, the *JAMA* ads omitted certain required warning information, including advice that patients be carefully watched for signs of a serious blood disease.

In the Food and Drug Administration, a decision was made that the *JAMA* ads for the product, originally called Miluretic but by then renamed Pree MT, would be the basis for the first criminal prosecution under the advertising provisions of the Kefauver-Harris Amendments to the Food, Drug, and Cosmetic Act. Word of this apparently leaked to the company, which then made an urgent request to *JAMA,* as a result of which the false claim "Contraindications: None Known" was physically removed from the printing plate. Although the claim had been misleading to the AMA's own members, and a threat to the helpless patients who depended on those members, *JAMA* never disclosed this astonishing action to its readers. It should be realized, however, that there was an unusual financial relation between the company and *JAMA*. In 1964, when all of this was happening, and also in 1963 and 1966, according to a tabulation prepared by the Library of Congress for Senator Gaylord Nelson, Wallace Laboratories was the single largest advertiser in *JAMA*. In those three years and in 1965, when the firm ranked third, it bought a total of 2,113 pages in the publication.

Despite all of this, a prosecution was initiated on the basis of the published claim of no contraindications. The defendant was the company. The law has no provision for prosecution of medical publications. The firm first entered a plea of innocent. But after the *Washington Post* publicized the case, the company switched its plea to no contest. As in the Richardson-Merrell and CIBA cases, such a switch had the advantage of precluding the further exposure that might now reasonably be expected from a trial. On January 17, 1966, in Federal Court in Trenton, New Jersey, Judge Arthur S. Lane imposed the maximum penalty, a fine of $1,000 on each of two counts. In 1964, the year of the offense, the after-tax income of the parent company, Carter-Wallace, Inc., was 5,650 times as large as the fine.[19]

Pharmaceutical executives have a unique reason for gratitude that their track record in avoiding imprisonment is as solid as that of the unincarcerable corporations for which they labor. This possibly fanciful thought was stimulated by a fine piece of investigative reporting which, in 1970, won a Pulitzer Prize for Harold E. Martin, editor and publisher of the *Montgomery Advertiser* and *Journal* in Alabama. His investigation concerned clinical testing of drugs in prisoners, who usually participate in experiments in hopes of amelioration of their bleak condition. The prisoners, while confined in penitentiaries in the states of Alabama, Arkansas, and Oklahoma, were used for blood plasma projects. After Martin broke the story, Walter Rugaber developed it further in a long piece for the *New York Times*. Rugaber said:

> The profits generated by these activities have gone to an enterprising contractor [Dr. Austin R. Stough] for the nation's biggest pharmaceutical manufacturers.
>
> The immediate damage has been done in the penitentiary systems of three states. Hundreds of inmates in voluntary programs have been stricken with illness and serious disease. An undetermined number of the victims have died.
>
> In a broader sense, countless millions of Americans have been involved.

Potentially fatal new compounds have been tested on prisoners with little or no medical observation of the results. . . .

Several major pharmaceutical manufacturers have recognized that some of the methods employed by Dr. Stough were extremely dangerous. They have continued to support him with large sums of money.

An executive of Cutter Laboratories [identified by Rugaber as Byron Emery] once acknowledged, for instance, that gross contamination was apparent in the areas where the largest blood plasma operations were conducted. The rooms were "sloppy," he observed.

When a Government doctor asked why Cutter continued to reward such an enterprise with hundreds of thousands of dollars' worth of business, the executive explained that the Stough group enjoyed crucial "contacts" with well-placed officials.

These contacts involved, among other things, the payment of sizable retainers to influential lawyer-legislators and the establishment of "partnerships" for a number of physicians who remained on the public payrolls.

Rugaber said he was told by an official of the Food and Drug Administration that since 1963 Dr. Stough had carried out some 130 investigational studies for thirty-seven drug companies.

The companies included the Wyeth Laboratories Division of American Home Products Corporation; the Lederle Laboratories Division of American Cyanamid Company; the E. R. Squibb & Sons Division of Squibb-Beechnut, Inc.; the Merck Sharp & Dohme Division of Merck & Co. and the Upjohn Company. These concerns, according to the current directory published by Fortune Magazine, are among the 300 largest corporations in the United States.[20]

In the spring of 1967 a Convair 580 operated by Lake Central Airlines crashed in Ohio. Thirty-eight persons were killed. The Federal Aviation Administration investigated. The agency concluded that the cause of the crash was a defect, a "soft" piston, which caused a propeller to separate and penetrate the fuselage. The FAA also reported that the manufacturer of the propeller, the Allison Division of General Motors, had known of the defect before the crash but had not advised the airlines, which together own a total of eighteen Convair 580's, to ground them for thorough disassembly and inspection. The FAA fined the company $8,000.[21]

In May of the same year Ralph Nader charged in a speech that the Greyhound Corporation, the giant conglomerate parent of Greyhound

Lines, was operating buses with extremely dangerous regrooved tires. Three days later, near Hackettstown, New Jersey, a Greyhound bus skidded on a wet mountain highway, went over an embankment, and hit a tree. One passenger was killed and eleven were injured. State police who investigated the accident blamed it on "the nature and quality of the tires." The Justice Department filed a criminal complaint. It was the first of its kind, although, Nader has pointed out, there have been other such violations that also have resulted in serious accidents. About two years later, on October 6, 1969, Greyhound unexpectedly appeared before Federal Judge Anthony Augelli in Newark to plead no contest. Learning of Greyhound's abrupt abandonment of its original plea of innocent, acting United States Attorney Herbert J. Stern literally rushed to the courtroom to oppose the plea. His effort failed. Greyhound received the maximum penalty, a $500 fine.[22]

Trivial punishments for corporate crime must be presumed to have less deterrent effect than would publicity reasonably proportionate to the seriousness of the offense and the importance and prestige of the client. Such publicity has been highly exceptional, although the situation has begun to improve. The absence of the public shame which, Edwin Sutherland said, "is an important aspect of all penalties," does help make corporate crime pay.[23] In the CIBA Pharmaceutical, Wallace Laboratories, and Greyhound Lines cases, sentencing proceedings went unreported by the *New York Times, Time,* and *Newsweek.* In the MER/29 case Richardson-Merrell's plea of no contest, climaxing a case without precedent in the prescription drug industry, also drew minor notice.

White-collar crimes and crimes of violence are related. The relation is aggravated by multiple standards in the law, the administration of justice, the media, and, as well, the business community and the public at large. No one has expounded this proposition with better credentials than Robert Morgenthau. For nine years, as United States Attorney in New York City, he provided an outstanding example of courageous and evenhanded law enforcement. On June 26, 1969, at a meeting of the National Industrial Conference Board in Manhattan, he discussed the connection between the two kinds of crime.

White-collar crime, he said, frequently is "not even discoverable without substantial investigation." Even when detected it leaves a trail of evidence that "is difficult, if not impossible to follow." In contrast, crimes of violence often "are readily discovered," and they "are generally committed by the poor." Morgenthau, who appealed to law enforcement agencies "not to follow the path of least resistance" by concentrating on crimes committed by the poor, said that those who "flagrantly disregard the law," and whom "we so often . . . must prosecute," include "prominent and supposedly responsible leaders." He recalled that in the last few years alone his office brought prosecutions

> against three law professors, numerous lawyers in private practice, many prominent doctors and surgeons, the executive vice president of a major bank, the treasurer of the New York State Committee of one of our major political parties, the executive vice-president of a major publishing firm, the president of the Board of Trade, partners in one of the country's largest accounting firms, a New York Stock Exchange member firm and a number of its partners, and numerous other corporate executives and businessmen.

A society that "does not condemn such conduct among its affluent citizens can also expect crimes of violence," Morgenthau said. He added:

> Equal justice under the law must mean more . . . than the right to free counsel or the right to remain silent in the precinct stationhouse. If the indigent who is brought into that precinct stationhouse rightly believes that the affluent are going unpunished for their crimes, then we have not only failed to achieve our goal of equal justice, but we have also created the conditions that will breed further disrespect for the law.

Morgenthau, who pioneered in the prosecution of the use of numbered, secret foreign bank accounts for illegal purposes, said in his June 1969 speech that perhaps better than any other white-collar crime this offense illustrates

> what the poor would call a "rich man's crime" which frequently goes unpunished. It is a white collar crime whose dimensions and seriousness have only recently begun to be appreciated. Of all the white collar crimes it is perhaps the most difficult to investigate and uncover. And perhaps most disturbing of all, we have discovered that the persons who use these secret accounts are all too frequently highly respectable corporate executives, businessmen, brokers, accountants and lawyers—men who would be the first to complain about a robbery or a mugging in their neighborhood.

Several months later, at a hearing of the House Committee on Banking and Currency on December 4, 1969, Morgenthau estimated that "hundreds of millions of dollars" are held for illegal purposes in secret bank accounts abroad. This may be an understatement, as indicated by the following article from the *Wall Street Journal* of November 11, 1970:

> How much money is stashed away in Swiss banks to evade U.S. income taxes?
>
> A whopping $5 billion in the last four years is the estimate pieced together by Arie Kopelman, a New York tax lawyer and UN consultant. Kopelman says his estimates are "admittedly incomplete," but he offers them as "very well supported hypotheses." They are based on something called the "errors and omissions" account in balance-of-payments figures.
>
> That account covers money that shows up in one country without being recorded as leaving another. Tourist spending and cash sent to relatives abroad are entries, but studies suggest that short-term capital flows (which include bank deposits) are most important. Kopelman finds that over the last 10 years, the U.S. has had an enormous $12.86 billion deficit in errors-and-omissions with Switzerland. Much of this was normal commercial deals, handled through Swiss banks, he says, but allowing for this still leaves billions in an unexplained flow of funds in 1966–69.
>
> *"The great bulk" of these billions is quite likely tax-evasion money, Kopelman contends. A U.S. Treasury aide says it has made no estimate, but adds that Kopelman's figure is "certainly not unthinkable."* [Emphasis in the original.]

At the December 1969 hearing on Capitol Hill, Will R. Wilson, head of the Criminal Division in the Justice Department, said, without elaboration, that a confidential survey by the Post Office disclosed that "thousands" of Americans have secret bank accounts in Switzerland. Not all of these are highly respectable executives, Morgenthau testified. "The foreign bank with its secret accounts is the place where the organized underworld and the purportedly respectable businessman meet," he said. Neil Sheehan of the *New York Times* has reported that "the line between entrepreneur and crook blurs in this gray world." He went on to say:

> The major American banks have been acting in concert to fight off any intrusion in the Swiss area. They, in turn, have rallied support at times from the State Department and the Treasury.
>
> The Treasury wants Swiss co-operation in maintaining the international balance of payments and monetary stability. The State Department is intent on preserving good relations because the Swiss have been helpful in intelligence gathering activities, while the banks, and their allies, the

274

brokerage houses, have a financial stake in unhampered commerce with the Swiss. They covet the commissions and interest charges on the enormous Swiss business.

Sheehan pointed out that in 1968 alone, Swiss banks bought and sold $11.3 billion worth of American stocks and bonds. With immense profits at stake, Sheehan said,

> Many big American banks are, in fact, seeking legal precedents that would allow their Swiss branches the same immunity from American courts and authorities that Swiss banks have. If they are successful, an American grand jury or court will be unable to subpoena as evidence of crime the records of an American bank branch in Switzerland.[24]

The First National City Bank of New York already had parried a subpoena for records concerning a $200,000 deposit certificate which was purchased from its branch in Geneva for an American broker and which was evidence in a stock fraud case. "I find it shocking that an American bank, by opening a branch abroad, can lend its facilities to citizens who are . . . violating our laws and then successfully deny its obligation to make account records available to the Department of Justice by claiming that the laws of a foreign country would be violated," Morgenthau testified at the House Banking and Currency Committee hearing.

At the time, it appeared that the Nixon Administration and Morgenthau held a common view about the seriousness of the problem of secret foreign accounts and agreed on the urgency of remedial action. They appeared to be united about the need for a bill of the kind sponsored by the committee chairman, Representative Wright Patman (D–Tex.). This measure would be effective mainly by requiring persons and corporations to report annually to the Treasury transactions with any foreign bank which does not make records available to American law enforcement agencies. A failure to make such a report would be a felony. Officials of the Justice Department and Treasury Department helped members of the committee staff draft the bill. Assistant Attorney General Wilson endorsed it when he testified on December 4. Two Treasury officials, Randolph W. Thrower, Commissioner of Internal Revenue, and Eugene T. Rossides, Assistant Secretary for Operations and Enforcement, were scheduled to testify on December 10. Thrower submitted a statement in advance. It said that the bill would not impose "unreasonable" record-keeping on the banks and was needed "desperately." Rossides, in a separate advance statement, also endorsed the bill. But, Neil Sheehan reported in the *New York Times:*

> In the meantime, the banks intervened. Mr. Rossides met representatives of the American Bankers Association and a number of major banks, including the Chase Manhattan, Morgan Guaranty and First National City.
>
> On Dec. 10 he and Mr. Thrower appeared before the committee with completely different statements. The bill would be too burdensome on the banks and would interfere with international commerce, Mr. Rossides said.
>
> Mr. Thrower echoed the view of Mr. Rossides. When Frank Bartimo, assistant general counsel of the Defense Department, supported the bill in testimony . . . calling it helpful in ferreting out military corruption, a Treasury spokesman said Mr. Bartimo "hasn't gotten the word" and that Treasury spoke for the Nixon Administration. The White House acquiesced.[25]

Prosecutor Morgenthau, a Democrat, had remained in office for almost a year after the Nixon Administration came to power. In December 1969, after Attorney General John N. Mitchell sent him a letter asking him to step aside, he resigned. "It appears to me that the White House, for all its statements about law and order, has failed to recognize that in law enforcement, as elsewhere, the customs and principles of 'the old politics' are no longer relevant," Morgenthau said in an interview with Victor S. Navasky.[26]

The Administration, Neil Sheehan reported, evidently was stung by accusations that it "favored tough law enforcement for poor people but lax treatment for rich criminals who could afford the secrecy of Swiss banks." Surely that was the most likely explanation of why, on March 2, 1970, it reached an apparent accommodation with the Banking and Currency Committee, with Assistant Secretary Rossides endorsing a version of the legislation substantially similar to Representative Patman's. "The accommodation came after the Justice Department exerted pressure on the Treasury to withdraw its opposition," Sheehan reported the next day in the *Times.* He said that Rossides "denied that the objections of the banks had had anything to do with the Treasury's opposition to the bill." The Treasury promised to submit detailed amendments within a few days. "Provided these changes follow the lines described by Mr. Rossides," Sheehan said with the valuable intuition of a reporter who does not want to get stung, "the wrangle over the bill between the Treasury and . . . Patman . . . will be ended."

276

Sheehan's caution proved to be warranted. The Administration tried to substitute a measure giving the Secretary of the Treasury *discretionary* authority to require a six-point record-keeping program. On March 17 the Committee rejected the substitute. On May 25 the House passed the legislation in a form which would require banks and other financial institutions to microfilm checks and other records of all foreign transactions and of domestic transactions by themselves and their clients in which the face amount of the check exceeds $499.99. Patman argued that a "disastrous loophole" had been created which "will make the check for $499.99 the standard medium of exchange." The bill then went to the Senate. The Administration and the banks began at once to press for weakening efforts in that body's Banking and Currency Committee. Surprisingly, these efforts proved to be largely ineffectual; and on October 6 Senate and House conferees approved what Neil Sheehan, in the *New York Times* the next morning, called "the first solid legislation to check crimes hidden by Swiss bank accounts." The conference committee, Sheehan added, had dealt "a rebuff to many of the country's major banks and to the Treasury Department, which have repeatedly sought to soften the measure considerably." And Congressman Patman, despite his earlier protestation about the "disastrous loophole," and despite another loophole amendment procured by Senator Wallace F. Bennett (R–Utah) to allow sums less than $5,000 (say, $4,999) to move in and out of the country without a report to the Treasury being required, was understood to be pleased.

Most men in business and industry fall considerably further short of perfection than did William H. Danforth of Ralston Purina. Yet they would like to see a much narrower chasm between business behavior and the ethical codes society professes to observe. How strongly they would prefer it, how many sacrifices they would make for it—such questions are valid but reach beyond our primary concern. It is not to be doubted that some uneasiness besets the business community, especially because young people, public interest law firms, new organizations to protect the environment and the poor, new leaders—all have been forcing significant elements of business, universities and other institutional stockholders, and the government to open their eyes to the public consequences of conduct and loyalties that in the past rarely had been challenged. Even in 1961, which seems a long time ago, significant evidence was provided in this shadowy area. The Reverend Raymond G. Baumhart, S.J., a former student of the Graduate School of Business Administration at Harvard, sent a questionnaire to five thousand readers of the *Harvard Business Review*. Summarizing and commenting on the results, Bernard Nossiter said:

> Seventeen hundred replied and of these, nearly three-quarters described themselves as members of either "top management" or "middle management." Nearly half said they agreed with a statement that American businessmen tend to ignore ethical laws and are preoccupied chiefly with gain; four of seven thought that businessmen would breach a code of ethics if they figured they could get away with it; four or five said there are practices generally accepted in their own industry which they personally regarded as unethical. Among these generally accepted unethical practices they cited: lavish entertaining to seek favors, kickbacks to customers' purchasing agents, price fixing and misleading advertising.
>
> These replies do not reflect a world of amoral executives, accepting the business life for what it is; instead, Reverend Baumhart's respondents display a marked uneasiness about their own role and that of their fellows. The late Professor Benjamin M. Selekman of the Harvard Business School once declared: "Outside of church circles, I find nowhere so much moral ferment as among corporation executives and teachers of business."
>
> Mencken would have scoffed at that but Sinclair Lewis might have agreed. If "ferment" means distress and confusion, then Selekman's observation is reinforced by Reverend Baumhart's questionnaire.[27]

The "ferment" has produced wholly insufficient overall and lasting improvement. "Distress and confusion" are feeble forces against the overwhelming power of the profit-making imperative. Actually, this kind of "ferment" is no match, either, for the self-serving rationale. In *White Collar Crime* Edwin Sutherland pointed out that "the businessman who violates the laws which are designed to regulate business does not customarily lose status among his business associates. Although a few members of the industry may think less of him, others admire him." There is, Sutherland said, "a general principle that a violation of the legal code is not necessarily a violation of the business code." Thus Harold Werner, the Richardson-Merrell vice president who pleaded no contest in the MER/29 case, remained as a member of the firm's executive heirarchy.

"We even find persons who publicly denounce crimes of violence while privately committing more 'socially acceptable' white collar crimes," Robert Morgenthau told the National Industrial Conference Board. Some white-collar crimes transcend mere hypocrisy to contribute directly to large-scale violence against human beings. This is attested by the problems of occupational safety and health. In 1969, occupational accidents killed 14,000 persons, or at least 55 every workday, and disabled 2.2 million, or 8,500 every workday. Of the year's toll of injured, 90,000 were permanently disabled, meaning that they never again could return to the jobs held when the accidents occurred. These figures are gross underestimates, not only because they exclude black lung, cancer and other diseases suffered by vast numbers of persons whose jobs expose them to hazardous fumes and dusts, but also because they exclude large numbers of industrial accidents that are not reported and tabulated.[28]

The key question was whether this wreckage might be in significant degree preventable. It is. In 1958, for example, Congress enacted the Maritime Safety Amendments to the Longshoremen's and Harbor Worker's Compensation Act. The amendments produced the first official, major safety regulations for a highly hazardous occupation. By 1968, a decade later, the rate of disabling injuries had decreased 52 per cent, to 18.6 per million man-hours. By the "guarded estimate" of George P. Shultz, then Secretary of Labor, "over 37,800 injuries were prevented in the nation's shipyards and docks."[29]

Organizations such as the Chamber of Commerce of the United States and the National Association of Manufacturers have responded to the situation on at least two levels. First, in the case of conduct that legally was not criminal but was certainly inhumane in its results, they undertook major lobbying campaigns to defeat truly effective remedial legislation; and not until the end of 1970 was a sound law finally enacted, thanks to, among others, Senator Ralph W. Yarborough (D–Tex.), Senator Harrison A. Williams, Jr. (D–N.J.), Representative Dominick V. Daniels (D–N.J.), former Labor Secretary W. Willard Wirtz, and Ralph Nader. Second, they did little if anything to counter the widespread violations of such feeble laws and regulations as do exist. "Thousands of American industrial concerns violate the Federal Government's occupational safety and health requirements every year, but the available penalties are almost never invoked against corporate offenders," Walter Rugaber said in the New York Times. His report was restricted to the Walsh-Healy Act, which applies to only those workers, about 25 million, in plants holding federal contracts. With a budget of $530,000 a year, inspectors reach a mere 2 to 3 per cent of the 750,000 contractors covered. Even so, Rugaber continued, a tiny force of twenty-seven engineers and five hygienists

> discover hazards in more than 90 per cent of the factories they enter, [although] only about 1 percent of the companies responsible are ever called to formal account, and barely one in a thousand is ever punished.
>
> Records at the Department of Labor show that during the six-year period from 1963 through 1968 the authorities filed safety and health complaints against only 154 companies and imposed sanctions against only 15 of them.[30]

If they are moved to file charges against corporations at all, many agencies of government, whether federal, state, or local, and prosecutors do not also charge the individuals responsible for the purported misconduct, even when it is feasible to do so. With personal responsibility thus eroded, Edwin Sutherland's observation should not be surprising:

> Businessmen customarily feel and express contempt for law, for government, and for governmental personnel. In this respect, also, they are similar to professional thieves, who feel contempt for law, policemen, prosecutors and judges. Businessmen customarily regard governmental personnel as politicians and bureaucrats, and the persons authorized to investigate business practices as "snoopers." Businessmen, characteristically, believe that the least government is the best, at least until they desire special favors from government. . . . The businessman's contempt for law, like that of the professional thief, grows out of the fact that the law impedes his behavior.[31]

To impede improper use of funds for foreign aid, the Agency for International Development adopted regulations which prohibited the use of these funds for sales commissions, allowances to importers for promoting trade names, or kickbacks. In 1963 a federal grand jury in New York City returned the first indictment against an American manufacturer for violation of the regulations. The defendant was the giant Olin Mathieson Chemical Corporation, then the parent firm of the pharmaceutical house of E. R. Squibb & Sons. The charges against Olin were that it conspired with other defendants, including the Philip Bauer Company, an exporter, to provide, and that it provided, false certifications of compliance with the regulations, and to defraud the United States. The indictment involved the shipment to Vietnam and Cambodia, over a five-year period, of antibiotics valued at $1.5 million.

The company eventually pleaded guilty to the conspiracy count and to two of twenty-three substantive counts. Judge Harold R. Tyler imposed the maximum sentence, $30,000. At the sentencing proceeding on September 23, 1965, the prosecutor, Richard A. Givens, an assistant to Robert Morgenthau, put into the record 152 exhibits which he would have used had the case gone to trial, and his own affidavit about the case. These documents disclosed, among other things, that the Bauer firm had made deposits of between $30,000 and $40,000 in the Banque Ferrier Lullin et Cie, Geneva, Accounts No. 41–22 and 41–23, for the benefit of a French national named Dr. Jacques Arnaud. He was the major stockholder in a drug importing firm in Cambodia. Olin Mathieson "was well aware" that the Bauer firm was making these deposits but used the exporter "to shield itself from responsibility," the Givens documents said. One of the prosecutor's exhibits was an Olin Mathieson internal document which recalled that at a meeting at the company's offices in Manhattan, Arnaud revealed to Olin officials that he had not divulged the bank-deposit procedures to his fellow stockholders.[32]

Olin Mathieson was by no means the only member of the drug industry found to have violated AID regulations. Daniel Cohen, of the agency's Price Analysis Branch, and, later, LaVern J. Duffy, assistant counsel of the Permanent Subcommittee on Investigations of the Senate Committee on Government Operations, established that six additional major pharmaceutical firms had paid kickbacks and illegal commissions in connection with AID-financed exports to Vietnam. Thanks to the efforts of Cohen and Duffy, the firms repaid the government more than $1 million, as follows: American Cyanamid, $313,383; Chas. Pfizer & Company, $306,796; Merck & Company, $144,970; Olin Mathieson, Philip Bauer, and Squibb International, $115,984; Parke, Davis & Company, $50,745; Schering Corporation, $61,929; and the Upjohn Company, $14,621.[33]

Such illegal behavior should not be presumed to be rare merely because it is underpublicized. In 1958 the Federal Trade Commission charged that the Pfizer firm, aided by Cyanamid, had committed fraud on the Patent Office to procure a patent on tetracycline, an antibiotic which is effective against a broad spectrum of infections. After a decade of legal contests the Sixth Circuit Court of Appeals upheld the FTC and, in March 1969, the Supreme Court let the ruling stand.

Immediately after the patent was granted, in January 1955, Pfizer made Cyanamid its exclusive licensee. This was even more advantageous than it might appear. The reason was that Pfizer already held the patent for oxytetracycline (Terramycin), one of the two principal competitors to tetracycline, and Cyanamid had the patent for the other, chlortetracycline (Aureomycin). With tetracycline locked up, Pfizer and Cyanamid now could assure that none of the three products competed in price with the others.

Even in 1955, however, the picture began to change. The Bristol-Myers Company, which had tried desperately to be dealt into the tetracycline market, succeeded after it learned that Pfizer had hired a private detective to tap phones used by its executives as well as those used by Squibb. With the tapping episode as a club, Bristol won a license to produce and sell tetracycline, and to supply it in bulk to Squibb and Upjohn.

In 1961 a federal grand jury in New York City handed up an indictment charging Pfizer, Cyanamid, and Bristol with having conspired to fix the prices of all three "wonder" antibiotics, with having conspired to monopolize a $100 million-a-year market, and with in fact having achieved the desired monopoly. Squibb and Upjohn were named co-conspirators but not defendants. At the trial in 1967 the prosecutor, Harry G. Sklarsky of the Antitrust Division of the Justice Department, produced devastating disclosures. Using data from the companies' own files, he showed that from 1953 to 1961, the period covered by the indictment, the manufacturing cost for one hundred capsules of tetracycline in the 250-milligram dosage was as low as $1.52. But the price to druggists was an unvarying $30.60, or twenty times as much. The standard retail price was $51. A reasonable wholesale price, according to specialists in these matters, would have been $6. With the same percentage markup by the pharmacist the retail price then would have been $10, or $41 less than the price that prevailed for at least eight years. In the six years ended in 1955, Cyanamid's own data showed, its revenues from antibiotics totaled $407 million. Of this $342 million was gross profit.

On December 29, 1967, a jury convicted the three firms. The companies appealed. An unusual sequence of events ensued. Long afterward, in May 1970, by a 2 to 1 decision, the Court of Appeals for the Second Circuit reversed the conviction and remanded the case. Next, the Justice Department sought an *en banc* rehearing. The court granted this on

November 12, with Judge Leonard P. Moore, who with Judge Henry J. Friendly had voted in May to reverse, retracting one of the major points he had made six months earlier. The vote was 5 to 3. The rehearing was set for mid-December. Two weeks before it was to be held, however, the court reversed itself and upheld the May remand order of Judge Moore and Judge Friendly. The vote this time was 4 to 3, with Friendly signing the new order. The Department has appealed the case to the Supreme Court.

Meanwhile, the Department had filed a $25 million damage suit against Pfizer and Cyanamid for overcharges on federal purchases. The government asked that the patent be canceled. In the first seven years of the life of the patent, which expires in 1972, Pfizer collected royalties of $17.1 million, the suit said.[34]

"The white collar criminal does not conceive of himself as a criminal because he is not dealt with under the same official procedures as other criminals and because, owing to his class status, he does not engage in intimate personal association with those who define themselves as criminals," Edwin Sutherland said. But, he added,

> they do customarily think of themselves as "law violators." This is another aspect of a different word for the same essence. In their confidential relations businessmen speak with pride of their violations of the law, and regard the enactment of the law rather than its violation as reprehensible. Their consciences do not ordinarily bother them, for they have the support of their associates in the violation of the law.[35]

The durability of Sutherland's observations was demonstrated in an extraordinary—indeed, sensational—case involving the Colonial Pipeline Company. This firm, based in Atlanta, is owned by nine oil companies (American, Cities Service, Continental, Gulf, Phillips, Sinclair, Socony-Mobil, Texaco, and Union) with assets of approximately $35 billion, and itself had assets of $385 million as of December 31, 1968. Colonial undertook to build, and completed in 1965, the largest privately financed construction project in history—a 1,531-mile pipeline, costing $390 million, which carries 40 million gallons of petroleum products each day from Houston, Texas, to the New York harbor area.

While the project was under way, a federal inquiry into union racketeering in pipeline construction turned up a mysterious check made out for $20,000. Investigation led to the completely unexpected discovery that in 1963 and 1964 Colonial Pipeline had paid, through intermediaries, a total of $110,000 in cash to two municipal officials of Woodbridge, New Jersey, Walter Zirpolo, the mayor, and Robert E. Jacks, president of the Municipal Council. The purpose of the payments, which was never in controversy after the matter was brought to light, was to get easements through five city-owned lots and to get, without the required public hearing, a building permit for twenty-two large storage tanks.

In February 1967 a federal grand jury in Newark returned indictments charging two conspiracies to use interstate mails, phones, and travel for purposes of bribery, one conspiracy involving procurement of the building permit and the other the rights-of-way. The indictment also alleged several substantive violations, each concerning delivery of bribe monies.

In addition to Colonial, Zirpolo, and Jacks, the defendants included Ben D. Leuty and Karl T. Feldman. They were, during the payment period, president and executive vice president, respectively, of Colonial. Another defendant was the Bechtel Corporation of San Francisco, the world's largest engineering firm, which was a contractor on the New Jersey section of the pipeline. After a lengthy trial, closing arguments of compelling interest were made to the jury.

"Rarely if ever," said Herbert J. Stern, then a special attorney for the Justice Department, "has the United States been able to pull back the curtain and to display before you or any jury the kind of naked corruption that we have displayed in this case, the intimate details of corrupt public officials met and joined, furthered and promoted by big businessmen who were equally corrupt for their own reasons."

Stern went on to say that "rarely if ever has the United States been able to prove such a deliberate, knowing, intentional and willful flouting of the laws. . . . Let me suggest to you the reason that these cases are so rare is because the men don't often get caught. . . . the reason they don't get caught is because generally they hide it too well, and if you doubt it . . . look how well it was hidden in this case."

Ben Leuty's counsel was Simon H. Rifkind, the former federal judge. Rifkind's argument to the jury was consistent with Edwin Sutherland's book. Thus Leuty was not the perpetrator of the crime of bribery; he "capitulated" to the crime of extortion. His character was "superlative." He authorized the payments to avoid the "national disaster" that would befall the country if the pipeline were not to be built and reliance had to be placed on tankers which are vulnerable in wartime to enemy sub-marines. "All of the evidence showed conclusively that what Leuty and his people tried to do was to prevent the officials of Woodbridge from acting dishonestly and illegally." Just as Leuty's reputation was "stainless," so was Colonial's, and the oil companies which owned it, in turn, were owned by "more than one million men, women, children, orphans." To-ward the end of his appeal to the jury Rifkind said, "Yours will be the glory when you wipe the tear off his lovely wife's cheek."[36]

The jury agreed with the prosecution and, on January 23, 1969, convicted all of the defendants (except for Zirpolo, who was convicted later in a separate trial but then won a new trial). There followed, on June 27, a sentencing proceeding that in its own way was at least as interesting as the closing arguments. The trial judge, Reynier J. Wortendyke, Jr., presided. He said he was fully aware of all of the explanations for the bribe-paying but "cannot yet understand why a corporation such as the Colonial Pipeline Company would pay any money." There then emerged a striking duality. He said that the case "was a liberal education [in] the amorality of business, politics and human relations in this democracy of ours." The conduct of the corpora-tions "shakes my faith in business in this country." But he had visited federal penitentiaries. Only the day before he had had to listen to "alleged testimony" from "some of the most degraded occupants of Atlanta Penitentiary that I have ever run into." Deeply upset as he was by the conduct of the men now awaiting sentencing before him, he could not bring himself to send any of them to prison. With Jacks, the Municipal Council president, standing before him, the judge said, "I'll tell you this: If you had committed a crime of violence I would have given you the maximum period of imprisonment because I have no patience with it."

In behalf of Ben Leuty, Simon Rifkind said that his client was "a man of impeccable character" who was felled by "all the elements of a Greek tragedy"—"loyalty to the laudable and honorable mission on which he was engaged," "fidelity to the interests of those who had entrusted a vast fortune to his keeping," and "a patriotic concern . . ." As to punish-ment, has not "Ben Leuty, in the context of his prior experience, . . . already been punished and lashed and flagellated far more intensely and far more cruelly than any punishment which this civilized court could now administer?"

Judge Wortendyke needled Rifkind "on having such an affluent client," one who surely "makes your colleagues envious." Addressing Leuty, he said he understood "that you have followed the guidance of your conscience. That is why I cannot understand why you and your company ever paid this money."

Warren W. Wilentz, who in 1968 was the Democratic candidate against Senator Clifford P. Case (R–N.J.), spoke for Colonial. He depicted it as a corporate lamb. "I know I represent a corporation, and rather a young corporation, if your Honor please, which I am afraid lost its way," he said. The wayward corporation "got lost somewhere around Woodbridge, sadly enough," Wilentz added.

Judge Wortendyke imposed the maximum allowable fines on all of the defendants. Colonial had to pay $90,000 and Bechtel $20,000. He gave each of the individual defendants a suspended sentence of a year and a day and put them on unsupervised probation for five years. About a year and a half later, in Philadelphia, the Court of Appeals for the Third Circuit overturned the convictions on the ground that the Grand Jury which had returned the indictment had been selected by a process that discriminated against women.[37]

It is tempting to wonder whether the incarceration of men such as Ben Leuty would serve to galvanize one of the most neglected of causes, penal reform. That aside, no one familiar with the Colonial Pipeline case, and no one who was in the courtroom for the sentencing proceeding, as was one of the authors, could fail to be impressed by the authenticity of Judge Wortendyke's integrity and compassion. Even if Rifkind's hamming may have tended to obscure it, Leuty and the other individual defendants of course had been through a dreadful ordeal. There are the most serious questions about what useful purposes, for anybody, would be served by locking up Leuty, Feldman, or Jacks, or Harold Werner of the MER/29 case, or Robert Keefer of the Swiss bank case. The kind of compassion shown these men apparently is felt even by the President. "Perhaps the closest of Mr. Nixon's friends" is Elmer H. Bobst, who says the Chief Executive "is like a son to me," a *New York Times* article on "Nixon's Inner Circle" said. The same article said that in 1941, before Bobst retired as president of the Warner-Lambert Pharmaceutical Company, "he was fined $3,000 in Federal Court on a charge of conspiring with German and other European interests to restrain the import and manufacture of medical hormones."[38]

The trouble is, the President, hard-liners at all levels of government, and many judges too often seem to run short of compassion when it comes to ordinary human beings who, in Rifkind's words in the Keefer case, "have slipped on the ice of some regulation or some emotion." In keeping with his campaign promises, Mr. Nixon, in fact, has made harsh retribution a distinguishing feature of his approach to street crime and the problems of marijuana and narcotics. Is it to be doubted that one of the roots of alienation and unrest is the multiple standards of justice, one for blue collars, another for white collars, still another for youths with long hair, and yet one more for corporations?

The following is reproduced in its entirety from the *Washington Post* of February 26, 1970, p. A6:

1,000-YEAR SENTENCE

DALLAS—Joseph Franklin Sills, 50, was sentenced by a jury, angry over a spate of assault robberies here, to one thousand years in jail for holding up a dry cleaning establishment. He netted $73.10 in the robbery, for which he was convicted by the same jury.

So far as victims are concerned, amoral corporate conduct and organized crime can have identical results. Both can produce death, injury, or other harm. In *Theft of the Nation* Donald R. Cressey, an outstanding authority on organized crime, presents a catalogue of the ruthless brutality of the Cosa Nostra, which he believes to be a more accurate descriptive phrase than "the Mafia."[39] A man borrows $10,000 from a Cosa Nostra loan shark, for example. The interest cost per year can be $104,000. The borrower is unable to meet the payments. Then "the usurer hires a goon to hang the borrower out a hotel window by his legs, to break his arms, to kick him in the stomach, or to take similar action." The breaking of arms, Cressey said, is a technique that the Cosa Nostra also uses against its own underlings, such as a field man who "was not turning in all the bets he collected."

Murder is of course another standard technique. Fred J. Cook, writing in the *New York Times Magazine,* provided one of the least forgettable examples. There is in Livingston, New Jersey, a wooded plot of several acres. On it is a great stone mansion. The owner is Ruggiero (Richie the Boot) Boiardo, a "flashy Prohibition mobster, complete with a $5,000 diamond-studded belt buckle" who, Cook said, achieved great political and economic power in Newark. Citing FBI transcripts of taped Cosa

Nostra conversations, Cook said that "some shudderingly sinister things have happened" at Boiardo's estate:

> On Jan. 7, 1963, according to the F.B.I. tapes, [Ray the Gyp] DeCarlo and Anthony (Little Pussy) Russo—a mobster who once bragged that he had Long Branch [New Jersey] in his hip pocket—discussed some of the macabre events that had taken place on the Boiardo estate. Russo warned DeCarlo never to go near the place alone if Boiardo tried to lure him there. According to Russo and DeCarlo, there was an incinerator for human bodies at the rear of the estate, up behind the Boiardo greenhouse. ". . . Ray, I seen too many," said Little Pussy. "You know how many guys we hit that way up there."
> DeCarlo: What about the big furnace he's got back there?
> Russo: That's what I'm trying to tell you! Before you go up there . . .
> DeCarlo: The big iron grate.
> Russo: He used to put them on there and burn them.[40]

Ordinary household products, by estimate of the Department of Health, Education, and Welfare in 1968, cause, or are associated with, 20 million injuries a year. To investigate this astonishing toll Congress created the National Commission on Product Safety. There is a new human "right," the right of the consumer "to be protected against unreasonable risk of bodily harm from products purchased on the open market for the use of himself and his family," Congress said in a joint resolution. In hearings around the country, the commission established beyond dispute that a great proportion of the injuries, some of them lethal, caused by products used in and around households are avoidable. One example to be provided here involves the breaking of arms. The other involves burnings.

In 1958 there was published in medical literature the first report on how electrically operated wringers on home washing machines catch fingers, hands and arms between their revolving rollers and break and mangle them. In the late 1940s there became available to manufacturers an "instinctive release," which stops the rollers when the victim pulls back. Also developed was a form of "deadman's control," long used in railroad operations, among others, which operates the machine only so long as the user applies pressure to a special switch. The cost per machine was $1 to $3. Surprisingly, there were as of 1969 about 14 million wringer-type washing machines in use, and in the previous year 379,000 of them were produced. Not until October 1968 did the industry adopt a voluntary standard under which manufacturers agreed to provide the safety devices. Meanwhile, an estimated 200,000 persons a year, about half of them children, were being injured.[41]

Particularly in temperate climates where home heating is needed only on infrequent occasions, gas-fired floor furnaces are widely used. The burner unit is suspended below the floor. There is nothing but air between it and the grille. As of 1969, approximately 4 million of these furnaces were in use, mainly in the dwellings of low- and moderate-income families but also in beach cottages and mobile homes. These devices are an extraordinary hazard to little children. As many as 60,000 of them each year were estimated to have crawled, toddled, or walked onto the searing hot grilles and suffered serious burns.

The Product Safety Commission made the furnaces the subject of a hearing at which the initial witnesses were Public Health Service physicians and injury specialists. Starting in the late 1950s they had tried to persuade the American Gas Association, which is composed mainly of gas utility companies, to deny its seal of approval to the furnaces if they could not be made safe. The AGA seal is of critical importance in the marketplace. Most gas companies that sell appliances, for example, sell only those approved by the AGA. However, the AGA said that nothing could be done. It continued to use a standard for approval of floor furnaces which allowed a temperature of 350 degrees Fahrenheit an inch above the grille, although a one-second exposure of the skin to 158 degrees can produce a second-degree burn.

At the commission hearing, witnesses for the AGA delivered a prepared statement which did not deal with the problem of floor furnaces but which expressed pride in a new $4 million research facility. Finally, the commission took testimony from Wiener Associates, a small engineering consultant firm in Baltimore to which the commission staff had quietly let an $800, nonprofit contract. Within three weeks, the firm testified, it had devised not one but several ways to eliminate the hazard of grille burns from floor furnaces. The simplest and cheapest was the placement of a loosely woven fiberglass mat over the grille.

On hearing this Arnold B. Elkind, the commission chairman, angrily summoned the Gas Association to comment. Frank E. Hogdon, director of laboratories for the AGA, candidly expressed admiration for the accomplishment of the Wiener firm (and the Association later used it as the basis for remedial action). Why, Elkind wanted to know, had the industry failed to protect possibly 60,000 children a year from serious burns? Hogdon's answer, a classically banal one, was that it "simply did not know of any technology and didn't perhaps have enough incentive."[42]

It is important to be meticulously precise about the distinctions between arm-breakings and burnings by organized criminals and arm-breakings and burnings by washing machines and floor furnaces. Organized crime is reasoned and systematic crime. Victims are deliberately chosen. A rival or a potential rival must be eliminated. Revenge must be had. A lesson must be taught. Debased though the techniques are, the victims are selected by a rational process, and the victims understand the system as well as their tormentors, or killers, if it comes to that.

But rationality of this kind does not attend the amoral behavior of large corporations. They seek to survive and prosper, not commit crime. Victims fall at random. Vengeance is not sought. No lesson is taught. It is, we may say, as impersonal as a decision in the Pentagon, or the White House, which results in the dropping of bombs on villages in Vietnam.

The title of Chapter 13 in *White Collar Crime* is "White Collar Crime Is Organized Crime." Sutherland meant this literally. That is, he presented evidence to show that a substantial proportion of the law violations committed by corporations is "deliberate and organized." For example, he said, businessmen organize to violate the laws against restraint of trade. They organize "formally, also, for the control of legislation, selection of administrators, and restriction of appropriations for enforcement of laws which may affect themselves." Sutherland did point to differences between the two forms of crime, the most significant one being that business offenders conceive of themselves, and are conceived of by the public, as respectable citizens.

Despite the validity of Sutherland's comparison between white-collar and organized crime, it raises problems today. The principal reason is that he measured white-collar crime against the organized crime of professional theft. Today, however, organized crime is a phrase which has become almost synonymous not with professional theft, but with the far more sinister Cosa Nostra.

Donald R. Cressey, the leading criminologist, was a research assistant to the late Professor Sutherland at Indiana University, and the two men had a close and extensive association. As has been noted, Cressey went on to become an authority on the Cosa Nostra. He wrote *Theft of the Nation* twenty years after publication of Professor Sutherland's book. The subtitle is noteworthy: *The Structure and Operations of Organized Crime in America.* This of course tends to make "organized crime" and "Cosa Nostra" interchangeable phrases.

Organized crime is a sociological category of crime. So is white-collar crime (*crime*, not simply amoral behavior). Cressey, like Sutherland, sees "obvious" similarities between white-collar crime and organized crime, including the Cosa Nostra brand. But Cressey is right to draw careful distinctions between white-collar crime and crime of the kind practiced by the Cosa Nostra:

> Organized criminals, to a much greater extent than white-collar criminals, directly corrupt police and other officials to insure that they can violate the law with impunity. . . . White-collar criminals are not organized for corruption, and only occasionally are they organized for crime. And even when they are organized for crime, they do not kill witnesses or potential witnesses against them.

Further, with emphasis in the original, Cressey said:

> *An organized crime is any crime committed by a person occupying, in an established division of labor, a position designed for the commission of a crime,* providing *that such division of labor also includes at least one position for a corrupter, one position for a corruptee, and one position for an enforcer.*[43]

This definition has standing. It was accepted by President Johnson's Commission on Law Enforcement and the Administration of Justice, to which Cressey was a consultant. Insofar as the corporation is concerned it makes clear that the fundamental problem is not evil men but a milieu that too often channels ordinary and even good men into activities that produce evil results.

An organization of small size is not automatically characterized by goodness. An organization of large size is not automatically characterized by badness. But there *is* something about bigness which should make us wary. It tends to fragmentize and even atomize personal responsibility, whether in a business, a bureaucracy or the military. "The very determination of what is a responsible decision and who is to be held

AMERICA, INC.

responsible is neither simple nor clear," Bernard Nossiter said. "There
is no formula that explains how competing claims are to be gratified;
there is no theory that fixes responsibility on specific actors in the corporate drama."[44]

On April 17, 1962, Shirley Sue Barth, a mother of two minor children, was driving a 1961 Chevrolet station wagon on a flat, straight highway in San Mateo, California. Five women friends were passengers.
Without warning the left rear tire blew out. Mrs. Barth lost control of
the car. It went over an embankment, struck a guard rail and, finally,
turned over end-over-end. Mrs. Barth and one of her friends were killed.
Her husband, Theodore H. Barth, and three of the surviving passengers
filed suit against the B. F. Goodrich Company, manufacturer of the
tire. It was a replacement purchased six months before the accident,
but was of the same quality and size as General Motors had provided as
original equipment.

At the trial, expert witnesses for Goodrich testified that rear tires
specified by GM for the vehicle in question were overloaded by 232
pounds, or 25 per cent, when six passengers weighing an average of 150
pounds each occupied the station wagon (which, incidentally, was a
nine-passenger model). One of the defense experts, who had been with
Goodrich for nine and a half years, testified that an overload of only 10
per cent would be excessive, by the standards of the industry's own Tire
and Rim Association. The trial ended with a judgment of $207,375 for
the Barth family. Goodrich appealed, but the judgment was affirmed by
the California Court of Appeal.

In its opinion, the court raised acute questions of responsibility.
"Goodrich knew that its tires were subject to overload and asked the car
manufacturer to be more observant of recommended loads," the opinion
said. "But it never informed the public or its individual customers of the
problem. Goodrich supplied the tires to the car manufacturer under
these circumstances as the business was a highly competitive one. It
knew that a certain percentage of tires sold would be exposed to overload-
ing conditions."

At the same time, Goodrich, when it sent its tires out, "did not know
what model car the tires would be used on as this was entirely up to the
automobile manufacturer," the court said. "Accordingly, if Goodrich
received from General Motors an order for a supply of the kind of tires

292

here involved, the order would be routinely filled and no inquiry made as to the use of the tire." As for GM, two of its experts, testifying for the defense, said that it "made no effort to fix the rated tire carrying capacity. The only criterion was whether the tires were performing satisfactorily on the car."[45]

When Harry S Truman was President he was justly praised for the sign saying THE BUCK STOPS HERE on his desk in the White House. But where did it stop, under what shell, at Goodrich? At GM? At CIBA Pharmaceutical, Wallace Laboratories, and the oil companies that own Colonial Pipeline? At Cutter Laboratories? At Richardson-Merrell? At Olin-Mathieson? For that matter, where does the buck stop today at the pharmaceutical firms, including Abbott Laboratories, Merck, and Parke-Davis, which manufacture prescription drugs that are powerful enough to injure and even kill, which give the necessary warnings to physicians in the United States because they are compelled to do so, but which deny the same warnings to physicians in the countries that do not compel them to do so?[46]

A common denominator of such situations, and the list could be extended almost indefinitely, is that those involved in bringing them about were remote from the victims. The mechanisms are such that a man who would flinch from striking a person will without giving it a second thought participate in processes which injure and kill people. In the most fundamental sense such decisions are not responsible. "A decision is responsible," the philosopher Charles Frankel says, "when the man or group that makes it has to answer for it to those who are directly or indirectly affected by it." This is true in public government as well as in private government. Garrett Hardin, a professor of biology at the University of California, Santa Barbara, measured the decision to build a supersonic transport by Frankel's definition. The taxpayers, not the corporations involved, were to pay at least 90 per cent of the $5 billion cost. If each of 240 passengers aboard earns $60,000 a year and, on a coast-to-coast flight, is saved two hours at $20 per hour, each planeload will save the passengers $9,600. But, Hardin said, "they don't have to pay the cost. The cost is paid by the 20 million people on the ground who suffer each time some 200 passengers save two hours. The decision to produce and fly the SST is, in the deepest sense, an irresponsible decision."

Why was it made? On April 1, 1970, the *Washington Post* was able to provide from the horse's mouth the answer that had been widely suspected all along:

> The controversial supersonic transport airplane is necessary to preserve the American aviation industry, Secretary of Transportation John A. Volpe said yesterday.
>
> "The aviation industry is essential to our nation," he said, adding that if the SST project is not pressed to completion, "then in six or seven years you would have tens of thousands of employees laid off and an aviation industry that would go to pot."
>
> He said President Nixon "feels the same way."

The President might feel differently if the SST's were to fly over the White House in Washington, the Western White House in San Clemente, and the Florida White House in Key Biscayne. Garrett Hardin said: "In passing, let it be noted that a responsible decision in the SST matter would be easily reached if all airline executives, all 45,000 employees of the FAA [Federal Aviation Administration] and all 535 members of Congress were compelled to live in the path of SST sonic booms, thus making them answer for their decisions, as Frankel recommends."[47]

To bring about a responsible decision, Senator William Proxmire, over a period of years, led a resourceful, tenacious battle. Gaylord Nelson, his colleague from Wisconsin, was another senator who made significant contributions. In late 1970 Proxmire and his allies achieved a degree of success that perhaps only a year, or possibly a few months, earlier hardly could have been imagined. By a vote of 52 to 41, the Senate voted to deny the $290 million for fiscal 1971 sought by the White House and SST advocates for development of a prototype. As if this had never occurred, a delegation from the Senate then went to a conference with a delegation from the House and joined in recommending passage of a "compromise" $210 million appropriation, as part of a money bill for the Department of Transportation.

On January 2, 1971, the last day of the Ninety-first Congress, Proxmire ended a minifilibuster after key senators made some concessions that, he predicted, would doom the SST project in the Ninety-second Congress. The proponents of the aircraft yielded, for example, to Proxmire's demand for separate votes on SST funding and the rest of the Department's appropriation. They promised that Senate conferees will not again give in to the House, should the Senate once more disapprove the SST and the House approve it. These and other concessions in hand,

Proxmire agreed to a compromise under which the Department will be funded for the year ending June 30, 1971, while the SST will be funded only through March 30, with $51.7 million rather than $210 million.

A responsible decision at, say, Cutter Laboratories might have the executives and their wives and children volunteer for clinical tests by Dr. Austin Stough. James M. Roche, the chairman of General Motors, might wish to specify that the GM cars in which he rides be equipped with tires that are overloaded. Officials of Parke-Davis might instruct their personal physicians to let them run the risk of fatal aplastic anemia by prescribing Chloromycetin for a cold, against which that antibiotic is ineffective.

Daniel P. Moynihan, a counselor to President Nixon until he returned to his Harvard professorship early in 1971, was a pioneer, in the 1950s, in calling public attention to the relation between automobile design and safety, before then most dimly perceived. A few years ago, in the *Public Interest,* he asked, "Why have the very large number of persons in business, industry and the law been impervious to the pleas to be rational about auto safety? Has it got to do with the nature of corporate organization, or is it simply that society is—as Reinhold Niebuhr suggests —easily corrupted in areas where individuals are asked to assume a personal relation to a collective responsibility?"[48]

Most likely the answer is not an either/or proposition, and certainly it may be more complex than we recognize here. But it seems reasonable to say that failures in auto safety, as in other areas, have some important roots in corporate organization; and they have other roots in the corruption, or anesthetizing, of conscience that easily occurs when individuals are asked to assume a personal relation to a collective responsibility. But the two are causally related: The large corporation diffuses ever more important collective responsibilities among more and more people and separates ever more acts from consequences—the decision-makers from those affected by the decisions. The buck seems to stop nowhere. This contributes to the corruption of which Moynihan spoke.

The evidence is that the corporate conscience, if it exists at all, is utterly undependable. To concentrate economic power, therefore, is to be even more catastrophically careless than we have been heretofore with the lives, health, environment, and economic welfare of our people.

9 THE DISPLACEMENT OF THE INDIVIDUAL

I was once obliged to introduce to the vice-president of one of our competitors the Assistant Sales Promotion Manager of the Small Appliance Division of the Merchandise Department of the General Electric Company. Try that sometime on your xylophone. —T. K. Quinn[1]

"Unchecked giantism—be it political, religious or economic—has never been compatible with individualism," Senator Philip Hart said a couple of years ago.[2] In corporations, giantism is most clearly a threat to the individualism of the managers and employees. Profits being the pre-eminent goal, and individualism being almost by definition a quality with a troublemaking potential, it is preferable that the bland lead the bland, that the bland lead the blind, that the blind lead the bland, that the blind lead the blind, or that all of these forms of leadership coexist. But "company-eating contests," as Hart called them, may bring previously independent men into the bland-blind world, thus further depleting the supply. There is an inevitable adverse effect on democratic values in society as a whole. Thus we see, Hart said, "an ever-growing paradox. Free enterprise—long idolized as the last bastion of rugged individualism—may be leading to the greatest institutionalized thwarting of individualism in the country: Big, Big Business."[3]

T. K. Quinn was tapped at one time to become president of General Electric. He preferred to quit and strike out on his own. GE's top management was surprised if not uncomprehending, just as, years later, GM's top management would be incredulous to hear from its private eyes that Ralph Nader was not venal. Even in 1953, when Quinn's *Giant Business* was published (and, incidentally, widely ignored), GE had long since stood as an example of corporate giantism and of the problems that giantism creates.

"The President of the General Electric Company kept what he called a PYM list of promising young men," Quinn said, as a starter. "The very existence of such a list was an unconscious acknowledgement of the over-size of the corporation. In a one million, ten, twenty, or even thirty-million-dollar company, the President is in continual personal contact with all of the key men. He knows them and their performance and qualifications personally. He needs no PYM paper list. Yet in billion-dollar General Electric, it was a compliment to the President of the Company that he had one. At least it indicated that he was making an effort, however distant and impersonal, to keep track of deserving candidates for advancement."[4] But he could not keep in touch even with the full vice presidents, so numerous were they. Consequently, there was interposed "another layer of super vice-presidents called 'executive vice-presidents' to whom from three to six other, ordinary vice-presidents report," Quinn said.

Just as a man could be on a PYM list, so could his name appear on, in effect, a UYM list of unpromising young men. "Many ambitious, able young men in giant organizations become wrongfully stamped as being 'unsound,' or 'too emotional,' or 'impulsive,' or 'disinterested,' or they are given some other negative mark, when in fact there is no true reason for any such reflection upon them," Quinn said. "Often it is mere political jealousy or prejudice. In smaller organizations the man or men in charge would know them and quickly disregard any unfair characterizations. But in giant organizations, the bosses must rely upon reports and paper ratings."[5]

From the time he became chairman of the Senate Subcommittee on Antitrust and Monopoly in 1963, Senator Hart said, he had tried through hearings on economic concentration "to measure the power of the supergiants—the conglomerates." But he noted: "There are no charts or graphs, no thoughtful statements, no acknowledgement actually as to what company-eating contests mean to the desire for individualism. Unfortunately, too often they mean that individualism is mummified."[6] We, too, lack charts and graphs, but we do have illustrative evidence, some from Quinn and some from an industry which has been disrupted by a series of conglomerate takeovers in recent years.

Quinn said:

The presidents of the independent smaller companies which we purchased usually became department managers, continuing their old activities but as subordinates. Without exception their whole attitudes [*sic*] changed. They were no longer primarily responsible, and began to speak in terms of pleasing the big boss. At a company meeting I once sat with Governor Trumbull, President of Trumbull Electric Company, which G.E. acquired. He had been a definite, outstanding personality, but now he had to court favor. He was scheduled to make a speech. "What shall I say?" he worriedly inquired. When his turn came he spoke like a man from another world—as though he were ill. It was a disappointment to everyone, including himself. Returning to his seat beside me, he whispered with great concern, "Was it all right? Did I say anything objectionable?" I answered him he had not, without adding that actually he had said nothing at all.[7]

From a succession of such incidents, and from seeing subordinate managers and officers become dependents of their superiors, catering to them and trying to get more recognition, Quinn concluded that the economic concentration of his day already had produced a "new, dependent generation":

Every one of the thousands of absorbed and merged corporations represents a lost opportunity for the young men of tomorrow to find more important places, where a man could assume responsibility and develop his ability and serve the community in the spirit of independence. Where will the leaders of the future come from? Surely not from the bureaucratic-minded subordinates of the third and fourth generations in giant corporations who line up and move from specialty jobs automatically to the next level as death or resignation overtakes their predecessors. They are not creative towers of strength; they are more like the trusting, clinging vines which hug these towers for their weak existence.[8]

It does not detract from Quinn to say that the Temporary National Economic Committee was sounding similar prescient warnings more than a decade before he did. In language that has a distinctly contemporary ring, the TNEC said in its report in 1939, "Democracy, which surely comprehends economic as well as political freedom for the natural person, cannot endure when the natural person cannot shape the policies and activities of the collective agencies which control all the materials of his economic life." The committee, which was set up to probe some of the nation's more vexing problems, also said in the report:

298

The American ideal of living has not changed, but the forms of our economic life have changed and most radically. The new forms of industrial organization are such that competition has become a vastly more difficult status to maintain and the American ideal of free living for people is not nearly so easy of achievement as before organizations superseded men in the economy.[9]

Book publishing obviously is unrepresentative of the bulk of industry. It has no blast furnaces, oil rigs, or assembly lines for bodies, engines, and frames. It is relatively small. It also has an extraordinarily large component of articulate, intelligent, and sensitive human beings whose value systems track poorly with those of giant conglomerate corporations. Thus the nature of these corporations was destined to be detected and recorded as if on a seismograph when, a decade ago, they began to send the tremors of acquisition through book publishing. In the evocative phrases of Henry Raymont of the *New York Times,* publishing had been "a stately ocean liner of industry," but was transformed by takeovers into "a jet of corporate flightiness, moving executives and authors from one house to another faster than they have ever moved before."[10] Frank E. Taylor, who for five years had been editor in chief and general manager of the trade book division of McGraw-Hill Book Company, said on resigning, "I have seen the unnecessary erosion of hundreds of creative editorial relationships."[11] Early in 1970, as was noted in an earlier chapter, Funk & Wagnalls, a division of the Reader's Digest Association, fired its entire editorial staff.[12]

Raymont sensed "a feeling of homelessness." Frederic Morton, whose *Snow Gods* was issued by World Publishing, the Times Mirror Company subsidiary, provided an example. "They reorganized so much they never got organized," Morton told Raymont. "The over-all problem for authors and editors in these big houses is that you are part of an enormous corporate image without an identity of your own—the book becomes merely an item on a long agenda."[13]

The week that Macmillan published Yakov Lind's *Counting My Steps* his editor left abruptly for World Publishing. Just previously, Lind told Raymont, the editor had phoned him in London, told him that Macmillan considered the book a masterpiece and that the reviews were wonderful—and asked him to come to New York "to help promote it." By the time Lind arrived the editor had left, as had Macmillan's publicity director. "It was the last, horrible blow," Lind said. "Not one

editor was left who had read the book and nobody cared. It was awful."
He was moved to tell the reporter, "We are human beings and not just
pieces of baggage."

In advertising and speeches, in the unsigned, canned editorials they
buy for circulation among the unsuspecting readers of weekly and small
daily newspapers, and through financial support of certain institutions
and causes, giant corporations cultivate the notion that they worship
individualism and are in the vanguard of its protectors. William H.
Whyte, Jr., accorded this notion its due in *The Organization Man*.[14]
He said that "the harsh facts of organization life simply do not jibe"
with the traditional idea "that pursuit of individual salvation through
hard work, thrift, and competitive struggle is the heart of the American
achievement." But, he said, the corporation man

> is not being hypocritical, only compulsive. He honestly believes he follows the
> tenets he extols, and if he extols them so frequently it is, perhaps, to shut
> out a nagging suspicion that he, too, the last defender of the faith, is no
> longer pure. Only by using the language of individualism to describe the
> collective can he stave off the thought that he himself is in a collective as
> pervading as any ever dreamed up by the reformers, intellectuals, and the
> utopian visionaries he so regularly warns against.[15]

Of necessity, the man who gets along and prospers in a collective
is more likely to be a conformist than an individualist. He may conform
with awareness, even when violation of the law is clearly involved, and
even when the results are highly adverse to the public interest.

Consider violations of the antitrust laws. These add billions of dollars to the prices paid by consumers. In just one major case, the prosecution in 1967 of the three drug manufacturers who for several years
forced consumers to pay fifty-one dollars for a hundred antibiotic capsules
which would have been fairly priced at ten dollars, the take was hundreds
of millions of dollars. The fines imposed on each of the three defendant
companies, Chas. Pfizer, American Cyanamid, and Bristol-Myers, were
the maximum allowable—$50,000 on each of three counts. In 1969 four
giant petroleum companies, American Oil (Standard Oil, Indiana), Mobil
Oil, Gulf, and Humble (Standard Oil, New Jersey), were convicted of
antitrust violations. The fines totaled $300,000, or approximately one-

tenth of one per cent of their total net incomes, in the preceding year, of $2 billion.

These penalities are obviously trivial. They fail to deter the kind of conformity that becomes a criminal conspiracy to violate the law. At a hearing of the Senate Subcommittee on Antitrust, Chairman Philip Hart and Walker B. Comegys, who is top aide to antitrust chief Richard W. McLaren, agreed on this point. The problem, Comegys said, is that the additional profits produced by prolonged violation of the laws vastly outweigh the possible fines. With such profits in prospect, Comegys testified, top management in typical corporate hierarchies exert constant pressure on middle management to produce. "Unfortunately," he said, "our experience has been that under this pressure, some middle managements succumb to hard-core antitrust violations—notwithstanding the substantial risk of personal indictment."[16] Managers who under pressure from the top violate the law hardly can be claimed to be worthy examples of individualism.

Conformity in a corporate collective is more easily achieved when blatant offenses such as antitrust violations are not at issue. In the broadcasting industry, say, there were men who in 1969 and 1970 fought a long, hard battle to keep cigarette commercials on television for nine months beyond the date when the cigarette manufacturers had agreed to end them. They "haggled with the [Senate Commerce] Committee for every possible extra year, month and day of cigarette advertising revenues, turning [the] Committee into a Turkish bazaar," Senator Frank E. Moss said.[17] In the advertising industry men of talent labor to contrive ads that are successful if, without being demonstrably illegal, they serve to mislead physicians into prescribing medicines which may be unnecessary, inferior to rival preparations, needlessly hazardous, or all of these things at once. In the retailing and finance industries merchandisers and lenders have scored awesome triumphs in persuading millions of consumers to forego paying cash for items they do need in favor of paying exorbitant credit charges to buy items which often they do not need.

Men who engage in such activities often win merit badges for good citizenship, but win them for activities outside the corporation. In a psychological sense, they may need the opportunity to serve a worthy outside cause such as the United Givers Fund as much as the help of the UGF is needed by some of its beneficiaries.

It is simply not in the nature of things for executives and employees of a giant organization, in which final responsibility is elusively dispersed, to question, or possibly even to think about, the nature of the ends served by the source of their livelihoods. "Scientists and engineers employed by corporations privately tell me of their reluctance to speak out —within their companies or outside them—about hazardous products," Ralph Nader has said. "This explains why the technical elites are rarely in the vanguard of public concern over corporate contamination. Demotion, ostracism, dismissal are some of the corporate sanctions against which there is little or no recourse by the professional employe."[18]

In *Functionaries,* F. William Howton said the giant organization "dehumanizes the individual by turning him into a functionary," that is, into "a new kind of man" who in his role of serving the organization "is morally unbounded. . . . The only limits he knows come from rationality applied to the choice and use of means to a given end—in other words, functional rationality. His ethic is the ethic of the good soldier: take the order, do the job, *do it the best way you know how,* because that is your honor, your virtue, your pride-in-work. . . . The logic of the functionary's work situation forbids him to take account of ends, because to do so would introduce an irrational element into his choice of means."[19]

To appreciate the improbability that men in a large organization reliably will take ends into account, one has but to consider the situation in enterprises that produce weapons such as napalm and chemical and biological warfare agents. The Dow Chemical Company produced napalm under government contracts. Herbert L. Doan, president of Dow, said the firm did so "because we feel that simple good citizenship required that we supply Government and our military with those goods they need." Rejecting such a justification, Harold Kasinsky, a University of California biochemist, asked in a letter to Melvin Calvin, who was elected a director of Dow in 1964, three years after winning the Nobel Prize in chemistry, "Do you honestly feel that if President Johnson were to ask Dow Chemical to provide vast quantities of potassium cyanide for gas chambers, that you would vote 'aye' at the board of directors meeting?"[20] The point is that such fundamental questions, when raised at all, usually are raised *outside* of the organization which produces weapons of horror. Seldom is there serious discussion *within* the organization, as Seymour M. Hersh discovered in researching his excellent book *Chemical and Biological Warfare: America's Hidden Arsenal*:

> The moral vacuum concerning CBW production and research is pervasive. One former germ warfare researcher at Aerojet-General Corp. told me the Rothschild book [*Tomorrow's Weapons,* a classic exposition of the case for CBW by General J. H. Rothschild] was not required, but suggested, reading on the job—"to get us a little ideologically oriented."
>
> She added that workers there "never talked about the implications of their work." Company officials "don't like you if you're inquisitive," she explained. "You get the feeling that the people higher up make all the decisions."[21]

Hersh also told of a letter he received from a former Army enlisted man who, in the 1950s, did a thirteen-month stint at Dugway Proving Grounds, the CBW base in Utah. The letter noted at one point:

> One seldom heard objections to the use or development of CBW. This did not bother me a great deal. . . . No one seemed very concerned with the inhumane possibilities of the stuff. What the Chemical Corps did have there was a group of pretty able young science graduates who gladly would have worked contentedly at the most dastardly of weapons had the situation been even faintly resembling a research or development laboratory.[22]

When Hersh himself visited Dugway in June 1967, he recalled, "one secretary told me she had 'found that after five or six weeks I'd forgotten what they're doing here.' "[23] Surely the insights Hersh obtained in researching his book on chemical and biological warfare helped to prepare him to do the reporting on the slaughter by American soldiers of hundreds of Vietnamese civilians at Mylai which deservedly won him a Pulitzer Prize.

Unpleasant as it is to do so, it is necessary to caution that, when carried to extremes, concern for means without concern for ends produces an Adolph Eichmann, the Nazi SS official who organized the transportation of Jews to extermination centers. William Howton said in *Functionaries,* "Eichmann appears to have been the type of man who was impersonal about the content of his work but took its method to heart; he was conscientious, skillful, ingenious in devising new and better procedures—in short, he was the very model of the dutiful functionary. . . . His defense at court was that he was not responsible for the policy, he merely carried it out."[24]

In 1954, in *Ethics in a Business Society*, Marquis W. Childs and Douglass Cater discussed the strains which the concentration of power puts on "an ever smaller number of managers in big business, big labor, big government." One of these strains, they said,

> has its origins in the growing awareness of the unreal relationship between the authority of the economic unit and the authority of the political unit. The individual participates, if he is a good citizen, in the politics of his city, his county, and perhaps even his state. But decisions taken by the mayor, the city council, the county manager, the governor of the state have comparatively little bearing on the daily life of the average citizen. It is his relation to the business for which he works that conditions his whole life. About this relationship he has little or nothing to say, particularly if he is one of the many millions of Americans who work for corporations employing a thousand or more workers.[25]

Sweden is not plagued by the problems that commonly are identified as those that are tearing our own society apart. No war in Vietnam. No vast military-industrial complex. No race problem, no black militants. No political conspiracy trials conducted by Judge Julius Hoffman. No poverty. But there is in this small, peaceful, rich, and civilized welfare state a great concentration of industrial power. This concentration had caused enough apprehension by 1968 that the government appointed a committee to investigate it. The committee reported that seventeen families, headed by the Wallenbergs, controlled more than one-third of all manufacturing industry. "This concentration of inherited industrial power is unparalleled anywhere in Europe, except possibly in Belgium," Anthony Sampson, of the *Observer* of London, said in a report from Stockholm. "Sweden may be a forerunner of the kind of patriotic complex towards which other European countries are moving. But she may be a forerunner, too, of the kinds of troubles and discontents that lie ahead."[26]

A research body financed by the big companies, called SNS, commissioned a survey of one thousand Stockholm students. Sampson said it showed, for example, that only a quarter of the students wanted to go into big private companies, against 33 per cent who wanted to work on their own; that 47 per cent of the students thought that private enterprise disregarded the interests of society; that 45 per cent thought the concentration of power was too great; that two-thirds of them wanted to boycott trade with South Africa; that 61 per cent thought that advertisements persuade people to buy things they don't really want.

In August 1969 SNS held its annual conference for heads of industry at a seaside resort. The conference was devoted to the student criticisms. The tycoons arrived, Sampson said, "quite obviously worried about their positions—not least because some were under attack from their own children. It was as if they had spent their careers climbing to the top of a tree, only to find that it was the wrong kind of tree." Sampson, who himself spoke at the conference, "about the international perspective," said in his article:

> What is now clear in Sweden is that the new generation of students— and not only left-wing students—find the big business structure intolerable. They attack the concentration of industry, its lack of social responsibility, its mendacious advertising, its wrecking of the environment, and its dealings with foreign dictatorships, such as Portugal and South Africa. . . .
>
> The debates about the concentration of power were the most outspoken, for most of the tycoons were themselves managers rather than owners and resented the financial powers and bankers in the background. . . .
>
> How far, I wondered, as I left this strange two-day confessional, is Sweden showing us some of our future problems? Certainly there is an important thread in the student revolt, quite apart from the protests about Vietnam or university professors, through all the rich industrialized countries of the west—which is the revival of discontent with the structure of big business, and a sense of alienation from the methods and implications of modern capitalism. Whatever happens to the Vietnamese or the professors, this discontent is likely to continue.

In "the great urge to merge" in Europe, and in the continent's "current obsession with balance of payments," Sampson wrote, "the questions of industrial democracy and genuine participation have gone into abeyance. But they are questions which—as the Swedes have found— simply will not lie down."

Just as the questions will not lie down for private socialism, they will not lie down for public socialism. Radical youth, Michael Harrington has said, "have set themselves against *all* bureaucratic styles, benign as well as arbitrary. They refuse to distinguish between corporate bureaucrats who plan antisocially and welfare bureaucrats who, for all the abstract heavy-handedness of their operations, do try to right wrongs."[27]

"The search of the young today is more specific than the ancient search for the Holy Grail," William O. Douglas, the Associate Justice of the Supreme Court, has said. "The search of the youth today is for ways and means to make the machine—and the vast bureaucracy of the corporation state and of government that runs that machine—the servant of man. That is the revolution that is coming."[28] But there are others searching, too—middle-aged and old, conservatives and liberals. This search will be in vain unless it leads to a vital new perception: that the condition of individualism in the giant corporation—frustrated, submerged, denied democratic processes—will, as corporate power concentrates, tend to become the pervasive condition of individualism in the total society.

10 PLAYING GOD

Largely free of effective checks and balances—including a reliable conscience, adequate government regulatory mechanisms, or a genuinely competitive marketplace—the giant corporation has been free to proceed without much regard for the consequences in such spheres as health, safety, the quality of life, and traditional institutions and values.

Large organizations frequently provide a depressing atmosphere for invention and innovation, as has been detailed in the Prologue and Chapter One. But here we will focus on the unfortunate impacts of this atmosphere on public safety and the integrity of the environment. The highly concentrated automobile industry will be used to illustrate this contention. It is an industry with a record of "probably unparalleled" technological stagnation, to use the phrase of one of its many critics, Yura Arkus-Duntov, who spent a quarter-century in engineering, mainly in the design and development of power plants.[1] And it is an industry in which, Donald N. Frey, while a vice president of Ford Motor Company, said a few years ago, "engineers can invent practically on demand. Almost any device we can dream up, the engineers can make. It may not be economically feasible or optimized, but it can be made and made operational."[2] Even allowing for Frey's caveat, something obviously has been amiss with the demands made upon the engineers. In a statement two years earlier, in January 1964, Frey said, "I believe that the amount of product innovation successfully introduced in the automobile is smaller than in previous times and still falling. The automatic transmission [which was used on buses in London as early as 1926, and which was adapted for mass auto production in 1938–1939] was the last major innovation of the industry."[3] Frey also has said, "It is a sad commentary, but some of the most reactionary people in industry

307

are engineers. Fresh new departures that require creative thinking and innovation can wind up in the file marked NIH—Not Invented Here."[4]

Seat belts were used in aircraft in the 1920s. During the 1950s there was a surge of interest in their application to automobiles. But the industry "lobbied around the country" against proposed legislation to make them compulsory, Senator Gaylord Nelson has said. In 1959, when he was governor of Wisconsin, and a bill was pending in the legislature, "one of the major companies came to my office, privately, and said they wanted me to know—privately—they were not against seat belts but did not want to say anything publicly or make any disclosures because it would infuriate the other auto companies."[5] The reason for the opposition, Ralph Nader said in an exchange with the Senator at a hearing, was that the industry feared that the safety belt would put "a spotlight on interior safety in the automobile."[6] A great advance came in Sweden, where Volvo, a relatively small company, began installing a convenient-to-use combination of lap belt and shoulder harness, or upper torso restraint, starting with the 1963 models. In January 1964 Studebaker, smallest of the full-line producers in the United States, broke ranks and became the first American company to make lap belts standard equipment.

The lifesaving potential of such devices had long been known, but in the mid-1960s Volvo made a study which produced startling data. The firm reviewed 28,000 accidents to determine death and injury rates when the belt-harness combination was used and when it was not. When the devices were used drivers had 83 per cent fewer fatalities and 40 per cent fewer serious injuries than when they were not. Front-seat passengers had 72 per cent fewer deaths and 68 per cent fewer serious injuries. Not one death either among drivers or front-seat passengers in belt and harness occurred at speeds of less than 60 miles per hour, while unrestrained occupants died in crashes at speeds as slow at 12 miles per hour.[7] The Department of Transportation used the Volvo data to overcome the bitter-end resistance of the automakers in Detroit to a proposal to require belt-harness combinations in the 1968 model cars. Once again, a small manufacturer had pioneered.

The engines produced by the auto industry are responsible for approximately half of the total tonnage of pollutants emitted into the atmosphere. Yet it was not the industry but a professor at the California

Institute of Technology, A. J. Haagen-Smit, who discovered that in sunlight hydrocarbons and oxides of nitrogen, both emitted by motor vehicles, can combine to form photochemical smog, the type from which Los Angeles suffers. Later, when the state of California was proposing to require that the 1966 model cars meet certain standards for emission of hydrocarbons and carbon monoxide, auto industry spokesmen said it would be impossible to have exhaust-control devices ready in time. Thereupon smaller firms developed such devices, and these were certified by the state during the first half of 1965—in ample time for the 1966 models. Faced with this competitive threat, Detroit, with suspect suddenness, discovered that, after all, it could provide satisfactory control systems of its own on the 1966 autos.

Let us return to the speech made earlier, in 1964, by S. Smith Griswold, then the air pollution control officer of Los Angeles County. In the speech, which was cited briefly in the Prologue, Griswold said:

> Everything that the industry has disclosed it is able to do today to control auto exhaust, was possible technically 10 years ago. No new principles had to be developed, no technological advance was needed, no scientific breakthrough was required. Crankcase emissions have been controlled by a method in use for at least half a century. Hydrocarbons and carbon monoxide are being controlled by relatively simple adjustments of those most basic engine components—the carburetor and ignition systems [this was to become the approach taken by the Chrysler Corporation].
>
> Why has this action required ten years? One is forced to ascribe it to arrogance and apathy on the part of this, the nation's largest industry. Control of air pollution does not make cars easier to sell, it does not make them cheaper to produce, and it does not reduce comebacks on the warranty. To people interested in profits, expenses for the development and production of exhaust controls are liabilities.[8]

At the time Griswold spoke he did not know of the existence of the corroboration of his point which Alfred P. Sloan, Jr., had implied twenty-five years earlier in the correspondence with Lammot du Pont about the use of safety glass in Chevrolets. Griswold went on to say in the 1964 speech:

> For nearly a decade, the auto industry has been telling us they have been spending a million dollars a year on air pollution control. Their announced expenditure has totaled about $9 million during that period. This provides an interesting contrast with a recent survey which revealed the earnings of

the 44 highest paid executives in the country. Of these, one half, 22, are employed by the auto industry. Their combined 1962 earnings were about $9½ million. In short, during the past decade the industry's total investment in controlling the nation's number one air pollution problem, a blight that is costing the rest of us more than $11 billion a year, has constituted less than one year's salary for 22 of their executives.

The industry is spending over $1 billion to change over its models this year. Their annual expenditures for air pollution control development is one-tenth of one per cent of $1 billion. For that, the industry has bought ten years of delay and unhampered freedom to pour millions of tons of toxic contaminants into the atmosphere.

As noted in the Prologue, Griswold was vindicated in 1969 when the Justice Department, in a civil antitrust suit, charged the big car makers and the Automobile Manufacturers Association with having conspired to suppress development and installation of technology to control pollution. The matter was settled with a consent decree in which the defendants promised not to engage in similar conduct thereafter. Those whose health had been impaired, who choked and coughed, whose eyes watered, who were deprived of fresh air—these millions of people might wonder why it is that

> *The law locks up both man and woman*
> *Who steals the goose from off the common*
> *But lets the greater felon loose*
> *Who steals the common from the goose.*

Yura Arkus-Duntov, who after leaving the practice of his profession of engineering became the executive officer of a group of mutual funds, has discerned connections between concentration in the auto industry, its technological stagnation and air pollution. "It is not surprising that, when the industry was faced with problems such as air pollution and safety in the last two decades, it was incapable of responding to them," he testified at a hearing held by Senator Gaylord Nelson.

> When problems such as safety and air pollution arise, no attempts are made to solve them through innovations but, rather, through "fixes" which do not require major changes in existing manufacturing facilities and usually do not achieve the desired results. This, of course, is to be expected, as the primary goal of the corporation is profit.[9]

Although Henry Ford II and others in the auto industry have, in 1970, been proclaiming dedication to the abruptly popular cause of pollution control, Ford himself had provided confirmation of Arkus-Duntov's essential thesis. In an interview published in *Look* on May 28, 1968, he gave this reply to a question about electric, steam, or other nonpolluting vehicles of radically different design: "We have tremendous investment in facilities for engines, transmissions and axles, and I can't see throwing them away just because the electric car doesn't emit fumes."

Ford, who earns admiration for personal candor of a kind that rarely comes out of the disembodied leaders of other giant corporations, was perhaps inadvertently casting doubt on the standard auto industry claim that it gives the customer what he wants. The first Henry Ford was reputed to have said the customer could have any color he wanted so long as it was black. His grandson is saying the customer can have any color he wants so long as it is on a car that pollutes.

Shortly after the appearance of the *Look* interview, the Senate Committee on Commerce and the Subcommittee on Air and Water Pollution of the Senate Committee on Public Works held a joint hearing on steam cars.[10] The hearing brought out persuasive if not compelling evidence that these are, and *long had been,* practicable and safe, and too, a most hopeful answer to serious urban problems. These things being true, some of the witnesses dealt with the question of why the steam car idea had not gotten anywhere.

One was Richard S. Morse, senior lecturer at the Sloan School of Management of the Massachusetts Institute of Technology, who in 1967 headed a fifteen-member panel appointed by the Secretary of Commerce to examine the technical and economic feasibility of present and future automotive power sources. "It appears that the auto industry has devoted little effort to the steam cycle as a viable concept with potential applicability for personal vehicle transport," Morse said. "On the basis of an informal survey of some dozen engine manufacturers, it appears that this industry has given no serious consideration to steam."[11] In further testimony consistent with that of Yura Arkus-Duntov, Ralph Nader, and other witnesses, Morse said:

> Essentially all enthusiasm for steam currently resides within a small group of so-called "steam car buffs" (inventors and mechanics) who, unfortunately by and large, have not had access to advanced technology nor are associated

311

with any management and industrial base essential to effective implementation of development activity.[12]

Morse concluded that "innovative ideas in the steam field will probably come from outside the automotive industry."

Morse's views are shared even within the Nixon Administration. "You can't expect the industry to produce major innovations," S. William Gouse, Jr., technical adviser on alternative engines in the President's Office of Science and Technology, has said. "They have their vested interests. It's not to their advantage to put a lot of money into coming up with the [sic] new engine."[14] In passing, it may be noted that Gouse made this observation about two months after Ford Motor Company and Thermo Electron Corporation of Waltham, Massachusetts, announced agreement on a joint program to develop commercial applications of steam engines. Apparently he was not especially impressed.

At the 1968 Senate hearing, Robert U. Ayres, a mathematician and physicist then with Resources for the Future, Incorporated, pointed out that steam cars do not need transmissions and conventional axles, the items cited by Henry Ford in the *Look* interview. But they also do not need, he said, clutches, starter motors, engine-block cooling systems, distributors, mufflers, or more than one spark plug per engine.

The internal combustion engine pollutes heavily because it burns fuel inefficiently. To achieve a drastic reduction in emissions, which as of now is a goal rather than an accomplishment, costly, hard-to-maintain "add-on" equipment must be provided. This equipment not only has inherent deficiencies, but cannot be relied upon to work well. When tested by the National Air Pollution Control Administration, about 80 per cent of production-line vehicles failed to meet emission-control specifications for carbon monoxide and hydrocarbons, Ralph Nader has charged. In a letter to Robert H. Finch, Secretary of Health, Education, and Welfare, he said the 80 per cent failure rate was achieved after 30,000 miles of driving—"which indicates that many vehicles are failing at substantially lower average mileage." The official standards required that maximum allowable emissions not be exceeded for 50,000 miles, provided there was a major tune-up at 25,000. Nader said a study of 1969 cars, made for the Pollution Control Administration by a contractor, showed that 68 per cent of the GM cars surveyed "failed for either carbon monoxide or hydrocarbons at an average of 12,000 miles." Yet the pollution control

312

agency, even while knowing for months of this "serious non-compliance with the law," had taken "no enforcement action."[15]

In contrast, the external combustion steam engine pollutes very little. It burns kerosene or other cheap fuel with high efficiency. It needs no "add-on" pollution control gear. The vast majority of motor vehicles always have been equipped with drum brakes. These have asbestos linings. Unavoidably, particles of asbestos are emitted into the atmosphere. These are a hazard to human lungs. A steam engine would substantially eliminate the problem because, Robert Ayres pointed out in his testimony, it "can provide instantaneous reverse acceleration . . . thus making mechanical brakes virtually unnecessary except for keeping the wheels locked when the engine is off." Bus and truck engines roar loudly during acceleration and gear-changing. This—"one of the greatest annoyances of urban living—would be eliminated" by steam engines, Ayres said. These by no means exhaust the list of advantages for steam and other forms of propulsion radically different from the internal combustion engine.

Existing institutions, as Henry Ford made clear, work to exclude from the market certain goods, services, *and* disservices. Smog, for example, is such a disservice. The price it exacts is paid by the public at large. In other words, Ayres said, because

> everybody "owns" the environment everybody can use it, without payment, as much as he pleases. Unfortunately some uses exclude others, as we all know: Thus if a paper mill or chemical factory exercises its right to unlimited free use of the environment as a place to dispose of residuals from its production processes, the rest of us are unable to exercise our rights to enjoy the natural environment clean and unsullied. . . . Every time any of us uses our car we impose uncompensated disservices on others.[16]

If the auto industry rather than society had had to pay for the disservice of automotive pollution we would have had non-polluting cars a long time ago; and if the industry had had to pay the costs of disposing of cars that are abandoned at an annual rate that reached 7 million in 1968, ways would have been found to make them more durable. We would not have had our streams and lakes so needlessly polluted had the industries that did it been compelled to compensate the rest of us for that very large disservice, and we would not have had the countryside littered with throwaway beer and soft-drink containers if the manufacturers had had to pay for cleaning up the mess.

This is conservative, not radical, economic doctrine. One who bears witness to this is Neil H. Jacoby, professor of business economics and policy at the University of California at Los Angeles, and a member of the President's Council of Economic Advisers during the Eisenhower Administration. Testifying before Senator Nelson, Jacoby said:

> Economists refer to externalities, external costs which do not appear in the profit and loss statements of the auto makers or the accountants of households. In my view, the automobile has imposed upon society very heavy external costs which ought now to be internalized. When the auto makers contend that they ought not to bear the costs of air pollution, I would argue that this is a cost they have imposed upon society, and that it is the role of Government to require them to bear these costs of minimizing air pollution, and also of making more safe vehicles.[17]

Governor Warren P. Knowles of Wisconsin, disturbed by conglomerate takeovers of companies owned by residents of his state, had a study made to see what the impacts were. The study was conducted by Professor Jon G. Udell, director of research at the Graduate School of Business at the University of Wisconsin.[18] One of his key findings concerned the rate of employment growth, or the rate at which new jobs become available. In the years 1960 through 1968, Udell found, the annual rate in firms acquired by out-of-state conglomerates had been 11.6 per cent in the years before merger, compared with a 1.8 per cent *decrease* after acquistion. In the case of firms acquired by other Wisconsin firms, the comparable rates were 4.7 and 1.4 per cent, or a pre-merger rate triple that of the post-merger figure. A similar finding was made for payroll expansion. The annual rate in firms acquired by out-of-state conglomerates was 15.6 per cent before merger and 2.1 per cent afterward. For in-state mergers the rates were 9.2 per cent and 6.5 per cent, respectively.

In cooperation with the Milwaukee United Fund, Udell looked at the rate at which donations had increased in the decade starting in 1959. Among thirty Milwaukee-area corporations that were acquired during the decade contributions increased 16 per cent. This was less than half the increase among a group of comparable locally owned companies, which increased their donations by 34 per cent. The decline in giving probably relates to a point made by Senator Philip Hart in a speech in

1968. He noted that "what today are 100 companies . . . 18 years ago used to be 500 companies," and that giant corporations insist upon mobility from men who want to advance within them. "With moves comes lack of identity with a community—not only for the man but his family as well," Hart said.[19]

Kansas in 1968 was the seventh largest oil producing state. The major oil firms therefore figure prominently in the economy and politics of Kansas and, for that matter, the region. An extraordinary assessment of the role of oil appeared on June 25, 1969, in Ted Brooks's "From the Oil Desk" column in the *Wichita Eagle*. In "A Letter to Major Firms," signed "The Independent Independents," Brooks said:

> We are writing to ask you to remove yourselves, your membership, your people and your influence from our trade associations and political groups. . . .
>
> By our nature we are tied to local and regional economic communities. The proceeds of our small achievements stay with us. In one way or another they are almost entirely spread among our neighbors and business associates. The harvest you reap goes elsewhere. And when the harvest ends, you go with it.
>
> Please do not tell us again about your contributions . . . in taxes, public works and doing good. We are grateful. . . .
>
> But on the corporate level you clog our courts with your reluctance to pay taxes. You subvert the interests of our politicians with contributions we cannot hope to match. Your money warps our legislative process. Our officialdom is constantly reminded that those who play your game go on to greater awards than those who act only in the public interest. And this they do. . . .
>
> Wherever power, money and threats will obtain allegiance, you obtain it. The conventions and pronouncements of the American Association of Petroleum Geologists, a great scientific body, are beginning to sound like waterfront precinct meetings. The American Association of Petroleum Landsmen is dedicated to proving your worth. You have terrorized almost all of the marketing and jobbing associations into rubberstamping your doctrines. The National Petroleum Council serves as your point of government infiltration and outright government-industry job-swapping. The American Petroleum Institute is your body and soul and the focal point of your political and ideological collusion. Your American Petroleum Institute seeds our civic organizations with its propaganda. Shockingly, you

315

even extend this to our schools, where our children are exposed to indoctrination in the beliefs that could insure the acceptability of your domination forever.

The complaint that major oil companies "invade public institutions" may not have been voiced before, as Ted Brooks further said, but it has a familiar ring. For example, the American Medical Association, which derives about half of its revenues from advertising, mainly of trade-name prescription drugs, long has taken policy positions on such economically sensitive issues as generic prescribing which are virtually indistinguishable from those of the Pharmaceutical Manufacturers Association. Indeed, much of the medical press pretty much has been an editorial captive of the drug makers. In 1963, the House of Delegates of the American Bar Association followed the recommendation of a study committee and summarily adopted a resolution condemning the truth-in-packaging bill. Senator Philip Hart has said, "Initially this action confounded me, but subsequently I examined the membership of the seven-man Advisory Committee of the Food, Drug, and Cosmetic Division of the Corporation, Banking and Business Section that made the recommendation, and discovered a possible explanation—that several of its top members were affiliated with the food industry."[20] The Society of Automotive Engineers has not set safety standards as if it were dominated by independent professionals, but as if it were made up largely of hired hands of the auto industry, which it is. A similar syndrome exists in other professional associations, including the American Society of Mechanical Engineers. In public forums, including hearings of the National Commission on Product Safety, the ASME has been shown to have given approval to safety standards, including those for natural gas and petroleum-products pipelines, which have been satisfactory to the oil industry but which have fallen far short of adequacy in protecting the public safety. If there is a pipeline explosion, after all, it likely will be on someone else's property.

In addition to eroding independence in the professions, giant corporations also have many questionable entangling alliances with universities. These have been adequately documented elsewhere. In *The Closed Corporation: American Universities in Crisis,* for example, James Ridgeway has an appendix listing university officials on the boards of directors of leading corporations, along with the shares of stock each holds.[21] Richard J. Barber provides another useful summary in his chapter "Business and Higher Education: The Emerging Alliance" in *The American Corporation: Its Power, Its Money, Its Politics.*[22]

The Civil Rights Act of 1964, the Southern States Industrial Council once charged, is "clearly of Communist origin and inspiration." The council is one of several organizations which frequently are found opposing civil rights legislation, among other social reforms. The council receives, Senator Lee Metcalf (D–Mont.) has said, "regular contributions from major corporations of America—including General Electric, General Motors, the Chesapeake and Ohio Railroad, Firestone Tire and Rubber, Household Finance, and electric utilities all the way from Middle South Utilities (of New York) to Idaho Power."[23] Groups such as the council purvey the fantasy that there is some kind of equation between giant corporations and individualism. At the same time, they do not go out of their way, needless to say, to call attention to the real correlation between giant corporations and racial discrimination.

The electric power industry is the nation's largest. It grows ever more concentrated. In 1945, for example, there were about one thousand privately owned utility systems. As of mid-1970 there were only three hundred. The three hundred firms had assets of $100 billion, but the ten largest accounted for more than 35 per cent of these assets. The power industry is for the most part an assemblage of monopolies. Strikingly, it is these monopolies that have the worst record among all major industries for hiring members of minority races. William H. Brown III, chairman of the Equal Employment Opportunity Commission, has told utility companies:

> At the White House Conference in 1968 your dismal employment record was revealed to the nation. A year later, we produced statistics showing a negligible improvement. Among 115 electric utility companies, blacks held only 4.8% of all jobs, up just 0.7% from the year before. They held just 2.8% of all white collar jobs, up only 0.7%, mostly in clerical positions. Spanish-surnamed Americans fared just as poorly. They held 1.2% of all jobs, and 0.5% of all managerial and professional positions. . . .
>
> A survey of 1969 data from over 100 major utility firms . . . shows that this industry employed blacks at only about half the rate for other major industries.[24]

A decade earlier, the auto industry, an oligopoly, had 38,000 franchised dealers. None was a Negro. Lack of capital hardly could be the whole explanation. In *My Years with General Motors,* Alfred P. Sloan, Jr., said that since 1929 Motors Holding Corporation, a GM division, had searched out qualified operators and "backed them with adequate capital."[25] Approximately the same score of 38,000 to 0 prevailed until about 1965, Ralph Nader testified before Senator Nelson. As of early 1969 there were 8 black dealers, and as of May 1970, following unprecedented publicity about the matter, GM counted 10 blacks among its 13,000 dealers.

William G. Shepherd, an associate professor of economics, made a study of associations between market power and racial discrimination in employment.[26] He focused on white-collar jobs because these are more thoroughly subject to independent management control than are blue-collar jobs, which in varying degrees are influenced by union apprenticeship programs. Relying heavily on Equal Employment Opportunity Commission data on almost all plants with one hundred or more employees as of 1966, he found clear-cut associations between the degree of monopoly and racial bias. "The 100 largest industrial and service firms with New York headquarters were surveyed in 1967," he said. "Their rate of Negro employment in white-collar jobs generally, and particularly in higher managerial positions, was lower than in the other categories of enterprise, such as smaller firms, firms in other sectors, non-profit entities, etc. The firms' headquarters had substantially lower rates of Negro hiring than did their own branches elsewhere, even though New York City had an unusually abundant supply (in both absolute numbers and percent of workforce) of qualified Negroes."

Shepherd gave appropriate weight to the few large firms that had been motivated by one or another special reason to hire an unusually large proportion of Negroes. "But these exceptions," he said, "accentuate the rule; most large firms apparently discriminate more than smaller firms, especially in their higher echelons." Data from nine major metropolitan areas produced a generally similar conclusion: that "open hiring of Negroes is found mainly in competitive industries, in some lesser firms in concentrated industries, and in non-profit entities."

The economist said that "one must surely be optimistic to anticipate that action by large and/or secure firms can substantially solve or alleviate the whole range of minority problems in urban areas. Doing so would rub against the corporate grain." But, he said, "policies to promote competition generally may successfully and appreciably reduce discrimination in employment."

A different kind of discrimination has been shaped by the auto insurance industry, which, while having a large number of companies, grows increasingly concentrated. A few more background facts may be useful. As American society became more and more dependent on the automobile, auto insurance became an all but indispensable investment for millions of people. It is also needlessly expensive. In research exhibits that broke new ground, Dean L. Sharp and Charles E. Bangert, who are lawyers on the staff of the Senate Subcommittee on Antitrust and Monopoly, established that in the decade ended December 31, 1968, motorists paid premiums totaling $81.5 billion. They got back in benefits $47.7 billion, or $33.8 billion less than they had paid in. Of the benefits, $5 billion went to claimants' lawyers. The companies' expenses came to $33 billion. This included $5 billion for defense lawyers and $11.3 billion for agents' commissions. The companies earned an after-tax profit of $3.2 billion on investments of the $81.5 billion in premium revenues. A check of the after-tax earnings of 1,200 firms selling all kinds of insurance disclosed a rate of return on mean net worth of 10.5 per cent. This was only 0.3 per cent less than the return for the nation's fifty largest banks. Among the 1,200 carriers, prospering as well as struggling, the profit leaders were Government Employees Insurance Company with 23.6 per cent and Allstate (Sears, Roebuck) with 21.6 per cent.[27]

The insurance industry's profitability was achieved in part at the expense of various groups—charging them extra-high rates, for example, or refusing to insure them at all, or canceling or refusing to renew existing policies. Such tactics were ruthlessly employed against persons whose driving records were without blemish but who happened to be black, to have a Spanish-sounding name, to have a ghetto address, or to be old. In 1967, David O. Maxwell, then the State Insurance Commissioner of Pennsylvania, said in a speech that one major insuror had a list of "hazardous" occupations, members of which were "unlikely to be insured." The list included actors, radio and television announcers, athletes, caterers, chauffeurs, members of the armed forces, farmhands, manicurists, masseurs, newspapermen, salesmen, and waiters.[28] One leading carrier, the Great American Insurance Companies, making

319

specific comments in the 1967 edition of its underwriting guidebook on customers of "average desirability," offered some words of caution about clergymen. They are "as a group probably not very skilled drivers," Great American said. They "must drive at odd hours." One may expect from them a "lack of attention while mentally composing sermons, etc." In sum, clergymen are "a consistent group of losers."[29]

There are certain humane values which our common heritage would have clergymen (and others) impart to the young. These values include caring, compassion, courtesy, gentleness, kindness, and thoughtfulness. I. F. Stone, the independent journalist, does not, as we do not, share what he called "the revolutionary outlook." It is, he has said, "gimmicky, another 'instant' recipe in our world of commercials. The problems of war, racism, bureaucracy and pollution are everywhere. No society has solved them; their roots are deep in the ancient conditioning of man and in his inability to control technology. Man himself is obsolete unless he can change. That change requires more altruism; more kindness, more —no one need be ashamed to say it—love."[30]

In pamphlets prepared for young people the automobile manufacturers exalt civilized values. For good reason: such values are essential to the safe operation of motor vehicles. Further, drivers under twenty-five are responsible for a disproportionate share of accidents. Albert Benjamin Kelley, vice president of the Insurance Institute for Highway Safety, has pointed to a three-year study by two researchers at the University of Michigan which reached the conclusion that "the onset of adulthood just before age 21 is an intersection point of several motivational trends: hostility and thrill seeking are still high, driving confidence is rising, and life changes and responsibilities are maximum. This turbulent combination may help to explain the excessive hazard of the 18-to-20 year old driver."[31]

But while the pamphlets emphasize themes such as the need for "driving with courtesy and consideration for others," other industry activities undermine them. General Motors gives its cars names such as Sting Ray, Tiger, and Cutlass. Ford picked Cobra, Cougar, and Maurauder; and Chrysler chose Fury, Charger, and Barracuda. Particular components are similarly designed. Thus a Chrysler engine rated at more than 450 horsepower was called the "King Kong." And while relatively trivial sums are spent for pious pamphlets, immense sums are spent to direct contrary themes at young people in advertisements in such popular publications as *Road & Track, Hot Rod, Motor Trend,* and *Car and Driver.* The message in the pamphlets is that safety pays for the driver; the message in the ads is that aphrodisiacs which act on the lust for horsepower pay for the auto industry. In November 1966, the staff of the Federal Trade Commission made a report which assembled some of this advertising material.[32] Ford, for example, promoted "a new kind of car: a brute—but a very very smooth brute.—A 97-pound girl can herd this 7-Litre and never know it has 345 horses and 462 pounds-feet of torque—unless she gets mad and stamps her foot. Then she'll know!" A Dodge Coronet ad called it "the *rambunctious* rebel that's leading Dodge's charge on *Dullsville.*" Buick ads suggested "billing yourself as the human cannonball," and driving a 400-plus horsepower model "like *you hate it*—it's cheaper than psychiatry."

A persistent critic of these base appeals, Jeffrey O'Connell, professor of law at the University of Illinois, put some typical statements from the safe-driving pamphlets and from the ads in parallel columns in the *Columbia Journalism Review.*[33] One of many pamphlets he used was GM's "RIGHT behind the wheel." It said that for infantile motorists who roar around with unmuffled exhausts, "normal driving is, of course, unthinkable. The engine must be revved up at stops, not idled. Starts must resemble a successful missile launching." O'Connell put alongside these derisive remarks an ad headlined, "A *Howitzer* With/Windshield Wipers/The New Buick Skylark Gran Sport." The text said that owning this car "is almost like having your own personal-type nuclear deterrent." Another GM pamphlet, "The Best Drivers Make It Look Easy," ridiculed the "novice" whose devices for calling attention to himself include a "screaming start from the curb." For contrast, O'Connell came up with an ad for a Pontiac 2 + 2: "It's what you might call a sudden automobile. Meaning that if it had started accelerating when this sentence began you would now be feeling enormous pressure in the abdomen."

By 1969 there were millions of "hot," "performance," and "muscle" cars on the roads. In that year alone the production of intermediate-size models with engines of 300 or more horsepower as standard equipment exceeded 600,000. Each was capable of delivering "orgiastic acceleration," as it was called in an article in *Esquire.* The results were predictable. At a hearing of the Senate Subcommittee on Antitrust and Monopoly in October 1969, Nationwide Insurance Companies told of a special actuarial study which showed that "these superpowered cars are producing, on the average, 56 per cent more losses than standard-powered cars." The National Highway Safety Bureau, in a report on the year 1967, said that as many as 12,000 highway deaths were associated with crashes occurring at speeds above 60 miles per hour. As horsepower and the emphasis on it have increased, so have driving speeds—and so have the risks of death and injury.

Privacy, the right to be let alone, is a precious civilized value. Louis D. Brandeis, the late Associate Justice of the Supreme Court, once called it "the most comprehensive of rights and the right most valued by civilized men." The large corporation, a person at law, values privacy for itself. It goes beyond this to put a high premium on secrecy. This has distinct advantages. A corporation can say that "higher costs" make a price increase necessary. But it is frequently impossible to determine if this is so. How does one know, say, whether a higher cost of materials has been canceled out by an increase in production efficiency? Or whether the price increase isn't much larger than is warranted by a true increase in costs? Or whether publicized rises in costs are being offset by unpublicized cutbacks in the duration and scope of warranties and guaranties? Such questions are not fanciful. To cite but one example: General Motors blamed an increase of $23 to $32 in the price of new cars, effective January 1, 1968, on the added cost of shoulder harnesses which had been made mandatory by the National Highway Safety Bureau. "These shoulder harnesses are being purchased by the domestic manufacturers for under $3 a pair," Ralph Nader protested in a letter to the Council of Economic Advisers.[34]

In January 1966 the attorney general of Iowa invited the heads of GM, Ford, and Chrysler to testify at a public hearing on auto safety. All refused. GM *does* supply guest lecturers. One of them has been Marilyn Van Derbur, a former Miss America.[35] What she could reveal is of unquestioned interest but of doubtful relevance. A couple of years ago, a group of seniors at Princeton University scheduled an open forum on corporate responsibility. They invited the attendance of the chairman, president, or chief executive officer of each of fifteen large corporations. None accepted.[36] Rarely do such private men testify before congressional

322

committees, preferring instead to send officials of trade associations who always can fend off sensitive questions by saying they are not authorized to speak for a particular company. Rarely do such private men face questioning by panels of newsmen. They prefer that public men, such as senators and governors, go before the television cameras.

But corporations that are themselves secretive want to know a good deal of information about the rest of us. In certain cases private detectives or investigators are used, and they gumshoe around using such pretexts for interviews as a claim that they are making a "pre-employment" check. This was true not only in the General Motors–Ralph Nader case, but also in the much less well-known case of the American Home Products Corporation and Jay B. Constantine three years later.

Constantine is a member of the staff of the Senate Finance Committee who had helped to draft legislation introduced by the chairman, Senator Russell B. Long (D–La.), which the prescription drug industry bitterly opposed for an obvious reason: it would permit Medicare and Medicaid financing for high-priced trade-named medicines only if they are recognized to be therapeutically superior to rival pharmaceuticals that are priced substantially lower. American Home Products, which with sales exceeding $1 billion ranked ninety-fourth among all industrial corporations in 1969, has two prescription drug divisions, Ayerst Laboratories and Wyeth Laboratories.

Early in 1969, Gilbert S. McInerney, who as vice president, secretary, and general counsel of American Home was its third-ranking official, and who was a member of the board of directors, as well, retained the Retail Credit Company to inquire into Constantine's personal affairs. Investigators inquired among neighbors and fellow employees on Capitol Hill about Constantine's mode of living and personal finances. Some of those interviewed were suspicious about the agents' explanation that he was looking for a new job, because they knew that he was pleased to be where he was, and alerted him and Tom Vail, chief counsel of the committee, who summoned American Home executives to explain. Company chairman and president William F. Laporte immediately stopped the investigation, which he said McInerney had initiated on his own, without the knowledge of either of his two superiors.

After Constantine threatened to sue for invasion of privacy and harassment, Laporte tendered what Senator Long, in a Senate speech on September 21, 1970, termed "a complete letter of apology" to Constantine and made a $10,000 settlement. Constantine's lawyer deducted his fee and, at the Senate aide's direction, donated the balance to the Children's Hospital in Washington. Long, who refrained in the speech from naming anyone even though the *New York Times* and the *Washington Post* had published detailed stories in July 1969, said that the investigation "affronted the integrity of the Senate" but elicited the apology and settlement only after the company's "stupidity was uncovered." At the risk of redundancy, it should be emphasized that Constantine has a long and unblemished reputation for integrity. As for McInerney, he left American Home early in 1970.

Far commoner than private investigators making inquiries of congressional aides is a much more modern phenomenon: the increasing use of computers which have a capacity to store data that approaches the infinite, and which have processes for data retrieval that are almost instantaneous. When such computers are linked with sophisticated methods of electronic transmission, it becomes possible to retrieve and send a person's complete credit history to any city in the country in less than a minute. At the urging of the Bank of America, the nation's largest bank, and one which itself is computerized, there was created the Credit Data Corporation of San Francisco. Its first customer was the Chase Manhattan Bank, which was followed by several major oil companies. By 1968 Credit Data had computers in New York and San Francisco which "talk to each other." In testimony in 1968 before the Senate Subcommittee on Antitrust and Monopoly an even greater potential for abuse was disclosed. The Associated Credit Bureaus, Incorporated, which has approximately 2,000 members, mainly in the United States and Canada, said that it was planning a vast computer network which would make the credit records of 100 million Americans instantly retrievable.

With such technology, a person's credit record becomes immediately accessible on a national basis. When a mistake is made, it, too, becomes national. And, as is common knowledge, mistakes *are* made. The consequences can be grievous. They can include, as was shown in hearings held by the Senate Antitrust Subcommittee, employment blacklisting, or inability to get a home loan. "A New Yorker who shall be called Charlie Green was unable to get a job for seven years in the industry for which he was trained because of a clerical error in the files of pre-employment investigators," Karl E. Meyer reported in the *Washington Post.* "Green's personnel card erroneously stated that he had been dishonorably discharged from the Army and that his landlord had found him an undesirable tenant. When Green finally discovered these errors, he also made another sad discovery—he had no legal redress. The law is weighted entirely on the side of the investigators."[37] A person who falls victim to a computer mistake, after aggravation and anguish, sometimes gets an acknowledgment of error from the company involved. The blame is then put on "the computer."

"At the very time when the need for sensitivity to interpersonal relationships is increasing, we find transactions losing their personal identity through the computerization process," Clifford E. Graese, a partner in Peat, Marwick, Mitchell & Company, a certified public accountant firm, has said. "The implications have been underestimated."[38] But not by Arnold J. Toynbee, the British historian and philosopher. "What we are really exasperated by is by being dehumanized, by being processed, being made into cards to punch through computers," he told an interviewer. "Treated as nonhuman beings. Treated as computers natives [*sic*]."[39]

Sometimes one of the natives becomes unfriendly. A vast private bureaucracy pushes him too far. He rebels and, with luck, achieves something. John Donovan is a classic case. He is dean of students at Ascension Academy in Alexandria, Virginia. Over the years, he built up a modest business transporting children to eight private schools in the Washington area. The time came when he needed new equipment. He ordered three new GMC V–6 school buses, 1969 models, at a cost of $8,146.80 each. The manufacturer of the chassis was the General Motors Truck and Coach Division in Pontiac, Michigan. The P. A. Thomas Car Works in High Point, North Carolina, installed the bodies. In early September 1969, Donovan, two of his drivers, and the GMC dealer from whom he bought the buses went to High Point to take delivery. On the 300-mile return trip to the Washington area, they had to make at least twelve stops for repairs. One bus required sixteen quarts of oil. On another bus an accelerator spring snapped, causing the engine suddenly to race. On the third bus all went well until nightfall, when it was discovered that the headlights would not work.

Donovan, then a thirty-four-year-old father of two children, eight months and three years of age, kept a meticulous diary of what happened thereafter. Aided by the diary and other records which Donovan preserved, Colman McCarthy told the entire story in a remarkable series of articles in 1969 and 1970 in the *Washington Post*.[40] Early on, Donovan told the writer, "I've never had a more frustrating, nightmarish period in my life. Caring for the buses—to keep them safe for the kids who ride them—so dictates my life that nearly everything else is blacked out."

Soon after the trip from High Point, an inspector at the District of Columbia motor vehicle inspection station found that a brake line on one of the buses was, during turns, being abraded by a wheel part. This created the ultimate possibility of a failure of the brake system. At a Virginia inspection station a second bus failed to pass because a faulty hanger was allowing the long exhaust pipe to dangle. If the pipe were to snap, carbon monoxide would be released under the passenger compartment.

By mid-December Donovan had spent 225 hours personally making repairs to the three buses or ferrying them to and from Central Motors in Alexandria, which does repair work for GM under contract (and which Donovan warmly praised). In addition, he had had to pay his drivers for 90 hours of similar work. Soon a routine developed. Each evening the drivers told Donovan of the latest mishaps and malfunctions. Donovan then drove an ailing bus to Central Motors. His wife, Virginia, and the two children followed in the family car, so that they could drive him home after the bus was dropped off. (It is a half-hour drive between their apartment in northwest Washington and the repair shop.) McCarthy wrote:

> After telling the mechanics what needs repairing, Donovan and family come home. The children are fed and put to bed. He and his wife have supper. They then wait for a phone call from Central—which is open until 2 a.m.—saying the bus is ready. Usually the call comes between midnight and 2 a.m. The Donovans wake the children—it is impossible to get a sitter at this hour—dress them, get in the car and head for Alexandria. Donovan gets the repaired bus and drives it to Newark and Idaho [an intersection near his apartment where he parked the buses], his wife and two children following.
>
> Donovan's records show that he has done this approximately 25 times since buying the '69 General Motors buses [14 weeks earlier]. On occasion, two buses malfunction in one day, so two round trips are needed. Some-

times Donovan gets less than three hours sleep a night, since he needs to be up at 5:45 every morning to call the drivers for the morning run.

In his initial article on December 15, McCarthy provided this partial list of troubles which had occurred since early September, a period during which each bus was operated about 6,000 miles:

Oil was leaking on the engines [of each bus]. This continued until Nov. 4, when after repeated pleas by Donovan, Central got factory approval to replace the gaskets on two and tighten the third.

All three buses leaked gasoline extensively from the extension on the neck of the gas tank until they were finally fixed Nov. 11. To prevent spilling by the cupful, which many waiting chauffeurs and parents noticed in alarm as they stopped for their children to board or alight, the tanks could be only half-filled. Since the gages on the dashboards didn't work on two of them, a stick had to be inserted for measuring.

At least two tires did not hold air. The proper air pressure is 70 pounds, but they held only 40. These are 9 by 20 ten-ply Firestone tires which GMC sells with its chassis.

The rear exhaust pipe hangers came loose after less than 1500 miles of operation on all three buses. Donovan repeatedly tightened them. Central finally put heavier straps on one. . . .

All buses have suffered broken motor mounts. The bolts either snapped or fell out.

One bus has burned out two clutches, the other two have burned out one each. The first clutch burned out Sept. 19, after ten school days.

The transmissions in the buses rattle, even with the clutches adjusted or newly replaced.

"I'd rather lose my business than lose the life of a child in my bus because of faulty equpiment," Donovan told McCarthy. "If GMC replaces these buses I can stay in business." But John Donovan and the GM collective—"General Motors Is People"—have different value systems. Early in December, McCarthy reported, Robert Stelter, general sales manager of GM's Truck and Coach Division, "said the company had no intention of replacing Donovan's buses. He seemed surprised that Donovan had even had the thought." At the start, Donovan's thought had been that no one would knowingly sell unsafe buses to the public.

As a result of McCarthy's reporting, two GM engineers flew in from Detroit and, for two weeks, checked over the buses and repaired everything that seemed to need repairing. But McCarthy said on March 2, 1970:

Incredibly, since getting the buses back in early January, Donovan has hauled them into his local GM garage *eight* separate times: the wheels wobbled on two buses (an alarmed motorist spotted this one time), a horn and a governor broke on two, five quarts of oil were needed in one bus's rear end after being out of the shop only one day, the brakes needed adjustment on one, another—loaded with children—wouldn't start one afternoon, and finally one bus failed D.C. inspection.

As if that weren't enough, Donovan received a bill last week from the Firestone Tire Company for $349.62—even though in December, Kimball Firestone, Harvey's grandson [Harvey Firestone was the founder of the company], personally promised Donovan 18 new tires—at no cost—to replace some defective ones. With new tires on his buses that he was told were given free of charge, will Donovan pay Firestone? "Sure. The same day GM pays me for the hundreds of hours of work and bother their three lemons have caused me."

Donovan, a former Marine officer, did not suffer his ordeal submissively. He wrote to James M. Roche, president of GM, and to Richard M. Nixon, President of the United States, among others. Apart from repairs covered by his warranties, he got nothing from GM—until he got the ear of Colman McCarthy. Only then did the corporate mammoth become seriously interested. The corporation and the National Highway Safety Bureau each announced an investigation. In February 1970 GM recalled 4,269 of its 1969 buses for a check of possible brake defects (although other safety-related factors also were clearly involved). Previously, GM had recalled about 10,000 of the 1967 and 1968 models.

McCarthy obtained from GM a list—which proved to be incomplete—of forty-four owners who had bought five or more 1969's. "It soon became clear that the safety and mechanical problems . . . were not isolated," he said. For example, a GM dealer, located by McCarthy although his name was not on the company list, bought fifteen 1969 buses and was "delighted that the truth was finally being told about GM." McCarthy said:

> He has had massive safety and mechanical problems also. "The power steering cannot be fixed, no matter what"; one new bus being driven back from the factory nearly killed his driver because the gas tank had a hole in it that dropped the fuel onto a heated exhaust line; "the brakes aren't worth a damn and won't stay adjusted. Overall, things have gotten to the point that I hate to face customers."

Another GM dealer, whose name also was not on the company list, "was so fed up with his seven 69s that this year he bought Fords," McCarthy said. "Asked if he thought it odd that a GM dealer would buy a competitor's product, he answered: 'What should I do—keep on buying buses that I know are nothing but trouble?' "

In the final article of four, neatly headlined "The Mark—Or Is It the Mock?—of Excellence," McCarthy reported that the trouble had started with the 1967 model year. Major changes were made at that time. With "a plain ruler and average eyesight," McCarthy said, "a few facts can be learned. First, the front bumper on the '66 bus—if a local vehicle is representative—is $1/4$ inch thick; on the '69, it is $1/8$ inch thick. . . . A second discovery is that behind the front bumpers of earlier year models is a piece of steel extending from the frame in each direction for about one foot. This reinforces the bumper. On the '69 model, however, this piece of reinforcing steel is gone." Thomas Gist of Sykesville, Maryland, who told McCarthy that his two 1969's ond one 1968 had given him more trouble than he had had in twenty-five years of operating school buses, measured the leaf springs that support the body of the '69 bus. He found them to be seven inches shorter than on earlier models. These are obvious symptoms of a general cheapening. To what end? To reduce costs, naturally. After all, what has changed since 1929, when Alfred P. Sloan, Jr., resisting safety glass for Chevrolets, had said, "Accidents or no accidents, my concern in this problem is a matter of profit and loss"? Perhaps one thing. GM has gotten much bigger. There are more executives among whom responsibility can be atomized, more executives who never go through the experience of meeting a John Donovan face to face, more executives to judge the success of GM on the basis of a balance sheet which looks better when profits are fatter even if bumpers are thinner.

But fundamentally nothing has changed. Henry Ford was asked, in the *Look* interview in 1968, to name the number one problem of the Ford Motor Company. "That's easy," he said. "Making more money." In a truly competitive market "making more money" is a desirable and necessary goal, from the viewpoint of society as well as the entrepreneur. Competition generally works to protect the public interest. But in a concentrated market the goal of "making more money"—because of the absence of genuine competition to direct and temper it—has a real potential to injure society.

11 FOREIGN AFFAIRS

In the fall of 1954, the International Telephone and Telegraph Corporation and certain subsidiaries opened multinational negotiations to secure "landing rights" for "Deep Freeze," the code name for a proposed 3,600-mile submarine cable system. The cable was to originate in the United States; continue to Canada, Greenland, and Iceland; and terminate in the United Kingdom, where ITT intended to spend $17 million of a total cost of $25 million. ITT hoped Deep Freeze would replace its old cable system and was prepared to assume full financing for it.

At the same time, the United States Air Force, seeking to improve its communications network in the North Atlantic region, put contract proposals before the private communications carriers. This led to a contract with ITT. The Air Force agreed to lease 11 per cent of the original capacity of the Deep Freeze cable. It also agreed to assist in "providing foreign cable landing sites and other facilities or approvals necessary to the performance of the contract." Eventually the project fell through. In 1960 the Commercial Cable Company, an ITT subsidiary, filed a suit in the Court of Claims charging the United States with breach of contract and asking $804,000 in damages. The primary issue was the extent of the Air Force's obligation under the assistance clause. On April 5, 1968, a court commissioner dismissed the complaint. Commercial Cable did not appeal.

While the suit was pending in 1967, the Federal Communications Commission was holding a hearing on ITT's proposal to acquire the American Broadcasting Companies. The Justice Department was opposing the merger on several grounds. One of its contentions was that the nature of ITT's normal foreign involvements made it an improper owner of one of the top three television and radio networks in the United States.

To support this position, Justice produced twenty-three documents, collectively labeled exhibit J261, which it had introduced in evidence or received in the Deep Freeze litigation in the Court of Claims.

The J261 papers have attracted almost no public notice although they provide rare and sometimes startling insights into the *modus operandi* of a giant conglomerate dealing with sovereign governments. The papers cannot be considered mere curiosities, because international corporations such as ITT play a role of transcendent importance in the world economy.

Indeed, if present merger rates continue, three hundred giant international corporations will dominate the economies of the principal non-Communist countries of the world by 1985.[1] We will explore this potential domination shortly, but our immediate concern is with the rare disclosures about ITT. It is truly an international corporation. "We now employ over 200,000 persons in more than 50 countries, representing an extensive involvement and responsibility in the economies and societies in which we operate," President Harold S. Geneen told the 1966 annual stockholders' meeting. In the same year, ITT was earning almost 60 per cent of its revenues outside of the United States, mainly from the sale of telecommunications equipment. One of the members of its board was John A. McCone, a former director of the Central Intelligence Agency. Among the officers and directors of ITT's foreign subsidiaries were a former Premier of Belgium, two members of the British House of Lords and a member of the French National Assembly. In a number of Latin American countries ITT owns large utility operating companies. Its telephone subsidiary in Chile has three directors who are appointees of the government of Chile. ITT is a minority stockholder in Indian Telephone Industries, Ltd.; the Indian government is its principal ownership partner. In France, ITT owns 20 per cent of a telecommunications research company; the French government is the majority owner.

In the case of Deep Freeze, ITT dealt with the governments of Great Britain, Canada, Denmark (for Greenland), Iceland, and the United States. Summing up ITT's campaign to win the requisite government approvals for "landing rights" for the proposed cable, the Justice Department said: "ITT had occasion to engage in discussions at the highest levels of a number of foreign governments, to make use of, and benefit from, personal friendships with some of the highest officials of these governments, and to seek out (and receive) confidential information about the internal deliberations of these governments and the probable actions which they would take."

The phrases "highest levels" and "highest officials" were not hyperbole. They referred to, among others, Harold W. Macmillan, who was Great Britain's Minister of Defence during the Deep Freeze episode (and who later became Prime Minister); Lester B. Pearson, then Canada's Minister of External Affairs, but later Prime Minister; and in the United States, John Foster Dulles, Secretary of State, and also the Joint Chiefs of Staff.

The principal figure in the Deep Freeze negotiations was a retired United States Navy admiral, Ellery W. Stone, who in World War II had been chief commissioner of the Allied Control Commission in Italy. Now he was president of Commercial Cable. Later, he would become vice president and director of ITT, vice chairman of the board of ITT Europe, and chairman of the board of ITT's American Cable and Radio Corporation. Along with other ITT officials, he was, the Department said, "on very close terms with high officials in the British government." Stone himself alluded, almost incessantly, to these friendships in the J261 documents. In a letter of June 20, 1954, for example, he told Sir Thomas Spencer, chairman of the board and managing director of Standard Telephones and Cables, Limited, ITT's British subsidiary:

> I know Sir Roger Makins, your Ambassador here [in the United States], very well, and also Sir Harold Caccia who is now in the Foreign Office [but who later became director of Standard Telephones]. Caccia was my British political adviser in Italy for one year. Also Harold Macmillan, who is being mentioned over here as successor to Mr. [Anthony] Eden if and when Sir Winston [Churchill] retires. I served with General John Harding in Italy when we were both under Alex [Field Marshal Sir Harold Alexander], and Admiral McGriger, First Sea Lord, served under me in Italy, *so I am hoping at least to be received by these gentlemen should we run into serious trouble.* [Emphasis supplied.]

Four months later, when Macmillan, who in World War II had been Britain's resident minister in the Mediterranean Theater, became Minister of Defence, Stone sent him a congratulatory note. Sir Harold's private secretary responded with word that he would "like to see you some time if you have time to call in." They met on November 3. Two days later, Stone reported in a cable to Forest L. Henderson, executive vice president of American Cable and Radio Corporation, of which Commercial Cable is a subsidiary:

> Had meeting with Harold Macmillan Minister of Defence Tuesday, 20 minutes of which were devoted to briefing him on Deep Freeze with full representations of JCS [The United States Joint Chiefs of Staff] position. . . . Half way thru our meeting he dictated memo to permanent Secretary of his Ministry, advising of his relationship with me during the war, my present position, the cost and route of Deep Freeze and the JCS support saying that he understood our application had been pending for some time. . . . He suggested that he be informed soonest where the matter stood. . . . *I asked for an opportunity to be heard at highest level* if there should be possibility of a negative or restrictive decision. . . . I really feel much good was accomplished becos [*sic*] of Macmillan's strong position in Government. . . . [Emphasis supplied.]

Commercial Cable already had offices in the United Kingdom to handle traffic with the United States. If Deep Freeze were to be built, the efficiencies of the then most modern technology could come into play against British-owned facilities. Thus there was an understandable wariness about Deep Freeze in the British General Post Office. Although it was not the Post Office but Cable and Wireless Ltd., a nationalized British corporation, which was an international cable and radio carrier, the Post Office had a stake in the matter because it was C. and W.'s agent within the British Isles.

ITT had as a supporter of Deep Freeze none other than the board chairman of Cable and Wireless, Major General Sir Leslie Nicholls. He provided ITT officials with "confidential information" from inside the British government, the Justice Department said. Evidence of this is in a letter that Admiral Stone hand-wrote to Forest Henderson two days after meeting with Sir Harold:

> I am writing—not cabling—this because I'm always afraid of getting Gen. Nick [Nicholls] in trouble—he is so very frank with me and tells me so much more than I'm sure he should. I called him this a.m. [Nov. 5] to see if he had received the new P.O. [British Post Office] paper. He had & said— "They're still 'agin' you. But I've got my staff shooting holes in it & of course I'll go back at them again. They say they haven't consulted the Ministry of Defence yet. They wind up saying—'We can't recommend it at this time.' But the paper hasn't gone to any Minister yet. It's only being circulated within the P.O. & to me." . . .

Another thing to note is that the **P.O.** emphasizes that their paper doesn't touch on the military aspect at all. That means that it probably *is* going to the Cabinet—where the Defence position will be presented directly. Nick has also said that Radley [Sir W. Gordon Radley, deputy director general of the branch of the British Post Office responsible for international telecommunications] has told him they want him to give his views directly to the Cabinet, when the Cabinet considers it. . . . The big guns in our favor will have to come from Defence & Treasury. The latter own and receive dividends from C & W [Cable and Wireless] & are the ones who will appreciate our $17,000,000 expenditure in U.K. & the saving of expense on the proposed NATO-U.K.-Iceland cable. . . .

On November 10, Sir Gordon called a meeting about Deep Freeze with, among others, representatives of the Ministry of Defence and the Foreign Office. Nicholls provided ITT with the names of the organizations represented, the positions they took, and, the Justice Department said, "further advice that the final decision on the project would be made at the very highest level after the Canadian Government's views had been received." Admiral Stone, in a cable to Forest Henderson, commented, "Note that the meeting took place exactly one week after my meeting with the Defence Minister." The next day, Sir Harold said in a note to Stone that: "A number of difficult and complicated issues are involved. I am afraid, therefore, that I cannot say when the British Government will be in a position to give its views." But Stone remained hopeful. "I am sure that his interest in our project is going to be helpful because he ranks next after Eden in the British Government," he told an associate in a note on December 7.

Later, Stone would admit to his board of directors in Commercial Cable that in the United Kingdom and Canada he had been able "to force any form of active consideration only through the pressures of personal friendship and U.S. Government support." He applied such "pressures" where necessary. "Yesterday, I had a satisfactory meeting with Harold Macmillan, Minister of Defence (there is talk that he may be the next Foreign Secretary if Churchill does retire)," Stone reported on April 1, 1955, in a letter to a high ITT official. He said that Sir Harold had shown "extreme friendliness and helpfulness," credit for which may have been owed in part to General Nicholls: "The military person did a fine job in briefing Mr. Macmillan in our favor two days before I saw him yesterday."

334

Meanwhile, ITT began efforts in behalf of Deep Freeze in Ottawa and Washington. These were at the highest levels of government, of course, but not at the highest levels of candor.

On September 14, 1954, Forest Henderson met with Lester Pearson in Ottawa. The next day, in a cable to Stone in London, Henderson said: "Feel would be able to get assistance from Joint Chiefs in Washington by having them call attention to defense officials UK of the urgent need for speed for military reasons to complete cable on target dates without bringing into picture any of the commercial aspects."

Pearson provided ITT with "information of a confidential nature," the Justice Department said. The information related to "the status of the Canadian Government's position, the possible participation by NATO, and the impact of NATO participation." In addition, "ITT's representative had numerous conversations with Mr. Pearson and other Canadian officials relating to the negotiations." The Department also said that R. B. Bryce, who as clerk of the Privy Council in Ottawa coordinated the various Cabinet departments, provided ITT with "reports on the positions of high Canadian officials."

The Justice Department based its summary on several documents in the J261 file, including a thirty-eight-page itemized bill for services from the law firm Commercial Cable retained for Deep Freeze negotiations in Ottawa, and a cable from Henderson to Admiral Stone.

The law firm was Maclaren, Laidlaw, Corlett & Sherwood; but the partner directly involved, "our Counsel," was Gordon Maclaren. "We have had strong support from our Counsel, who as a result of his political position and friendships has been able to bring the arguments in favor of our project directly to a number of the Ministers of the Cabinet and to secure consideration of the project at Cabinet level," Stone told his company's board.

The law firm's itemized bill, which lists $15,000 in fees for services from July 27, 1954, to December 27, 1955, contains this item for November 25, 1954: "Telephone call from L. B. Pearson and he to try to stir things up and let us in on the great difficulty they have run into and bring us into the picture if possible (Confidential)." The next day, Henderson said in the cable to Stone that he had just talked with E. A. Martin, Commercial Cable's representative in Canada for Deep Freeze, who had received a call from Pearson. The Minister

> requests us keep following information completely confidential. He advised
> that his department had received a note from the Canadian High Com-

missioner's office in London to the effect that the United Kingdom was opposing our application at this time and that it might be desirable for Canada to hold off making an immediate decision pending further exchanges between the two governments. In addition he told our counsel that NATO was now involved and that various countries within NATO were going to consider it. . . . If NATO gets into the picture as informed would add considerably to delay. . . . Martin called Bryce . . . after receiving this information and explained situation to him. . . . Bryce replied that he was going to consult immediately with the various ministries involved and would give Martin a report today. . . . This report from Bryce will also be strictly confidential but it will help us to know the lay of the land and guide us in making further plans and decisions.

There follows an enlightening disclosure on how to manipulate a branch of the public government for the benefit of a private international government:

We feel that it is high time for our State Department to step into this picture with a strong message to the FM's [foreign ministers] of all countries involved requesting immediate attention to our project and favorable action on same. If you agree Kennedy [James A. Kennedy, vice president and general counsel of American Cable and Radio and its subsidiaries] and I will be in Washington Monday to work on same, but because of following sentences and strictly confidential nature of above information we do not propose to divulge same to State Department. It is of greatest importance that above information coming from highest government source must not be mentioned to anyone, including military person [General Nicholls]. It is pointed out that should the above become known the consequences would be disastrous. Same will also apply information to come from Bryce later.

In May, Stone himself enlisted the State Department. At a conference of foreign secretaries in Paris, he pleaded his cause with Assistant Secretary of State Livingston T. Merchant. Ever the name-dropper, he gave Merchant a memo in which he said that he had twice discussed Deep Freeze with Sir Harold, "having known and served with him during World War II . . ." The memo expressed the hope that during the conference Secretary of State John Foster Dulles "will find opportunity to mention the matter to Mr. Macmillan . . . with a view to stimulating favorable action by H.M.G." The meeting with Merchant was "satisfactory," Stone said the same day, May 12, in a cable to New York.

Merchant concluded by saying he would make strong recommendation to Dulles to speak to Macmillan today but if Dulles unable because of heavy conference load, he (Merchant) will definitely take up with Sir Harold Caccia, Macmillan's deputy on British Delegation here and in Foreign Office for European Affairs. . . . Caccia was my British political adviser in 1944 in Italy and Jim [James Kennedy] will remember our assistance to Caccia last fall on personal matter.

The same evening, Under Secretary of State C. Douglas Dillon, who also was in Paris, said in a telegram to Washington that Dulles had asked Sir Harold "to give matter push on return to London. Macmillan agreed to do so."

Despite intervention from such exalted diplomatic and military levels of government, and despite leaks of information from high officials who acted as ITT's errand boys in London and Ottawa, the project failed. Critical government resistance in London and Ottawa never was overcome. Commercial Cable's law firm in Ottawa, for example, had this revealing entry for May 20, 1955, in its itemized bill: "Mr. Pearson advising me that he is advised that the British will not give us outlets there under any circumstances, and on my suggesting Britain was waiting to see what Canada did, he said that is not his information but he would check into it immediately to make certain." There were other problems, including the distractions to the British government caused, at critical points in the negotiations, by election campaigns and dock and rail strikes.

Perhaps most important, ITT had little going for it but what Admiral Stone called "the pressures of personal friendship." He was aware that by themselves these could be an insufficient basis for successful negotiations. "We are not in a position here," he once said in a cable from London, "to Quote insist Unquote upon an equal footing or, in fact, to Quote insist Unquote on anything except free dental treatment."

ITT's failure in the Deep Freeze case is much less significant than the exposure of efforts by a global corporation to translate economic power into political power at the international level. Other such efforts, of course, routinely occur. As noted, just three hundred international corporations will dominate the economies of the principal non-Communist countries of the world by 1985, if present merger rates continue. Not surprisingly, two hundred of these corporations will be the ones that now control two-thirds of the manufacturing assets of the United States. Al-

337

ready, these American-chartered corporations operate as international organizations—or, in some respects, as *de facto* international governments. Among such corporations there is a tendency to shed national identity and, perhaps, even national allegiance. This makes it difficult for any one nation to exercise effective control over the operations of businesses which are international—just as the individual states have found it difficult to regulate American Telephone and Telegraph or insurance firms and their holding companies which are national in character.

Employment figures provide one measure of the magnitude of giant international corporate operations. In 1968, to carry out its worldwide operations, General Motors, for example, employed more than 740,000 persons; Ford, 388,000; General Electric, 350,000. Among corporations based abroad, Siemens (West Germany) employed 257,000, Unilever (primarily British) 300,000, Phillips (the Netherlands) 244,000, Royal Dutch/Shell Group (primarily the Netherlands) 174,000, Fiat (Italy) 134,-000, and Dunlop (Britain) 104,000.

A second measure of magnitude comes from listing in order of dollar rank the gross national products of leading nations and the net sales of the largest corporations. The top forty include eight corporations. As of 1966, General Motors, with net sales of $20.2 billion, fell between the Netherlands' GNP of $20.8 billion and Argentina's GNP of $18.7 billion. With net sales of about $12.2 billion each, Ford and Standard Oil of New Jersey fell between the GNP of Czechoslovakia, $13.4 billion, and the Union of South Africa, $11.9 billion. The net sales figures for Royal Dutch Shell, General Electric, Chrysler, Unilever, and Mobile Oil interlaced with the GNP's of Venezuela, Norway, Greece, Colombia, and New Zealand.[2]

Many companies operate in more than fifty countries and derive from 25 per cent to more than 50 per cent of income from sales outside their home country—which, in the majority of cases, is the United States.[3] Included in this list are such American-based companies as International Telephone and Telegraph, Standard Oil Co. (New Jersey), National Cash Register, Colgate-Palmolive, Chas. Pfizer, General Electric, General Motors, Goodyear, and IBM; and such foreign-based companies as Unilever, Royal Dutch Shell, Volkswagen (West Germany), Fiat, Sony (Japan), and Nestlé (Switzerland).

Direct investments—generally, book value of corporate stock—that American companies make abroad far exceed the direct investments that all foreign-based companies make in the United States—$70 billion compared with $12 billion in 1969. In the same year, however, other long-term investments, generally bonds, notes, and inventory, by foreign companies in the United States amounted to almost $30 billion.[4]

Of greater significance is that the two hundred largest American-based corporations accounted for almost 80 per cent of the direct foreign investments made by all American companies. And a handful of these giant enterprises accounted for one-third of these investments.[5]

The vast size and frequency of mergers and of joint ventures among American and foreign firms, and among foreign firms alone, has been amply documented.[6] Clearly, the United States has not been unique in experiencing a conglomerate merger movement. Other industrialized nations also have undergone a similar phenomenon of comparable dimensions, often with the blessings of the governments involved.

The international corporation, ballooning by direct investment and, increasingly, through merger, is tending to dominate already highly concentrated economies.[7] Arthur Barber, former Deputy Assistant Secretary of Defense, International Security Affairs, has described the effect:

> In an ever increasing degree, the decisions affecting economic growth are not only international decisions but corporate decisions. A decision concerning the location or removal of a plant, a transportation terminal or a research and development laboratory is made more often in the office of a corporate executive than in the government. The government is more often a pleader than a negotiator or administrator.
>
> It would be a mistake, however, to believe that international corporations are instruments of the government. Two years ago the United States government learned that a French subsidiary of the Fruehauf trucking company had received an order for trucks from the People's Republic of China. The United States government ordered Fruehauf not to deliver. The French government seized the French firm and the trucks were delivered. The international corporation is the instrument of no government; it is responsive only to the laws of the lands where it operates and its own board of directors.

"What is this new international institution that challenges governments?" Barber asked.

> While corporations have long operated across international borders, the post-war period has seen the emergence of the truly international corporation. These corporations play an increasingly dominant role in the world

economy. They have international staffs, international funding, international communication networks, and—in the computer—even an international language.[8]

International corporations walking the cracks between the laws of the myriad countries in which they operate may be developing into a super-international government of their own. Conceivably, the role of the sovereign state thus could come to be subordinate to that of the corporation state.

Jean-Jacques Servan-Schreiber, author of *The American Challenge,* told a subcommittee of the Congressional Joint Economic Committee: "Because of the world-wide empires which they are carving out for themselves, the multinational corporations are also able to create a new jungle. Widely spread out in their component parts and commanded from geographically remote bases, they account to no single national authority. And since international law is feeble, or non-existent, they are free of international authority as well."[9]

Interrelationships between the sources of money, predominantly the banks, and the corporation, although not as clearly delineated as in the United States, also exist. Corporations, as we have shown, do not, for the most part, generate their own income. They seek it from outside sources. Inasmuch as American corporations play such a major role in the internationalization of business, it seems apparent that the previously cited studies by Representative Wright Patman's House Banking and Currency Subcommittee, showing the influence of the banks on the corporations, are equally valid when assessing international operations.

Indeed, the top banks named in the Patman staff study tend to dominate international money markets, or at least to play an important part in them.[10] Testimony before the Senate Antitrust and Monopoly Subcommittee in 1966 revealed that a small number of banks dominate international lending by American financial institutions. For example, 80 per cent of all foreign credit is held by only sixteen banks. As of March 31, 1966, thirteen American banks operated branches abroad, with the number of branch offices totaling 213. One expert witness said: "The most extensive foreign bank services are operated by the three largest banks in the country and these systems virtually encircle the globe."[11] A mere seven of the largest American banks held $6.23 billion in foreign assets—68 per cent of the foreign assets held by all American banks. The partnership between banks and other U.S. corporations extends to the world in which the international corporation operates.

Servan-Schreiber pointed out to the subcommittee of the Congressional Joint Economic Committee: "Our capital markets are also dominated by American controlled institutions. Indeed the banking centers of London, Zurich and Frankfurt seem to be at the mercy of the mighty, and occasionally not so mighty, Eurodollar. And it is an extraordinary paradox that the savings of Europeans are used to finance the acquisitions of local industries by U.S. companies."

What is happening internationally is analogous to the industrial development of the United States. At the turn of the century, industrial cartels dominated our economy. Up to World War II, cartels also dominated world markets. In his minority views in the *Report of the Attorney General's National Committee to Study the Antitrust Laws,* Eugene V. Rostow wrote in 1955:

> The international cartel problem is one of the most thoroughly studied issues in public life. Years of effort by committees, governments, foundations and individual scholars have fully documented the significant role of cartels in the world economy. The importance of foreign cartels to our own economy has long been generally understood. The problem was perhaps most vividly dramatized in public thought by the Senate investigations before World War II, of the business connections between American and German firms, and by our earlier experiences as purchasers of quinine, rubber, diamonds, and certain other products produced and sold under cartel conditions. . . . *In the last 30 years, government reports alone have reviewed cartel plans with respect to more than 120 commodities or services of significance in world trade,* including aluminum, diamonds, wood pulp, nickel, copper, rubber, various chemical and electrical products, dyes, cocoa, shipping, magnesium and machinery of many types. [Emphasis supplied.]

After World War II many industrial countries developed laws patterned after our antitrust laws; and the European Common Market came into being with its own rules patterned after our Sherman Act. The cartels then became less obvious, although cartel-type arrangements existed and still exist.

A report prepared for the State Department by Professor Corwin D. Edwards in 1964 stated:

Although cartels in Western Europe are fewer, more informal, and less restrictive than before the Second World War, they still include price fixing often enough to impede competitive adjustment of prices; control of discounts often enough to affect channels of distribution; rigidities such as joint marketing, quota systems, and allocations often enough to be obstacles to competitive pursuit of efficiency; and aggregated rebate systems, eligibility requirements, and exclusive or preferential dealing arrangements often enough to handicap independent business. The impact of most cartels is local or national, not international. Information about export cartels and international cartels is scant, but there is enough to indicate that there are significant instances of each.[12]

The internal operation of cartels, of course, is kept secret by the participants. Rarely is it possible even to glimpse the inner workings. So it was an impressive coup that the Senate Subcommittee on Antitrust and Monopoly brought off when it obtained the secret minutes of seventeen meetings held by the quinine cartel. The first of these meetings was held on December 2, 1959, and the last on September 21, 1962. The usual meeting sites were hotels, including the Plaza in Brussels, the Amstel in Amsterdam, the Europa in Heidelberg, and the Selsdonpark in London, and the offices of a J. R. Roques in Paris. Dr. John M. Blair, who directed the investigation, laid out the story of these meetings at a subcommittee hearing in March, 1967. The story developed from that hearing, from an earlier one in May, 1966, and from the subcommittee's 1967 report, *Prices of Quinine and Quinidine,* follows.[13]

Quinine and quinidine are found naturally in the bark of the cinchona tree. Since the end of the nineteenth century nearly all of the world's quinine has been derived from Javanese bark. Manufacturing plants in Holland and Germany do most of the processing. The owners are a Dutch company, N.V. Nederlandsche Combinatie voor Chemische Industrie (commonly referred to as "Combinatie" or "Nedchem"), and two West German firms, C. F. Boehringer & Soehne G.m.b.H. and Buchler & Company. The firms produce the great bulk of the quinidine consumed today by chemically converting it from quinine, to which it is closely related in molecular structure. Persons who suffer from irregular heartbeat, or cardiac arrhythmia, take quinidine to restore and maintain a normal heart rhythm. "In this country alone," the Antitrust Sub-committee report said, "the drug is used for varying intervals by about a

342

quarter of a million people, most of whom are older persons. Many require the drug every day and for them it is quite literally a matter of life or death." Consequently, it was an extremely serious matter when in 1964 and 1965 the retail price of quinidine increased more than 300 per cent. "I cannot continue to pay these high prices for quinidine, yet my doctor tells me I cannot live without it," an elderly patient said in a letter cited in the report.

A key element in the price increase was a huge stockpile of quinine owned by the United States government. In January 1955, when 13.8 million ounces had accumulated, the General Services Administration declared the stockpile surplus. From that time until the GSA formally published a disposal plan in August 1958, the report said, "negotiations were conducted secretly and exclusively among GSA, State [the State Department], the Dutch Embassy, and representatives of the cartel." Making a memorable translation of economic power into political power on an international scale was the First Commercial Secretary of the Netherlands Embassy. Acting for the cartel, he submitted the conditions which it had set for acquisition. This was shown by an internal GSA memorandum of September 7, 1956: "In general, Mr. Moerell summed up the position of the Dutch by saying they would be interested in the U.S. Government's quinine under two conditions: (1) that the Dutch be permitted to purchase the total quantity, and (2) that there be no general advertising of this sale through the Federal Register."

In 1961 and 1962, the GSA sold off 9.5 million ounces of stockpiled quinine. The cartel did not get it all, as it had wished, but it did get all but 1 million ounces. Even this was more of an accomplishment than it may seem, because it was done in defiance of a GSA commitment to set aside half of the surplus quinine for sale to small business. The Small Business Administration and the Comptroller General had forced the commitment out of the GSA. The frustration of the commitment was achieved largely by the State Department working as an ally of the Netherlands Embassy, which, as noted, was indistinguishable in this instance from the cartel.

The GSA carried the stockpiled quinine on its books at 63 cents per ounce, which presumably fairly represented the price the government had paid to acquire the quinine from the cartel in the first place. When Nedchem, the Dutch firm acting for the cartel, bought back the quinine from the stockpile, it paid only 21 cents, or one-third as much. Yet, at the end of 1964, the cartel was reselling the 21-cent quinine at more than $2.00, and at the end of March, 1966, at more than $3.00.

"Where does the blame lie?" Senator Philip A. Hart, the subcommittee chairman, asked in closing the first set of hearings in 1966. "Principally," he said, "in the operations of an international cartel, with the Dutch firm in the driver's seat." But, he continued, blame also goes to government officials, "particularly in the State Department, [who] rendered valuable assistance to the cartel." The record clearly supports this charge. At one point, for example, the administrator of the GSA showed how the economic power of the quinine cartel, albeit indirectly, had come to influence the Department of State. The administrator wrote that the Department "has indicated that it would strenuously oppose domestic sales of the stockpile as this would seriously disturb relations with the Netherlands and with the Government of the Republic of Indonesia."

The actual minutes of the cartel's meetings, efficiently kept by its secretary, disclosed brazen price-fixing, division of markets, and evasion of the antitrust prohibitions of the United States and the European Common Market.

Cartel control of quinine and quinidine dates back three-quarters of a century, to an initial agreement in 1892 between Dutch and German quinine processors. In 1913 the European quinine manufacturers and the producers of Javanese bark organized a full-fledged cartel. Fifteen years later a federal grand jury indicted the cartel and American conspirators for antitrust violations which included restricting the production of bark, allocating the bark among participating manufacturers, establishing sale prices for bark and quinine derivatives, setting up a profit-pooling arrangement for participating manufacturers, engaging in price discrimination among customers, and coercing manufacturers into participating under threat of deprivation of bark supplies. The case was settled with a perpetual consent decree, but it had no significant effects on the operations of the cartel (in fact, in 1968, the Justice Department undertook a highly successful new antitrust prosecution which involved many of the same kinds of arrangements even if there were changes in the cast of characters).

In late 1959, the international quinine cartel was reactivated or reestablished, as the subcommittee demonstrated. It embraced all of the

344

world's producers with the exception of the factory in Bandung owned by the Indonesian government. The cartelists, it was developed in the subcommittee report, "entered into a series of restrictive agreements designed to control prices, distribution, and production in every aspect of the quinine industry," with a key objective being "the elimination of competition among the various producers in securing the U.S. stockpile." Their operating "convention" consisted of a stockpile agreement under which Nedchem, the Dutch firm, alone would bid for the stockpile and then would share it with the others on a basis of previously established quotas; an export agreement under which prices would be fixed and other restraints imposed in world markets *outside* the United Kingdom and the countries of the European Economic Community; a gentlemen's agreement under which prices would be fixed and other restraints imposed *within* the EEC and the UK; and, finally, a bark pool agreement under which efforts would be made to hold down the price for the raw material, to set selling prices for cinchona bark, and to pool purchases.

The subcommittee report identified the participating companies and their officials who customarily attended meetings as follows: England: Rexall Drug Co., Ltd., Mr. J. R. Lumley; Carnegies of Welwyn, Ltd., Mr. F. Chapman; and Lake & Cruickshank, Ltd., Mr. G. N. Cruickshank. France: Société Nogentaise de Produits Chimiques, M. L. Augustins and M. P. Jacob; Pointet & Girard, M. L. Girard and M. A. Pointet; "President of the French Group," M. J. R. Roques of Ets. Roques. Germany: The Boehringer and Buchler firms, mentioned earlier, were represented by Mr. G. Tessmar and Dr. W. Buchler, respectively. Holland: the "Combinatie" or "Nedchem," also identified earlier, was represented by Mr. C. N. van der Spek and Mr. C. W. van Heeckeren van der Schoot.

The minutes of the cartel's third meeting, held on February 4, 1960, provide some representative insights into how the game was played. Here is one:

> *Dr. Buchler* says that since a convention cannot buy the stockpile, how can we hope to acquire same?
>
> *Mr. van der Spek* says that the convention will not be advertised and that manufacturers are not going to be too obvious about it. The cartel between Boehringer and the Dutch is public, but not published. *GSA will not ask information about cartels.* [Emphasis supplied.]

The prediction that the GSA would not raise embarrassing questions about cartels "proved to be accurate," the subcommittee report noted.

At another point, the meeting was concerned with how to try to translate their economic power into political power:

> *Dr. Buchler* asks how to proceed about the stockpile. Could not all manufacturers induce their governments to approach the U.S. Government? . . .
>
> *Mr. van der Spek* says that the U.S. Government then would have to choose to which manufacturer or manufacturers it should sell and which governments the United States would have to disappoint.

The conferees also took up a dilemma that was to plague them for months to come: Should they raise the world price of quinine and thus reap an immediate increase in profits, or should they keep the price at its existing and rather low level, and thus make it possible to buy the stockpile at a lower price?

> *Mr. van der Spek* . . . Now if we make a convention and put up the price by say Hfl.3—that means a million guilders a year, which we let go if we do not make a convention to better our chances to get the stockpile.

The allocation of markets, to make certain geographic markets the exclusive preserve of one or more manufacturers, caused much dissension. "It has always been so," van der Spek said at a meeting on December 2, 1959, "France for the French, Germany for the Germans and the Netherlands for the Dutch." Nothing was said about Britain for the British, leading to a logical protest by Chapman of Welwyn, Ltd., that "it follows that the United Kingdom is for the British only." But van der Spek said it would be asking too much of the Dutch to abandon their "old tradition" of selling in the UK. Roques, the French group leader, agreed. "France for the French is a historical principle, whereas the Dutch have been selling quinine to the United Kingdom since the existence of quinine," he said. It turned out that "France for the French" meant not merely continental France, but also the North African colonies, Central Africa, Vietnam, Laos, and Cambodia.

Ultimately, the British felt forced to accept an agreement which bound them to halt further sales to French or German customers, while their own national market remained open to the Dutch and the Germans. "It is a bitter pill to swallow," Chapman said, "that France is for the

French, Germany for the Germans, Holland for the Dutch, while the United Kingdom should be the exception." In response, the meeting minutes reported, van der Spek "points to the great English tradition of liberalism." There *was* evidence of British liberalism, of a sort. Among other things, they gave up their right to compete for the large amount of low-cost quinine in the stockpile, paid a fee to the Dutch for their expenses in getting 84 per cent of the stockpile for themselves, and persuaded British importers and distributors to withdraw support from U.S. Quinine, a company which had been Nedchem's most serious rival for the stockpile.

For the Dutch, the convention served an essential purpose: to eliminate competition by other producers for the American stockpile. On June 29, 1962, Nedchem accomplished that purpose when it signed a contract for final disposal of the stockpile. Surely, that triumph must be the explanation of why, four months later, Nedchem demolished the convention which it had been the leading force in creating. Nothing else in the record could seem to account for what the report called "the paradox of an enterprise deliberately undoing 2 years of the hardest form of co-operation." Once Nedchem had the stockpile and had broken the convention, it shared it with—and only with—Boehringer, the German firm with which it had made a cartel agreement in 1958. This was a prime example of how a cartel not only can thwart competition, but also ban competitors. In blunt terms, it played the British and French for suckers.

Concentrated industries in the United States increasingly tend to replace clearly illegal hard-core price-fixing agreements with lockstep pricing, which is certainly more subtle and at least not obviously illegal. Now, with concentration increasing in international markets, the rigid pricing that attends concentration can be expected to become more commonplace everywhere. For reasons explained in Chapter One, giant conglomerates that operate in many industries feel restrained from engaging in price competition with each other. Perhaps ironically, growing international concentration thus will diminish the *raison d'être* for cartels.

However, the steel industry is apparently taking no chances. *Business Week* reported on September 3, 1966:

Europe's cartels, those blocks of big business bent on regulating production, prices, and market, are reappearing. They aren't quite the same as the prewar ones, but they have the same basic aim—limiting competition. The trend is becoming increasingly evident:

Two weeks ago, the German steel industry announced that 31 steel producers had grouped themselves into four marketing cartels. Competition would be eliminated among the member companies of each cartel.

France already has a secret cartel operating in steel. . . . The new cartels in Europe are distinct from corporate mergers which both the Common Market and the coal and steel community are trying to encourage. . . . By contrast, the new trend toward cartelism involves the classic pattern of settling production quotas, fixing domestic and export prices, and imposing severe penalties on companies that violate the cartel agreements. It is reminiscent of the maneuvering that led to the establishment of the International Steel cartel . . . in 1926.

On October 11, 1966, *The Times* of London reported:

The conviction is growing among industrialists of many companies who buy special varieties of steel that they are being held to ransom to pay high prices by international cartels among steel makers. The decline in the prices of more common varieties is making the cartel activities conspicuous. Mounting indignation from customers is expected to force more than one government to act before long.

There followed in 1967 a report on the domestic and foreign steel industries by the Rev. William T. Hogan, S.J., a steel economist generally sympathetic to American corporations. He said:

One of the most significant and promising steps toward international co-operation in steel taken to date by the free world steel community is the establishment of an international iron and steel institute "IISA." . . . The founding member companies met in May of 1967 and agreed to meet again on November 11 & 12th in Brussels. Also attending this meeting will be other important contributors to the free world's production of raw steel.

Leading the list of founding member companies were four American firms, United States Steel, Bethlehem, Armco, and Republic. Then came the major steel firms of Japan, Germany, France, Italy, Canada, Australia, Belgium, Luxembourg, and the Netherlands.

The American companies had lost no time in reacting to the threat of a foreign steel cartel. Their answer, in effect, was "Don't fight them, organize them." *Iron Age* reported in November 1967: "The free world's leading steel makers recently launched the International Iron and Steel Institute in Brussels. They hope it can help the industry from floundering on reckless competition trends." ("Reckless competition," of course, is another phrase for "price competition.") The *New York Times* reported on March 23, 1968: "The Japanese steel industry soon will inform the United States industry that they have adopted a voluntary company by company export quota plan to insure orderly marketing of steel in the United States."

Also in 1968, with the aid of the United States government, American, Japanese, and European steelmakers entered into agreements to reduce imports into the United States. The world's steelmakers appear to be cooperating through an international organization. While their operation is technically not a cartel, it has had cartel-like effects, at least so far as the American consumer is concerned.

The ultimate in concentration is the operation of international markets in the same manner as concentrated domestic markets. The international aluminum industry has achieved the ultimate and may well be the model which other industries will attempt to emulate. The situation in aluminum was outlined to the Senate Subcommittee on Antitrust and Monopoly by Professor Heinrich Kronstein of the Institute for International and Foreign Trade Law at Georgetown University and of the University of Frankfurt.[14] He testified that the problem of concentration is necessarily international. It is not, he said, understandable when seen as merely a national phenomenon. Professor Kronstein pointed to a series of mergers, agreements, and other anticompetitive actions by the world's leading integrated aluminum producers which have resulted in this highly concentrated international industry's acting for all practical purposes as a global monopolist. He stated that the world market in aluminum is such that a look at the United States market is at the same time a look at the international market, and vice versa. And, he said, other industries acting in the same monopolistic way include copper, zinc, tin, and oil.

Senator Hart summed up:

> You are telling us, as I understand it, that some of these basic raw material industries can be immunized both from competition and from government action. . . . If that is true, then . . . private forces, operating outside of any social control, direct elements of our economy that are critical. And in that

sense and to the extent that these things are basic to the economy . . . then you are telling us that all of these things, our economy and our life, are dependent on the benevolence of private interests, which are not even national but are international in scope.

Just as economic concentration displaced the old-fashioned trusts and much old-fashioned price-fixing, so it is now displacing international cartels. For consumers seeking relief from high prices such changes offer little if any hope. In a legal sense, in fact, there has been a step backward. The laws of most industrialized countries could effectively deal with cartels, provided there was aggressive enforcement; but the laws are far less effective against concentration. As we have seen in the case of steel, the political power represented by its economic power has translated itself into government activity to help restrain international competition.

In the international field the United States is faced with a supreme irony. By allowing its own corporations to merge freely with those in other countries, it has encouraged other countries to retaliate in kind; i.e., to encourage mergers among their own domestic firms supposedly in order to compete more effectively with the American giants. Yet the impact will be to further assure that there will be effective competition neither in the United States nor in the other industrial countries of the world, nor in the world as an economic entity.

No one has given greater impetus to public support of the movement toward European concentration than Jean-Jacques Servan-Schreiber, author of *The American Challenge*. This provocative book quickly became an international best-seller. Regrettably, one of its basic themes, that to combat an invasion by American corporations the Common Market countries must foster the development of European companies equally giant-sized, is invalid. The premise is that modern technology can thrive only in the context of giant corporations. As demonstrated in Chapter One, modern technology in most cases does not require giant corporations; indeed, giantism may thwart the acceptance of modern technology.

In this regard, a statement of Stuart T. Sanders, former chairman of the Penn Central Railroad, before a House of Representatives subcommittee on July 21, 1970, is instructive. He said that the Penn Central went bankrupt not because of mismanagement, but because it was unmanageable. And in December 1970, the United States government moved to bail out the leading defense contractor, Lockheed, one of the top fifty corporations.

Which are the giant corporations with the technology and innovative capacity that disturb Servan-Schreiber? Among the top fifty American corporations are three automobile companies, eleven petroleum companies, at least two patchwork conglomerates, two steel companies, six aerospace companies, and two food and soap companies.

The impact of imports of automobiles, from Common Market countries and Japan, and the specific criticism of both the safety and durability of American automobiles in congressional committees and by informed critics should make it clear that American companies have no monopoly on advanced technology. Indeed, as we demonstrated in Chapter Two, they have generally lagged behind available technology developed by others. The petroleum companies owe much of their success to government tax and import policies rather than to technological prowess. As far as technology is concerned, hosts of firms in Europe either equal or surpass American companies. Indeed, British Petroleum and the Royal Dutch/Shell Group have successfully invaded the American markets.

The American steel companies have been notorious for their failure to adopt new technologies. European firms developed the major breakthroughs in steel. Their tough competition forced the advances on reluctant American companies.

The aerospace companies depend almost entirely on the federal government for their sustenance. They cannot be compared with firms that do not get gigantic federal subsidies. Indeed, Murray L. Weidenbaum, Assistant Secretary of the Treasury for Economic Policy, has found a pervasive lack of knowledge of non-defense industries in the aerospace industry. In testimony before a House Government Operations subcommittee in November 1970, Weidenbaum explored how far-ranging the lack of knowledge can be. "It often includes," he said, "ignorance of products, production methods, advertising and distribution, financial arrangements, funding of research and development, contracting forms, and the very nature of the civilian customer's needs."

As to General Foods and Procter & Gamble, certainly they owe their primary success not to true innovation and technological superiority, but to massive saturation advertising—unless, of course, one considers sugar-coated cereals or enzyme detergents (which have raised serious health questions for many users as well as for the workers who produce them) to be technological breakthroughs.

The glamour conglomerates among the top fifty firms, such as Ling-Temco-Vought and Litton Industries, at this writing, hardly had distinguished themselves by any breakthroughs, either—except possibly to lead the downward plunge of the stock market in 1970, or, in Litton's case, to consummate a development contract with the military junta in Greece.

Also high on the list of the top fifty corporations is General Electric, which, with all of its financial power, has been unable to touch IBM in the computer market. Because of the unprofitability of its computer division, GE, in 1970, sold its computer manufacturing business to a subsidiary of Honeywell, Inc.

In the entire list of the top fifty, IBM stands almost alone as any kind of technological giant. But its success has been due to a myriad of factors, including leadership in a newly developed field, government support in the formative years, aggressive and dynamic management—and a lack of enforcement of the American antitrust laws. It would be a pity if the European countries were to consider giantism the answer to all of their problems, based on the example of IBM.

Nor could Servan-Schreiber have been aware, when he wrote his book, of *Fortune* magazine's survey of June 1970 which showed that the American corporations in the second group of five hundred were more profitable—and, therefore, more efficient—than the top five hundred. Indeed, a second *Fortune* survey in August 1970 showed that the top one hundred foreign corporations fared better in 1969 than the top five hundred American companies in both sales and profits, despite disparities in size.

Europe would make a tragic error to accept the Servan-Schreiber thesis that giantism is the answer to American corporate penetration.

The investment by foreign firms in the United States, which totaled $12 billion by 1969, indicates the extent to which such expansion can be two-way. The British Petroleum company, as pointed out, is now established in America. In addition to the ubiquitous automobile imports, other foreign industries have invaded the American market. For example, the Good Humor man works for Good Humor Ice Cream Co., owned by Unilever, the British-Dutch organization that also owns the Lever Brothers soap company. Wishbone Salad Dressings are made by a British-owned company. Shell gasoline is marketed by the huge Royal Dutch/Shell Group. Nestlé Company chocolate products are Swiss-owned, and

International Nickel Company, whose stock is one of the thirty used in the Dow-Jones Industrial Average, is Canadian.

There is no question that giant American firms have been aided in getting into foreign markets by their access to both domestic and foreign capital. But this is an attribute of power, not efficiency. And there are solutions other than compounding an already bad situation by creating giants to deal with other giants.

What has allowed American firms to get a foothold in the Common Market countries is not their giant size. Rather, it has been the cartel mentality of many European businessmen. In addition, until the advent of the Common Market, European businesses were conditioned to thinking of marketing in terms of their own national boundaries. This severely limited their markets and the need to develop means of .production. It has been a notion difficult to shake, for many of the old family-owned businesses in particular.

Servan-Schreiber, in his book, quotes from a UNICE (an organization of European businessmen and executives) report:

> It has been clear . . . that certain American firms have been badly informed about the price mechanisms used in the European market—mechanisms which the various Continental rivals respect. A joint study of production costs has allowed us to set up rules which, while safeguarding competition, prove beneficial to all. We must not allow the American firms, from lack of knowledge of our methods, to provoke a price war that would cause serious difficulties in the market.[15]

The same point was made in hearings of the Senate Antitrust and Monopoly Subcommittee in 1966 by Mark S. Massel, then a senior staff member of Brookings Institution. He testified:

> I would like to suggest further that on many occasions American companies have made excellent use of our antitrust laws in making certain, from the standpoint of their own selfish business interests, that they are not tied up with cartels and are not tied up with restrictive business practices so that they can avoid the fetters of the kinds of cartel arrangements that companies are accustomed to in other countries.
>
> I know of instances—because I participated—in which American companies were able to avoid the restrictions that were set down by other business organizations in other countries, on the ground that the antitrust laws stopped the American company from getting into arrangements of that type—and that on several occasions, with which I am quite familiar, the

American companies found over a period of time that it was highly profitable for them to avoid the restrictions in order to be able to push ahead on their own.[16]

An obsession with giantism only masks the basic problem. The real answer is learning how to compete by utilizing the advantages of smaller enterprises to outperform the giants. Computerization, as we have pointed out in Chapter One, generally has helped smaller corporations to compete effectively with giants. Instead of rushing pell-mell to match the size of American rivals, European companies might better be utilizing the advantages of smaller size to develop and market new technologies. And government policy in Europe, rather than encouraging mergers, might well be redesigned to make research funds available to smaller producers. Inasmuch as the movement of American firms into European markets has been largely through merger and joint venture—which itself negates the idea of superior technology—European policy also should be directed to stopping such marriages.

Servan-Schreiber understands well the beneficial effects of competition. He says:

> At a time when the nations of Eastern Europe are trying to get back to such economic mechanisms as the price system, interest rates, and profits, it is hard to deny that the market economy is, as Churchill once said about democracy, "the worst, except for all the others." It has its obvious limitations. But where competition comes into play, the market provides services that a gaint computer programmed by supermen could hardly perform: it points out consumer needs, regulates investment according to demand and cost of materials, and shows by means of deficits which production is unnecessary and which behavior inefficient. The market takes advantage of freedom in a way that the Russians would like to be able to use themselves, so that they could get a better return from their economic system.[17]

He also understands why both the right and left in Europe distrust competition:

> It is striking that conservatives are more attached to the fetters which the pure market economy imposes on the collective will than to the freedoms it provides for individual initiative. Even today they are apt to ask the government simultaneously to release them from the discipline of the plan [government planning of the economy] and also, by closing professions or frontiers, to spare them the risks of competition. . . .

On the Left the same distrust of man leads to a cult of coercive planning. Many progressives still dream of setting up a society where an omniscient bureaucracy, the repository of moral order, will dictate to consumers the enlightened decisions they are incapable of making for themselves.[18]

Men of the Right may ultimately approve the giantism Servan-Schreiber proposes in the belief that they will control the mechanisms; the Left may ultimately approve it in the belief that it is a necessary preliminary to government control of the same mechanisms.

One must hope, however, that the experience of Germany, Italy, and Japan before World War II will not be lost on Servan-Schreiber and his followers. In those countries, it should be remembered, highly concentrated economies facilitated military takeovers. Control of the economy is a prerequisite to control of the political structure.

After World War II in Germany and Japan the old cartels were broken up, and under the aegis of American occupiers competition deliberately was fostered. Swiftly, both economies achieved growth rates that far outstripped all others.

This, too, is an important lesson. Ironically, the same policies which fostered this growth now are being thwarted under the guise of reacting to competition from American corporations.

Servan-Schreiber postulates that meeting the American challenge requires (1) the liberation of intiative and (2) the creation of a handful of giant corporations. Yet, the two are inconsistent.

History shows that concentrated economic power eventually thwarts individual initiative. One would have hoped that Europe, at least, had learned this lesson. Three hundred corporations sitting atop the free-world economy will produce an international establishment in which the individual will be helpless to pursue his liberated initiative.

Only real competition, unrestrained by cartels, cartel agreements, artificial government trade barriers, or concentrated industries, will enable Europe to compete effectively with American companies and to develop the innovation and technological advances which Servan-Schreiber so desires. Only a competitively structured marketplace offers hope to liberated initiative.

Servan-Schreiber, in his appearance in July 1970 on Capitol Hill before the Joint Economic Committee's Subcommittee on Foreign Economic Policy, pointed out that "economics and politics have become so intertwined that one cannot be considered without the other." He also said, "from the radicalism of the young stems a deeply-felt conviction that a system which allows the excesses of economic competition to ride herd over social life is basically immoral."

And he expressed the crux of a basic problem facing the world today. "Economic and political power must be separated as much as possible if each is to fulfill its mission. . . . The separation of economic and political power is, therefore a primary task for the future."

But economic power will continue to play a greater and greater role in translating itself into political power as it increases in size. Economic power, as we have attempted to demonstrate, is political power. Therefore, only by thwarting economic giantism will the separation for which Servan-Schreiber so devoutly wishes have a chance to develop.

12 CONCLUSIONS AND RECOMMENDATIONS

Diffusion of economic power is indispensable to a society that aspires to be responsive to the rightful social and economic claims of free citizens. This does not mean a return to the backyard foundry, any more than diffusion of political power contemplates a return to the township as the ideal unit of government. But it does mean that the giant corporation must be broken up. Neither the giant corporation nor giant government should be the regulator of the economy; competition should be, almost always. But it cannot be so long as the corporation is permitted to exercise sovereign power.

There is nothing sacred about the corporation. No process of God or nature controlled the evolution which produced it. Rather, it developed as a method for accumulating capital and for shielding the user of that capital from individual liability. Thus, it is a mere legal device. And what the law has created, the law must be free to control. The corporation cannot be permitted to be above the law, just as the citizen cannot. For too long, the corporation, as a device for doing business, has exploited and manipulated the very society that gave it life.

A corporation exists because one or the other of the fifty states has granted it a charter that, under the Constitution, must be honored throughout the land. This is absurd. The modern corporation operates in several states, or in all of them, and in many countries. Yet, the laws of the single state that incorporated it govern its operations. Often the corporation chose that state as its legal home because its management could have maximum freedom from legal strictures.

Early in the American experience, the states kept a relatively tight rein on corporations. They limited total capitalization, conditioned charters on fairness of business operations, and restricted the scope of

357

those operations. During the nineteenth century, however, significant expansion occurred in the nature and range of commerce. Single corporations began to operate on a national scale. They raised capital in one state. They took raw materials from a second state and processed them in a third. Then they sold the finished products everywhere.

In the last quarter of the nineteenth century there began a trend to relax state restrictions. New Jersey set the pace, on the theory that by encouraging more enterprises to incorporate in Trenton it would harvest more taxes. New Jersey even legalized holding companies and became the home of the Standard Oil trust.

But Delaware would go on to win the potlatch by enacting, in 1896, a law that gave the most away. Thus Delaware became the favored state for incorporation. In 1899 a waspish article in the *American Law Review* said:

> Meanwhile the little community of truck-farmers and clam-diggers have had their cupidity excited by the spectacle of their northern neighbor, New Jersey, becoming rich and bloated through the granting of franchises to trusts which are to do business everywhere except in New Jersey, and which are to go forth panoplied by the sovereign state of New Jersey to afflict and curse other American communities. . . . In other words little Delaware, gangrened with envy at the spectacle of the truck-patchers, sand-duners, clam-diggers and mosquito wafters of New Jersey getting all the money in the country into her coffers,—is determined to get her tiny, sweet, round baby hand into the grab-bag of sweet things before it is too late.[1]

Emulating Delaware and New Jersey, other states relaxed their laws so as to compete for corporate taxpayers. For the most part, the new laws shifted ever greater control of the corporation from stockholders to management. Delaware, New Jersey, and the states which followed their lead cut back the rights of shareholders to challenge management activities, eliminated preemptive rights, made shareholders' derivative suits more difficult, and, most important, removed charter limitations on the scope of corporate business.

In effect, changes in state law for the purpose of attracting taxes started a race among the states to transfer their legitimate prerogatives to private management. Simultaneously, the states beat back efforts to regulate corporate activity, fearing that tighter regulation would drive corporations to looser jurisdictions. State governments so humbled themselves to court corporate managements that they fairly could be viewed as adjuncts of them. This self-abasement by the states continued even into the 1960s, as evidenced by the preamble to the 1963 revision of the corporation laws of Delaware:

> WHEREAS, The State of Delaware has a long and beneficial history as the domicile of nationally known corporations; and
>
> WHEREAS, The favorable climate which the State of Delaware has traditionally provided for corporations has been a leading source of revenue for the State; and
>
> WHEREAS, Many States have enacted new corporation laws in recent years in an effort to compete with Delaware for corporate business; and
>
> WHEREAS, There has been no comprehensive revision of the Delaware Corporation Law since its enactment in 1898 [sic]; and
>
> WHEREAS, The General Assembly of the State of Delaware declares it to be the public policy of the State to maintain a favorable business climate and to encourage corporations to make Delaware their domicile. . . .

This led one knowledgeable observer to remark:

> The sovereign state of Delaware is in the business of selling its corporation law. This is profitable business, for corporation law is a good commodity to sell. The market is large, and relatively few producers compete on a national scale. The consumers of this commodity are corporations, and as we shall see, Delaware, like any other good businessman, tries to give the consumer what he wants. In fact, those who will buy the product are not only consulted about their preferences, but are also allowed to design the product and run the factory.[2]

In 1969, Delaware reached a new high, or low, when it passed a law under which a corporation chartered in that state could skip its annual meeting altogether. The exclusion of state controls once the corporation is launched and the final elimination of a shareholder voice under the Delaware law make clear that state corporation laws are in varying degrees a charade.

This brief history points to our primary recommendation. It is that federal chartering replace state chartering of corporations. It is an old idea, and it is a conservative one, most of all, in the profound sense of promising to check and balance tyrannical power. Indeed, the idea is believed to have first come up in a conflict between two of the Founding Fathers, Alexander Hamilton and Thomas Jefferson. Hamilton had proposed a federally chartered United States bank. Jefferson opposed it. The Constitution, he held, nowhere specifically authorized the federal government to charter a corporation. However, Jefferson had a deeper concern: that a federally chartered bank would become a magnet for large aggregations of capital that ultimately could overwhelm the states and dominate the country's economy. Jefferson prevailed over Hamilton.

More than a century later, the states—and almost the federal government—actually were being overwhelmed, but ironically by corporations which the states had chartered. In this wholly new factual setting the idea of federal chartering enjoyed a brief renaissance.

In July 1911 Senator John Sharp Williams introduced a bill for federal chartering. The Senate Committee on Interstate Commerce then held hearings to consider "what changes are necessary or desirable in the laws of the United States relating to the creation and control of corporations engaging in interstate commerce." One witness indicated that such corporations should be licensed by a federal commission and the license should be revoked for improper behavior. He claimed that corporate concentration had much to commend it, but said that in "order to protect the people against imposition on the part of the managers of these aggregations of wealth there should be some government control." The witness was none other than Judge Elbert Gary, chief executive officer of United States Steel.[3]

Those who consider themselves liberals should not be put off. Just eight years later another Chief Executive also endorsed federal chartering. "These great corporations are economic states," President Woodrow Wilson said in a special message to Congress on August 8, 1919. "They are no longer private corporations." He went on to recommend formulation of a law requiring a federal license of all corporations in interstate commerce. Such a license, or the conditions under which it would be issued, would embody specific regulations designed to secure competitive selling and prevent unconscionable profits in methods of marketing. He was responding to the problems created in the country's economic life by unfettered corporate trusts: inflated prices, inferior goods, and manipulation of government for their own ends. Because Wilson went unheeded the problems persisted, even though the trusts were restructured. In 1937, the late Senator Joseph C. O'Mahoney responded by reviving the concept of federal chartering. He, too, went unheeded. Today, we are beset by the great conglomerates and we still suffer the same antisocial effects as we did in the days of the trust —but on a grander scale.

The federal charter, foremost, provides the mechanism to clarify the appropriate roles of the government and the corporation. A rational society has long-term economic goals and priorities. The legitimate government should set these goals and priorities free from undue influence by the corporation.

In most cases, such economic goals as better products and service at lower prices, and such social goals as maximum individual freedom and initiative, can best be achieved in a society in which competition is the regulator of the economy. Economic concentration obstructs the fulfillment of such goals.

Federal chartering would allow the government to define the role of the corporation. It could be used to restructure certain concentrated industries to introduce competition. In some cases the restructuring alone would suffice; in others new competitors would be encouraged to enter the field.

The charter would limit the business activities in which a business could engage. The conglomerate that is economically and socially unjustified would become legally impermissible. Thus, General Motors, say, could be permitted to make automobiles—but not to make locomotives, refrigerators, or any other unrelated product; and GM could be sharply restricted even as to the auto parts it could produce and as to its role in distribution of cars and trucks. International Telephone and Telegraph, if it chose to make telecommunications equipment, could be required to abandon such unrelated businesses as the baking of Wonder Bread and Hostess Twinkies, the housing and feeding of transients in Sheraton Hotels, the leasing of Avis cars, and the making of consumer loans to customers of the Aetna Finance Company. RCA could be compelled to get out of book publishing and CBS to free the New York Yankees.

Federal chartering then could halt and reverse the conglomerate tide; it could provide a more competitive economic structure and hold companies to sizes commensurate with human managerial capacities and effective competition. And we could be rid of those particularly abhorrent enterprises that exist not to make and sell products, but to deal in corporations and thus to enable the tycoons who run them to amass great personal power.

Decisions of this kind, of course, would be made by a chartering authority, subject to safeguards such as a special court of appeals. However, we do not pretend to do more than present an outline and to indicate the general direction a federal incorporation law should take. Nor do we pretend it is the total answer to all of the problems of society. But it can create the setting in which other fundamental reforms can move ahead.

A federal charter also could be the instrument to make management genuinely responsible not merely to itself but to a broader shareholder and public interest as well.

An attempt to accomplish this result was undertaken in Washington by a tiny band of dedicated young men and women, mostly lawyers, called the Project for Corporate Responsibility. In February 1970 the Project unveiled its "Campaign to Make General Motors Responsible." "Campaign GM," as it also was known, had very limited resources and very little time, yet it achieved truly impressive results—if the measuring rod is, as it should be, expansion of public awareness of the hitherto largely unperceived responsibility of GM (and, by implication, of other giant corporations) for problems such as pollution; carnage on the highways; the denial of a pittance from the massive Highway Trust Fund for mass transit; the needlessly extravagant costs of insuring, maintaining, and repairing cars; and the discrimination against blacks and women in executive and dealer echelons. Campaign GM generated significant attention and support on campuses across the country, in the Carnegie and Rockefeller foundations, in religious groups, among individual stockholders, and elsewhere.

But Campaign GM induced few stockholders, large or small, actually to vote their shares for its proposals, such as the addition of three "public interest" directors to the board of GM. Everyone knew from the start that the stockholder proposals would fail overwhelmingly, and they did. Such efforts are destined to go on failing, because the imperatives of investing (consider the university treasurer who is impelled to seek a maximum return to meet rising costs) and the dynamic of the corporation (if making maximum profits is not to be the primary goal, what is?) will make them fail. Appeals for sacrifice for the sake of broader interests can achieve only partial, fleeting success. But Campaign GM greatly enlarged public understanding of the need to change the rules to make those broader interests ascendant. Thus, it improved the climate for possible true reform—by which we mean federal charters.

Another advantage of the chartering process is that change could take place in a measured and reasonable manner over a period of time, so as not to disrupt the economy or cause stockholders needlesss shock. Indeed, past divestitures often have increased rather than diminished corporate efficiency and stockholder profits.[4]

Federal chartering would allow the public government to regain its proper role as quarterback of the economy, without massive new bureaucracy and without that meddling which is rightly condemned. The government would do this by utilizing its powers to grant, modify, and implement or revoke charters to achieve adherence to national goals and priorities as set forth in federal statutes, such as those intended to preserve the environment. Yet, the day-to-day implementing of national goals would be in private hands.

Federal chartering, however, would not be sufficient in all cases. In certain areas of the economy, at least at certain times, competition simply does not work adequately, even where a "natural monopoly" does not exist. For example, adequate health services are lacking. Insurance firms often refuse to write new policies on inner city businesses, homes, and cars. Should government through regulation force corporations to do that which they do not want to do? Should the government itself take over the activities? Or should the government "bribe" the corporations with subsidies or tax favoritism?

A better solution would be government-owned enterprises to provide the services that any society purporting to be rational and humane must provide. Private industry would be free to compete with such government-owned enterprises whenever it determined it could do so. Surely veterans of the armed forces will appreciate this. The net cost to one of the authors for his $10,000 "term" insurance policy with the Veterans Administration has been as low as $16.00 a year. No private company can match this, or could be expected to. But the availability of "GI" insurance has been invaluable to millions, has provided a yardstick for measuring the value offered by private policies, and has, withal, hardly prevented the insurance industry from prospering mightily.

The largest and most successful of the few government-owned corporations in the United States is the Tennessee Valley Authority.

363

By making available abundant low-cost power, it has infused economic vitality into an entire region, in good part by enabling that region to compete with others for new industry. The TVA's costs and procedures are out in the open for all to see. Thus, it provides "yardsticks" for utilities, particularly in the Tennessee Valley. These private companies manage to survive and prosper, as does TVA. Clearly, then, a government-owned corporation can be a spur to competition. Without competition, however, a government-owned enterprise can stagnate or arrogate excessive power unto itself, no less than can a private one.

To help depose the government of oil, the legitimate government should establish a corporation of the TVA type to develop, exploit, and sell oil shale, the black rock that, under heat, yields oil. In the Green River formation in Colorado (and spreading into Utah and Wyoming) there is enough of it to supply the needs of the United States for two thousand years, at present levels of consumption; enough, to put it another way, to be worth $25,000 to every man, woman and child in the nation. The public already owns four-fifths of the oil shale reserves. This public ownership makes them an especially grave potential threat to the multibillion-dollar investment of the major petroleum companies in reserves of liquid oil, pipelines, and tankers. These companies have shown no zeal to develop oil shale. And, so long as they govern the government, oil shale will continue to remain significantly underdeveloped.

The idea of a government corporation of the TVA type was brought up by Morris Garnsey, a University of Colorado economist, before the Senate Subcommittee on Antitrust and Monopoly.[5] Ronnie Dugger of the *Texas Observer* gave it another airing in a review of Chris Welles's book *The Elusive Bonanza: The Story of Oil Shale.*[6] Such a corporation, Dugger said, "could fabulously endow the government" and in addition, could

> end or curb the pollution of oceans and beaches around the world by liquid oil. Producing oil from rock, either limiting the pollution to the one area of the Green River formation or avoiding pollution entirely by producing the shale oil *in situ*, the government could provide a yardstick against which the performance of the heavily subsidized oil industry could be tested. Obviously the national security would be better served by having all our oil inside the country.[7]

CONCLUSIONS AND RECOMMENDATIONS

What should be the function of federal regulatory agencies? A short answer as good as any once was given by Nicholas Johnson of the Federal Communications Commission. "People ask how you can improve the FCC," he said. "You cannot improve the FCC until you improve the political process of which it is a part."[8]

Applicable as that observation may be for all regulatory agencies, there is a case to be made for regulation of "natural" monopolies. There are a few of them. The telephone system comes closest—but even here, the FCC has obstructed certain avenues for competition, an example being its long-lasting insistence that only those phones manufactured by Western Electric, the wholly owned subsidiary of American Telephone and Telegraph, could be used on AT&T lines. This has changed only recently. Indeed, even here modern technology may make feasible competitive communications systems.

Where a "natural" monopoly is not present, there is scant justification for the government to restrict entry—to bar, for example, anyone meeting essential requirements from opening a new bank, launching a new airline, entering the trucking business, or starting to haul barges on inland waterways. Still less justification exists for the government to set rates, as it does in interstate transportation industries.

Just how is the Civil Aeronautics Board serving the traveling public when it allows Eastern Airlines to charge $27.00 for the 205-mile hourly shuttle flight between New York and Washington, or 13.1 cents per mile, while PSA, an airline that operates intrastate in California and, fortunately, is therefore beyond the reach of the CAB, charges $16.20 for the 347-mile hourly shuttle flight between Los Angeles and San Francisco, or 4.6 cents per mile?

The CAB might argue it must allow higher rates to subsidize unprofitable service elsewhere which the public requires. However, such situations are likely prospects for the government-owned corporation.

Competition must be developed in the industries that are now regulated; entry barriers must be lowered, and prices should be allowed to fluctuate freely with the market. The contrast between the fares for Eastern's New York–Washington shuttle and PSA's Los Angeles–San Francisco shuttle makes the point, even allowing for Eastern's guarantee that it will provide another plane if the shuttle fills up. PSA provides other airlines with real competition. Had San Francisco been in one state and Los Angeles in another, the CAB probably would have raised a barrier to PSA's entry. Had it gotten into the market, it surely would be charging higher fares—maybe $45.00 instead of $16.20, on the basis of Eastern's per-mile rate.

Certain industries always will require a specific type of regulation—such as for solvency in banking—but such regulation should be restricted to the specific areas where competition is not adequate to protect the public.

At a minimum, a plan proposed by Milton Friedman, the University of Chicago economist, would make better sense than the present system. He has said:

> Suppose, however, that the government, in its infinite wisdom, decides to limit the number who may engage in any activity to a smaller number than wish to do so. The least it can do is to avoid giveaways. It can adopt the method Alaska used to assign oil leases; decide how many people it is going to permit in an activity, specify the terms and conditions, announce these publicly, and hold an open auction to decide which particular persons will engage in the activity.
>
> This is a simple and direct way to end giveaways. TV licenses can be auctioned off instead of assigned without charge. . . . Rights to particular air routes, to establish one of a limited number of liquor stores, to operate one of a limited number of cabs—each and every one of these can be auctioned off. The public will still suffer from governmentally created monopoly, but at least it will recover some of its loss in the form of revenue.[9]

It is clear, however, that where health and safety are concerned competition alone cannot be relied upon to protect the public. A person who buys a sirloin roast will be utterly unaware that it may contain residues of antibiotics, transmitted from animal feeds, to which she or a member of her family may be allergic or sensitive. Thalidomide taught us that the human embryo can be deformed or otherwise injured by a chemical ingested by its mother at critical points in pregnancy. If that chemical is a potent medicine prescribed by a physician, and if the physician has been misled into prescribing it by a false claim in an advertisement, how can the supremely defenseless fetus protect itself? Surely not with competition.

One need only look at the enormous bloodshed inflicted by unsafe household products for incontrovertible evidence about the folly of trusting totally to competition in this area. According to an estimate by the Department of Health, Education, and Welfare, these products inflict at least 20 million injuries per year, of which 30,000 are fatal, 110,000 permanently disabling, and 585,000 serious enough to require hospitalization.[10]

The National Commission on Product Safety found that competition can work *against* safety. For example, manufacturers of oil-based furniture polishes compete, in part, by tinting their products to make them identical in color with cherry or lemon soda pop. This explains why children by the thousands swallow them and suffer sometimes fatal chemical pneumonia.[11] The impersonal forces of the marketplace have not been shown to be willing to reward, to take another example, the manufacturer of a safe rotary lawnmower any more than the manufacturer of a machine that amputates fingers or throws a stray pebble with such force that it blinds a boy in the next yard.

But there *can* be competition to make safer products if the government stimulates it. The Product Safety Commission recognized this when, in its report to President Nixon and Congress, it said "that the greatest promise for reducing risk resides in energizing the manufacturer's ingenuity." Consistent with this, the commission recommended—and we endorse—an omnibus new product safety law. It would create a new safety agency to develop, set, and enforce mandatory product safety standards where voluntary means fail. The agency would be empowered to compel manufacturers to recall and stop distributing unsafe products and to warn consumers. The President would appoint an independent safety advocate, or "ombudsman," who would work to overcome the bureaucratic rot that so often afflicts regulatory agencies.

This legislation would complement the proposals for an independent consumer agency which, among other things, would be empowered to represent the consumer interest before federal agencies, including the Federal Trade Commission, the Federal Communications Commission, the Justice Department, and the Food and Drug Administration, and in the courts. In 1970, a bipartisan coalition came close to getting such legislation through Congress, and in 1971 they should succeed.

The government, so often derided as a parasitic enemy of business, has an enormous untapped, and generally unrecognized, potential to stimulate socially useful competition. The bill recommended by the National Commission on Product Safety is but one example. Elsewhere in the consumer marketplace, the government should require suppliers to give buyers the full facts about their products, as the Federal Trade Commission moved to do in December 1970 in the case of gasoline octane ratings.

Consider the food industry. Processors of fruits and vegetables should be required to disclose on container labels the quality of the contents as graded under a simplified federal system, the date of processing and the weight of syrups or other "fillers." Packers of sausage and bologna products should be required to disclose on the label not only the proportion of fat, but also the protein value. Makers of "fruit drinks" should disclose the percentage that is fruit and the percentage that is water. Similarly, the buyer of a can of "mixed nuts" should be able to determine at a glance what is the proportion of peanuts, and the buyer of a chicken pot pie should know just how much chicken is present. And the FTC should adopt the proposal by the Center for Study of Responsive Law to make advertisers provide substantial evidence for claims about efficacy, performance, and safety. Such simple and even homely reforms would do much to bring about true competition, which presumes fully informed buyers as well as fully informed sellers.

If competition is to work effectively—even within the parameters we have outlined—tough enforcement of the antitrust laws remains necessary.

Since 1890, the Sherman Act—the basic antitrust statute—has been the law of the land. And the basic premise of antitrust legislation, as described by Justice William O. Douglas, is this:

> Industrialized power should be decentralized. It should be scattered into many hands so that the fortune of the people will not be dependent on the whim or caprice, the political prejudice, the emotional stability of a few self-appointed men. The fact that they are not vicious men, but respectable and social-minded is irrelevant. That is the philosophy and command of the Sherman Act. It was founded on a theory of hostility to the concentration in private hands of power so great that only a government of the people should have it.[12]

The problem, however has been not with the philosophy of the Sherman Act, but with a chronic failure to enforce it.

In 1950, Congress enacted Section 7 of the Clayton Act to prohibit any corporation from acquiring another, in whole or in part, where the effect of such an acquisition may be substantially to lessen competition or to tend to create a monopoly of any line of commerce in any section of the country. The Supreme Court, in a series of decisions over a period of years up to the present, has been a "strict constructionist" of Section 7 and other antitrust legislation. But the tide of economic concentration, while it may have been slowed, has not been held back.

That the laws have not worked as well as they should have is, again, less a criticism of their intrinsic merit than a tribute to the efficacy of interlaced economic and political power. Insufficient action has been taken against existing concentration because of the shackles that economic power clamps on political power. After all, even existing antitrust statutes as interpreted by the Supreme Court allow attacks to be made on highly concentrated markets. Yet the Justice Department and the Federal Trade Commission, unfortunately, have not fully exercised the franchise given them by the Court, even if they have attacked certain mergers. It suffices to say that the leaders of the antitrust agencies have for the most part been good and capable public servants—but not foolhardy. It cannot be said that deconcentration is an insuperable task, assuming it could be undertaken untrammeled by economic-political power. At hearings of the Senate Antitrust and Monopoly Subcommittee, Dr. John M. Blair has pointed out that deconcentration of a mere eight industries would reduce the share of the industrial economy that is highly concentrated from one-third to one-sixth.[13]

With federal chartering as a method of achieving deconcentration, the antitrust agencies could concentrate on anticompetitive behavior and on keeping a more watchful eye on the mergers such chartering would allow. Thus, federal chartering and antitrust would complement each other and the work of the antitrust agencies could become more effective.

Steps consistent with our thesis could make important contributions to protection of the environment. As in the case of safety, for example, one of the government's roles should be to stimulate competition in the development of products and processes that minimize pollution. This is an eminently practical concept. Senator Magnuson has put it to work in a proposal, incorporated in the 1970 "clean air" amendments, which provides what amounts to a bounty to motor vehicle manufacturers who are willing to supply the large government market with cars that are significantly less polluting than their competitors.

Another way to attack pollution is to make it pay its way. A company that contaminates the air makes those of us who breathe pay the bill, in terms of damage to life and our surroundings. Such a company "externalizes" its costs, that is, makes others pay them. If such costs were to be "internalized" there would be less pollution.

Finally, there must be an end to the permissiveness which has characterized the handling of corporate polluters by the Justice Department and other prosecutors and the courts. Through the first six decades of the twentieth century, federal laws against pollution of the nation's waterways went totally unenforced, with calamitous result. While the clear waters were turned into brown, purple, and red cesspools; while aquatic life became extinct; while great rivers became unfit for recreation; while all this was happening, a vagrant was likely to be arrested for urinating in the Hudson River. Who are the "coddled" criminals?

On many of the relatively infrequent occasions when giant corporations have been charged with and convicted of crime, they have eluded the publicity that normally would attend similarly unfortunate human beings. In addition, government agencies often have shown a peculiar disinclination to charge the executives responsible for their corporations' criminal behavior. For example, the *Physicians' Desk Reference,* the most widely used prescribing guide, says in its foreword that each description therein of a drug product "has been prepared by the manufacturer, and edited and approved by the manufacturer's *medical department, medical director,* or *medical counsel."* [Emphasis supplied.] In other words, human beings, who were paid to do so, wrote each entry. During the mid-1960s, under the spur of Dr. Robert S. McCleery, a dedicated physician then with the Food and Drug Administration, the FDA, through the Justice Department, filed criminal charges against pharmaceutical firms that published false and misleading entries in the *PDR* (and medical journals as well). But never did the charges—usually filed without announcement—name an individual in any accused corporation.

The National Commission on Reform of Federal Criminal Laws, whose chairman is Edmund G. Brown, the former governor of California, has productively examined such questions. In June 1970, in its *Study Draft of a New Federal Criminal Code,* the commission bit the bullet. It recommended revisions of the code under which:

CONCLUSIONS AND RECOMMENDATIONS

First, a person would be "legally accountable for any conduct he performs or causes to be performed in the name of an organization or in its behalf to the same extent as if the conduct were performed in his own name or behalf." In addition, he would be legally accountable for failing to perform an act required by law or regulation in an area in which he has "primary responsibility."

Second, a person responsible for supervising "relevant activities" in a corporation would be "guilty of an offense" if by willful default within the range of his responsibility he "contributes to the occurrence of an offense for which the organization may be convicted."

Third, when an organization is convicted, the court, in addition to or in lieu of "other authorized sanctions," can "require the organization to give appropriate publicity to the conviction by notice to the class or classes of persons or sector of the public interested in or affected by the conviction, *by advertising in designated areas or by designated media, or otherwise.*" [Emphasis supplied.][14]

In its *Final Report*, issued in January 1971, the Commission wholly ignored the recommendations for publicizing convictions. Possibly its thrust toward even-handed justice was too strong for some business-oriented members.

The voters may look to the government to countervail corporate power, but it does not. Instead, the government enhances it, joins with it, and begins to operate a welfare state for corporations. The voters may want to protest, but in the polling booths they can register their frustrations only on a diffuse, incoherent level; they have no reliable way to make particular protests known. A citizen who votes for candidates promising to repress, say, crime in the streets and high prices in the marketplace may reasonably look forward to repression of civil liberties—but not of inflation.

We are not likely to get fundamental reforms, including a fair tax structure, so long as candidates for public office remain indentured to the concentrated industries that finance their campaigns. Thus, it is of great importance to limit the sums that can be spent on campaigns. Anthony Lewis, chief of the London bureau of the *New York Times*, said in a column:

> The ideal in a democracy presumably ought to be that a candidate's wealth, or his party's, should not substantially affect the outcome of an

371

election. The British approach that ideal in practice. In the crucial battle-ground of the modern campaign, money is simply excluded as a significant factor. That is the way the rules work.

No candidate or party may buy television time or advertising. There are no political spot announcements. Instead, each major party is allotted a number of free ten-minute periods for straight political broadcasts. The number is worked out by consultation with the parties, according to their relative strength. In this election [in 1970], Labor and the Conservatives had five each.

But the main political impact of television, and it is great, comes from straight news and feature coverage. The networks cover the main speeches and the daily press conferences by the party leaders, and invite them in for interviews and other special programs.

In short, the display of politicians on television depends mainly on professional news judgment, rather than money. That is subject, naturally, to a general requirement of equal treatment.

Compare the situation in the United States—the scandalous situation. There, antique and ill-drawn statutes provide no effective limit on what may be spent in campaigns. . . . Surely it is wrong to make the most power-ful office in the world [the Presidency] depend on how many spot announce-ments a candidate can buy.[15]

Lewis said that the United States should by now be ready to prohibit television advertising and time purchase altogether in presidential elec-tions. Had this been done in time for the 1968 election, various industries might not have been able to provide a winning margin to elect Richard Nixon. If Lewis's advice is heeded in time for 1972, the electorate actually might choose the President. Lewis acknowledged that his proposal "would still leave great advantages for the moneyed in presidential primaries and in all other elections." But, he said, "it would be a beginning." Amen.

In an act of singular courage, the American Broadcasting Company's Frank Reynolds urged the abolition of televised political spot announce-ments. These commercials are "made to order for trickery, innuendo, im-plications of treason, smear and irrelevance," he said on ABC's evening news program on October 13, 1970. The day before, in an act of singular cynicism, President Nixon had vetoed a bill to limit the sums candidates could spend on TV and radio. Extremely modest though it was, the bill was the first significant reform of its kind that Congress had enacted since the Corrupt Practices Act of 1925. "I am as opposed to big spending in campaigns as I am to big spending in government," Mr. Nixon said in his veto message. This was as piously hypocritical as it was pompously symmetrical. "The Republican Party's five national committees expect to spend a record $11 million in this year's campaigns," Bernard D. Nossiter reported in the *Washington Post* five days after the veto. "The total, disclosed in interviews by party officials, is *nearly twice* the previous off-year peak recorded in 1966 and about *five times* as much as three comparable Democratic committees are raising and spending." [Emphasis supplied.]

The "ultimate goal" in handling campaign financing long has been, in President Johnson's words, "to finance the total expense for this vital function of our democracy with public funds, and to prohibit the use or acceptance of money from private sources."[16] This would give the public one of the greatest bargains of all time, because men in public life would be better insulated from pressures to sell out the public interest.

"Without criticism and reliable and intelligible reporting, the government cannot govern," Walter Lippmann once said. "For there is no adequate way in which it can keep itself informed about what the people of the country are thinking and doing and wanting. The government intelligence service is an insufficient provider of the knowledge which the government must have in order to legislate well and to administer public affairs."[17] But Lippmann, as we understand him, was thinking exclusively in terms of conventional national and foreign issues. We go further. We say there must be, in addition, reliable and intelligible reporting about the subgovernments of business and about the media's own faults and errors. These, as the Commission on Freedom of the Press said more than two decades ago, "have ceased to be private vagaries and have become public dangers."

The views of an owner obviously make an impact on media content and comment. This has become of greater concern with the growth of the chains and the emergence of local press monopolies in all but a few cities and towns. To be sure, there are, as Bryce W. Rucker, professor of journalism at Southern Illinois University, has acknowledged, "other rich sources of national and international news."[18] Yet, he said, "in most cities it falls to the newspaper to provide more than cursory local news and comment." He continued:

Those who own the mass media, unfortunately, have extensive non-communications financial investments. Newspaper publishers own large interests in the oil industry, mining, manufacturing, transportation, farming, ranching, timbering and so forth. [In 1970 Field Enterprises, owner of the *Chicago Daily News* and the *Chicago Sun-Times,* launched a large cosmetics firm, Field Creations.] The noncommunications holdings of broadcasters are even more extensive and varied. Need I review the holdings of Radio Corporation of America (NBC) . . . or Metromedia (a large chain)? The grave danger here is that consumers of their information and comment are unaware of the special interests for which the mass media plead. Under these circumstances how can we evaluate the news and editorial content of a newspaper or broadcasting station when events under discussion affect the financial well-being of the owners? Can we trust those who profit from war to discuss over their networks the relative merits of war and peace in a given situation? Can we trust the editorials of those who own oil interests to be untainted when they discuss oil depletion allowances or shale oil? To what extent are these people using the mass media to enrich themselves and to the detriment of their communities and their nation? These questions go to the heart of the matter.[19]

In Canada, a special committee of the Canadian Senate did go to the heart of the matter, in a study of the mass media that lasted twenty months and fills three volumes. "Rarely has any previous document had such free-swinging frankness as to term Nova Scotia and New Brunswick 'journalistic disaster areas' or to refer to 'the flatulent nature' of some editorial products," Robert H. Estabrook of the *Washington Post* wrote. Newspaper chains control 77 of Canada's 116 dailies. The most fundamental conclusion in the report about the effects of such concentration was that Canada "should no longer tolerate a situation where the public interest in so vital a field as information is dependent on the greed or good will of an extremely privileged group of businessmen."[20] Neither should the United States tolerate such a situation.

As a beginning, Congress should enact a bill advocated by Senator Thomas J. McIntyre (D–N.H.) to arrest the trend toward media concentration. In its tentative form, this legislation would prohibit an owner of five or more daily newspapers from acquiring any additional newspapers hereafter. To thin out local media monopolies, the bill would prohibit an owner of a daily newspaper from henceforth owning or controlling any radio or television station in the same standard metropolitan statistical area in which his paper is published. Existing newspaper chains would not be required to divest themselves of any newspaper properties, but existing newspaper-broadcast combinations in specific markets would have to sell off one or more of their properties within three years.[20] And progress toward assuring an independent, democratic, and robust press could be achieved with numerous other devices—for example, a court interpretation of the First Amendment to give access for comment and rebuttal in publications that refuse even to print letters to the editor, including the *Reader's Digest,* the *New Yorker,* and *U.S. News and World Report.*

Commercial broadcasters could be taxed for their use of the public's airwaves, with the proceeds to go to public broadcasting. Networks should be licensed. Public hearings on the granting, transfer, and renewal of broadcast licenses should be automatic in the case of large operations and mandatory in other cases if a significant number of requests is made.

Useful as all of these proposals may be, we would take the basic precaution of including in any legislation for federal chartering a ban on ownership of communications media by unrelated interests, or vice versa, except for house organs and other special situations. Most of all, that means there could be only minimal ownership of such media, including book publishers, by conglomerate industrial corporations and banks. For the very reasons that we object to ownership of communications media by public governments we must also object to such ownership by private governments.

We take the same approach to banks. They wisely had been restricted to banking. Now, because of the insidious one-bank holding company device, they have moved far from their proper role into numerous other areas of the economy. There has been no more alarming example of creeping (or is it sprinting?) private socialism. If anything, an economy controlled by the sources of money can be more hostile to an enduring free society than an economy controlled by the owners of the means of production.

All national banks, which already are federally chartered, should be restricted to banking only, and their charters should fix limits on their total assets. Certainly, they should not be allowed to interlock with any corporations or to make large loans to enterprises in competition with one another.

Inexorably, over any substantial period of time, economic power translates into political power. The process fattens on itself, increasing its mass as it gains momentum. Once the process is under way, once it builds a private socialism in which ownership of communications media, of banking, and of the means of production is concentrated in a few corporate hands, democratic institutions cannot flourish and, indeed, are undermined.

State socialism suffers from similar handicaps. When political power and economic power are concentrated in the state, the corporation is the state, or the state is the corporation—take your pick. The bureaucracy set up to run the system owns it, in all but a literal sense. "The Soviet Union today is like a huge company town," I. F. Stone, the independent journalist, has said.[21] To say, as some do, that the citizen owns the means of production is to be absurd. An Englishman who disapproves of government management of the nationalized coal industry can do no more in the polling place to change it than could a small English stockholder who previously disapproved of private management. The root of the evil is concentrated economic power. It cannot be entrusted to either private or public hands.

Gabriel Kolko, the brilliant radical historian, has said: "Ever since the days of Theodore Roosevelt and Woodrow Wilson corporate monopoly has been not just another interest group in American life, but . . . the keystone of power which defines the essential preconditions and functions of the larger American social order."[22] The more conservative editors of the *Antitrust Law and Economics Review* have a similar message:

> The complaints of our young and disadvantaged are not directed to the workings of small scale enterprise in our atomistic industries, but to the country's industrial heartland, to the several hundred firms that hold leading positions in our major oligopolies, and that, by virtue of those positions, exercise a significant amount of power—both economic and political—over vast numbers of other human beings in our society.[23]

Now that modern technology is making the giant corporation obsolete, there is no remaining justification for excessive corporate power. Neither private socialism nor public socialism is permissible for a society that seeks to fulfill democratic aspirations and to free the individual to exercise independent choice and initiative. Concentrated

376

economic power lies at the core of much of the unrest, injustice, and unresponsive government that beset us. Until it is removed we can fiddle with this and that, but true progress will elude us.

POSTSCRIPT

It is the vice of a vulgar mind to be thrilled by bigness, to think that a thousand square miles are a thousand times more wonderful than one square mile, and that a million square miles are almost the same as heaven.

—Uncle Ernst in the late E. M. Forster's *Howard's End* (New York: Knopf, 1921), p. 36.

NOTES

PROLOGUE

1. Speech to the American Society of Newspaper Editors, Washington, D.C., January 17, 1925.

2. New Haven: Yale University Press, 1937, p. 268.

3. Testimony of Joseph A. Califano, Jr., in hearings before the Executive and Legislative Reorganization Subcommittee of the Committee on Government Operations, House of Representatives, Ninety-first Congress, First Session, Part 1, *Organizing Federal Consumer Activities,* September 16, 1969, p. 111.

4. Daniels, claim manager for the Detroit Automobile Inter-Insurance Exchange, criticized the adoption of "entirely decorative" bumpers in a paper given before the American Society of Body Engineers on October 2, 1968. The paper has been reprinted in Hearings before Subcommittees of the Select Committee on Small Business, United States Senate, Ninetieth Congress, Second Session, *Planning, Regulation, and Competition: Automobile Industry—1968,* pp. 471-73.

5. Testimony of Mack W. Worden, vice president of General Motors for marketing, at Hearings before the Subcommittee on Antitrust and Monopoly of the Committee on the Judiciary, United States Senate, Ninety-first Congress. First Session, *Automotive Repair Industry,* October 14, 1969.

6. Opening statement of Senator Philip A. Hart, Hearings before the Subcommittee on Antitrust and Monopoly of the Committee on the Judiciary, United States Senate, Ninetieth Congress, Second Session, Part 1, *Automotive Repair Industry,* December 3, 1968, p. 3. Donald A. Randall of the Subcommittee staff developed the $1-billion estimate on parts.

7. New York: Grossman, 1965.

8. Speech at the annual meeting of the American Association for the Advancement of Science, December 30, 1967.

9. Statement for a Hearing before the Committee on Commerce, United States Senate, Ninetieth Congress, Second Session, *Implementation of the National Traffic and Motor Vehicle Safety Act of 1966,* April 25, 1968, p. 322.

10. *Unsafe at Any Speed, op. cit.* (above, note 7), p. 92.

11. Some of the pictures, along with related data, are reproduced in *Implementation of the National Traffic and Motor Vehicle Safety Act of 1966, op. cit.* (above, note 9), pp. 368-81.

12. Daniels, *op. cit.* (above, note 4), p. 473.

13. Hearings before the Subcommittee on Monopoly of the Select Committee on

Small Business, United States Senate, Ninety-first Congress, *Competitive Problems in the Drug Industry,* May 7, 1969, pp. 5029–30.

14. *Washington Post,* June 20, 1968, p. A3:1.

15. *Competitive Problems in the Drug Industry, op. cit.* (above, note 13), p. 5165.

16. The dependence of the *Journal* on pharmaceutical advertising, and the repeated use of that publication for advertisements which the Food and Drug Administration has deemed false and misleading, is documented by Morton Mintz in *By Prescription Only* (Boston: Beacon and Houghton Mifflin, 1967) and in numerous articles in the *Washington Post,* the *New Republic* and the *Progressive.*

17. "The Massive Statistics of General Motors," *Fortune,* July 15, 1966.

18. Testimony of Ralph Nader, *Planning, Regulation and Competition, op. cit.* (above, note 4), p. 102n.

19. Arnold made the statement, cited in *Planning, Regulation and Competition, op. cit.* (above, note 4), p. 147, in 1959 in testifying before the Subcommittee on Antitrust and Monopoly of the Committee on the Judiciary, United States Senate, in behalf of a bill to divest GM of the General Motors Acceptance Corporation.

20. Hearings before the Subcommittee on Antitrust and Monopoly of the Committee on the Judiciary, United States Senate, Ninetieth Congress, Second Session, *Economic Concentration,* Part 7, April 2, 1968, p. 3446. Dr. Sohmen is a member of the Department of Economics, University of the Saar, Saarbrucken, Germany.

21. *Private Power and American Democracy* (New York: Knopf, 1966), p. 39.

22. *The New Freedom* (New York: Doubleday, 1913), pp. 57–58.

23. Remarks to the Lawyers Club of the University of Michigan, Ann Arbor, Michigan, April 8, 1969.

24. Hearings before the Subcommittee on Antitrust and Monopoly of the Committee on the Judiciary, United States Senate, Ninety-first Congress, First Session, *The Newspaper Preservation Act,* June 20, 1969, pp. 294–98.

25. New York: Simon and Schuster, 1968, pp. 432–33.

26. *Congressional Record,* April 15, 1969, p. S3757.

27. "Oil-Gas Industry Is Powerful Lobby Force," *Congressional Quarterly,* November 29, 1968.

28. Speech to the National Press Club, Washington, D.C., December 9, 1969. Gardner was then chairman of the Urban Coalition Action Council. He later founded, and heads, Common Cause.

29. Speech to Consumer Assembly '69, Washington, D.C., January 30, 1969.

30. Consumers' Protection Message, March 15, 1962.

31. *By Prescription Only, op. cit.* (above, note 16), p. 184.

32. This was established in Hearings before a Subcommittee of the Committee on Government Operations, House of Representatives, *Drug Safety,* Parts 3 and 5, 1965 and 1966, and summarized in *By Prescription Only, op. cit.* (above, note 16). An example, involving an antidepressant tradenamed Parnate, is set out in *Prescription* on pp. 199–213, and 213d–g.

33. *Washington Post,* July 9, 1969, p. A13:1.

34. *Washington Post,* May 17, 1969.

35. Statement by Thomas P. F. Hoving, chairman of the National Citizens Com-

mittee for Broadcasting, New York City, November 10, 1969. The statement assembled documentation from *Broadcasting* magazine and the *New York Times*.

36. Edited by Marvin Barrett (New York: Grosset and Dunlap, 1969), p. 5.

37. Statement of Commissioner Nicholas Johnson of the Federal Communications Commission to the National Commission on the Causes and Prevention of Violence, Washington, D.C., December 19, 1968.

38. *Ibid.*

39. *Ibid.*

40. Boston: (Houghton Mifflin, 1964), pp. 44–45.

41. *Ibid.*

42. *The Federalist*, No. 47, 1788 (New York: Modern Library), p. 313.

43. Hearings before the Subcommittee on Antitrust and Monopoly of the Committee on the Judiciary, United States Senate, Eighty-ninth Congress, *Economic Concentration, Part 2*, April 21, 1965, p. 810.

44. Speech before the Georgia Bar Association, Savannah, Ga.

45. Special message to Congress endorsing what became the Public Utility Holding Company Act of 1935.

46. *American Individualism* (New York: Doubleday, 1922), p. 18.

47. *Studies by the Staff of the Cabinet Committee on Price Stability* (Washington: 1969).

48. Speech to the Economic Club of Detroit, January 27, 1969.

49. Cited by Senator Philip A. Hart in a speech to the Antitrust Section, American Bar Association, Washington, D.C., April 4, 1968.

50. *Ibid.*

51. Hearings before the Subcommittee on Monopoly of the Select Committee on Small Business, United States Senate, Ninety-first Congress, First Session, *Role of Giant Corporations*, Part 1, July 10, 1969, p. 2.

52. *Giant Business: Threat to Democracy* (New York: Exposition Press, 1953), p. 106.

53. *The Screwtape Letters and Screwtape Proposes* (New York: Macmillan, 1961), preface.

54. *Giant Business, op. cit.* (above, note 52), p. 145.

55. *Commercal Banks and Their Trust Activities: Emerging Influence on the American Economy*, Volume 1, Ninetieth Congress, July 8, 1968. The cited findings are taken almost entirely from the "Summary and Conclusions," pp. 1–5.

56. *San Francisco Examiner and Chronicle*, September 7, 1969.

57. "The General Electric Company is, justly, one of the most respected of American corporations," Berle said in *The Twentieth Century Capitalist Revolution* (New York: Harcourt, 1954), p. 83. "Its management has been able and of unquestioned integrity." Of course, GE "was the kingpin of the greatest criminal price conspiracy known to the antitrust laws," as Nossiter points out in *The Mythmakers, op. cit.* (note 40, above), p. 85.

58. New York: Doubleday, 1921.

59. *Ibid.*, p. 4.

60. *Ibid.*, p. 7.

61. *Ibid.*, p. 82.

62. *Ibid.*, p. 87.

63. *Ibid.*, p. 134.

64. *Ibid.*, pp. 162–64.

65. *Ibid.*, p. 169.

66. *Ibid.*, p. 140.

67. *Ibid.*, p. 312.

68. *Ibid.*, p. 282.

69. *An Inquiry Into the Nature and Causes of the Wealth of Nations*, (New York: Modern Library, 1937), p. 460.

70. *Planning, Regulation, and Competition, op. cit.* (above, note 4), pp. 910–12.

71. *Fortune, op. cit.* (above, note 17).

72. *Planning, Regulation, and Competition, op. cit.* (above, note 4), pp. 910–12.

73. *Ibid.*

74. Boston: Houghton Mifflin, 1967.

75. *Ibid.*, p. 382.

76. Hearing before Subcommittees of the Select Committee on Small Business, United States Senate, Ninetieth Congress, First Session, *Planning, Regulation, and Competition*, June 29, 1967, p. 12.

77. "The Corporation: How Much Power? What Scope?" *The Corporation in Modern Society*, edited by Edward S. Mason, (Cambridge, Mass.: Harvard University Press, 1959), p. 99.

78. Speech to the American Political Science Association, New York, September 7, 1966.

79. *The Liberal Hour* (Boston: Houghton Mifflin, 1960), p. 111.

80. "How to Prevent Organizational Dry Rot," *Harper's Magazine*, October 1965, p. 20.

81. *A Free and Responsible Press* (Chicago: University of Chicago Press, 1947), p. 3.

82. *Washington Post*, January 15, 1969.

83. *Washington Post*, December 5, 1968.

84. *Washington Post*, December 28, 29, 30, 1969.

85. "The ABC-ITT Merger Case: Reconsideration, Dissenting Opinion of Commissioners Robert T. Bartley, Kenneth A. Cox, and Nicholas Johnson," June 22, 1967, pp. 8–9.

86. *Ibid.*, pp. 84–86.

87. *Washington Post*, January 12, 1970, Bl:1.

88. Winter 1967/1968, p. 3.

89. "Proposed Conclusions and Brief Submitted by the Department of Justice, before the Federal Communications Commission," May 29, 1967, p. 67.

90. "Merger Case," *op. cit.*, (above, note 85), pp. 28–33.

91. *Washington Post*, July 8, 1967.

92. Speech on CBS Radio Network, June 27, 1968; published in *Nixon Speaks Out* (New York: Nixon-Agnew Campaign Committee, 1968), pp. 9–19.

93. "Reflections on the McCarthy Campaign," *Harper's Magazine*, May 1969, p. 94. During the 1968 presidential campaign Goodwin wrote speeches for Senator McCarthy and the late Senator Robert F. Kennedy. Tom Hayden is a leader of the New Left.

94. *The New Industrial State, op. cit.* (above, note 74), p. viii.

95. "The Case Against Big Business," *Fortune*, May 1952.

96. *Planning, Regulation, and Competition, op. cit.* (above, note 76), pp. 12–13.

97. *The New Industrial State, op. cit.* (above, note 74), p. 76

98. Testimony of Ralph Nader, Hearings before the Subcommittee on Executive Reorganization of the Committee on Government Operations, United States Senate, Ninety-first Congress, First Session, *Establish a Department of Consumer Affairs,* March 20, 1969, p. 383.

99. Address to the Eighth International Congress of Accountants, New York City, September 24, 1962.

100. Hearings before the Subcommittee on Antitrust and Monopoly of the Committee on the Judiciary, United States Senate, Eighty-ninth Congress, First Session, *Economic Concentration,* Part 3, pp. 1313–14. Lehman's biography was *This High Man, the Life of Robert H. Goddard* (New York: Farrar, 1963).

101. "Big Steel, Invention and Innovation," *Quart, J. Econ.,* May 1966; reprinted in *Economic Concentration, op. cit.* (above, note 100), pp. 3098–111.

102. *Planning, Regulation, and Competition, op. cit.* (above, note 76), p. 14. The citation to *Business Week* was November 16, 1963, pp. 144–46.

103. *Giant Business, op. cit.* (above, note 52), pp. 192–94.

104. *The Federalist, op. cit.* (above, note 42), cited by Edward Mead Earle in the Introduction, p. xx.

CHAPTER ONE: A TOUR THROUGH A STATE OF CONCENTRATION

1. *Washington Post,* June 2, 1966, p. A21. Eleven days after the column was printed, the U.S. Supreme Court decided *U.S.* v. *Pabst Brewing Co.,* 384 U.S. 546. Justice William O. Douglas used the column as the appendix to his concurring opinion.

2. Hearings before the Subcommittee on Antitrust and Monopoly of the Committee on the Judiciary, United States Senate, Ninety-first Congress, Second Session, *Economic Concentration,* Part 8: *The Conglomerate Merger Problem,* November 4, 5, 6, 1969, January 28, February 5, 18, 19, 1970, p. 4544.

3. *Economic Report on Corporate Mergers,* prepared by the Bureau of Economics, Federal Trade Commission, Commerce Clearing House Edition, p. 3.

4. Hearings before the Subcommittee on Antitrust and Monopoly of the Committee on the Judiciary, United States Senate, Eighty-eighth Congress, Second Session, *Economic Concentration,* Part 1: *Overall and Conglomerate Aspects,* July 1, 2, September 9, 10, 11, 1964, p. 203.

5. *Op. cit.* (above, note 2), p. 4544, Table I.

6. See testimony of Dr. John M. Blair, Hearings before the Subcommittee on Antitrust and Monopoly of the Committee on the Judiciary, United States Senate, Eighty-ninth Congress, First Session, *Economic Concentration,* Part 2: *Mergers and Other Factors Affecting Industry Concentration,* March 16, 17, 18, April 13, 14, 15 and 21, 1965, p. 651ff.

7. *Corporate Mergers, op. cit.* (above, note 3), Chapter 4.

8. *Economic Concentration,* Part 2, *op. cit.* (above, note 6, pp. 667–68).

9. *Corporate Mergers, op. cit.* (above, note 3), figure 8–8.

10. *Economic Concentration,* Part 1, *op. cit.* (above, note 4), p. 155.

11. *Corporate Mergers, op. cit.* (above, note 3), pp. 5–33.

12. *Economic Concentration,* Part 8, *op. cit.* (above, note 2), p. 4815.

13. *Newsweek,* March 2, 1970, p. 61.

14. *The Business of Acquisitions and Mergers,* edited by G. Scott Hutchison (New York: Publishing House, Inc., 1968), p. 5.

15. *Op. cit.* (above, note 3), pp. 2–48.

16. Hearings before the Antitrust Subcommittee of the Committee on the Judiciary, House of Representatives, Ninety-first Congress, Second Session, *Investigation of Conglomerate Corporations,* Parts 1–7: *Government and Private Witnesses,* July 30, 1969, to May 15, 1970.

17. Boston: Houghton Mifflin, 1967, pp. 68–69.

18. *Giant Business: Threat to Democracy* (New York: Exposition Press, 1953), p. 117.

19. *Ibid.,* p. 177.

20. Hearings before the Subcommittee on Antitrust and Monopoly of the Committee on the Judiciary, United States Senate, Eighty-ninth Congress, Second Session, *Economic Concentration,* Part 5: *Concentration and Divisional Reporting,* September 12, 13, 19, 20, 1966, p. 1940.

21. Testimony of Dr. John M. Blair at Hearings before the Subcommittee on Antitrust and Monopoly of the Committee on the Judiciary, United States Senate, Eighty-ninth Congress, First Session, *Economic Concentration,* Part 4: *Concentration and Efficiency,* August 24, 25, 26, September 9, 10, 1965, pp. 1536, 1554.

22. The basic study is by Professor Samuel Richardson Reid, *Economic Concentration,* Part 5, *op. cit.* (above, note 20), p. 1914. Studies confirming his findings are by Professor Thomas F. Hogarty and Eamon M. Kelly, *Economic Concentration,* Part 8 *op. cit.* (above, note 2), pp. 4632, 4647.

23. *Studies by the Staff of the Cabinet Committee on Price Stability* (Washington: Government Printing Office, January 1969), p. 83.

24. *Op. cit.* (above, note 3), pp. 2–18.

25. *Economic Concentration,* Part 1, *op. cit.* (above, note 4), p. 248.

26. *Economic Concentration,* Part 8, *op. cit.* (above, note 2), p. 4603.

27. *Ibid.,* p. 4657.

28. Joe S. Bain, "Economics of Scale, Concentration and the Condition of Entry in Twenty Manufacturing Industries," *American Economic Review,* vol. 44, 1954, pp. 15–39. See also *Corporate Mergers, op. cit.* (above, note 3), pp. 2–19, 2–20 and footnotes.

29. Testimony of Dr. John M. Blair, *op. cit* (above, note 20), p. 1541.

30. *American Capitalism: The Concept of Countervailing Power,* (Boston: Houghton Mifflin, 1952), 1956 edition, p. 86.

31. Hearings before the Subcommittee on Antitrust and Monopoly of the Committee on the Judiciary, United States Senate, Ninety-first Congress, First Session, *Economic Concentration,* Part 3: *Concentration, Invention, and Innovation,* May 18, 24, 25, 27, June 17, 1965, p. 1075.

32. *Ibid.,* p. 1133.

NOTES

33. Hearings before the Subcommittee on Antitrust and Monopoly of the Committee on the Judiciary, United States Senate, Ninety-first Congress, First Session, *Economic Concentration*, Part 6: *New Technologies and Concentration*, September 19, 20, 22, 25, 26, 27, October 2, 3, 4, 6, 1967, pp. 2757ff.

34. See Hearings before the Subcommittee on Antitrust and Monopoly of the Committee on the Judiciary, United States Senate, Eighty-ninth Congress, First Session, *Economic Concentration*, Part 4, *Concentration and Efficiency*, August 24, 25, 26, September 9, 10, 1965.

35. *Economic Concentration*, Part 5, *op. cit.* (above, note 20), p. 1888.

36. Hearings before the Subcommittee on Antitrust and Monopoly of the Committee on the Judiciary, United States Senate, Eighty-ninth Congress, Second Session, *Possible Anticompetitive Effects of Sale of Network TV Advertising*, Parts 1 and 2, May 24, 25, 26, June 2, 3, December 12, 13, 14, 1966.

37. *Federal Trade Commission* v. *Procter & Gamble,* 386 U.S. 568, in which the Court ruled that the acquisition of Clorox by Proctor & Gamble was a violation of the antitrust laws.

38. October 15, 1968, p. 30.

39. May 15, 1967, p. 30.

40. *Economic Concentration,* Part 8, *op. cit.* (above, note 2), p. 4774.

41. July 24, 1969.

42. April 3, 1967, p. 3.

43. *Ibid.*

44. *Op. cit.* (above note 3), pp. 2–59.

45. *Ibid.,* pp. 2–73.

46. *New York Times,* May 24, 1970.

47. Hearings before the Subcommittee on Antitrust and Monopoly of the Committee on the Judiciary, United States Senate, Eighty-seventh Congress, Second Session, *Rail Merger Legislation,* Part 1, June 12, 13, 14, 15, 19, July 3, 5, 6, 11, 1962, p. 26.

48. April 18, 1968, p. 9.

49. February 15, 1967, p. 38.

50. These accounts are taken from Hearings before the Subcommittee on Antitrust and Monopoly of the Committee on the Judiciary, United States Senate, Ninety-first Congress, First Session, *The Insurance Industry,* Part 15: *State Regulation for Solvency, Conglomerates and Insurance Companies, and Case Study of One Non-Renewal,* February 24, 25, 26, March 4, 5, May 7, 1969. Testimony of Arthur Levitt, Jr., President of Cogan, Berlind, Weill and Levitt, Inc., p. 9443. Testimony of A. Addison Roberts, president, Reliance Insurance Co., p. 9515. Testimony of Marvin Finell, Chairman, Operating Committee, Great American Insurance Company and general counsel, National General Corporation, p. 9533.

51. *Ibid.,* p. 9524.

52. *Ibid.,* p. 9552.

53. *Forbes,* April 15, 1970, p. 26.

54. *Business Week,* November 30, 1968, p. 77.

55. The classic work is A. A. Berle and Gardiner C. Means, *The Modern Corporation and Private Property* (New York: Macmillan, 1933). The thesis has been generally

accepted since then and has been most eloquently stated by John Kenneth Galbraith, *The New Industrial State, op. cit.* (above, note 17).

56. Clem Morgello, "The Big Get Bigger," *Newsweek,* May 4, 1970, p. 80.

57. *The Insurance Industry,* Part 15, *op. cit.* (above, note 50), p. 9556.

58. Staff Report for the Subcommittee on Domestic Finance of the Committee on Banking and Currency, House of Representatives, Ninetieth Congress, Second Session, *Commercial Banks and Their Trust Activities: Emerging Influence on the American Economy,* Volume 1, July 8, 1968, p. 18.

59. *Ibid.,* p. 19.

60. *Ibid.,* p. 17.

61. Staff Report for the Committee on Banking and Currency, House of Representatives, Ninety-first Congress, First Session, *The Growth of Unregistered Bank Holding Companies—Problems and Prospects,* February 11, 1969, p. 1.

62. *U.S.* v. *The Cleveland Trust Co.,* Civil No. C–70–301, filed March 27, 1970, in the United States District Court in Cleveland, Ohio.

63. Hearings before the Subcommittee on Antitrust and Monopoly of the Committee on the Judiciary, U. S. Senate, Ninetieth Congress, Second Session, *Competition in Defense Procurement,* June 17 and 21 and September 10, 1968, p. 82.

64. New York: Macmillan, 1955, p. vii.

65. For an excellent case study of government subsidization of big business, see Leonard Baker, *The Guaranteed Society: A Jolting View of America's Degeneration into an Industrial Welfare State* (New York: Macmillan, 1968).

66. Report of the Committee on the Judiciary, United States Senate, Made by Its Subcommittee on Antitrust and Monopoly, Eighty-ninth Congress, First Session, together with Individual Views, *Antitrust and Monopoly Activities, 1965,* August 17, 1966, p. 17.

67. Hearings before the Subcommittee on Antitrust and Monopoly of the Committee on the Judiciary, United States Senate, Eighty-eighth Congress, Second Session, *Legislation Making Antitrust Treble Damages Non-Tax Deductible,* July 27, 28, 29, 1966.

68. Hearings before the Subcommittee on Antitrust and Monopoly of the Committee on the Judiciary, United States Senate, Ninety-first Congress, First Session, *Governmental Intervention in the Market Mechanism: Petroleum Industry,* Part 1: *Economists' Views,* March 11, 12, 24, 25, 26, April 1, 2, 1969; Part 2: *Industry Views,* May 20, 21, 22, 27, 28, 29, 1969; Part 3: *Complainants' Views,* July 22, 23, 24, 29, 30, 31, 1969, Part 4: *The Cabinet Task Force on Oil Import Control: Majority and Minority Recommendations,* March 3, 26, 1970, Part 4, Ninety-first Congress, Second Session.

CHAPTER TWO: HEAR NO EVIL, SEE NO EVIL, SPEAK NO EVIL

1. *United States* v. *Associated Press,* 52 F. Supp. 362 (S.D.N.Y.) (1943).

2. *Associated Press* v. *United States,* 326 U.S. 1 (1944).

3. *Red Lion Broadcasting Co. Inc.* v. *Federal Communications Commission,* 89 S. Ct. 1794 (1969).

NOTES

4. "News as a Byproduct: What Happens When Journalism Is Hitched to Great Diversified Corporations," *Columbia Journalism Review*, Spring 1967, p. 8.

5. "Separate Statement" in a case before the FCC involving WBAI, a New York City radio station, March 26, 1969.

6. Boston: Atlantic–Little, Brown, 1970.

7. Testimony in Hearings before the Committee on Banking and Currency, House of Representatives, Ninety-first Congress, First Session, *Bank Holding Company Act Amendments*, April 21, 1969, pp. 248–49.

8. *Op. cit.* (above, note 5).

9. Transcript of extemporaneous remarks to the National Citizens Committee for Broadcasting, New York City, November 6, 1969.

10. "The Silent Screen," *TV Guide*, July 5, 1969.

11. New York: Holt, Rinehart & Winston, 1961, p. 39 (Foreword by Donald R. Cressey).

12. "Pastore's All-Purpose Program," *New Leader*, January 5, 1970, pp. 30-31.

13. Hearings before the Subcommittee on Antitrust and Monopoly of the Committee on the Judiciary, United States Senate, Ninety-first Congress, First Session, *The Newspaper Preservation Act*, June 12, 13, 20, 1969, pp. 223–37. The *Washington Post* carried an article and a photograph on June 14, 1969, the morning after disclosure of the "Pig Document."

14. *Newspaper Preservation Act, op. cit.* (above, note 13), pp. 102–33.

15. *Washington Post,* July 21, 1969.

16. Hearings before the Subcommittee on Antitrust and Monopoly of the Committee on the Judiciary, United States Senate, Ninetieth Congress, Second Session, *The Failing Newspaper Act*, Part 7, February 27, 28, March 18, 19, 26, 27, April 16, 1968, pp. 2992–93. See also *Washington Post,* March 28, 1968.

17. In addition to Senator Nelson, the Democrats who voted against the bill were Quentin N. Burdick of North Dakota, J. William Fulbright of Arkansas, Philip A. Hart of Michigan, Edward M. Kennedy of Massachusetts, George McGovern of South Dakota, Thomas J. McIntyre of New Hampshire, Walter F. Mondale of Minnesota, and Edmund S. Muskie of Maine. In addition to Senator Percy, the Republicans who voted against the bill were Norris Cotton of New Hampshire, and Charles E. Goodell, and Jacob K. Javits of New York.

18. "A Story for Our Times, or What Is the Chairman of General Foods Really Trying to Say to Mary Jones," April 1965.

19. "Time . . . Fortune . . . Life . . . Luce," *Profiles from the New Yorker,* (New York: Knopf, 1938), p. 310.

20. *Ibid.*, p. 311.

21. *Ibid.*, p. 311.

22. The primary sources for the account of the Digest episode were: *New York Times*, June 2, 1968, 88:1; "Indigestion at the Digest," *Time*, June 14, 1968, and "Look That Up in Your Funk & Wagnalls," *Saturday Review*, November 22, 1969.

23. *New York Times*, January 17, 1970, p. 1.

24. "The Nixon White House: Herrlichman and Co. Look Ahead to 1972," *Washingtonian*, February 1970, p. 37.

25. Speech by Senator Thomas J. McIntyre, *Congressional Record,* January 19, 1970, pp. S 67–71.

26. The testimony of Professor Rucker, who is author of *The First Freedom* (Carbondale: Southern Illinois University Press, 1968) is in Hearings before the Subcommittee on Antitrust and Monopoly of the Committee on the Judiciary, United States Senate, Ninetieth Congress, First Session, *The Failing Newspaper Act,* Part 1, pp. 281–95. Numerous other witnesses also deserve attention. Among them, in Part 1 alone, are Elmer Brown, president of the International Typographical Union, Eugene Cervi, William J. Farson of the American Newspaper Guild, and Brian McNamara. Part 1 covers testimony given on July 12, 13, 14, 18, 19, 25, and 26, 1967. In Part 2 (July 27, 28, August 7, 8, 9, 14, 15, 1967) is the testimony of consultant Malone, pp. 953–87, and publisher Clinton, pp. 634–81. The testimony of Hochstein, the former Newhouse executive, is in Part 7, *op. cit.* (above, note 16), pp. 2942–65.

27. Senator McIntyre, *Congressional Record, op. cit.* (above, note 25).

28. *New York Times,* July 25, 1969.

29. This was established by Senator Philip Hart in a colloquy with Rosel H. Hyde, then chairman of the FCC; *Failing Newspaper Act,* Part 7, *op. cit.* (above, note 16), pp. 2891–93.

30. *Ibid.,* pp. 3442–55.

31. *Ibid.,* pp. 3301–3411.

32. "Broadcasting in America and the FCC's License Renewal Process: An Oklahoma Case Study: A statement by Commissioners Kenneth A. Cox and Nicholas Johnson on the occasion of the FCC's renewal of the licenses of Oklahoma broadcasters for a three year term beginning June 1, 1968."

33. Dissents of FCC Commissioners Cox and Johnson in Saginaw FM grant; reprinted in *Failing Newspaper* hearings, *op. cit.* (above, note 16), pp. 3455–61.

34. Cited by Mayor Henry W. Maier of Milwaukee, *Newspaper Preservation Act, op. cit.* (above, note 13), p. 11, from the February 1969 issue of *The Quill.*

35. Speech to the Federal Bar Association, Washington, D.C., May 29, 1968.

36. Testimony of Charles de Young Thieriot, president of the Chronicle Publishing Company and editor and publisher of the *San Francisco Chronicle, Failing Newspaper Act,* Part 2, *op. cit.* (above, note 26), p. 560.

37. *Ibid., p.* 546.

38. *Ibid.,* p. 549.

39. *Ibid.,* p. 573.

40. *Failing Newspaper Act, op. cit.* (above, note 16), pp. 3113–14.

41. "News as a Byproduct," *op cit.* (above, note 4), p. 10.

42. "Case History: Wilmington's 'Independent' Newspapers," *Columbia Journalism Review,* Summer 1964, reprinted in *Failing Newspaper Act, op. cit.* (above, note 26), Part 4, "Articles, Miscellaneous Documents and Cases," pp. 1571–76.

43. "Houston's Shackled Press," *Atlantic,* August 1966, pp. 87ff., reprinted in *Failing Newspaper Act,* Part 4, *op. cit.* (above, note 42), pp. 1576–83.

44. *Failing Newspaper* hearings, Part 2, *op. cit.* (above, note 26) , pp. 894, 898.

45. "Friedmanism, n., doctrine of most audacious U.S. economist; esp., theory 'only money matters,'" Milton Viorst, *New York Times Magazine,* January 25, 1970, p. 80.

NOTES

46. *Commercial Banks and Their Trust Activities; Emerging Influence on the American Economy*, Vol. 1, Staff Report for the Subcommittee on Domestic Finance, Committee on Banking and Currency, House of Representatives, Ninetieth Congress, Second Session, July 8, 1968, pp. 503–09. A note of caution may be appropriate. In at least one case, involving the Long Island paper *Newsday*, the material was obsolete as of the date of publication. The report lists Morgan Guaranty Trust as holding, and having partial rights in, 49 per cent of the Class A stock. At the time, however, a *Newsday* spokesman said, "No stock of *Newsday* is in the hands of Morgan Guaranty Trust or any other bank."

47. *Washington Post,* July 9, 1968, p. A10:1.

48. *Commercial Banks, op. cit.* (above, note 46), p. 55.

49. Publication of the American Newspaper Guild, AFL-CIO, Washington, D.C., July 26, 1968, p. 4.

50. *Bank Holding Company Act Amendments, op. cit.* (above, note 7), pp. 242–46.

51. *Ibid.*

52. "The News on TV and How It Is Unmade," *Harper's Magazine,* October 1965, p. 80.

53. New York: Trident, p. 60.

54. Speech in Iowa City, Iowa, November 13, 1969.

55. Quoted in "Spiro Agnew's Candles: What the Vice-President Kept Dark," Morton Mintz, *New Republic,* January 17, 1970.

56. Testimony of Richard W. McLaren, Assistant Attorney General in charge of the Antitrust Division, *Newspaper Preservation Act,* op. cit. (above, note 13), pp. 294–98. On September 25, 1969, after the Commerce Department made the surprise disclosure that President Nixon supported the bill, McLaren essentially repeated his earlier opposition testimony before the House Antitrust Subcommittee. Chairman Emanuel Celler (D–N.Y.), unable to recall a precedent for the Commerce Department's speaking for the President on an antitrust bill, told a bitterly disappointed McLaren that the White House was trying to "light one candle for Christ and one for the Devil and take no chances." See *Washington Post,* September 26, 1969, and "Spiro Agnew's Candles," *op. cit.* (above, note 55).

57. *Failing Newspaper Act,* Part 1, *op. cit.* (above, note 26), p. 368.

58. Federal Bar speech, op. cit. (above, note 35).

59. *Violence and the Media: A Staff Report to the National Commission on the Causes and Prevention of Violence,* prepared by Robert K. Baker and Dr. Sandra K. Ball (Washington: 1969), pp. v–vi.

CHAPTER THREE: TOLLS ALONG THE HIGHWAY

1. *Wall Street Journal,* May 18, 1970.

2. *Economic Report of the President Together with the Annual Report of the Council of Economic Advisors,* transmitted to the Ninety-first Congress, First Session, January 1969, House Document No. 28, p. 107.

3. *Studies by the Staff of the Cabinet Committee on Price Stability,* January 1969, p. 40.

4. Hearings of the Executive and Legislative Reorganization Subcommittee of the

House Committee on Government Operations, Ninety-first Congress, First Session, *Organizing Federal Consumer Activities,* Part 1, September 16, 1969, p. 111.

5. Much of the pioneering work in the area of administered prices has been done by Gardiner C. Means; see *Pricing Power and the Public Interest* (New York: Harper, 1962) and *The Corporate Revolution in America* (New York: Crowell, 1962). Others have modified the concept and have made substantial contributions toward illuminating the problem. See Hearings before the Subcommittee on Antitrust and Monopoly of the Committee on the Judiciary, United States Senate, Eighty-eighth Congress, First Session, *Administered Prices: A Compendium on Public Policy,* 1963 and citations. See, further, *Guidelines, Informal Controls and the Market Place,* edited by George P. Shultz and Robert I. Aliber (University of Chicago Press, 1966) and citations therein.

6. *A Primer on Monopoly and Competition,* (New York: Random House, 1970), p. 110.

7. Article by Alfred L. Malabre, Jr., October 22, 1968.

8. Louis B. Schwartz, "A Law Professor's View of the Sherman Act—Fluid Fronts in the War Against Excessive Concentration of Economic Power," 27 *A.B.A.* Antitrust Section, p. 87.

9. *Economic Report on Corporate Mergers,* prepared by the Bureau of Economics, Federal Trade Commission, Commerce Clearing House edition, p. 140.

10. See Walter B. Erikson, *Price Fixing Under the Sherman Act: Case Studies in Conspiracy* (doctoral dissertation, Michigan State University, 1965).

11. See David R. Kamerschen, *An Estimation of the "Welfare Losses" from Monopoly in the American Economy* (doctoral dissertation, Michigan State University, 1964), discussed in *Antitrust Law and Economics Review No. 1* (Summer 1964).

12. Vol. 3, No. 1, (Fall 1969), pp. 12–13.

13. See *Antitrust Law and Economics Review,* Vol. 3, No. 4, (Summer 1969).

14. Hearings before the Subcommittee on Antitrust and Monopoly of the Committee on the Judiciary, United States Senate, Ninetieth Congress, First Session, *Consumer Credit Industry,* Part 1, May 16, 17, 18, 19, 1967, and Part 3, Ninetieth Congress, First Session, November 27, 28, 29, 30, December 18, 1967.

15. Remarks of Senator Philip A. Hart at New York Consumer Assembly, March 7, 1970.

16. Edward McCreary, Jr., and Walter Guzzardi, Jr., "A Customer Is a Company's Best Friend," *Fortune,* June 1965.

17. *Consumer Credit Industry, op. cit.* (above, note 14), Part 3, p. 2348ff.

18. *Consumer Credit Industry, op. cit.* (above, note 14), Part 3, p. 2527ff.

19. These techniques were outlined by Matthew Josephson in *The Robber Barons* (New York: Harcourt, 1962).

20. Hearings before the Subcommittee on Antitrust and Monopoly of the Committee on the Judiciary, United States Senate, Eighty-ninth Congress, Second Session, *Distribution Problems Affecting Small Business,* Part 2, January 18, 19, 20, 26, 27, 1966, p. 583.

21. Hearings before the Subcommittee on Antitrust and Monopoly of the Committee on the Judiciary, United States Senate, Eighty-ninth Congress, First Session, *Price Discrimination Legislation—1965,* June 21, 22, 23, 30, 1965, p. 62.

NOTES

22. *Ibid.*, p. 138.

23. See generally the following hearings before the Subcommittee on Antitrust and Monopoly of the Committee on the Judiciary, United States Senate: *Price Discrimination Legislation—1965, op. cit.* (above, note 21); *Distribution Problems Affecting Small Business*, Part 1, *Franchising Agreements*, Eighty-ninth Congress, First Session, March 2, 3, 4, 1965; and Part 2, *op. cit.* (above, note 20); *Price Discrimination Legislation—1969*, Ninety-first Congress, First Session, September 23, 24, 1969; and *Dual Distribution*, Part 1, Eighty-ninth Congress, First Session, September 15, 16, 17, 1965; and Part 2, Eighty-ninth Congress, Second Session, March 29, 30, 31, 1966.

24. *Dual Distribution*, Part 1, *op. cit.* (above, note 23), p. 69.

25. Hearings before the Subcommittee on Antitrust and Monopoly of the Committee on the Judiciary, United States Senate, Ninety-first Congress, Second Session, *Economic Concentration*, Part 8: *The Conglomerate Merger Problem*, November 4, 5, 6, 1969, January 28, February 5, 18, 19, 1970, p. 4847.

26. *Wall Street Journal*, March 7, 1968.

27. *Congressional Record*, December 12, 1950, pp. 16613ff.

CHAPTER FOUR: THE POLITICIAN AS AN INVESTMENT

1. Speech cited by Alfred Balk, "Beyond Agnewism," *Columbia Journalism Review*, Winter 1969–70, p. 19.

2. Speech in the Senate on a proposal by Senator Long to permit the individual taxpayer to earmark $1 of his income-tax payment for a presidential campaign election fund, *Congressional Record*, April 4, 1967, pp. S4582–83.

3. "Oil and Politics," *Atlantic*, September 1969, p. 83.

4. *Ibid.*, p. 90. The size of the chemical division of Jersey Standard was noted by John M. Blair at Hearings before the Senate Subcommittee on Antitrust and Monopoly of the Committee on the Judiciary, United States Senate, Ninety-first Congress, First Session, July 22, 1969, *Governmental Intervention in the Market Mechanism*, Part 3, p. 1176.

5. "Oil and Politics," *op. cit.* (above, note 3).

6. September 16, 1968.

7. "The Ticklish Problem of Political Fundraising—and Spending," *Reader's Digest*, January 1968.

8. Herbert E. Alexander and Harold B. Meyers, "A Financial Landslide for the G.O.P.," *Fortune*, March 1970, p. 104.

9. Statement during debate on the Long proposal, *op. cit.* (above, note 2), p. S 4580.

10. Speech by Senator Long, *op. cit.* (above, note 2), p. S 4586.

11. *Washington Post*, January 5, 1969, p. A1.

12. John S. Lang of Associated Press, *Washington Post*, October 5, 1969.

13. *New York Times*, May 5, 1967, p. 22.

14. *Ibid.*

15. Speech by Senator Long, *op. cit.* (above, note 2).

16. December 25, 1966, p. A1.

17. Speech by Senator Long, *op. cit.* (above, note 2), p. S 4574.

18. *Washington Post,* May 11, 1968.

19. "Financial Landslide," *op. cit.* (above, note 8), p. 187.

20. *Washington Post,* May 18, 1968.

21. The text of the affidavit was released by Senator Wayne Morse (D–Ore.) on December 21, 1966.

22. The guilty plea and the contribution to Senator Russell were reported by the *Los Angeles Times* on November 4, 1969. The presence of Maurice Stans on the Fluor firm's board was noted in the *Cleveland Plain Dealer* in an article later cited in the *Congressional Record,* December 1, 1969, p. E 10,163.

23. *San Jose Mercury,* October 17, 1969, and *Los Angeles Times,* October 28, 1969.

24. *Los Angeles Times,* October 18, 1969.

25. *Washington Post,* June 18, 1969, p. A2.

26. *Washington Post,* February 8, 1970.

27. *Washington Post,* January 3, 1970.

28. Report by *Congressional Quarterly, Washington Post,* March 12, 1970, p. E3.

29. *Ibid.*

30. The commission's report, issued September 30, 1969, was reprinted in the *Congressional Record,* October 3, 1969, pp. E 8113–27.

31. "Financial Landslide," *op. cit.* (above, note 8), p. 189.

32. The Report of the subcommittee is ably summarized in the *Congressional Quarterly Almanac,* Vol. 13 (1957), pp. 187–8.

33. Herbert Alexander and Harold B. Meyers, "The Switch in Campaign Giving," *Fortune,* November 1965.

34. *CQ, op. cit.* (above, note 28).

35. "Financial Landslide," *op. cit.* (above, note 8), p. 104.

36. *Ibid.*

37. *Ibid.,* p. 187.

38. Taken from the Nossiter interview, *Washington Post,* p. A1, January 31, 1971.

39. "Financial Landslide," *op. cit.* (above, note 8), p. 187.

40. Testimony before the Subcommittee on Administrative Practice and Procedure of the Committee on the Judiciary, United States Senate, on S. 3434 and S. 2544, July 21, 1970.

CHAPTER FIVE: THE EXECUTIVE

1. New York: Macmillan, 1961.

2. *Ibid.,* p. 9.

3. New York: Simon and Schuster, 1968, pp. 426–27.

4. *Ibid.,* p. 427.

5. *The Politics of Oil: A Study of Private Power and Democratic Directions* (New York: Macmillan, 1961), pp. 404–11.

6. *Ibid.*

7. *Case Against Congress, op. cit.* (above, note 3), pp. 428–29.

8. *Ibid.,* p. 429.

NOTES

9. Drew Pearson and Jack Anderson, "Washington Merry-Go-Round," *Washington Post*, October 15, 1968, p. B11.

10. *Washington Post*, November 13, 1968, p. A1, and January 31, 1971, p. A25.

11. *Washington Post*, January 31, 1971, p. A25.

12. Erwin Knoll, "The Oil Lobby Is Not Depleted," *New York Times Magazine*, March 8, 1970, p. 27.

13. *Ibid.*, p. 103.

14. February 16, 1969, p. A-6.

15. September 1969, p. 75.

16. "Oil and Politics," *The Atlantic*, September 1969, p. 90.

17. Herbert E. Alexander and Harold B. Meyers, "A Financial Landslide for the G.O.P.," *Fortune*, March 1970, p. 104.

18. *Washington Post*, March 28, 1970, p. A3.

19. *Politics of Oil, op. cit.* (above, note 5), p. 419.

20. *Op. cit.* (above, note 12), pp. 26–27.

21. "Oil and Politics," *op. cit.* (above, note 16), p. 71.

22. *Ibid.*, pp. 67, 71–72.

23. "Oil Lobby," *op. cit.* (above, note 12), p. 27.

24. *Ibid.*, p. 109.

25. *Ibid.*, p. 106.

26. *Ibid.*, p. 106.

27. *Ibid.*, pp. 26, 104–05.

28. *Washington Post*, February 21, 1970, p. A1.

29. *Washington Post*, March 4, 1970, p. A3.

30. "Consumer Be Damned," March 7, 1970, p. 12.

31. "Nixon's Announcement Hailed by Oil Industry," *New York Times*, February 21, 1970, p. 47:1.

32. February 24, 1970.

33. "The Regulatory Agencies: What Should Be Done?" *Washington Monthly*, August 1969, p. 48.

34. October 7, 1968.

35. January 28, 1970, p. 19:1.

36. Morton Mintz, *By Prescription Only* (Boston: Beacon and Houghton Mifflin, 1967), pp. 95–96.

37. *To Hell in a Day Coach: An Exasperated Look at American Railroads* (Philadelphia: Lippincott, 1968), p. 221.

38. Morton Mintz, "The Culture of Bureaucracy: Rebuke at HEW," *Washington Monthly*, December 1969.

39. Morton Mintz, "FDA and Panalba: A Conflict of Commercial and Therapeutic Goals?" *Science*, August 29, 1969; and "Public Swallows FDA Mistakes," *Washington Post*, November 23, 1969, p. B1.

CHAPTER SIX: THE CONGRESS

1. New York: Harper, 1965 (revised edition), pp. 22–23.

2. *Ibid., pp.* 47–48.

3. "Congressional Staffs: The Third Branch of Congress," *Washington Post,* January 18, 1970, p. A1.

4. *Washington Post,* December 2, 1969, p. A1.

5. October 16, 1968, p. A1.

6. "Wall Street: The Big Get Bigger," *Newsweek,* May 4, 1970.

7. Jerry S. Cohen, "The Washington Lawyer—A Contrived Legend," *George Washington Law Review,* May 1970, pp. 769–70.

8. "Congressional Staffs," *op. cit.* (above, note 3).

9. *Ibid.*

10. "Inside Capitol Hill: How the House Really Works," *Harper's,* October 1968, p. 68.

11. "The Tax-Exempt Foundation: A New Major Threat to Clean Politics." *Congressional Record,* July 1, 1968, pp. H 5858–61.

12. New York: Simon and Schuster, 1968, p. 102.

13. William J. Eaton and Robert Gruenberg, "Dirksen Irons in Many Fires," *Chicago Daily News,* July 11, 1969.

14. *Ibid.*

15. *Case Against Congress, op. cit.* (above, note 12), pp. 119–20.

16. *Ibid.,* p. 120.

17. "Out-of-State Fund-Raiser Is New Twist," September 22, 1969.

18. *New York Times,* March 13, 1970, p. 1.

19. Testimony before the National Commission on Product Safety, September 30, 1969; reprinted in *Congressional Record,* September 30, 1969, p. E 7976.

20. *New York Times,* September 16, 1969, p. 1.

21. *Washington Post,* January 6, 1969, p. A2.

22. *Responses to Questionnaire on Citizen Involvement and Responsive Agency Decision-Making,* committee print submitted by the Subcommittee on Administrative Practice and Procedure to the Committee on the Judiciary, United States Senate, Ninety-first Congress, First Session, September 9, 1969, p. 126.

23. *Washington Post,* April 24, 1969, p. A2.

24. *Deficiencies in Administration of Federal Insecticide, Fungicide, and Rodenticide Act,* a report by the Committee on Government Operations, Ninety-first Congress, First Session, November 17, 1969.

CHAPTER SEVEN: THE REGULATORY AGENCIES

1. *Office of Communication of United Church of Christ* v. F.C.C., 359 F. 2d 994, 1003.

2. Testimony before the Subcommittee on Administrative Practice and Procedure of the Committee on the Judiciary, United States Senate, on S. 3434 and S. 2544, July 21, 1970.

3. *Washington Post,* March 31, 1970, p. A1.

4. *Responses to Questionnaire on Citizen Involvement and Responsive Agency De-*

cision-Making, committee print submitted by the Subcommittee on Administrative Practice and Procedure to the Committee on the Judiciary, United States Senate, Ninety-first Congress, First Session, September 9, 1969, p. 134.

5. *Washington Post,* July 2, 1967, p. A1.

6. Cited by Representative Richard L. Ottinger (D–N.Y.) in testimony before the Subcommittee on Transportation and Aeronautics of the Committee on Interstate and Foreign Commerce, House of Representatives, November 17, 1969.

7. *Ibid.*

8. *Washington Post,* March 17, 1970, p. A1.

9. *Washington Post,* November 27, 1968, p. A1.

10. Ottinger testimony, *op. cit.* (above, note 6).

11. "We Need the Pastore Bill [by Louis L. Jaffe]; No We Don't [by Nicholas Johnson]," *New Republic,* December 6, 1969, p. 17.

12. *Op. cit.* (above, note 6).

13. Cited by Morton Mintz in *By Prescription Only* (Boston: Beacon and Houghton Mifflin, 1967), p. 176.

14. New York: Putnam, 1968, p. 9.

15. *Ibid.,* p. 11.

16. *Ibid.,* pp. 320–21.

17. *Ibid.,* pp. 327–38.

18. *Ibid.,* p. 341.

19. *Ibid.,* 208–219.

20. New York: McKay, 1967.

21. *Washington Post,* April 13, 1969.

22. *Ibid.*

23. October 23, 30, 1967.

CHAPTER EIGHT: "CRIME IN THE SUITES"

1. Cited by J. Ernest Bryant of Searsport, Maine, in a letter the *New York Times* published on July 18, 1968. Bryant recalled Collins, the keeper, in connection with a *Times* editorial suggesting that a strong health warning be required not only on cigarette packages, but also in cigarette advertising. "But Congress has discovered that the type of businessman referred to by Emerson . . . is apt to be found in industry today," Bryant said.

2. With a foreword by Donald R. Cressey (New York: Holt, Rinehart & Winston, 1961). The foreword recalls that Cressey tried to persuade Sutherland to identify the seventy corporations he studied, but that, warned by attorneys for the original publisher (New York: Dryden) of possible libel actions, the author deleted the identifications.

3. *The Rich and the Super-Rich: A Study in the Power of Money Today* (New York: Lyle Stuart, 1968), p. 76.

4. New Haven: Yale University Press, 1937.

5. *Ibid.*, pp. 185, 186, 189.

6. *Globe Woolen Co.* v. *Utica Gas Co.*, 224 N.Y., 483, 489; 121 N.E. 378, 379 (1918).

7. Letter from Johnny H. Killian, Legislative Attorney, American Law Division, December 6, 1968, to Benjamin Gordon, staff economist, Senate Select Committee on Small Business.

8. *The Mythmakers* (Boston: Houghton Mifflin, 1964), p. 85.

9. The correspondence between du Pont and Sloan is Exhibit 220 of Hearings before Subcommittees of the Select Committee on Small Business, United States Senate, Ninetieth Congress, Second Session, *Planning, Regulation and Competition: Automobile Industry—1968*, pp. 964–69. The letters originally became public documents in *United States of America* v. *E. I. du Pont de Nemours & Co., et al.*, U.S.D.C. N.D. Ill. Civil Action No. 49C–1071 (1952). The Justice Department brought this antitrust case to require du Pont to divest itself of its stock in GM. Starting on April 28, 1952, Sloan made depositions that were to become the du Pont company's defense exhibits 299 through 362. Hugh B. Cox of the Washington law firm of Covington & Burling, which was counsel for du Pont, attempted through these exhibits to bolster the defense contention that the company's stock in GM did not influence the automobile maker's purchasing. The Sloan–Lammot du Pont letters were among the exhibits and were numbered 346 through 354. However, the correspondence was not introduced in the trial. The District Court decided the case for the government, forcing du Pont, the single biggest shareholder in GM, to sell the stock. The court's opinion at the conclusion of the trial is reported in 126 F. Supp. 235. The Supreme Court affirmed: 353 U.S. 586 (1957).

10. Ralph Nader, in *Unsafe at Any Speed: The Designed-in Dangers of the American Automobile* (New York: Grossman, 1965), quotes the court in the course of a detailed discussion of this case, pp. 42–51.

11. *Ibid.*, pp. 52–3.

12. All of these data were supplied by James M. Beggs, Under Secretary of Transportation, in an exchange of letters in July 1969 with Senator Philip A. Hart (D–Mich.), who as chairman of the Senate Subcommittee on Antitrust and Monopoly was conducting hearings on the automotive repair industry.

13. Morton Mintz reported the wheels case in the *Washington Post*. The publication dates of some of the more important stories, from which the account here derives, were October 15, 1969, and July 2, September 16, October 1, November 5, 7, 1970.

14. *Unsafe at Any Speed, op. cit.* (above, note 10), p. 296.

15. *Washington Post*, February 21, 1970, p. A1.

16. December 1, 1969, p. 42.

17. The story of the MER/29 case is told by Morton Mintz in *By Prescription Only* (Boston: Beacon and Houghton Mifflin, 1967). The sentencing episode is on pp. 244–45.

18. *Ibid.*, pp. 92j, 92k, gives background on the CIBA case. The *Washington Post* reported the outcome on October 27, 1968.

19. *By Prescription Only, op. cit.* (above, note 17), pp. 92b-92e. The Library of Congress report on the volume of drug advertising in *JAMA* and other medical journals is published in Hearings before the Subcommittee on Monopoly of the Select Commit-

NOTES

tee on Small Business, United States Senate, Ninety-first Congress, First Session, *Competitive Problems in the Drug Industry,* Part 11, pp. 4863–4998.

20. July 29, 1969, p. 1.

21. Ralph Nader, "Corporate Crime," *Business Today,* Summer 1969; reprinted in *Congressional Record,* June 2, 1969, p. E 4544.

22. *Washington Post,* October 8, 1969.

23. *White Collar Crime, op. cit.* (above, note 2), p. 39.

24. December 1, 1969, p. 42.

25. February 15, 1970.

26. "A Famous Prosecutor Talks About Crime," *New York Times Magazine,* February 15, 1970, p. 30.

27. *Mythmakers, op. cit.* (above, note 8), pp. 84–5.

28. The estimates, and the judgments that they are inadequate, were made by Secretary of Labor W. Willard Wirtz in testimony in 1968 before the Senate Committee on Labor and Public Welfare and the House Select Committee on Labor, and by his successor, George P. Shultz, in 1969 before the same committees. A series of articles dealing at length with occupational health and safety, written by Thomas O'Toole and Morton Mintz, appeared in the *Washington Post* on December 28, 29, 30, 1969, and was reprinted in the *Congressional Record,* January 19, 1970, pp. S 106–110.

29. *Ibid.,* December 28.

30. January 2, 1970, p. 17.

31. *White Collar Crime, op. cit.* (above, note 2), p. 220.

32. *Washington Post,* April 10, 1966, and *By Prescription Only, op. cit.* (above, note 17), pp. 383g–383j.

33. Report of the Committee on Government Operations, United States Senate, made by its Permanent Subcommittee on Investigations, Ninety-first Congress, First Session, 1969, *Improper Practices, Commodity Import Program, U.S. Foreign Aid, Vietnam,* pp. 33–34.

34. Despite such sensational disclosures as those about patent fraud, corporate wiretapping, and profit rates exceeding 80 per cent, the antibiotics antitrust trial received insufficient attention in most news media. After it was over, the *Columbia Journalism Review* said in its Winter 1967/1968 issue, a researcher for the review checked to see how the conviction was reported by twenty-five daily papers "of national consequence." Five of the papers had put the story on page one, nine put it inside and eleven ran nothing. The *Review* suggested, "first, newspapers still underestimate stories that cut close to readers' essential concerns of life and health; second, . . . editors may have lacked advance warning of the importance of the story because only *The Washington Post* covered it regularly. Neither the New York papers nor the wire services did."

35. *White Collar Crime, op. cit.* (above, note 2), p. 223.

36. *Washington Post,* February 24, 1969, p. A3.

37. *Washington Post,* June 28, 1969, p. A2, and the official transcript. The Appellate Court decision, announced on February 19, 1971, was reported the next day by the Associated Press in a story in the *Washington Post,* p. A3, and was expected to be appealed to the Supreme Court.

38. January 17, 1970, p. 1.

39. New York: Harper & Row, 1969.

40. "The People v. the Mob; or, Who Rules New Jersey?" February 1, 1970, p. 32.

41. Morton Mintz, "Product Safety Gains Impetus," *Outlook* section of *Washington Post*, May 11, 1969, p. B3.

42. *Ibid.* and *Washington Post,* February 20, 1969, p. A2.

43. *Theft of the Nation, op. cit.* (above, note 39), pp. 311–19.

44. *Mythmakers, op. cit.* (above, note 8), p. 85.

45. Senator Gaylord Nelson (D–Wis.), chairman of the Senate Subcommittee on Monopoly, has for several years led the fight in Congress for tire safety. At a hearing on July 9, 1969, Thoman C. Mann, president of the Automobile Manufacturers Association, asserted that the industry "makes a great effort to make these cars as safe as they possibly can." Disagreeing, Nelson said that "finally the proof came through that original equipment tires put on according to the specifications required by the automobile manufacturers themselves were inadequate. Many of those automobiles were overloaded the moment you put in the normal number of passengers for which the automobile was built, and in some of them, without putting in more than one passenger." His point was "proved beyond any doubt" by the Barth case, he said. He published the court opinion in Hearings before the Subcommittee on Monopoly of the Select Committee on Small Business, United States Senate, Ninety-first Congress, First Session, Part 1, *Role of Giant Corporations,* 1969, pp. 103–16.

46. This practice, along with another in which drug manufacturers sell medicines in foreign countries for less than in the United States where they are made, is described in Morton Mintz, "The Great Drug Robbery," *Progressive,* September 1968, and in his "Medical Safety is Geographic," *Washington Post,* July 12, 1970, p. C1.

47. "We Trouble the Earth," *Outlook* section of the *Washington Post,* February 22, 1970, p. D1.

48. "The War Against the Automobile," Spring 1966, p. 10.

CHAPTER NINE: THE DISPLACEMENT OF THE INDIVIDUAL

1. *Giant Business: Threat to Democracy* (New York: Exposition Press, 1953), p. 107.

2. Remarks on accepting Distinguished Public Service Award from National Council of Salesmen's Organization, Inc., New York City, December 2, 1968.

3. *Ibid.*

4. *Giant Business, op. cit.* (above, note 1), p. 138.

5. *Ibid.,* p. 139.

6. Remarks, *op. cit.* (above, note 2).

7. *Giant Business, op. cit.* (above, note 1), p. 83.

8. *Ibid.,* p. 278.

9. Cited by Marquis W. Childs and Douglass Cater in *Ethics in a Business Society* (New York: Harper, 1954), p. 106.

10. January 27, 1970, p. 46:1.

11. *New York Times,* February 10, 1970.

12. This episode was described in Chapter Two.

13. *Op. cit.* (above, note 10).

14. New York: Simon and Schuster, 1956.

15. *Ibid.,* pp. 5–6.

16. *New York Times,* March 5, 1970.

17. "The Real Issue of Cigarette Advertising," speech in the United States Senate, *Congressional Record,* November 11, 1969, S 14095.

18. "The Profits in Pollution," *Progressive,* April 1970, p. 21.

19. Chicago: Quadrangle, 1969, pp. 5–6.

20. *Chemical and Biological Warfare: America's Hidden Arsenal* (Indianapolis: Bobbs-Merrill, 1968), p. 259.

21. *Ibid.,* p. 262.

22. *Ibid.,* p. 140.

23. *Ibid.,* p. 138.

24. *Functionaries, op. cit.* (above, note 19), p. 5.

25. *Op. cit.* (above, note 9), p. 162.

26. *Washington Post,* December 14, 1969, p. G1:6.

27. "Whatever Happened to Socialism?" *Harper's* February 1970, p. 104.

28. *Points of Rebellion* (New York: Vintage, 1970), p. 96.

CHAPTER TEN: PLAYING GOD

1. Hearings before the Subcommittee on Monopoly of the Select Committee on Small Business, United States Senate, Ninety-first Congress, First Session, *Role of Giant Corporations,* July 9, 10, 11, 1969, p. 402.

2. "Plugging Science into the Market Place," remarks before the National Industrial Research Conference, Purdue University, Lafayette, Indiana, January 10, 1966.

3. Cited by Ralph Nader in *Unsafe At Any Speed: The Designed-In Dangers of the American Automobile* (New York: Grossman, 1965), p. 230.

4. "Plugging Science into the Market Place," *op. cit.* (above, note 2).

5. Hearings before the Subcommittees of the Select Committee on Small Business, United States Senate, Ninetieth Congress, Second Session, *Planning, Regulation, and Competition: Automobile Industry—1968,* July 10, 23, 1968, p. 331.

6. *Ibid.,* p. 331.

7. *Washington Post,* October 10, 1967, p. A1.

8. Speech before the Air Pollution Control Association, Houston, Texas, June 1964.

9. *Role of Giant Corporations, op. cit.* (above, note 1), p. 402.

10. Joint Hearings before the Committee on Commerce and the Subcommittee on Air and Water Pollution of the Committee on Public Works, United States Senate, Ninetieth Congress, Second Session, *Automobile Steam Engine and Other External Combustion Engines,* May 27, 28, 1968.

11. *Ibid.,* pp. 64–65.

12. *Ibid.,* p. 100.

13. *Ibid.,* p. 100.

14. *New York Times,* July 11, 1970, p. 1:1.

15. *Environmental Health Letter,* April 1, 1970.

16. *Automobile Steam Engine, op. cit.* (above, note 10), p. 4.

17. *Role of Giant Corporations, op. cit.* (above, note 1), p. 540.

18. *New York Times,* May 24, 1969.

19. Remarks on accepting Distinguished Public Service Award from National Council of Salesmen's Organization, Inc., New York City, December 2, 1968.

20. "Can Federal Legislation Affecting Consumers' Economic Interests Be Enacted?" *Michigan Law Review,* May 1966, p. 1266.

21. New York: Random House, 1968, pp. 240–49.

22. New York: Dutton, 1970.

23. Speech to the Midwest Association of Railroad and Utilities Commissioners, Bismarck, North Dakota, June 21, 1968.

24. Remarks at National Energy Policy Conference, Washington, D.C., February 18, 1970.

25. New York: Doubleday, 1964, p. 288.

26. "Market Power and Racial Discrimination in White-Collar Employment," *Antitrust Bulletin,* Spring 1969, pp. 141–61.

27. *Washington Post,* December 1, 1969, p. A7.

28. *Washington Post,* July 21, 1968.

29. *Washington Post,* March 8, 1969.

30. *I. F. Stone's Bi-Weekly,* March 5, 1970, p. 4.

31. "About Hot Cars," speech to the annual meeting of the Greater Jacksonville Safety Council, Jacksonville, Florida, December 17, 1969.

32. Reprinted in *Planning, Regulation, and Competition, op. cit.* (above, note 5), pp. 457–62.

33. Fall 1967, pp. 21–29.

34. *Planning, Regulation, and Competition, op. cit.* (above, note 5), p. 543.

35. "The Hidden Executives," *Business Today,* Winter 1968.

36. Ralph Nader, "Consumer Protection and Corporate Disclosure," *Business Today,* Autumn 1968.

37. March 12, 1970.

38. "News Item: Man Bites Ford," *Consumer Reports,* March 1970.

39. *New York Times,* April 2, 1969, p. 49:1.

40. "Three GMC School Buses And One Man's Ordeal," December 15, 1969; "Troubled School Bus Operator Begins to 'Get Action,'" December 22, 1969; "Bitter Tales From the GM Lemon Groves," February 23, 1970, and "The Mark—Or Is It the Mock?—of Excellence," March 2, 1970. All of the articles appeared on the editorial page of the *Washington Post.*

CHAPTER ELEVEN: FOREIGN AFFAIRS

1. This estimate is based principally on an article by Howard V. Perlmutter, "Super-Giant Firms in the Future," *Wharton Quarterly,* Winter 1968. He is consistent with other commentators in the field, who generally have come up with a figure of from 300 to 350.

NOTES

2. "Money Power," *War/Peace Report,* October 1968.

3. See Howe Martyn, "Multinational Corporations in a Nationalistic World," *Challenge,* November–December 1965, and Judd Polk, "The Rise of World Corporations," *Saturday Review,* November 22, 1969. See also Richard J. Barber, *The American Corporation* (New York: Dutton, 1970) Chapter Seventeen, "The Internationalization of Business."

4. See statement of Robert Stobaugh, Harvard University Graduate School of Business Administration, Hearings of the Subcommittee on Foreign Economic Policy of the Joint Economic Committee, Ninety-first Congress, Second Session, *A Foreign Economic Policy for the 1970's.* Part 4: *The Multinational Corporation and International Investment,* July 27, 28, 29 and 30, 1970, p. 874.

5. *Ibid.*

6. See Hearings before the Subcommittee on Antitrust and Monopoly of the Committee of the Judiciary, United States Senate, Eighty-ninth Congress, Second Session, *International Aspects of Antitrust,* Part 1, April 20, 21, 26, 27, 28, 29, June 6, 7, 8, 10, August 29, 30, 1966; especially useful is Appendix C, Table I, "Foreign Acquisitions Made by the 50 Largest U. S. Manufacturing Firms between January 1, 1958, and January 31, 1966." See also "The Fortune Directory: The 200 Largest Industrials Outside the U.S.A.," *Fortune,* August 1970, p. 142, and introduction and footnotes to this article.

7. The state of industrial concentration in the major industrial nations of the world is treated in Hearings before the Subcommittee on Antitrust and Monopoly of the Committee on the Judiciary, United States Senate, Ninetieth Congress, Second Session, *Economic Concentration,* Part 7: *Concentration Outside the United States,* April 2, 3, 5, 8, 10, 11, 17, 1968. See also Joe S. Bain, *International Differences in Industrial Structure* (New Haven and London, Yale, 1966).

8. "Emerging New Power: The World Corporation," *War/Peace Report,* October 1968.

9. *Multinational Corporation, op. cit.* (above, note 4), p. 935.

10. See Charles P. Kindleberger, "The International Firm and the International Capital Market," *Southern Economic Journal,* Vol. 34, No. 2, October 1967, pp. 223–230. See also Testimony of Robert L. Sammons, Associate Director, Division of International Finance, Board of Governors of the Federal Reserve System, *International Aspects of Antitrust, op. cit.* (above, note 6), p. 110; Hearings before the Subcommittee on Antitrust and Monopoly of the Committee of the Judiciary, United States Senate, Eighty-ninth Congress, First Session, *Antitrust Exemptions for Agreements Relating to Balance of Payments,* July 15, 16, 1965.

11. Sammons testimony, *op. cit.* (above, note 10).

12. "Cartelization in Western Europe," reprinted in Hearings before the Subcommittee on Antitrust and Monopoly of the Committee on the Judiciary, United States Senate, Eighty-ninth Congress, Second Session, *Foreign Trade and the Antitrust Laws,* Part 1: *General Considerations,* July 22, 23, 29, 1964, p. 475.

13. Hearings before the Subcommittee on Antitrust and Monopoly of the Committee of the Judiciary, United States Senate, Eighty-ninth Congress, Second Session, *Prices of Quinine and Quinidine,* Part 1, May 16, 17, 18, 23, 1966, and Part 2, Nine-

tieth Congress, First Session, March 22, 23, 1967; and Report of the Subcommittee on Antitrust and Monopoly to the Committee of the Judiciary, United States Senate, Ninetieth Congress, First Session, *Prices of Quinine and Quinidine,* August 16, 1967.

14. *Concentration Outside the U.S., op. cit.* (above, note 7), p. 3641.

15. *The American Challenge* (New York: Atheneum, 1968), p. 23.

16. *International Aspects of Antitrust, op. cit.* (above, note 6), p. 32.

17. *The American Challenge, op. cit.,* (above, note 15), p. 254.

18. *Ibid.,* p. 255.

CHAPTER TWELVE: CONCLUSIONS AND RECOMMENDATIONS

1. "Little Delaware Makes a Bid for the Organization of Trusts," 33 *Am. Law Review* 418, 419 (1899).

2. "Law for Sale: A Study of the Delaware Corporation Law of 1970," *University of Pennsylvania Law Review,* Vol. 117 (1969).

3. Cited in "Bigness, Efficiency and Antitrust," remarks by Assistant Attorney General Richard W. McLaren, Federal Bar Association Convention, Washington, D.C., September 15, 1970.

4. See Kenneth G. Elzinga, "Mergers: Their Causes and Cures," *Antitrust Law and Economics Review,* Vol. 2, No. 1, Fall 1968.

5. Hearings before the Subcommittee on Antitrust and Monopoly of the Committee on the Judiciary, United States Senate, Ninetieth Congress, First Session, *Competitive Aspects of Oil Shale Development,* April 18, 1967, p. 40.

6. New York: Dutton, 1970.

7. *Book World,* October 18, 1970, p. 6.

8. Remarks before a National Citizens Committee for Broadcasting luncheon, New York City, November 6, 1969.

9. Milton Friedman, "How to End Giveaways," *Newsweek,* February 23, 1970, p. 84.

10. Annual estimates of the National Center for Health Statistics of the Department of Health, Education, and Welfare and the National Safety Council for injury in and around the home by consumer products, excluding foods, drugs, cosmetics, insecticides, cigarettes, certain flammable fabrics, firearms and motor vehicles; cited in *Final Report* of the National Commission on Product Safety (Washington: 1970), p. 1.

11. *Washington Post,* June 23, 1970, p. C1.

12. *U.S. v. Columbia Steel Co.,* 334 U.S. 495 (1948).

13. Hearings before the Subcommittee on Antitrust and Monopoly of the Committee on the Judiciary, United States Senate, Ninetieth Congress, First Session, *Economic Concentration,* Part 6: *New Technologies and Concentration,* September 19, 20, 22, 25, 26, 27, October 2, 3, 4, 6, 1967, p. 2977.

14. *Study Draft of a New Federal Criminal Code* (Washington: Government Printing Office, 1970), pp. 31–32.

15. *New York Times,* June 20, 1970, p. 28.

16. Special Message to Congress on Election Reform, May 25, 1967.

17. Remarks before the International Press Institute, London, May 27, 1965.

18. Hearings before the Subcommittee on Antitrust and Monopoly of the Commit-

tee on the Judiciary, United States Senate, Ninetieth Congress, First Session, *The Failing Newspaper Act,* Part 1, July 18, 1967, p. 293.

19. Estabrook's story was published on January 2, 1971. Senator Keith Davey, of Toronto, a member of the Liberal Party, headed the special committee. The report, which was made public in December 1970, recommended such reform measures as the creation by the newspapers of a press council similar to that in Britain, a federal press ownership review board to represent the public interest whenever mergers come up for approval or disapproval hereafter, and withdrawal of special tax exemptions for the Canadian editions of *Time* and the *Reader's Digest.* The report found wide quality variations among the newspaper chains: the thirty dailies (and fifteen other papers) owned by Britain's Lord Thomson were "almost uniformly disappointing," but the eight papers in the Free Press group based in Winnipeg, the largest chain in terms of circulation, ranged from "competent to excellent." "The only reliable rule," the report declared, "appears to be that good newspapers usually happen when (a) the operation is financially secure and (b) people who care more about journalism than about balance sheets control the editorial product."

20. Senator McIntyre first introduced his bill, with an accompanying explanation, on January 16, 1970.

21. Quoted by A. Kent MacDougall, "Gadfly on the Left: I. F. Stone Achieves Success, Respectability, But Keeps Raking Muck," *Wall Street Journal,* July 14, 1970.

22. David Donald, "Radical Historians on the Move," *New York Times Book Review,* July 19, 1970, p. 23.

23. Vol. 3, No. 1, Fall 1969, p. 11.

Index